Raphael's Legacy

Author

Barry Hardy

Raphael's Legacy

Copyright © 2008 Barry Hardy publications which is part of BH Management Services Ltd, London UK

Pre Launch Discussion Version published in Great Britain 15th November 2008.

Limited First Edition published in Great Britain 22nd December 2008.

All rights reserved. No part of this book may be reproduced or transmitted in any form or by any means without written permission of the author.

ISBN 978-0-9559865-1-2

Discover more at www.barryhardy.com

I am the master of my own happiness, for its in my interests to live life to the full

Decency warning & insight

Please note that Raphael's Legacy contains strong, explicit views including the use of offensive language, which some may find unnecessarily gratuitous. Therefore please don't read this book if you are easily offended by:

- Strong views.
- Strong language.
- Personal suffering freely expressed.

And/or

- Grammatical inconsistencies

I am the master of my own health, for I take my quality of health seriously

DEDICATION

This book is dedicated to the battalions of helpless souls butchered in the killing fields of medical man. We who survive will do our level best to right their wrongs.

I am the master of my own happiness, for its in my interests to live life to the full

Disclaimer

The information provided in this book should not be construed as personal medical or clinical advice or instruction no action should be taken based solely on the contents of this book. Readers should consult appropriate professionals on any matter relating to their health and well being. The information and opinions provided here are for personal research purposes only. Readers who fail to consult appropriate professionals assume the risk of incurring injury and must accept any consequences directly or indirectly associated with their personal actions on any and all related matters.

I am the master of my own health, for I take my quality of health seriously

About the Author

Barry Hardy is a quite remarkable man, even amidst his own personal suffering he has the innate ability to lift the spirits and inspire those around him. His generosity, compassion, zest for life and comical sense of humour are simply infectious. I personally believe therefore that this book is a milestone in Barry's eventful and extraordinary life and so sincerely hope that at the very least; this book generates great personal insight for those who choose to read it.

Mrs. Edna Garrick

I am the master of my own happiness, for its in my interests to live life to the full

MY DESIRE TO INSPIRE

At a very early age it began to dawn upon me that 'anything and everything was possible when I applied the right approach, connected with the right people and sort out or learned the right skills' and that approach remains my personal life mantra. Collectively and as individuals in our own right, we are so much more than we could ever begin to believe that we are. All we need to do to experience our own unique magnificence is to understand that if we remain strong, if we remain courageous and if we remain true to our own ideals, nothing and I mean nothing is beyond our mortal potential.

This book really shouldn't have been written, because in reality I really shouldn't have been alive today to write it. But this book has been written, yet not from the comfort of some genteel authors office in a pleasant countryside backwater. It was written entirely amidst the heaving throng of a busy urban multicultural internet café, with only clarity of purpose, a degree of effort on my part and the unequivocal generosity of my hosts as its primary driving force. I hope that once you've read this book that it inspires you to be all that you were born to be.

I am the master of my own health, for I take my quality of health seriously

You see, even though I wrote this book on a background of intense personal suffering, my sincere hope is that all the readers of my books enjoy or at the very least are encouraged to explore their own fluid normality and personal perceptions as a result of some of what I have to say. With that desire very much to the fore and with all my imperfections clearly on show, I now hand this book over to you to explore the substance of all that I have to say.

I am the master of my own happiness, for its in my interests to live life to the full

Acknowledgments

My sincere thanks go out to:

My lovely Karina without who's love and support for and of me there would have been no mortal redemption or hope for me.

Dr Sarah Myhill and Hania Baker for all their support and generosity towards my wellbeing and clinical care.

Mrs Edna Garrick for her generosity in agreeing to proof read my manuscript for me.

John Brenan, Fred Anderson, Paul Berry and Janice Curwen, for making room in their own busy lives to hear at least some of my despairs.

My Mum, my sister Anne, Edna Garrick, Lucy Garrick, my accountant John O'Hare and my business banker Trevor Walker whilst all felt powerless to help me, they nevertheless had the decency to care.

David Beattie for his texts and updates about our mutual heroes; Glasgow Rangers Football Club, cheers for that Rangers Dave.

Mr. Stuart Korth registered Osteopath, for his continued professional input into my dreadful cranial and vestibular anomaly.

I am the master of my own health, for I take my quality of health seriously

Mr. Dave Martin from 'man in a hat' for your creative in put into the selection of the right image for this book cover. Explore Man in Hat @ www.maninahat.com.

Julian, Paul, John, Bill and Ian who gave me a job on the B315 documentation project, whilst others who knew me well simply knifed me in the back. Your faith and understanding of my predicament guys at that time simply enabled me to keep going at a simply horrendous time for me.

Mr Abdi Nur Ali, Mr. Dahir Nur Ali and Mr Abdikarin Mohamed for their generosity during the compilation of this book in their internet café on Westow Hill.

All the girls at 'The Café' on Westow Hill; Michelle, Sharon, Laura, Debbie & Ronnie, big thanks for your humour and sufferance of me in terms of my daily order of tea, biscuits and toast with jam.

Daniel, Terry, Peter, Harshid and Colin for their football crack and banter during my breakfast visits to The Cafe on Westow Hill, it's a real shame you guys all support rubbish football teams.

Dave, Ian and John from Court Crash Repairs on Westow Hill, thanks for the crack guys and I hope Canada works out well for you big John.

Finally to all the medical and clinical luddites and charlatans that I've encountered thus far, you are the only reason for this books production, you're a disgrace to decency and I hope one day that the tables will be turned on you all.

I am the master of my own happiness, for its in my interests to live life to the full

JUST SO YOU KNOW

I'm the first to admit that my writing style is both strange and highly challenging at times and I suspect perhaps that's a lot more to do with my personality than anything else. Nevertheless because I know that for some I have the propensity to confuse where my choice of words is taken literally rather than perhaps my original intent. It's therefore important that I present for you now a typical example of this just so that you know that when you're reading my work; that there may be other more abstract yet plausible intent where I've used specific words or indeed phrases etc. Okay enough of the waffle; let me give you a simple example, I have used the phrase 'whole body disease irradiation' in this book and have been asked why irradiation and am I implying that all sufferers of chronic disease need to undergo radiation treatment. Well my answer is no of course I don't believe that all sufferers of chronic diseased states need to undergo radiation treatment.

The context in which I use disease irradiation is based upon my own personal belief that we all have the ability to tap in to our own unique personal power i.e. our higher self wherever there is a particular need to do so. Therefore in my use of that phrase; I'm advocating that we can personally help destroy in fact irradiate and hence eradicate disease from our bodies. By simply applying a multipronged disease eradication process based upon nothing more than scientific root cause analysis whilst empowering our higher self to support all our endeavours.

I am the master of my own health, for I take my quality of health seriously

ESSENTIAL READING

Further personal insight and self help books written by Barry Hardy in relation to Raphael's Legacy include:

Stress at Close Quarters
Anxiety at Close Quarters
Exploring Fluid Normality
Arthritis at Close Quarters
Raphael Treatment Protocol
Depression at Close Quarters
Fibromyalgia at Close Quarters
Lymes Disease at Close Quarters
Manic Depression at Close Quarters
Gulf War Syndrome at Close Quarters
Toxic Body Syndrome at Close Quarters
Myalgic Encephalopathy at Close Quarters
Chronic Fatigue Syndrome at Close Quarters
Obsessive Compulsive Disorder at Close Quarters

You can purchase any of these books at www.barryhardy.com

I am the master of my own happiness, for its in my interests to live life to the full

CONTENTS

Decency warning & insight 3
Dedication 4
Disclaimer 5
About the author 6
My desire to inspire 7
Acknowledgments 9
Just so you know 11
Essential reading 12
Contents 13
Foreword 17
Personal empowerment - no pacts 21
In an earth gods company my story began 25
Luddites charlatans & rogues masquerading as healers 31
My journey through a book of hells 59
Psychological illness fact or fiction? 117
Hippocratic oath or merely hypocritical froth 135
When all else fails test for lymes disease 149
Depression expression and what we all need to know 163
Stop stressing about stress! 209

I am the master of my own health, for I take my quality of health seriously

Could our thyroid hold the key?	241
Fibromyalgia is not just a pain	257
ME, CFS & PVFS: illness or simply names?	271
Passionate, Obsession, Addicted or driven life force	287
Our invisible time bombs	303
Arthritis: the genetic links	317
Toxic body syndrome or TBS	331
Expensive Illness Syndrome or EIS	347
When testing has no sanity!	359
Analytical testing options	385
Last night the internet saved my life	391
Spare us all from the numpties of this world	405
Pursuing wellbeing a treatment explorer	415
Treatment abroad - er….what?	465
Insanity or irony you judge	475
Fantasy punishments and mind anger released	497
Putting a price on illness	507
Friends forever or until you get too ill baz	519
When harpies are your only companions	537
Exploring my own mortality	549
A few closing thoughts	557
Authors notes	565
Book images & contributors	571
Web sites you may wish to explore	573
Decency warning	574

I am the master of my own happiness, for its in my interests to live life to the full

I am the master of my own health, for I take my quality of health seriously

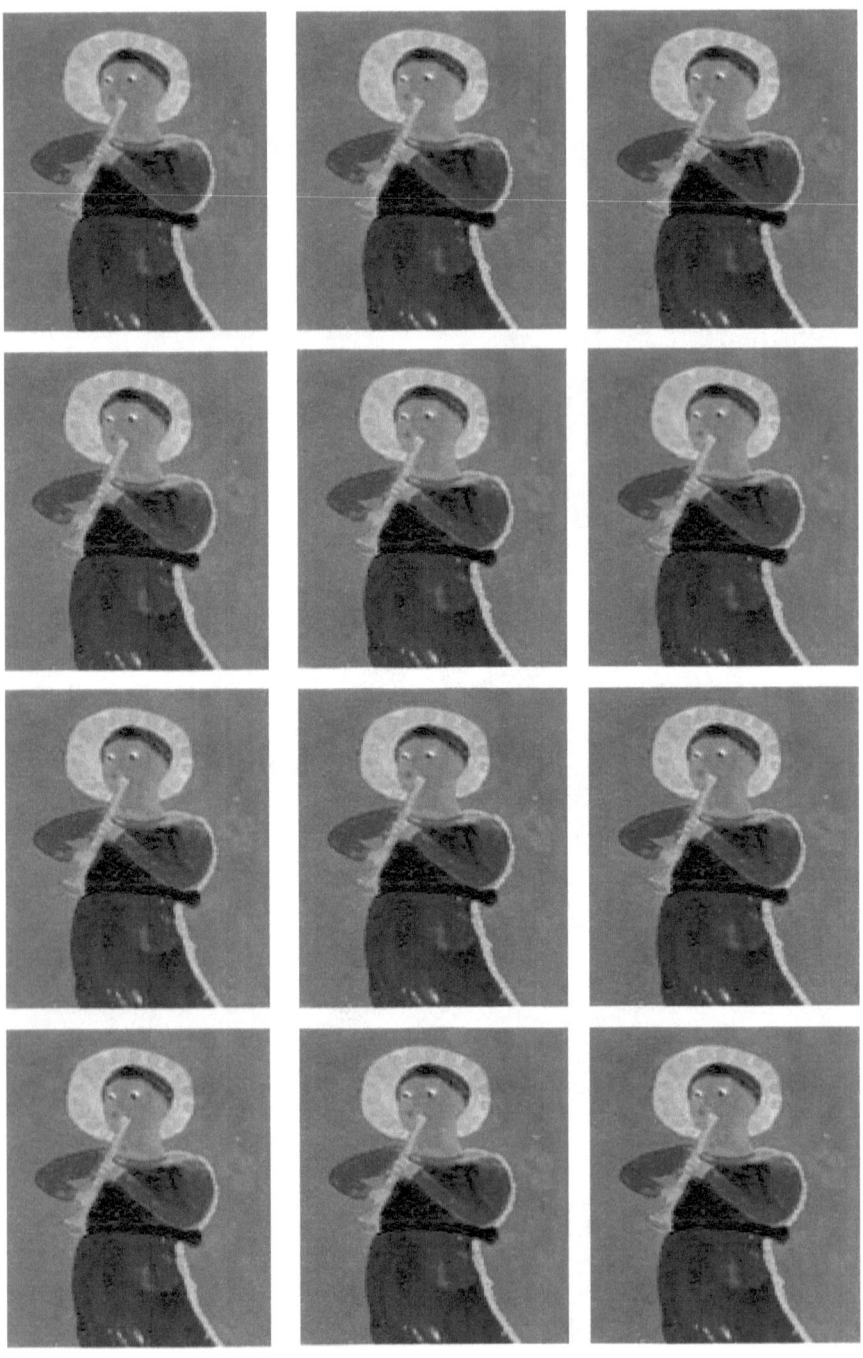

I am the master of my own happiness, for its in my interests to live life to the full

Foreword

Ark Angel Raphael is thought to be a master healer and one of the most inspirational angelic guides at our disposal. He helps us mortals to discover our own unique healing gifts and assists us on many fronts towards our goal of wholeness in mind, body and soul. He is thought to bring great strength to those in need to help them overcome seemingly insurmountable odds. I'm no angel for sure, yet paradoxically I'm no stranger to seemingly insurmountable health issues either. My life was nearly destroyed by a level of medical and clinical incompetence and abuse that even today seems simply incredulous.

As a mortal I am no different from you; my struggles are like your struggles, my pain is like your pain, my hopes, dreams and desires are like your hopes, dreams and desires. This book, 'Raphael's Legacy' offers nothing more than an insight into a different way of thinking, to challenge and to postulate but above all to allow you the reader to make your own value judgments about me, my experiences, my views, my assumptions, my conclusions and my prejudices and how they may or may not resonate with you.

This book took only sixty hours to write, however in its infancy it was very raw, angry and even brutal at times, however I sincerely hope that rawness now has given way to much softer perceptional expressions. Nevertheless it is still important to note that this book was written, from points of sheer desperation and isolation, from my heart, from my head,

I am the master of my own health, for I take my quality of health seriously

from points of extreme personal endurance, through my personal life experiences and because of the ignorance of my fellow man. It offers no salvation and requires no gratification; this book is simply what it is, one mans struggle and pursuit of peace and well-being laid bare. Raphael's Legacy is the phoenix from which I launch my ensemble of thoughts, visions, observations, contradictions, but above all my humanistic desires and expectations of life and everything that underpins that state of existence. From the Raphael process that I've worked through, I was able to compile my book: The Raphael Treatment Protocol 'RTP' but that's a book for you to read another day and only after you've read, Raphael's Legacy.

So, read on only if you're interested in a collection of thoughts, an exploration into medical incompetence, ignorance, prejudices and to connect with one man's innate ability to do battle with and fight for what is our most precious of gifts, the gift and right to life. Thirty years of struggle, thirty years of pain, a career and body destroyed and all because our medical industry is institutionally incompetent, ignorant and unsympathetic to basic scientific rationale, suffering or pain.

I am the master of my own happiness, for its in my interests to live life to the full

I am the master of my own health, for I take my quality of health seriously

I am the master of my own happiness, for its in my interests to live life to the full

Personal empowerment - no pacts

To those who failed me, who criticised me, who ridiculed me, to those who misdiagnosed me, who mistreated me and who clinically abused me I say to you now: may your god forgive you for all that you are for you are without doubt the lowest of all mortal life forms.

To those who could have, should have, yet chose not to heed me, to help me, to support me or to love me I say to you now, do not attempt to re-write my past by reaching out and connecting with me now or in the future. It's not for me to forgive you your prejudices, your ignorance, your selfishness or your cruelty towards me. As a mortal I merely wish for you strength, growth and humility as you pass through your own personal hells that I believe lay before you.

To those who loved me, who prayed for me, who laughed with me, who cried with me and to those who died with me many times I say to you now; we may be few, but we are the luckiest of all living things. We have loved, we have cared, we have given, we have shared, we have lived and we will die touched by the presence of unquestionable friends.

To those offering up prayers for some sort of miracle or divine intervention, I say only this, never forget that you are the true master of your destiny, and whilst it's okay to sit back and rest for a while, always keep your wits, strengths and friends about you.

To those who read this book and are able to balance the many negatives with the many positives, I say only this, the truth of any mans truth is only as good as the receptivity it generates in others, so I implore you to look further for the answers you desire, because you're already on the right path for you.

To those who read this book and who find themselves fearful of everything they read, I say only this, when you release the fear that you hold deep inside, you'll discover that it's not a fear of this books contents that you have, you're simply choosing to live a life filled with fear.

To those who recognise upon completing this book that they need different help, new sources of inspiration and greater more focused support, I say only this, rejoice in all that you are because you are free of the bonds that have been holding you back, the universe and all its majesty are now yours to explore.

Above all things never ever forget that:

'Anything and everything is possible with the right skills, the right people and the right approach'

I am the master of my own happiness, for its in my interests to live life to the full

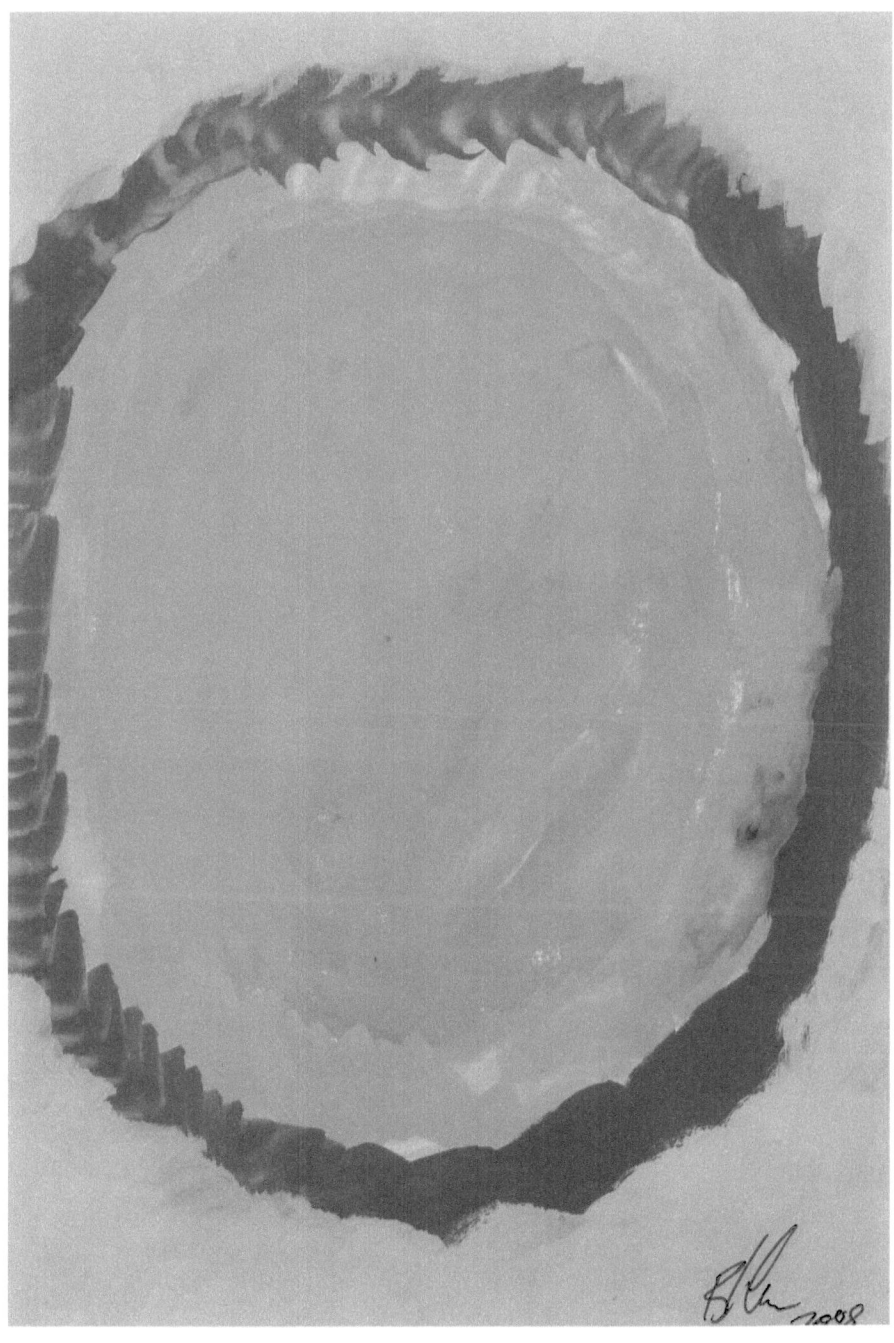

I am the master of my own health, for I take my quality of health seriously

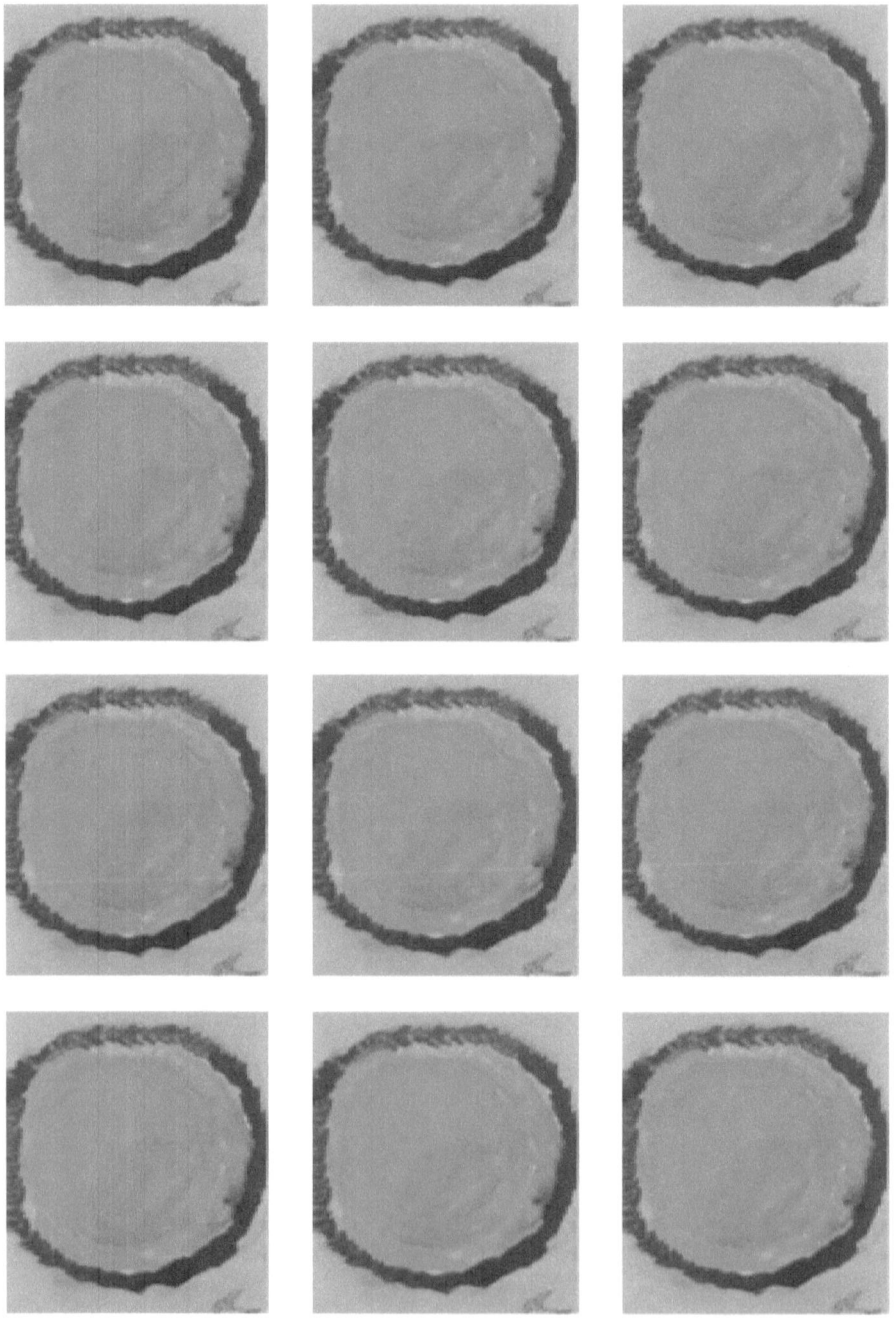

I am the master of my own happiness, for its in my interests to live life to the full

IN AN EARTH GODS COMPANY MY STORY BEGAN

Born into a family ravaged by sectarianism, prejudice and ignorance in the small West Cumbrian town of Whitehaven, mine was not the easiest of childhoods. My oldest brother William had been born with Down's Syndrome. Excluded by most and ridiculed by the majority he died at the tender age of two years four months. Whilst I never met him in the flesh, he was never far from my thoughts or far from my side as I grew up in what was a stereotypically dysfunctional working class environment. At first I didn't know just who my little, big brother was, when he visited me as a child at night, but over the years his presence, mission, love and support of me became all too clear, year upon year.

My older surviving brother on the other hand either felt incredibly threatened by me or he hated me with a vengeance because he was a truly surly child completely lacking in any compassion or personal generosity. He was only happy when our parents were absent from the domestic scene so that he could resume his beating, abusing and mistreatment of me. My sister, nine months my junior, for many years was my only ally at those times when my parents were not at home and to this day we remain caring and supportive friends.

I am the master of my own health, for I take my quality of health seriously

Despite my personal circumstances I was a naturally irrepressible kid growing up in my horrible home. I became the Friday night bill payer, the Tuesday family allowance collector, the general grocery and errand boy. In essence I was the families doer; the church magazine delivery boy, the bags of coal man handling boy, the wood chopper, the grass cutter, the house decorator, the worrier, the carer, the entertainer and yet ultimately I always seemed to be the family enigma too. At the age of nine I connected with my first ever guide and mentor, my granddad Robert Edgar, or big Bob. He was a collier by necessity and an earth god by nature. He loved his family, his TV, his cartoons, his food, his gardening and boy did he love and nurture me too. Escaping my brothers' hatred I spent my first long summers with my granddad, leaving my home at 7:30am every day and returning home only when I knew that it was safe to do so. I walked, talked, sat on benches, on beaches, in hedgerows and numerous allotments with my granddad.

During that time I learned so much about life, the meaning of life and the personal conduct required of a meaningful life. I worked the land with him and for him; we built green houses, sheds, cold-frames and seemingly anything and everything was possible, all with a sense of equality and great fun. All was love, all was hope, all was contentment and all was unmitigated friendship, laughter and joy.

However, right from those early years I was bitten many times by sheep ticks as we walked our local fields searching out only the finest and freshest of sheep droppings for my granddads beloved tomato plants. In time old fashion he would kill those damn ticks with the butt of his cigarette and we would both laugh with glee when my grandma Annie lost her cool as the incidents of our extended day came to light over our late afternoon tea. Little did I know then that my time with my granddad had both prepared me for my future struggles whilst simultaneously sowing the

I am the master of my own happiness, for its in my interests to live life to the full

seeds for a lifetime of despair and isolation through what I call my hellish years. A lifetime of despair created solely and simply by an unimaginable level of institutional medical incompetence, ignorance, neglect and misdiagnosis of what is an easily identifiable and initially easily treatable condition known merely as Lymes Disease. Having been brought up to feel privileged that a medic should see fit to acknowledge or treat me, those splendid men and women of learning seemed of far greater intellect indeed. Is it any wonder that their stupidity, ignorance and incompetence was initially never challenged or questioned by some one of my background. You see; I never stood a chance with my incongruent working class formative programming.

It seems however that fate can be our biggest liberator albeit difficult at times to rationalize or see. For it's only once we've been liberated that we can gleefully see that the baggage and crap that we inherited in our childhood is not ours at all and as such can be jettisoned and respectfully or disrespectfully in my case set free.

I am the master of my own health, for I take my quality of health seriously

This book does not claim to be the greatest of reads, it offers no miracles or cures it merely postulates my shift in perceptions which aided my physical, emotional and spiritual healing. But if you're on the path of personal advancement you'll know that the process of personal evolution never truly ends and so with that in mind, I hope you now enjoy your read.

I am the master of my own happiness, for its in my interests to live life to the full

I am the master of my own health, for I take my quality of health seriously

I am the master of my own happiness, for its in my interests to live life to the full

Luddites Charlatans & Rogues Masquerading as Healers

I'm somewhat embarrassed these days by the fact that whilst many turned their back during the greedy and wasted Thatcher and Major years. I spent a great deal of my youth campaigning and lobbying against local and central government with passion on a whole host of issues, not least of which was my desire to save what I felt was a laudable institution under threat, namely our glorious NHS. 'Boy did I get it wrong'. The institution and all the mechanisms that underpin that bullshit ridden and sedentary industry are rotten to the core. Fortunately I have no medical or clinical qualifications, I'm just a regular guy a, *Time Served Plumber* trained in engineering and engineering sciences and like most engineers I have an engaging and problem solving mind. As a regular guy I would respectfully suggest that having an enquiring, capable and problem solving mind is probably the most mandatory requirement for those engaged in a service delivery profession such as the medical industry. Now clearly the back room girls and boys appear to have that predisposition because we have all witnessed the tremendous advances that have been achieved over the past fifty years or so. I'm talking here however about medical scientists and scientific medical engineers, the people we should regard as the true heroes of medicine, the men and woman who steadfastly develop new tools, new tests and new treatments.

I am the master of my own health, for I take my quality of health seriously

However, the heroes of medicine are a stark contrast to the front end cretins, rogues and Luddites e.g. *Any Opponent of Industrial Change or Innovation* of the medical world that we the general public are unfortunately exposed to. The rogues that we're exposed to are only interested in one thing and one thing only: self gratification at the expense of their fellow man. I refer of course to the medical receptionist, the nurse, the general practitioner, the registrar, the specialist and the consultant etc, etc, etc. They may or may not start off life as rogues but certainly become very big rogues at the point they're allowed to administer their own unique brand of divisive, destructive and judgmental clinical administration and medical butchery. These people are the lowest form of mortal life, guilty of crimes against humanity that simply eclipse the acts and transgressions of the worst of all ruthless dictators. They are institutionally lazy, self obsessed, greedy, serial abusers with only one thing on their agenda, self preservation of their highly inflated status within what is the devil's own institutions. Forget all the waffle and Hippocratic oath bullshit, the bottom line for these people is themselves first, themselves second and what ever is left over; is all for themselves. These people don't solve problems, they don't hear suffering, they're not prepared to think outside of the box and why? Because they're the wrong people for the job, the wrong people who are gaining great rewards from an industry that is rotten to the core. For anyone misfortunate enough to develop a chronic illness I've mapped the actual clinical abuse process that most people are forced to endure during the course of their chronic illness. What the process loop cannot do is qualify the simply appalling nature, neglect and abandonment anyone experiences during that process. Where the cause of desperate conditions are often written off as psychological issues and placed directly back on the shoulders of the patients, identifying them as the originator and hence owner of the condition in totality.

I am the master of my own happiness, for its in my interests to live life to the full

RAPHAEL'S LEGACY

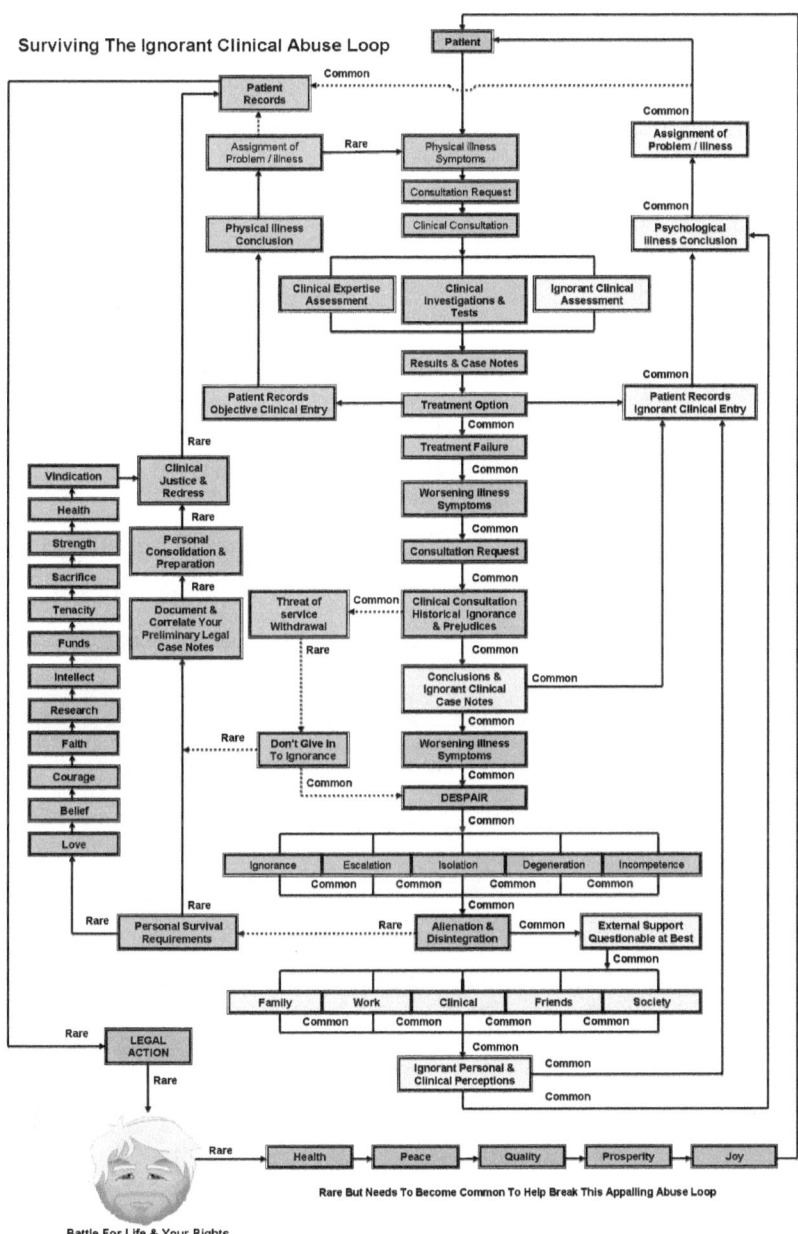

I am the master of my own health, for I take my quality of health seriously

That being said; it's eminently justifiable to suggest that the selection criteria for individuals entering the medical industry and the training they undergo is now by modern day standards both outdated and fundamentally flawed. If the selection criteria for those entering the medical industry and their subsequent training were right; then we wouldn't have such fundamentally flawed service delivery. You see;

- How can it be that we still have a sociologically biased industry that is controlled from within?

- How can it be that we still have a sociologically biased industry that protects and rewards underperformance from those who support it or are employed by it?

- How can it be that we still have a sociologically biased industry that is afraid to acknowledge advancement in thinking until that change in approach is decades old?

- How can it be that we still have a sociologically biased industry where those who are employed in it have no idea about the majority of diseases and conditions they encounter?

- How can it be that every unexplainable condition can be written off by those within this industry as simply being of a psychological origin?

- How can it be that they're programmed as a service provider within this industry not to hear, help or support suffering and pain?

I am the master of my own happiness, for its in my interests to live life to the full

- How can it be that no matter what your own personal or professional credentials are, as soon as you engage with this industry you're immediately considered an intellectual cretin by those providing even basic services within?

- How can it be that if you dare to challenge this industry from within you're immediately risking your career?

- How can it be that fighting for resolution from chronic illness can expose you to the pressure of clinical services being withdrawn from you?

You only need to be misfortunate enough to become ill to discover just how diabolically poor, unresponsive and uncooperative this industry really is. No matter which sector you seek help from, be it either the public or the private sectors, the service is abominable. No matter whom you consult or what level that representative may be, it doesn't matter what tests you participate in or what sort of investigation you undergo. These people know very little about very little and what they do know or articulate freely to you is generally outdated, self protectionist and complete and utter bullshit with no humanistic element to it. And yet they all assume the same grotesque air of arrogance about who they are and what they are and how complicated your particular situation may or may not be. This bullshit they offload is by default, simply an outdated facade designed for a bygone age when we the general public were considered by these rogues as intellectually inferior. This assumption still exists today to mask clear inadequacies, ignorance and fragile egos yet the reality is that it's probably more disrespectful to us now than it ever was because we're all much smarter than these cretins give us credit for.

I am the master of my own health, for I take my quality of health seriously

This crux of my irritation is that this industry and those who support it are an affront to everything that is both decent and good in our modern world. We don't expect or accept bullshit and ridicule from any other private sector or public service industry. So why do we accept this institutional misconduct from the clinical world? Well, the truth is that we really don't think that we have any power to change our situation; however I propose to the wider public that in reality we do.

Although we require the government to deliver significant changes to this completely unacceptable situation, we as individuals in our own right can make a difference by shifting our perceptions and taking action too. Given what I've been through I suggest that its not in the least bit inflammatory to suggest that this industry and the rogues who support it are still adopting a work ethic from the 19th century, and whilst our governments know that, they still seem terrified to challenge it for fear of a back lash from the old boy clubs that underpin it in totality. It's simply laughable to me that our government is so scared to take this industry on. I distinctly remember Thatcher smashing manufacturing in this country because she didn't like its outdated and troublesome cultures. She closed the mines and decimated our steel and shipping industries in a frenzy of North American business mantras tabled as helping to set our economy and entrepreneurs free. Er....... okay, well they didn't but what they did do was cause our people a lot of suffering and pain. The point is her radical and callous actions did create a dynamic of greater flexibility, uncertainty and the destruction of outdated cultural impediments and hence removing in the short term any resistance to change. My view is simply this; I see no difference and liken the institutions and cultures that underpin our medical industry to the old manufacturing, shipping and mining cultural views that Thatcher smashed. Our medical industry's perceptions, instincts and cultural dogma remain intrinsically linked symbiotically to an outdated old boy's club culture which I believe must

I am the master of my own happiness, for its in my interests to live life to the full

be raised to the ground. How can we have a 21st century medical model when we empower luddites and afford them ample opportunity to delude themselves into believing that they have acquired some form of earth god status. Is it any wonder that the majority of clinical problems are categorized simply as I don't understand this problem and so given that I'm the 'All Seeing Eye this problem can't possibly exist and must therefore be a manifestation of a deep seated emotional problem?

At which point it's a very simple matter of then offloading that problem back onto the individual who raised it in the first place, but unfortunately not before the patients clinical records have been corrupted with unqualified psychiatric and psychological assumptions and clap trap. Just who do these rogues think that they are? It doesn't matter if they're a receptionist, a nurse, a general practitioner, gynecology biased, ENT biased, endocrine biased, cardio biased, orthopedic biased, pediatric biased, geriatric biased etc, etc, etc.

At the point they can't solve a problem they instantly become an eminently qualified psychiatrist or psychologist. They can't do the bloody job we're paying them a fortune to do, but they think they have a god given right to make clinical judgments and entries into our clinical records from a place of complete ignorance.

How dare they, how bloody dare they. The problem is once that clap trap is on your records its there for a life time; you will never be free from the fall out and magnification of those ridiculous assumptions and prejudices. You are no longer a normal healthy functioning individual in your own right, you're from that point forward an attention seeking screwed up neurotic, who lurches from emotional instability to depressive cycles at a whim.

I am the master of my own health, for I take my quality of health seriously

But hey how laughable is this too, not only have you not had the original problem solved you will face an even greater uphill battle to sort it now because even when these rogues get it wrong their perception is that they got it right. Therefore it really can be a; lose-lose situation when we seek help from some of these cretins.

Let me be clear here because my rant is not simply an unjustifiable rant, I haven't just decided to have a rant at this industry and those who gain great benefit from it because one particular medic failed me. If only that had been the case I wouldn't have spent the vast majority of my life suffering in isolation. I would have spent some glorious years running my beloved Cumberland fells, building and changing industry all over the world. Instead I was forced to endure more than thirty years of medical ignorance which all but destroyed my life. So I'm not here now ranting in my book about their incompetence just for the hell of it, the horrible truth of the matter is I'm simply not alone here. Millions of lives are left wrecked each year by this industry and whilst some may gain some benefit from aspects of its care, there are far too many ethical, moral and technical competency issues that need to be improved before this industry can even begin to consider itself ready to join the 20th century, let alone the 21st.

It's only right as reasonable citizens that we expect and accept no matter what our own unique experiences with the medical industry are, that those undergoing medical or clinical training have at the very least some modicum of social interaction skills and an enquiring mind or intelligence? Regrettably it seems they don't and I believe that's a clear derivative of the industries fundamentally flawed selection process for those entering clinical or medical service careers.

I am the master of my own happiness, for its in my interests to live life to the full

The inevitable consequence of this is that it is us the end user who pay the heaviest price. We are disrespected, disenfranchised and very often clinically dispatched with no solution save for highly opinionated dogma every time we present ourselves to them with something they don't understand. But I will state again that these people are not earth gods, neither are they the most intelligent or highest form of human life, they are simply mortals like us who are employed by us and its simply unacceptable that they repeatedly fail us and yet apparently care not about any of that or their own incompetence's. We all make mistakes and there really is no secret in that, but the key to progression is realizing, accepting and learning from those mistakes, something completely lacking in the medical industry.

So whilst I would never advocate medical practitioner witch hunts just for the sake of it, since when all said and done we do need some tangible form of this industry at some level in our society. I do advocate that if it can be proven that they're unable to do their job with a high degree of competence then they should be released from front end service delivery as they would be in every other industry in the developed world.

No more jobs for life for these 'clowns' it's high time that the old boys' protectionist clubs that have served them so well for decades be raised to the ground. We must all demand accountability from them and commit to the pursuit of justice when they either fail us or they fail our loved ones. The public needs to accept that these people are mortals and as mortals they have the potential to be; deviants, paedophiles, alcoholics, drug addicts and gamblers. They shit every day like us, they screw every day like us, they mess up every day like us and they have lots of hang ups every day just like us.

I am the master of my own health, for I take my quality of health seriously

I advocate that the time old arguments that they frequently roll out to defend indefensible errors of judgment, transgressions, underperformance or incompetence using crap like; 'sorry that was an unforeseen complication' or 'I'm suffering from work related stress' should be grounds enough for seeking them to be removed from their posts with immediate effect. Because times have changed people, the good old boy lifestyle is over, my view is; if you wish to work in the modern medical world be prepared to take the consequences of shoddy service delivery too.

No more bullshit or froth, no more postulating the impossibility of performance demonstration. It's only reasonable for us to expect them to be able to demonstrate their capabilities in an open and transparent fashion just as we must do in our daily work. I think it's eminently acceptable for us to request each practitioner or service provider to qualify just how many people they've cured, how many chronic cases they have on their books right now, how many people they've removed from their books and the reason for their removal and how many hours they've undergone training or have actually worked in any given reporting period.

If they're unable to provide substance based support information then they're simply not in control of their work load and by default they're not providing the value added service that we that hard working and taxpaying public require. Now these requests are not unreasonable because every one of us today has much greater reporting compliances placed upon us than ever before in the work place and we just have to accept that. So much so that the majority of us normally compile this mandatory information on our own time with no cost applied to our employers or to the detriment of our work place commitments.

I am the master of my own happiness, for its in my interests to live life to the full

Try getting that sort of buy-in from a medic and for sure you'll get all the age old clap trap of working patterns, etc, being rolled out time and time again. These people really do believe that they have a hard and challenging job, which simply qualifies for me that the medical and clinical industries are truly out of step and out of touch with the realities and practicalities of living and working within the 21st century.

The thing that gets me is that we give our medics jobs for life, we award them exorbitant salaries and pensions and we the taxpaying public provide them with brilliant facilities too. We allow them to earn money privately in our facilities and we bestow upon them a status over and above their capabilities in most instances, so what is their problem? Well the answer is; they've had it to good for far too long. They're living in a bygone age and we all know from our own experiences that absolute power and self determination corrupts absolutely our perceptions and attitude towards acceptable standards and codes of conduct in life.

I believe that if we their employers cannot prove that they're good enough to stay in their posts, then they should be demoted immediately to a level more in keeping with their capabilities. If there is even the slightest insinuation or formal accusation relating to breaches in acceptable clinical care, including evidence or speculation of incompetence or impropriety. Then we should simply remove them from practice with immediate effect. We as a society must change our mind set, we owe the medical industry nothing save for respectful pleasantries where necessary and the continued funding that we pay out every year to ensure that they're able to provide us with the level of care that we believe we so richly deserve.

I am the master of my own health, for I take my quality of health seriously

As far as any mention of work related stress from this industry I would simply roll-out their own bullshit industry standard medical model for problem solving to assess their suitability to continue their role. The criteria for this would be if they're unable to cope with their workload due to work related stress etc, then they clearly have a deep seated psychological problem because psychological problems are the root cause of all illnesses. For that reason and that reason alone I advocate that any medic or clinician either reporting or being reported for underperformance through work related stress etc, should be suspended immediately with the complete cessation of any financial support. Equally they should be prevented from practicing again until they are able to prove via an independent body that they are indeed fit to meet our service delivery requirements of them as would happen in any other industrial environment or application.

Now whilst this may sound harsh it's important to note that I lost everything I had at the time I was misdiagnosed with stress. So what is good enough for me is good enough for anyone employed in the medical or clinical service sector industries.

You see the biggest joke for me is: simply ask any medic you encounter to define work related stress if that's a handle that they've placed upon you. I guarantee you that they will either go straight to the psychological bullshit model or they'll ramble on about the body being very complex and capable of many things etc, etc, etc. What they won't do is instigate a holistic line of investigation or attempt to qualify why you're feeling the way you're feeling. If you're lucky they'll do a flawed thyroid blood check on you, knowing full well that it will come back normal but they will not attempt to do any further root cause analysis.

I am the master of my own happiness, for its in my interests to live life to the full

Why should they? As far as they and your records are now concerned you're a neurotic, an incapable, a depressive and an antagonist if you object to their prescriptive suggestion that you should drug yourself up with SSRI's etc.

The appalling truth however is they haven't got a bloody clue. Can you believe that? Stress has been with us since time began and yet those in medical or clinical care still don't understand it. How can that be? I'm a time served plumber and I know what stress is, I know how you recover from stress and I cover it in a later chapter where I look specifically at stress. But the only reason I know all about stress is because I had to find ways to recover from bacterial, hormonal, neurotoxin and biotoxin stress including the fall out that chronic illness imposes upon the bodies' physical and emotional coping capabilities. I had to do this because the only thing the medical industry had to offer me was clap trap, SSRI's and the probability of being sectioned under the 'Mental Health Act' had I not withdrawn from their fraudulent care.

Now I'm a realist, I know that anything and everything I dare to postulate in terms of my views on medical or clinical care will be greeted with howls of derision from those either within or on the fringes of those industries. Some may misrepresent me, others may merely seek to challenge or criticize me from lofty spires just for the hell it.

I am the master of my own health, for I take my quality of health seriously

Cackling and deriding my views with sickening pomposity whilst articulating their retorts with typical bile and systemic industry biased lunacy. 'How can an ignorant plumber even dare think he has answers to such a complex clinical condition as; stress?'

However if those very same individuals didn't have such shallow egos and didn't instinctively fear change, people like you and me wouldn't need to seek or find answers to questions that they're just to ignorant to explore. It really is laughable but if the average medic ever managed to pull their head out of their own arse they would discover like normal people that the world can be such a beautiful place when one's life is not coated or wrapped up in bullshit or pain. That there are answers to every question and problems are no longer problems once the solutions have been found.

I liken the medical industry today to the blood letting charlatans of ye olden days in that they have absolutely no idea about the majority of conditions they encounter but are truly comfortable when working in their self made yet ignorant comfort zones. As for the patient well what matter if he or she lives or dies. As far as the medic is concerned they simply think; 'well I've done all that I could reasonably do and have nothing to reproach myself for. After all, everyone should be most very grateful for my involvement in that case because when all said and done as a medic I am a very busy and highly intelligent earth god'. It's that predisposition of comfort with an end product of failure and excuse that we as a society must bring crashing to its knees. We must drag our medical industry and the rogues who are employed in and by it kicking and screaming into a service delivery based industry where accountability not protectionism is king.

I am the master of my own happiness, for its in my interests to live life to the full

We must insist upon cultural change to service delivery within these industries including challenging outdated perceptions within the same. But more importantly we must create a climate where redress for transgressions and failures of due diligence are easily and sympathetically dealt with and at great speed. To achieve that however we must first accept our innocence in all clinical failures wherever they present and be fully prepared to take those rotten industries head on in pursuit of redress.

You see, clinical abusers and their underwriters are very adept in their clinical and litigation defense approach in making sure or attempting to make sure that we the victims are always made to feel that we are the primary cause for of all that went wrong. That we should be most humbly grateful for any in put from them including what they decide to cite as the cause of our problem. But we are not at fault and we must never consider ourselves as being in any way, shape or form responsible or the contributing party to any and all clinical failures of willful medical abuse. You see, we invariably enter into dialogue with a clinician lacking completely in mutuality of power because we are by default, vulnerable as a result of our presenting conditions. Often that which is said, reported, interpolated and recorded in our medical reports is simply millennia or light years apart. When seeking help from this industry we're immediately downgraded to a lower intellectual status. Because there is a fuzzy logic in this social intercourse which institutionally, albeit covertly, states that you as the patient challenge me as the medic at your peril. But that is exactly what we need to do. We need to challenge this industry's incompetence's, we need to challenge their intellect, we need to challenge their emotional stability and we need to challenge their integrity, because that is the ultimate doorway from which in time we will all secure better and more responsive medical and clinical care.

I am the master of my own health, for I take my quality of health seriously

We must face up to the fact that we can and have a right to seek redress and in doing so we must dispel any fears that we may have of reprisal and/or any reticence to believe that there is a real possibility of securing success. If we don't take these industries on, how will we ever bring about the change that we so desperately need? How will we ever eradicate the poor standards of service delivery and care which sees eminently recoverable diseases escalate to terminal conditions and lives filled with despair? I mean to say; how on earth can we love ourselves or love the people we say we love if we're not prepared to challenge the bastards who medically and clinically abuse and fail both us and them?

I am the master of my own happiness, for its in my interests to live life to the full

Look, I make no secret of the fact that I will sue the bastards who destroyed my life and left me with chronic disabilities. You see, I remember being struck off whilst still being incredibly ill because of who I was and my tenacity in pursuit of well being. Now the records will show that I was struck off because I requested a repeat prescription for some 0.5mg Clonazepan 'which is a controlled substance' whilst living down in Shaftsbury undergoing intense herbal treatment. It was cited by my practice that it was inappropriate to mail such a prescription via royal mail because of the potential danger of it falling into the wrong hands and that I should register with a GP in Shaftsbury. *I was actually on the books of medical practice down in Shaftsbury as a temporary patient, but I was too ill to go through all the torture of explaining my case to a new GP so I opted to contact my registered practice in a humanistic attempt to illicit their support.*

Well as ever I received very little understanding or support from them and whilst it might appear on the surface to be a very reasonable and fair stance for my practice to take in not sending me a prescription via royal mail even though I offered to pay for recorded delivery. The truth of the matter is that whilst the prescription issue and my temporary geographical residence whilst undergoing treatment were used as grounds for the removal of services from me. Both cited issues however were actually complete rubbish and nothing more that the opportunity they had been looking for to offload me, because they knew I had the potential to become a real thorn in their hypocritical sides.

I am the master of my own health, for I take my quality of health seriously

You see, I was a complete nightmare in their shallow eyes, I wouldn't go away quietly, roll-over or die, neither would I buy into the preposterously incompetent script that they had written for me and I kept proving those incompetent 'cretins' wrong. Time after time I secured clear clinical diagnosis as a result of intensive clinical research and great personal and financial expense as they perversely kept writing me off whilst corrupting my medical records.

The real issue was that they were completely unaware that I had been through a neurological procedure which only came to light as I made my application for this medication. *It is important to note here that my approach to using this medication in a very difficult situation was conservative to say the very least. I knew the potential for addiction etc, and I suffered greatly simply not to become too accustomed to this drug.*

Anyway I digress, as I endeavoured to secure a prescription the surgical procedure came to light and it was clear that AZ Saint Lucas had not informed my practice about my surgical experience. At first I was a little surprised about this and then it became clear that the reason for this was because my referring GP had been Dr Sarah Myhill and that's where clinical notification had been sent. Now the reason Dr Sarah Myhill was my referring GP was because she actually listened to my symptoms, she considered the personal research that I'd undertaken about my condition and she helped me find the diagnostic tools and facilities that were able to prove my micro vascular compression syndrome. In contrast the last clinical cretin that I saw in my practice was a complete shit of an individual, overflowing with clear insecurities and inadequacies about his own capabilities. He sat hands rested on his knees, 'as smug as a closet pedophile, who's found himself in a children's playground all alone with the kids' and asked me what I thought was wrong with me? I replied, 'well my research would indicate that I have micro vascular compression syndrome' and proceeded to hand over a portfolio of information that I had compiled to support my case. I have to say here that I was suicidal at the point I saw that 'incompetent cretin' because I'd been tortured by my Posterior Inferior Cerebella Artery (PICA) for over three months. *I'd had very little sleep since my PICA went psychiatric; the pain was unbelievable eclipsed only by the sheer intolerability of its insult to my vestibular nerve.* I was desperate and I really needed someone within the medical industry to help me and I desperately hoped this GP would consider my position from a place of clinical receptivity and expertise.

However, he just placed my report to one side of his desk, smirked and said, 'hmnnn....let me tell you what I think is wrong with you, I think you have a mental health issue'. Of all the rogues who have abused and mistreated me I have to say that I could do time for that 'bastard' because even two years after that incident I really want to hurt him ever so much. At the point he delivered his bombshell it dawned upon me that if I wasn't careful there was great potential of me being sectioned under the 'Mental Health Act' because I was likely to be considered high risk having committed to suicide in 2004 re: *my book of hells next chapter*. That being said, I felt the best and safest course of action for me was to retreat and to either get out of my body or out of West Cumbria full stop. Now that is a very long winded way of saying that the real reason I was struck off was because when the Clonazepan issue was raised and my practice decided to become as ever unsympathetically dogmatic about the situation. I inflamed the situation further because in complete contempt of their approach I forwarded them my discharge letter from AZ Saint Lucas and cited in that communiqué the reason they did not have updated records was because one of their staff wrote me off as having a mental health issue.

I am the master of my own health, for I take my quality of health seriously

Whereas Dr Myhill had listened to me and done her level best to help me resolve my 'CHRONIC PHYSICAL HEALTH' condition for me. Shortly after that I was notified via 'Royal Mail' to the 'Temporary Address' that I'd already vacated and they knew that, but they still informed me by communicating to that address that clinical service had been removed from me. Which was typical of the rogues, charlatans and luddites I'd unfortunately become accustomed to dealing with for so many disagreeable years within their practice. Nevertheless I wonder however; who amongst the players in that dynamic will ultimately have the final say on matters of decency and ethical conduct, perhaps it's a case of watch this space!

Having service removed from you is a very real possibility when you're chronically ill but determined to fight for your rights and your quality of life. It happens every day of the week; and what's worse is that it is underwritten and even proactively encouraged within the great British Medical Control Model as the most appropriate course of action to take with difficult patients.

But chronically ill patients in the most part aren't violent of abusive patients, they're not drug addicts or alcoholics, in general they're very decent people desperately trying to find an answer to real debilitating conditions. It is for that reason that I'm happy to cite that we must sue the bastards who impose a greater sense of suffering upon us, when we are desperately trying to resolve a chronic illness expression. You see, I will have my day by all the rogues who abused and mistreated me, in particular the anal cretin who insulted me the last time I was in my former GP's surgery. It is fact as sure as night follows day that the members of staff at my former GP's practice know only too well that I will put just as much effort into securing redress and justice from them as I was forced to commit to securing some form of return to health and life at the point they abandoned me.

I am the master of my own happiness, for its in my interests to live life to the full

Nevertheless and from my perspective I'm in no rush to sue my abusers, I may sue them next year, in 2, 10, 15, 20 or 25 year's time who knows? What's more it's not important. All I know is that this unfinished business hangs over them like the *sword of Damocles*, but that's okay because as sure as night follows day I will sue the bastards who destroyed my life. I will sue those bastards because:

(a) I have nothing to lose.

(b) Redress is only fair.

(c) Those very same bastards who destroyed my life are still destroying the lives of good people right now and that's not right.

It's no longer acceptable for these bastards to write us off, to offer no solutions or to complicate our conditions through ignorance and dogma. Its not really rocket science but some people really struggle to come to terms with the reality of they're innocence in terms of their clinical abuse experiences. I don't have any problem with my innocence; I was abused by a raft of clinical and medical abusers and the institution is a disgrace to humanity, end of story. Its time for retribution, time for a shift in this power dynamic, its time for the integrity of all our medics to be subjected to intense social, moral and ethical scrutiny in wide and open forums.

We as a society need to come to terms with the fact that our medical industry is shit and the fall out from that underperformance is costing innocent people their livelihoods and in a far too many instances; quite simply their lives. I remember all my abusers well, I remember each and every one of them, I remember their cruel incompetence and all their mortal imperfections and whilst some may already be dead, the others are still alive and kicking content; perversely to keep on abusing.

I am the master of my own health, for I take my quality of health seriously

Below is just a sample of some of my abusers. All incompetent healers but ironically I gained strength in time from their gross ignorance, stupidity and cruelty:

The gentle nervous wreck.
The snarling grumpy dwarf.
The nurses with sick perversions.
The snarling administration witches.
The anal surgeon only happy when humiliating his patients.
The pompous professor with shit for brains.
The sharp suited smiling assassin locked in his 1950's training.
The insane psychiatrists unable to see, hear or care.
The disabled know it all who actually knew very little.
The greedy charlatan happy to table his failures.
The midget with the big ego, big voice and obviously small…!
The game playing chick with the smelly pits.
The sarcastic jock with the cruel gob.
The masculine females or simply men without balls.
The Mr. touchy, feely, horrible and seedy.
The corn beef ego with absolutely no substance.
The vestibular imposters with sickening incompetence.
The approachable paella with little to no bottle.
The anal stick insect with massive insecurities.

I am the master of my own happiness, for its in my interests to live life to the full

I'm actually looking forward to the day when the rogues who abused me are finally brought to account and forced to face the music for their barbaric crimes against me. Because I'm simply interested to hear, read and see just how my protagonists of the, 'kop-out psychology is the root of all illnesses mantra' actually cope themselves on a psychological level when their world appears to fall apart.

I'm interested to hear, read and see just how they cope as their character, competency and integrity is brought into question time after time. I'm really interested to see how those rogues cope on a psychological level when hopefully their relationships start falling apart as their livelihood potentially ends up in the shredder.

Now you would think that personal retribution would be enough for any man but I'm afraid it's not enough for me. You see, I'm not only looking forward to my own retribution, I'm also interested in supporting, mentoring and aiding any kindred soul who is seeking their own medical abuse retribution, because that's just the sort of bloke that I am. Now hey, I'm no innocent, I know securing retribution will be no walk in the park, but I'm determined to take my case all the way and if that means taking my grievances to the European Courts of Human Rights, then so be it because that is what I will do.

I am the master of my own health, for I take my quality of health seriously

Personal Notes

I am the master of my own happiness, for its in my interests to live life to the full

Personal Notes

I am the master of my own health, for I take my quality of health seriously

Personal Notes

I am the master of my own happiness, for its in my interests to live life to the full

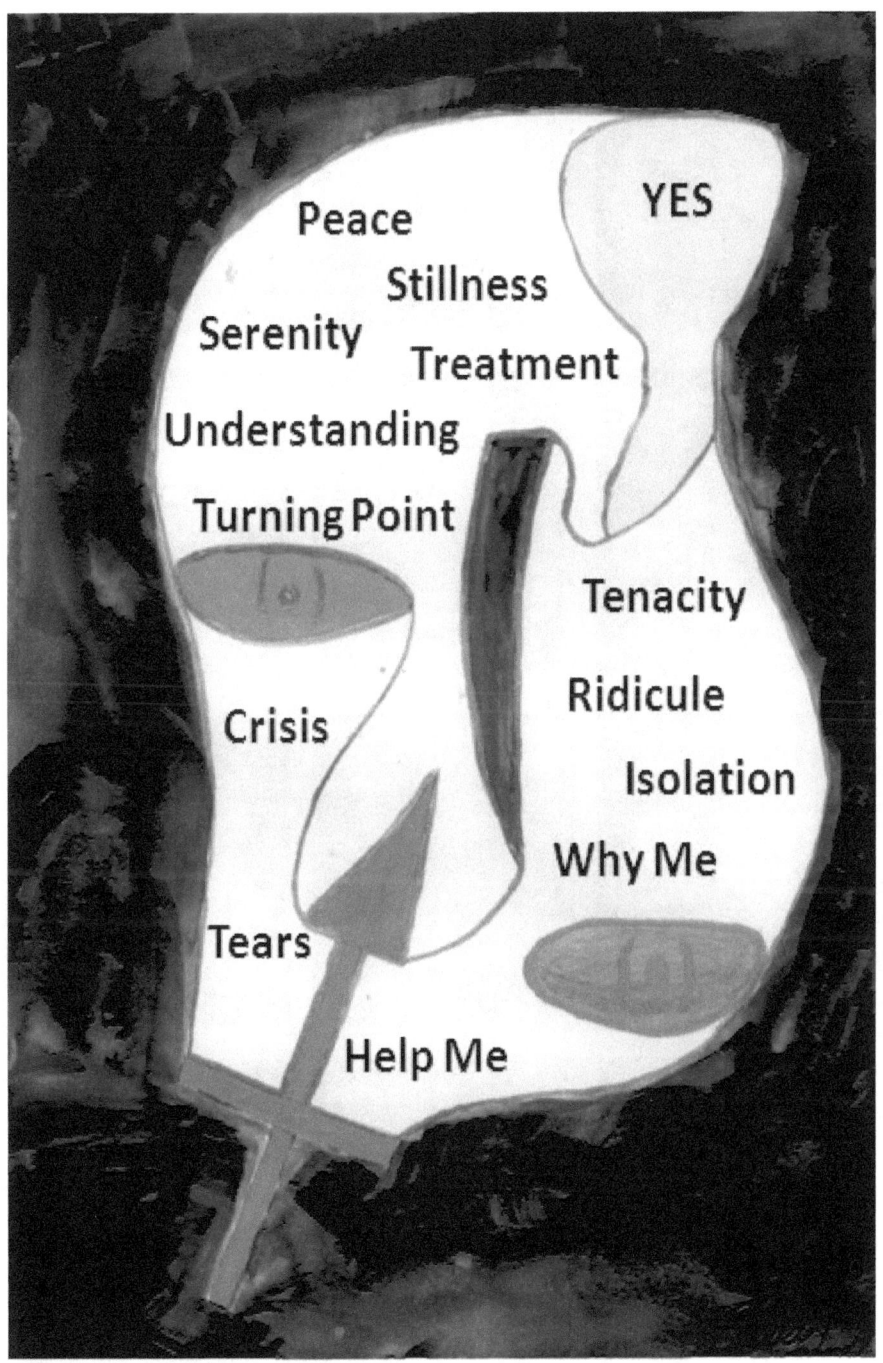

I am the master of my own health, for I take my quality of health seriously

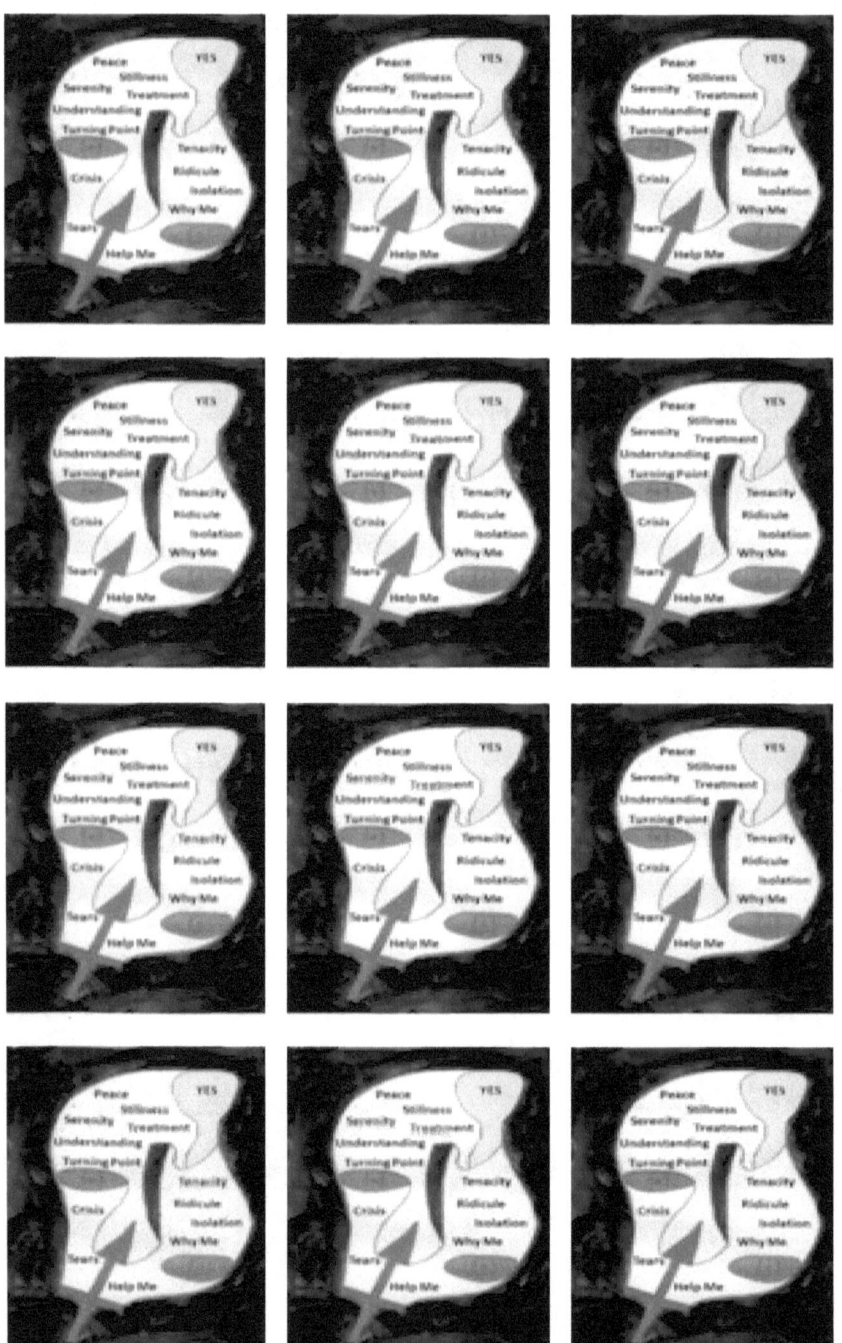

I am the master of my own happiness, for its in my interests to live life to the full

My Journey Through a Book of Hells

Growing up as a wee man on the Woodhouse council estate devoid of friends I sought out my cousin Danny on the playing fields of Kells. I remember being taken aback when I first heard of the book of Kells for in my innocence I thought it had been written about the fine people that lived, played and who worked on Kells. Ironically though, my fall into ill-health began in the playing fields, sheep fields and costal hedges of Kells and that's why this chapter has been worked up into my book of hells. I realise now that a fall from good health to that of a chronic diseased state is not always a straight forward process and can take many years and that no matter how brave or strong we are, poor health simply wrecks lives.

We have nothing without good health, no prosperity, no career or joy. Yet good health is something we all take for granted until it's ripped forever from our grasp. As a society we're not programmed to explore and look for answers when our health is in decline, because we absolve ourselves of that responsibility and empower only a select few. Therein we lose the connection that we need to plot and determine the origin and cause of our disease, because as our body's sole custodian we live the reality of our bodies every day of our life.

I am the master of my own health, for I take my quality of health seriously

As part of preparing this book it was important for me that I mapped and shared with you my decline, for in that process all the connections are clearly defined. With a simple red line mapping depression, blue line mapping physical strength and green line mapping my emotional strength over an entire forty year period.

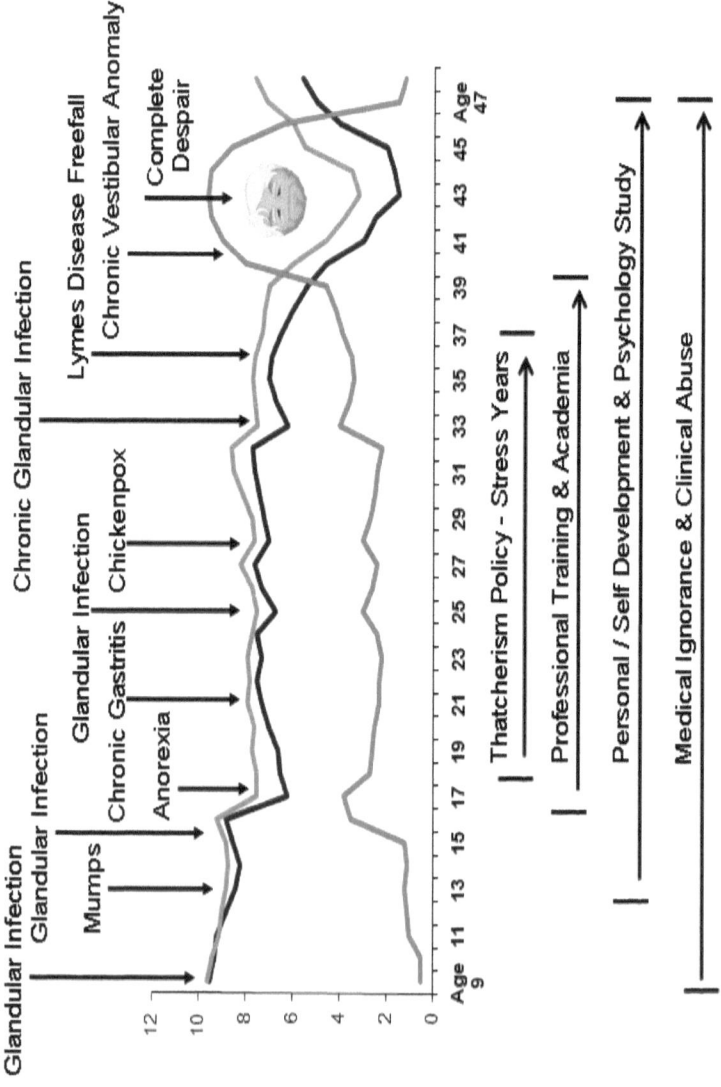

I am the master of my own happiness, for its in my interests to live life to the full

Before I elaborate further upon my own health decline however it's important that I cover emotional and depressive state perceptions because they are frequently cited by medical cretins as the originators of illness. When in reality they are nothing more than an expression of disease.

Nevertheless there is a big difference between emotional state and depressive state and they must never be confused or directly linked as one in the same because they are not, *but I will qualify this point further in subsequent chapters.*

Our emotional state in essence is our ability to cope, to rise to a challenge, to pick ourselves up after a set back and/or to project ourselves into the future and is nothing more than a derivative of our endocrine functionality.

Whereas depression I'm prepared to argue is nothing more than a symptom of disease and should not therefore be confused with subtle mood swings which are part of our normal emotional expressions.

As you will observe my health profile map starts way back at the point of formalized body awareness for me where I'm aware that I had exceptionally high levels of physical endurance and emotional strength with low depression intent i.e. I simply coped, laughed and got on with things.

Those expressions are mapped such that, physical and emotional scores at ten indicate high energy levels and equally very strong emotional stability. Whereas zero would indicate that I have no energy, no resilience, no emotional rigidity, no fight, in essence I'm simply burnt out.

In terms of depression expression, zero on the map indicates no depression present whereas ten would indicate chronic suicidal depression. As my health declined it's easy to see the correlation between physical strength and emotional strength and the impact that disease has

I am the master of my own health, for I take my quality of health seriously

upon all three states i.e. physical and emotional states decline in vitality and depression increases with paradoxical ferocity during chronic disease. Therefore my primary postulation is that the vast majority of depressive states are a direct result of a diseased state and that depression is not the generator of illness as most medics would have us believe.

Depression in itself is not an illness in the vast majority of cases rather it is a symptom that simply manifests through disease. Equally; psychological stress is not the originator of fatigue at best it is merely a bit player or derivative of that same diseased state. It is therefore very important that we all understand that the originator of chronic symptomology is not the fault of the patient because it is nothing more than an indicator of disease. Understand that and you're at least part of the way to accepting that you have a condition which needs treating and that you're not the entire cause of all your presenting symptoms. Now having covered that, it's back to my personal decline.

I am the master of my own happiness, for its in my interests to live life to the full

The beginning:- born with energy and vibrancy for life, head-strong and powerful I certainly caused myself strife. I wanted to understand, to know and to explore, but to my parents and siblings my questions and I were simply perceived as a complete bore. In isolation my only salvation was my beloved granddad who's generosity and receptivity towards me set free the lad from the boy, ultimately releasing through personal growth the man deep within. From his wisdom, his candor and his love for his family the boy alone in the summer of 1970 would discover the true blessings of life. There has not been a day, a week, a month or year since his parting that I haven't missed his voice, his views or his generosity of soul.

My journey into many hells began way back in those inspirational summer days, bitten to pieces by sheep ticks, midges and fleas. I remember at the age of nine being struck down by the most horrendous rash all over my body, followed by a glandular infection and fatigue after a heavy day of sheep droppings searching and being attacked by ticks, midges and fleas. That incident however was completely ignored by my parents and all concerned at the time because it was just a part of everyday life growing up on woodhouse and kells. What also didn't help the situation was the fact that I was out and about again as soon as I could even though I still felt extremely poorly.

Shortly after that event though, my body began to change with speed. I stopped being an energetic footballer, rugby player or athletic kid and became wracked with groin and leg pain. My ears were always sore and worse than that my body weight began to drastically grow. Cold hands and feet, night sweats and the most disgusting of body odor 'like decaying matter' were just some of the more noticeable changes that manifested themselves at that time in my life.

I am the master of my own health, for I take my quality of health seriously

At the age of ten I developed lumps in my groin the size of walnuts, but they were written off by GP's as an infection relating to athletes foot, even though I didn't have athletes foot. My mum hit the roof, she took it as a slant on her and that I hadn't been washing myself, even though she frequently told me it wasn't normal to have so many showers, which was my attempt to wash off my appalling body odor. This was a common theme from my mum however. She always lashed out verbally from a point of ignorance and always made things worse by not being there for me. As far as she was concerned whatever the GP said was correct and that was it.

This was a difficult place to be, difficult family situation to grow up in and probably why I closed down from them and did the best I could in any way possible just to get by and cope. I have to say here also that my dad never played any part in our formative development or education, as far as he was concerned he went to work, tipped the money over on Thursday night and that was all he had to do. No house repairs, no decorating, no washing, no cleaning, no caring and with no visible loving that was the way my dad chose to live his life. But hey my dad wasn't a bad man, he wouldn't help anyone, didn't think about anyone else's needs but he never ever directly harmed anyone either, he was just 'dad' and that was the way he was. I never received a birthday card, a gift or any form of encouragement from him in my entire life but equally I was never physically harmed by him either. Yet every night he came in from the pub, we all received a bag of our favourite crisps from him, I guess that was the only way he could show his love. As long has he had his cigarettes and his four pints of beer a night in Kells Royal British Legion he was happy, but I digress here so now back to my clinical decline.

I am the master of my own happiness, for its in my interests to live life to the full

Between the ages of eleven and twelve the pains in my legs, groin and now testicles became ridiculous. Again these symptoms were all written off this time as growing pains, even though I'd sort of stopped growing vertically but had begun to grow outwards. At the age of thirteen I developed mumps which was later changed to a glandular infection because it went on much longer than mumps would have been expected to last. Plus I was struck down several times during this period with instances of what I now know was vertigo, but I never told anyone. There was no point, mum was too ill and dad simply didn't want to know.

It was becoming difficult to swallow now and eating was becoming a real problem. In the dark days of the seventies convenience food in working class circles simply didn't extend much further than bread and jam, hot oxo and bread or cornflakes with milk and hot water. But they all became part of my staple diet because they were the only things I could sort of force down or swallow.

At sixteen I left Whitehaven Grammar school because with a brother now wanting to do his PhD, staying on in sixth form and university were not an option for a working class lad like me. I secured six engineering apprenticeships before opting for Albright & Wilson Marchon Chemicals on Kells.

All was fine on my basic engineering course until just before Christmas when I was struck down by my glandular infection once more. There was no room for sickness in training in those days. You either continued or you just simply lost your job.

So as I endeavoured to meet my work commitments, my condition declined over the following weeks and months and the swallowing problem simply went beyond a joke. But hey, I was working and had access to health food shops and literature and with sort of semi independence via my weekly apprentice allowance. I began taking a multimineral, vitamins B and C.

I am the master of my own health, for I take my quality of health seriously

In weeks my energy rose again albeit my groin and legs were still killing me. Things didn't improve much at home. Ever the clever bastard; my brother on one of his trips back from university to swell his student funds told my mum that my supplements were dangerous. As he was the clever one in the family I returned home one day from work to find that she'd thrown the lot away. In future my drive for better health would need to be more stealth like, I would tell no one anything about what I was thinking or doing, plus I needed to find somewhere to hide my stash away. A difficult situation because I lived in a home where my mum, continuously in a paranoid state, rummaged through my mail, my wardrobes and clothes; in fact she rummaged through everything, there was no space or grace in our house.

But where there is a will there is a way and it was time for me to get really fit again, to feel confident around the chicks, I didn't like the excess weight I was carrying and didn't feel that it was there because of me. I stored my vitamins in an old garden shed and I committed to jogging in the Easter of 78. In those days if you did anything like that in my area there was no support or reward, you were immediately discredited as a nutter and more often than enough ignored. Within two months I was flying and really starting to feel good. It was then whilst out running one night that I started to cough up not mucus but blood and boy did I feel rough physically. Very scary, no one to talk to and having no one who would know, my conclusion was to ignore it in the hope that it would simply go away. The next day I awoke as rough as a badgers bum. My throat was up again and I could hardly walk. I didn't eat anything for a week or maybe two and the weight just plummeted off me in a way it had never done before.

One month on I was in a right old state, exhausted, bloated with wind, terrible pains in my lower back, low emotionally and unable to cope. In steps my mum and she's read an article in a Sunday supplement and that's it our Barry is anorexic. It's back to the doctors again, no one is listening to any of my symptoms, the fact that I can only keep crushed apple down etc, is completely ignored and I'm now diagnosed with this most insidious of diseases. The stigma, the alienation and the ramification of that diagnosis was to be my Achilles heal for decades in my ignorant local community. What's more for the first time in my own personal life I was sucked into the mental health world by default, questions raised about my personality and sexuality. Answers twisted and misrepresented but again I had no help from anyone. I was in a difficult situation. I was ill, I was living in an unsupportive domestic situation and I was working in a callous and aggressive male dominated environment. I was the butt of everyone's jokes, I was a soft point of ridicule, and I was, 'the freak who was only happy when he was starving himself to death'. To my left I had arseholes full of bullshit and prejudices, to my right there was opportunist homosexuals masquerading as mental health carers, now how bad of a situation is that for a young lad to find himself in?

Nevertheless it was also around this time that two differing tradesmen took me under their wing, big Arthur Skelly and larl Alan Dixon 'dixie' Arthur could be an aggressive foul mouth oaf of a man at times but at heart he was a generous, caring and genuine family man. Dixie too, was a generous family man but unlike big Arthur he was, expansive, inspirational yet uncompromising and implicitly dogmatic most of the time. As I matured it was I suppose inevitable that our personalities would clash and they did and so my connection with both of them ended dramatically and that was the end of that.

I am the master of my own health, for I take my quality of health seriously

Nevertheless I have nothing but the uppermost respect for the part that those two guys played in my personal and engineering development, at was a very difficult time to say the least for me. I'm nearly fifty now but I also realised at this time just how special my 'granddads mentoring had been in my preparation for life.

During this difficult period I did the only thing I could do, I got my head down, worked through my problem on my own and I saw the harpies and charlatans for the rogues that they actually were. I read, I self medicated and began to explore the unknown about matters of psychology, spirituality and healing whilst living on the fringe of my family.

Was I any better? Well in truth not much because my throat and my groin were still painful to touch, my stomach ached daily now and became bloated with the slightest intake of food; irritable bowel syndrome IBS was the medical conclusion now but not a resolution to be found.

By the age of twenty I was sort of trying to lose myself in booze, but the stigma of anorexia like the Black Death followed me in the shadows everywhere that I went. Fathers distrusted me and brothers wanted to beat me up for daring to date or sleep with their sisters. At that time it seemed that I was never out of Kells Royal British Legion with my uncle Benny or Gordon Cottiers Paul Jones Tavern trashing myself with the likes of Jimmy Moore 'SW' the Raging Bull, Big D, Kikee, Norman Whiteside and Bense to name just a few.

Nevertheless I bumbled along, reading, exploring and trashing myself every weekend until at the age of twenty four when it was at last time to buy my own pad no more renting or lodging for me. What a risk that was, we were in the dreadful Thatcher years, there was no work, we had high interest rates and the nation was racked with despair. My energies were changing though and it felt the right time to open up new doors.

I am the master of my own happiness, for its in my interests to live life to the full

Free of local scrutiny my jogging commenced again and I met my first fell running hero, Steven Martin one of the true mountain men. This was a time of great physical, emotional growth and pain for me, tarnished by Thatcherism and the death of my girlfriend, Ann Marie through leukemia at just twenty three. Yet whilst the death of Annie was very hard to come to terms with, the worst part of all was the bigotry and hatred generated by her mum and her 'shit for brains brothers' towards me.

You see, Annie was a third generation 'Irish Roman Catholic' and her family simply hated me for being a Protestant. I was threatened with violence during our brief relationship and latterly if I visited her in hospital and finally if I attended her funeral albeit that I did because I thought to myself; screw them and their shit filled brains.

Shortly after Annie's death with a heart filled with rage I joined the Orange Order; I was tired of the 'Irish Rebel Roman Catholic Culture' and lashed out with equal hatred and contempt of that culture because I was sick to my back teeth of being victimized by it.

These were strange karmic learning years indeed, for I was a young man with far too much anger which I idealistically channelled into fighting for far too many ideological lost causes. I was a complete paradox, a true gentleman, considerate and caring, yet a young man also filled with far too much hate. I hated Roman Catholics, Tory's, Industrial Scabs, My Mum and my Dad but most of all I hated me because my life at that time always felt as if it was pointless and going nowhere.

At twenty seven however I had a very terrifying out of body experience where I was given a very clear message from an angelic form that there was a mountain before me that I had to climb because the welfare of mankind rested upon it, now how weird is that?.

I am the master of my own health, for I take my quality of health seriously

I took this experience very literally and began really pushing myself on my local Cumberland Fells. It was also the period that I picked up the nickname the chocolate fell runner from the late David Donald. He christened me that because whilst in training I would destroy my club mates climbing and descending the local fells, but when it came to race days I would either be too ill to race or too fatigued during the race to represent myself well. Hence DD put 2 and 2 together and arrived at 6 and decided I never performed in races because I didn't have the bottle.

He couldn't have been further from the truth; I was being eaten alive at the time by sheep ticks, pulling 3 or 4 out of my flesh during warm downs after being out on the fells for a few hours. It was just the way it was, sheep ticks burrowing into my back hair, chest hair, groins, and the back of my thighs every time I went out on the fells with my old Border Collie Jetblack. It was very normal at the time for us both to be eaten alive, God love him, no wonder he faded so fast in the end.

The cycle of monthly fevers, shivers, swollen glands, fatigue, hot flushes, mouth ulcers and chronic leg pains including the insidious lowering of mood made no sense, but I realise now that it was just low grade Lymes Disease and the beginning of deeper disease. Silly things would happen during this period.

For instance my heart would race to over 240 beats per minute for no apparent reason but when that worsened and went on for months and I brought it to the attention of my GP the inevitable result was; I was simply ridiculed as neurotic.

I would lose over a stone in weight in one week for no apparent reason and then gain it all back the following week, a presentation that I now know is the result of thyroid storms. Nevertheless at that time I had to weigh myself every day because if I trained during a weight loss cycle the anorexia jibes would start once again.

I am the master of my own happiness, for its in my interests to live life to the full

In one instance my body weight plummeted down as low as 8 stone 3lbs. All my body hair fell out over a period of six weeks yet when I brought it to the attention of my GP the response was; it's not normal to have that amount of body hair Mr. Hardy. One even joked 'have you not thought of buying a vest like the rest of us'? Not one of them suggested clinical testing to see what was going on, but I was offered the obligatory SSRI's.

When I raised the spectre of Lymes Disease, the qualification of 'neurotic' simply increased and the view was that I read too much, which was not a good thing because after all I was an intellectual cretin and not an earth god like them.

I would suffer appalling stomach cramps, foot cramps and even lost the sight in my left eye but time after time the symptoms would change, alternate or in some instances even disappear.

However the most insidious condition which almost brought me to my knees was the chronic gastritis which I'd had from my teens. This was a fantastic condition for my GP's because they simply wrote it off as a stress related disease because my profile did not fit that derived from Helicobacter pylori.

Now hey; there was no getting away from the stress I was under at that time for it was everywhere. But it was most certainly not the root cause of all my declining health issues of that I'm now one hundred percent sure.

I am the master of my own health, for I take my quality of health seriously

The 1980's and 90's were a difficult time; Thatcher had waged war on the country, community industry and hope had almost evaporated and this turned us into a nation in despair. Yet in my area the nuclear industry was sheltered from her rage, creating by default a culture of elitism and greed. In that industry it didn't matter if you were lazy, talent-less or lacking in any professional qualifications, you were guaranteed a job and life style which even now I personally consider to be obscene.

Nevertheless whilst some of us stood up and fought for what was right, decent and good, others just sat back and played their part in our greediest, soulless and darkest of days. Whole communities were thrown into a life of constant anguish. The best of our talent was thrown onto the scrap heap, it was a time when you could work for weeks and months and maybe never get paid. A time when you could have qualifications to die for, but never secure any paid work or work of any validity. All in the name of progress, all in the name of the free market and all at a time when society turned its back on everything it had previously believed in.

It was the time of the invisible SID, the time when we as a nation sold just about every corporate asset we'd ever owned. A time when a nation filled with greed trampled over the helpless, the dying or those simply in dire need. It was a time of injustice, social unrest and a social disease where working men were beaten over the head by policemen for simply daring to strike or defend their basic needs.

This was a time we must never forget, for it was a time when the lizards ruled our home lands, a time of hatred, prejudices and millions in despair as leading politicians and their sycophants lined their slimy pockets through debauchery, lies and greed.

I am the master of my own happiness, for its in my interests to live life to the full

So when we think about health and how it can decline we should never forget the part played by our governments and their self motivated policies which are often hidden and unseen. For the deviants who orchestrate our state imposed stress are always driven by dogma and greed.

I remember the constant stress of retraining, of reinventing myself, of trying to make 'ends meat' *West Cumbrian expression of poor finances and unable to buy even the scraggy ends of meat* whilst battling daily with my continuously failing health. Very little of that stress was of my own making; I simply did what I could in intolerable situations.

Yet the perpetrator of this cultural stress was no less than Britain's first modern dictator, a she devil who became despised in the end by her party, her people and her kith and kin. So whilst some may lament her passing when at last her mortal remnants must go, I will crack open the bubbly and shout with great cheer; fuck you Margaret Thatcher you butcher and slayer of men, may your God if you have one fuck you hard from now on and certainly until times end.

I am the master of my own health, for I take my quality of health seriously

During that dreadful period it seemed to me that every time I took one step forward there was no reward for me as I always seemed to be greeted by some other form of set back or personal misery. No work, no money and further training always to begin and all on the back of my tick bitten time bomb and a building momentum from deep within. Poor health, Thatcher's cruel crusade and working through the fallout of Ann Marie's death in totality did create a greater sense of isolation deep inside me, a sort of hidden grief and misery that simply tormented and hung over me.

Still challenged by cycles of intense fatigue, fever, lowering of mood, IBS and chronic gastritis, by the age of twenty six my daily medications included: 'Cimetidine' for my stomach and 'Salbutamol' asthma inhalers and a range of supplements including: amino acid building blocks, calcium/magnesium complex, multi-mineral, Vitamin B complex and Vitamin C with A and E. But still I could find no resolution to the ever increasing conditions which kept badgering, taxing and compromising me.

At twenty eight I was struck down by adult chickenpox, I hadn't a clue what was happening to me for eight weeks or so before it actually broke out. I could hardly put one foot in front of the other I was so fatigued. During this episode I was still working at the time in a manual industry and remember nearly crying with all the bodily pain and fatigue that I was experiencing.

When it was diagnosed it was greeted with great hilarity from those around me, not one single soul paid me a visit or enquired as to how I was doing as my condition pushed me into my bed. I lay in there for over six days wrecked unable to get up to make anything to eat or drink.

I am the master of my own happiness, for its in my interests to live life to the full

When I returned back to work, the first two remarks that I was greeted with were, 'has thou been starving thee sell again' and 'hey Baz I've got a spot here thou better not have given fucken chickenpox to me you skinny larl bastard'. Not one single person said, how you feeling Baz? Not one person cut me any slack in the work place. Instead I was thrown right back into all the shit jobs that the elites in my work place simply refused to do.

This was a major turning point in my life; I dropped all social links with the people I'd worked with for over seven years. On a daily basis I still had to interact with them, but they all filled me with revulsion and because of that I didn't want anything further to do with them. Here I was reinventing myself again; I was isolated now on all fronts and found only peace and solidity in my own home or on the Cumberland Fells. Reading, studying, resting and running became my only past times as I seemed to have nothing in common with anyone I knew except for the odd one or two.

At twenty nine I simply couldn't work any longer in the industry or with the people I'd forced myself to endure for so long so as I prepared to leave my current work situation behind I connected with a different crew of work place friends. Frank Vincent, Bobby Green, Jimmy Curwen, Gordon Nicholson, Ronnie Nicholson, Peter Donnelly, Larl Ronnie Savage, Big Bobby Stubs, Tommy Harper and big Joe Pulen to name but a few. All of whom encouraged me to move on and upwards because that in reality was all I could do.

I am the master of my own health, for I take my quality of health seriously

You see, as the highest qualified operational support engineer on the site at that time with highers in both mechanical and civil engineering I was unable to make any career progression because of the stigma around my illness in my teens. Within months I felt it was time that I put my professional qualifications to good use and I jumped into the ruthless world of contracting where external perceptions and internal realities are simply miles even light years apart.

I quickly learned that travel can be challenging, change difficult to understand, that people can be ruthless and home can seem like some distant or foreign land most of the time. For me there are no great rewards in contracting or opportunities to think about the higher things of life. Once you're on the contract treadmill it's dog eat dog, cat eat cat and all accompanied by the worst thing of all: those dreadful two legged rats.

Contracting is not the way a man should choose to live. It robs him of his grounding, of solidity, of prosperity of soul, for whilst he's chasing the illusive pound signs in his dreams, he's missing out on his own crock of gold. I contracted and I hated it, there was no money in it, no security in it, no home in it and no soul in it, but that was the tone of the Thatcher years when surviving was a man's only goal. Getting through the Thatcher years took a very great toll upon me. I struggled with so many things, declining personal health, governmental generated decline, and an insidious negative energy which invaded every single cell of my being including my psyche.

I am the master of my own happiness, for its in my interests to live life to the full

By the age of thirty I was frequently urinating protein i.e. blood stained pee, plus the pains in my lower back, groins and legs where a constant source of distress to me. The fevers every month would wipe me out for anywhere between one and five days, but I was fighter and as such theses cycles were just a part of my normal living days by then.

I became an even greater paradox to the people I worked with and the woman that I slept with. They all in general seemed to like me but would get very angry because they could not get close to understanding me or have immediate access to me. You see; I kept everyone at arms length, I was very sociable, very generous, and considerate but above all I valued my own space. I needed rest and my own agenda to allow me to do and cope with my condition in the best way that I could manage.

This was a lonely time, a time where I craved companionship but where none of my companions filled that gap. I was looking for knowledge, understanding and personal growth and a soul mate who could handle a companion committed to that difficult path. In the circles I worked and lived in though all I encountered were greedy or needy companions, each one for whatever reason transfixed by something they thought that I had deep within.

Laughably I knew in reality that hadn't anything near what they thought I had, I was just a bloke like so many other blokes simply doing my best just to cope. I was on the fringe of everything, I wasn't one of the boys, I didn't have young children, and didn't have visibly steady girlfriends. It was a very strange time because I became eminently more attractive to the twenty something wives, to the single mums with very small kids, to the mature woman with deeper thoughts and desires and to the freelancers and ladettes who just wanted me to explore their own sexual desires.

I am the master of my own health, for I take my quality of health seriously

The guys on the other hand seemed to despise me and took great delight in ridiculing me and my sport. They frequently questioned my morality and sexuality imposing their own ridiculous agendas upon me fueled through stupidity and ignorance of thought and nothing more. The funny thing was that some of the biggest offenders had no idea that in years gone by I had either slept with their girlfriends, daughters or wives.

The more I learned, the more aloof I became and greater became my isolation from main stream thoughts and perceptions. I didn't want any of the garbage that my peers appeared to want; I just wanted to live a life devoid of problems and manmade fears. I guess what I was looking for was simply contentment, rest and peace.

Yet my biggest Achilles heal remained as ever my receptivity to my parents and my sister for I was forever allowing myself to be dragged into their preventable dramas which continued to be a drain on my capabilities in wellness and in fatigue.

In the early 90's my parents were still living in the council house that I'd grown up in, but the estate had changed. No longer was it an estate of hard working, hard living, salt of the earth West Cumbrian's, it was a waste land of crime, of single mothers under twenty five with children from a wide range of men. There was no respect, no decency and no time for authority. The estate I had grown up on was by now a complete mire of mind, body and dole. Yet my parents for all their faults were decent people and worthy of a much better quality of life than they'd now acquired.

So it became my struggle by default to somehow extract them from their situation and hopefully give them a much better quality of life. In time I bought my parents a small two up/two down, decorating it from top to bottom in one week and I'm happy to say that from that day to this, their lives at that time was as contented as their lives had ever been.

I am the master of my own happiness, for its in my interests to live life to the full

At thirty two I spent a full year without leave in the Middle East just enough time to pay off my parents' new home, but I returned to the UK after three chronic glandular infections a shadow of my former self. I was experiencing a high degree of unexplainable anxiety and chronic muscular fatigue. My stomach was no better and so I went on a visit to my GPs for my medication and to explain to him exactly what I was feeling. Immediately the glandular infections were put to one side and the focus of this male GP's questions turned specifically to questions about me;

- You've a bit of a strange hairstyle and highly manicured beard there Mr. Hardy is that because you're gay?

- When was the last time you had sex?

- Are you afraid of having sex?

- Do you feel that you need to see a counsellor?

- Why are you so uncomfortable with this line of questions?

- Do you have something to hide?

I was bloody raging by this time because I had a bad stomach and symptoms that this cretin just didn't seem to be hearing. Now though all of a sudden he was either tapping me up or suggesting for some reason that I was gay. Here are some of the answers that I would love to have given that arsehole of a GP. But at that time I wasn't in a position to completely tell him to fuck off.

- No you areshole excuse the pun I'm not gay.

- I don't need counselling.

I am the master of my own health, for I take my quality of health seriously

- I need a bloody GP who knows what he or she is doing.

- Now give me a prescription for my cimetidine and let me get the hell out of here.

In the absence of that personal assurance of the impropriety of his line of questions, I did the best that I could just too simply fend them off and cope, because I knew that an outburst of the sensations and emotions I was feeling would have closed all the doors and given me no other place to go. Or at least that's what I foolishly thought at the time.

Now hey gay awareness in the 1980's and 90's and a preoccupation with a fear of homosexuality by insecure heterosexuals and/or reluctant homosexuals was indeed an insidious blight. If that preoccupation wasn't used to intimidate non conforming individuals it was certainly used in disproportionate frequencies as a tool of slander driven spite. The thing that really pissed me off with this insidious slant on life was that if I had been gay I wouldn't have had a problem admitting that I was indeed gay and that's because I have always worn my heart on my sleeve. I did however often wonder about the motives of the repressive and closet gays who for whatever reason frequently targeted me. Unlike them, I had known from nine years of age via my mums 'Little woods' catalogue and some cheer leaders I saw at a Rugby game that it was chicks in nice lingerie that did it for me, beautiful faces, breasts and shapely feminine hips did it every time for me O yeah!

Nevertheless gay or not gay that sort of rhetoric had no part to play in an ignorant GP's office and served only to make me more vulnerable from a clinical perspective and set off some massive alarm bells deep inside me. I had to find a way through my physical hells and that meant exploring alternative treatments because I wasn't going to put up with any more bullshit from anymore stupid GP's.

I am the master of my own happiness, for its in my interests to live life to the full

I wanted to talk to healers who were prepared to listen and help me. So during that period I continued to explore a wide range of alternative approaches including;

- Psychology training.
- Buddhist retreats.
- Philosophy study retreats.
- Indian sweat lodges.
- Tantric sex retreats.
- Yoga.
- Detoxing.
- Homeopathy.
- Remedial massage.
- Hellerwork.
- Bowen technique.
- Reflexology.
- Healing crystals.
- Tarot.
- Reike.
- Specific blood group diets.
- Acupuncture.
- Hot stones.
- Alexander technique.
- Ayurvedic medicine.
- Chinese medicine.
- Etc, etc, etc.

I am the master of my own health, for I take my quality of health seriously

Despite all my efforts my health continued to be up and down with symptoms that would simply come and go but there was only one constant just like there had been for so long and that was my health moving steadily into deeper decline.

At thirty six, whilst working away from home in 'Portugal' my stomach became almost unbearable with pain. My throat was so swollen I could hardly speak, I was losing weight quickly and unable to sleep and it was right at that time that I was struck down by panic attacks.

What could I have done? The alternative things weren't helping so in an act of desperation I resigned my post, headed off back home and reported once more to a practice GP. His conclusion was short and sharp 'your suffering from Anorexia again with clear symptoms of depression' handing me a prescription for some well know SSRI's, stating that it was common for people like me with 'issues' to have a nervous breakdown.

I was indeed weary of my life I didn't know whether I was coming or going and the depression was certainly picking up momentum as the uncontrollable anxiety grew inside me. I took one of those pills that very same afternoon and by 8:00pm I was out of my head. Sweat was pouring out of me, I was so dizzy I couldn't stand up, my anxiety was off the scales and now the depression inside me was so bad that I was ready to jump under a bus.

I somehow managed to get a further appointment the following day and explained to the shit GP what was going on. His reaction was there was no way that the tablet could have got into my system already and instead of taking one table I should now take two. *I explain hypo metabolism later in the Lymes chapter qualifying adverse reactions to small amounts of food, medication or supplements etc.* He made me an appointment for the same day in the psychiatric outpatients department at my local hospital and once again I was interrogated by a deviant proclaiming to be something that he clearly wasn't.

I am the master of my own happiness, for its in my interests to live life to the full

The entire line of questioning focused upon my sexuality and that there were places I could go and people I could see if I wished to discuss the problems I had about recognizing my sexuality. The GP had obviously either imprinted that line of questioning on my referral notes or this was just another deviant chancing his arm. Either way it was simply outrageous and I have to say that if I ever met any of the people who contributed to my thirty plus years of medical abuse, I would need to be held back from tearing them apart limb from bloody limb.

I didn't take two of the GP's tablets and I explained that to the deviant that I saw. For some reason he agreed and then at the end of our session his line manager wrote me a prescription for an alternative medication. At the time one of my cousin's wives worked in mental health care so I spoke to her about this new tablet. Her recommendation was; 'take it, its good for you and clearly just what I needed'. So I started taking the damn things and within a day I could hardly walk again because I was so fatigued. My head was splitting by now and I was unable to focus upon anything because my vision was blurred and my eyes just drifted in concentration and rolled around in my head. I listened to all her rubbish and I kept taking them for just over two weeks but I was getting worse not better so I simply threw the bloody lot out with my weekly rubbish. I thought Jesus Christ, there must be a way out of this hell hole and that perhaps it was all down to me.

In that frame of mind it was clear to me then that freedom through exercise could perhaps be the key again. So I put my fell shoes on day after day and simply walked the fells with 'Jetblack' the problem was however that my ego and identity were shattered once more and I knew I would have to reinvent myself yet again. These were bad times, indeed very bad times. I had chronic groin pain, chronic stomach pain, chronic anxiety, chronic fevers and chronic isolation whilst attempting to earn enough money just to get by once again.

I am the master of my own health, for I take my quality of health seriously

Reinvent myself I did. I started up my own engineering consultancy and secured immediately because of my expertise a project to help survey and base line the asset structures for the UK's first ever commercial nuclear reactor decommissioning project. So I profiled the facility's asset, system and building structures in double quick time. Then I implemented a computerized maintenance management system before handing over this new methodology to my client, winning unconditional approval from the nuclear inspectorate of industry that decommissioning could proceed. *I did all that on the back of Chinese whispers about my sanity, whilst battling with my illness of pain, depression and chronic fatigue.*

Despite my illnesses however I was still highly respected within my profession and in 1998 I was invited to enroll on a post graduate program at the University of Manchester studying my primary specialist subject Maintenance Engineering and Physical Asset Management. I agreed and self funded my entire program which cost me in excess of £30K. *I graduated in July 1999 despite all the personal self funding and personal health issues that I faced and became the FIRST full time postgraduate student to be awarded that degree from my faculty in the UK.*

The point I make here is that it is still possible to achieve major success during times of great illness when we are blessed with great reserves of inner strength and lots of emotional resolve. That's why I've always taken a great exception to the medical world playing the emotional liability and or stability card when dealing with the likes of me. They don't know me and I'm sure that none of the cretins that I've met in the past could have battled through my adversities like I have through-out the majority of my life.

I am the master of my own happiness, for its in my interests to live life to the full

In 2000 I was involved in a helicopter crash where we ditched into the Persian Gulf. The result of the crash was that upon compression of my neck in any direction I became dizzy and unable to see. I'm not going to labour this point but doubtless to say all subsequent medical investigations ultimately re-assigned the cause of that new symptom at the door of my weak psychology. Oh yes! As far as the medics were concerned this was not a physical condition it was indeed an emotional/psychological condition.

Little did I know then that a whole new clinical abuse loop had just been opened up to more suffering for me! I cover this incredibly debilitating condition and the abuse I endured in my book My Psychiatric Artery where I self-diagnose micro vascular compression syndrome which leads onto the unique discovery that I have a genetic and seemingly inoperable abnormality. I discovered that I was born with a Posterior Inferior Cerebella Artery (PICA) running directly though my vestibular bundle left side which also abuts my brainstem. The upshot of that is symptomology and suffering beyond the comprehension of mortal man, matched only by the medical abuse I endured at the same time.

My personal hardships continued to seem never ending when in 2001 I'm escorted off the Sellafield Nuclear reprocessing site. My contract was terminated abruptly because of my overt criticism of some of the company's directly hired staff, site operational techniques and standards of due care on the back of the site's horrendous MOX plant breaches in quality recording that almost brought that company to its knees. But hey that's another battle for another day. It's safe to say though that there are three of my former line managers from the mid 90's on that site that I would hope to pursue redress from in the fullness of time.

I am the master of my own health, for I take my quality of health seriously

Nevertheless I wasn't in the best of shape but it's clear that there would be no further work for me in my local area, the only good thing about this situation however was that the Labour party had been in for three years now and things were at last starting to move once again in the British economy.

As ever, I was financially broke and could see no way forward so I was forced to put my home on the market and sell it for what I paid for it way back in 1992. I gave most of my possessions away and put a few bits and bobs in storage and moved in with my parents for what I thought would be a matter of a month or two. But at the point I moved in it became very clear that something was not right with my dad.

He couldn't hold a line of thought or communicate without using bla bla etc, to plug the gaps in what I guess he was trying to say, more than this however he didn't really appear to know what he was doing anymore. Within days I'm thrust into a situation where I'm trying to get help for him because my mum and my sister are in denial as ever and not prepared to accept that he has dementia.

Once again I find myself karmically involved in a domestic situation I would rather not be in. My own health because of this additional stress continues to decline too, as the pressure of living in my parent's box room and my dad's deteriorating conditions impose greater and greater strain upon me.

Whilst I pick up little bits of work here and there for some dreadful, dreadful karmic reason it became very clear that I was simply not going to be able to break free of this new dreadful domestic situation that I'd found myself in. I had no space, no quality of life yet I became the buffer between my dad's condition and everyone else's life. My mum couldn't cope, my brother didn't give a shit and my sister with a vulnerable son was in the middle of a nasty divorce. 'Arrrrrrrrrrr' was my constant thought; I need an exit route out of here!

I am the master of my own happiness, for its in my interests to live life to the full

In 2002 I met and thought that I'd fallen in love with a new chick on the block, someone who appeared to offer all the things I'd always looked for in a partner. She was well travelled, had similar alternative views on life to me and seemed to like a lot of the values that I myself had always aspired too. However the red warning flags were every where right from the very first date.

In truth if I'd still had my own place and my own space I would never allowed myself to get to involved with her. Early into our relationship I thought this chick is certainly messed up and perhaps needed counselling, but that quickly changed to thinking that perhaps she was insane as her true personality began to be revealed. However it wasn't until 2004, long after I'd ended the relationship that I finally understood why she was so deadly and so emotionally abusive.

This person had many failed relationships under her belt which I suppose on the surface can be interpolated as part of life's rich tapestry. What was very bizarre however was that for some reason she felt the need to talk about them all the time, day and night.

For the short time we were together I allowed her deluded illusions of reality and what she believed was acceptable in a relationship to be a significant part of my life. It was neither healthy nor adult and as a result of which I lost any spark that I'd once had for her.

In essence I lived with ten or twelve of her failed former lovers for the entire time we were together, as she picked over the bones of what they were all like, the size of their dicks, their good points, bad points, how they hurt her etc, etc, etc. At first I was supportive but then became incredibly tired of; David, Gary, Sammy, Steve, Sayid, Steve, Abdul, Mike and the like, because no matter where we were they were in my face and in my life.

She was incredibly selfish, moody, manipulative and abusive when things from her perverse perspective were not going right. She would scream at me, you must be insecure if you can't handle my past. In reality however it wasn't me who had the problem it was her who kept dragging her baggage into every aspect of mine and her current life.

The guys who lived in her head were with us before sex, during sex, after sex, whilst shopping, talking or simply walking and yet if I so much as looked at another woman all hell would break loose because I had wondering eyes.

It was eminently acceptable for her to meet up with or contact former lovers because that was her simply being grown up and mature, but if I even dared to mention I'd met with a female friend for lunch, dinner or just a cup of tea she would scream like a lunatic at me about being unfaithful or words to that effect.

It was like living in a nightmare, every bloke on the planet fancied her in her mind; every bloke had the right to ask her out on a date and everything that was wrong in our relationship was simply down to me.

But I quickly discovered that she was a fantasist, a lost soul, unable to give or to love, but her worst trait of all was her ability to detach from people and situations at the drop of her hat when she could simply switch off, pack up her belongings and move on.

The number of times we went out to places and/or an event and she'd just stormed off in a manufactured rage or conduct herself like a complete and utter spoilt brat was simply insane. And whilst she never stopped wanting, once acquired nothing was ever good enough and she sort of rejoiced in the nickname of finicky that she'd inherited from her friends and frequently referred to herself as the princess from the book 'The Princess And The Pea'.

I am the master of my own happiness, for its in my interests to live life to the full

In all my years I've never quite met anyone as horrible and uncaring as her. Postulating to the outside world such an air of refinement and spiritual development when in reality she was just as fucked up as the people she was kidding. To live with her was to truly know her she was not a highly evolved soul at all; she was a sham and a fraud that simply enjoyed playing the victim out loud.

Now all that is a long winded way of saying that boy did I fuck up big time getting involved with her and it remains to this day the worst mistake I've ever made in my life. Yet the price that I paid for my failing even today feels disproportionate to the simple mistake that I made. Not only did she play with my head for a while but through our karmic connection I allowed her to infect me with a disease that nearly cost me my life and still to this day imposes a terrible load upon me. A disease that has tested every aspect of my physical, emotional, spiritual, strengths, beliefs and resolves and you know what I mean bloody Lymes Disease.

You see, from the very first night I slept with her in December of 2002 I awoke the next morning with a fever and virtually unable to breath, but worse than that I had a big red rash all over my penis, groin and testicles. Her immediate reaction was what on earth was wrong with me and I'd better not have given anything to me, meaning her. Well the truth of the matter was I hadn't and that she'd in point of fact infected me still further with her dreadful diseases herpes and Lymes Disease.

You see in her youth she'd spent some time in Canada exploring her sexuality with a range of ethnicities which she was always more than happy to talk about, the black hoodlums, the yoga teacher, the lumberjack twins, the gardener etc, etc, etc. However within years of returning home to the UK she'd become ill yet recovered from non-hodgkins lymphoma. Now what she didn't and probably doesn't know to this day is that she is a carrier of Lymes Disease.

I am the master of my own health, for I take my quality of health seriously

She's spent the best part of 30 years hiding behind non-hodgkins lymphoma when in reality she's been destroying guys' lives with her highly infectious yet hidden diseases. It's only when all the pieces came together that the true picture behind this individual became ever so clear. Whilst she frequently bleated on about her dysfunctional childhood citing it and her dad for all the freaky dudes she gone on to meet. The reality all the time if she'd ever cared to look was clearly there between her wide open legs. Once engaging in any form of sexual activity guys immediately became infected with her insidious bacterium which directly attacked both their body and brain with unrelenting ferocity. There's no wonder her former lovers got tired of her because she has always worn them down and made her guys ill.

Now either understanding or accepting responsibility for her part in the decline of her relationships or the stability of her men is not something she would ever entertain. You see; at that point she would need to turn away from being the victim mode which she relishes and become the true fiend that she actually is. That however would not sit at all well with her psyche or the illusions she worked so hard to fabricate for herself. You see; she's actually happy playing the victim because as the victim she never needs to grow up.

Now hey I'm no hero here, we all have issues, we all have shit to deal with it's just that some of us hold our hands up and try our best to deal with our shit whilst others simply enjoy playing the victim and simply choose to spend their lives procrastinating whilst either directly or indirectly abusing anyone stupid enough to move to close to them.

I am the master of my own happiness, for its in my interests to live life to the full

Nevertheless as I've stated I fortunately managed to drag myself out of that relationship which was difficult because for me, there was some sort of deep karmic bond attracting me to her at that time even though I was desperately ill by then. However in the end it was very easy to let her go when by letting her mask slip completely she made it very clear as my health declined by her pursuit of her next yoga lover that she wasn't worth any more of my energy, love or my time.

People have often asked me since my diagnosis if I'd ever informed her about her condition and further; would I ever help her get through Lymes Disease if she needed my help. My answers have always been no and there is no point because she's simply not evolved enough to accept or admit that at any point in her life it has been her and her alone that has been responsible for so much of her personal misery. Apart from that she is a great user and abuser, she takes what she needs and then moves on. The year we parted I did send her a very generous Christmas card wishing her well and thanking her for the part she'd played in my life, but ever the abusive child that she is, she retuned to my mums home covered in bile and crap. Some adults may have accepted my gesture in the spirit it was sent, whereas others who didn't wish to be reminded of a former connection may have just binned it or informed me that they'd moved on. She did unfortunately what she always does; she lashed out in her childish state which indirectly closed our karmic connection gate forever…..yay. Since we parted I've done an extraordinary amount of spiritual and karmic cleansing work to exorcise her and her energy from my life and there's no way I would ever let a dark soul like her back in.

I am the master of my own health, for I take my quality of health seriously

Today whilst I wish her no harm, I really don't give a hoot whether she's alive or dead, because she's out of my life, my heart and my head and that's the way it will always stay, believe me! Ironically two guys have contacted me about her and asked what she's really like, my advice has been on both occasions give her a big miss dude, the illusion she spins isn't worth her drama or the consequences that she will bring into your life.

I am the master of my own happiness, for its in my interests to live life to the full

By the end of 2003 I simply couldn't stand being in my body any more, the pain and pressure in my head were insane. I'd lost the sight completely in my left eye, couldn't stand sunlight, or the slightest of background noises anymore, the lumps in my groins where like boiled eggs and I'd lost all my body hair once more. Yet no one seemed to be able to diagnose me or listen to my despair, I was simply written off as a depressive with another nervous breakdown. My head pain was written off as tension headaches and all the other symptoms simply part of psychological stress. But that's the great British diagnostic medical model they're only happy when writing us off. I realise now that all those years of battling low grade lymes were simply insignificant to the load I'd picked up via sex in 2002 and 2003.

By now my thoughts were screaming and tormenting me, I was unable to sleep and simply too exhausted too cope. I was lost in a world of isolation, suffering and pain. My head had become sunken into my shoulders, I couldn't turn it in any direction for the horrendous pain, plus my neck ached like chronic toothache and felt like granite whilst my eyes felt as if they were going to explode.

The depression was unprecedented, no matter what I did or tried to do I was in agony and the only thing on offer for me was SSRI's or a long enforced stay in a psychiatric ward. I remember my brother called my mum one day and she passed over the phone to me where he starkly rebuffed me when I started to explain just how I was feeling; *'Why don't you just give yourself a shake, we've all got problems but we all just get on with them you seem to be only happy when you're making a drama out of every thing Barry now I just haven't got time for you or this'.* I've never spoken to that shit again from that day to this and in all that I hold dear I guarantee you I never will.

I am the master of my own health, for I take my quality of health seriously

It's not for me to forgive him or to excuse him his sins, my only obligation now is to cope with what I have left in this life and as for my brother well all I feel is fuck him and his kin. No matter how things evolve I will never allow him to rewrite my history or his simply because it's more comfortable for him. My brother and his family mean absolutely nothing to me now and I have no place for them in the years that I have left and what's more I'm more than happy with that.

I wasn't insane at this point of great suffering, despite what people like my brother thought and joked to their friends about me. I knew something was eating me alive in my body but I simply couldn't make anyone see. Yet the machetes' and pressure inside my head continued to crucify me.

I didn't have pressure in my head, I only had symptoms of pressure in my head was the response that I received from a so called eminently qualified professor of neurology in his private clinic over in the north east. No matter whom I saw, what investigation I sought, I was rebuffed, blocked and the blame for my condition placed firmly back upon me.

If I had a £10 for every minute I spent on the internet desperately looking for a solution I would be a multi millionaire. Yet I can say without any shadow of doubt that not one single person ever committed to any line of personal investigation on my behalf to try to help me.

I'd spent my entire professional life solving problems and my entire personal life helping to find answers for myself and others whom I'd allowed to drop their problems upon me. Yet here I was, I had a problem that simply couldn't be solved and no one wanted to help or support me. I can count on one hand the people who remained connected to me. The others whom I'd helped and supported over many years simply turned their back or ridiculed me. In terms of my spirituality and beliefs my life passage has certainly challenged and changed me.

I am the master of my own happiness, for its in my interests to live life to the full

Again I tried desperately to reinvent myself via the support of my life long friend John; I set up a one man plumbing business and simply tortured myself trying to earn a few bob in my chronic state. John and his partner Janice did so much for me during this period, they invited me into their home, made a little flat for me, supported me financially and yet still my health continued to decline.

In the summer of 2004 after reading Dianne Holmes 'Tears Behind Closed Doors' I began investigating the thyroid link and desperately tried to see if that was the defining holy grail that had been alluding me. I connected with Dr Gordon Skinner and a course of thyroxin I began.

My depression by now had gone past any rationale and I wasn't afraid to express my suicidal thoughts. I was tired of the medical profession, tired of my body but more than that I was tired of my life. I knew I didn't want to be sectioned because I knew that would simply not help me.

So after months of deliberation it was time to end the cause of the problem and that was me. But believe me, my attempt at suicide was no cry for help. I'd spent years screaming and begging for help but everyone had simply ignored me. To this day I know that I planned my exit with great detail and so there should be no reason why I'm still here today writing this book. But I was discovered by my mum and mortality was unfortunately extended and my consignment of suffering continued.

I came out of hospital, still in agony, under greater personal and social pressure and strain, enduring greater isolation and ridicule from people who now openly called me insane. By now my brain would shiver with pain, it was like I had six inch nails being knocked in all day long, the machetes in the front, top, back and sides never ever went away. I was unable to think through the sludge in my brain and only dark glasses in normal day light now allowed me to move around and cope.

I am the master of my own health, for I take my quality of health seriously

The clock on the wall and the arbitrary flies would almost drive me insane by their noise. I tried everything possible to cope with my problems I read, bought supplements and was tested and apparently cleansed galore including:

- Hair analysis.
- Mineral balancing.
- Fungal and parasite investigations and cleansing.
- Colonic irrigation.
- Spiritual healing.
- Indian head massage.
- Reiki.
- Psychic intervention.
- The list just went on and on

From my research it was clear that I had some form of chronic adrenal insufficiency issue going on so under the private guidance of Dr Barry Durrant Peatfield I began to support my adrenals. Whilst there were some improvements of sorts, the pain and the depression simply increased. I cover the adrenal axis connection in more detail in my chapter about stress.

In the winter of 2004 I met and fell in love again with Karina which was simply insane, I was feeling no better, had nothing to offer her and yet for some apparent reason she was still so keen. Why she was attracted to me I still find hard to fathom out, but her love and support of me has never wavered during my years of hell. We are best friends and companions and life is so easy between us but the reality is that our lives have been no fairy tales.

Things didn't get better when we first met, I was forced into deeper despair as my illnesses continued to progress. There were times when I simply screamed out in rage how much more punishment must one man endure. I wanted to leave my body almost every day, but now I had someone who cared deeply for me and in my ego felt that if I ended my life she would never recover, cope or live again. Despite how ill I was or how much time I spent in my bed she never ever gave up on me as hard as I tried to push her away. Instead she always greeted me with 'hi gorgeous' and love filled smiles, and we would frequently hug each other in a tear filled bed. To this day I never stop marvelling at her sexuality, sensitivity, integrity and talent with flare, she's my confidante, my best friend and my soul mate and the first person in my life who's ever truly cared. Some men may have been much luckier than me in this life in their careers and business endeavours, doors may have opened up for them when they closed for me and their fortune and finances simply grown. But I would find it hard to believe that in the midst of their glory that any man has ever had a finer and more loyal companion by his side than my lovely Karina has been to me.

I am the master of my own health, for I take my quality of health seriously

During all my years of suffering I had never come across anyone until 2005 who knew exactly what was wrong with me until I met a guy called Dr Andrew Wright. He diagnosed me straight away and my North American blood tests 5 days later proved that he was right.

I did in fact have Lymes Disease and my loading was just about off the official scales. That diagnosis brought no happy ending though as I learned to my great despair that getting diagnosed and making a good recovery from Lymes is as far apart as heaven is from hell.

Shortly after my diagnosis I experienced my first herx as part of the flawed lymes treatment protocol I'd just begun. The Herxheimer reaction also known as Jarisch-Herxheimer or herx occurs when large quantities of toxins are released into the body as bacteria typically Spirochetal Bacteria are killed, due to antibiotic or herbal treatments.

Basically what that means is that at the point you begin to kill the bacteria that are making you feel so ill, you are immediately made to feel much worse by the toxins they release into your blood stream, now how insane is that? Herxing until I found a way through it has for many years either been completely ignored or discounted by the medical world as a real phenomenon. Whilst paradoxically being raised by alternative practitioners as acknowledgement that progress is being made in treating diseases of a spirochetal nature.

Both view points are postulated from points of ignorance at worst and gross innocence at best. To anyone who suffers from spirochetal illness such as syphilis or Lymes Disease, herxing is a real issue and one that needs to be experienced to fully appreciate the ferocity of its action. Sufferers' symptoms simply increase ten fold or more when the spirochete infection has been killed and that in essence is the herx reaction. The problem is that herxing is not as simple as some would have sufferers believe.

I am the master of my own happiness, for its in my interests to live life to the full

It's not always about getting on top of an infection and that's because even the most informed simply don't understand the dynamics of neurotoxin and biotoxin loads. A patient my herx when their infection is killed, but equally they may herx when they burn body fat or when toxins from their liver are released. I'm not going to go into any further detail at this point, save to say that I was tormented by the so called herx phenomenon for the best part of two years until my research and self testing allowed me to break free of what is a dreadful condition and not the same as Lymes Disease. But that breakthrough didn't come with ease; there were no experts and no pioneers just thousands of sufferers making no progress from these conditions or disease.

So I did what I've had to do so many times; I self funded, self medicated and self theorised my way through the lymes and neurotoxin mire. I've reached a place now where I'm able to prescribe that whilst herxing is an inevitable part of the process of recovery it should not be considered an integral part of life and you will see that later when you explore time line recover maps in the chapter treatment explorer. Herxing should reach a climax in the process of recovery and there after serve only as a frequent reminder that we have a disease state which whilst uncomfortable at times does not need to rule or ruin our quality of life.

Things were getting a little bit better for me albeit I was far from well and then in 2006 my posterior inferior cerebella artery went into a psychiatric state. The damn thing which had bugged and taxed me for so long simply began insulting my vestibular nerve and brain stem with every single beat of my heart. I cannot begin to articulate my suffering because this condition is beyond comprehension. I'm talking here about a nerve that feeds information to our brains about our orientation and position in space being subjected to a vascular insult which our crude vestibular testing techniques simply cannot qualify. You have no idea the amount of abuse and insult I endured trying to get anyone from the NHS or private medical world to help me, it was like I was in some sort of insane horror story, indeed a proverbial mad house to say the very least.

With this arterial insult life became a whole lot worse I was in a desperate state, the pain in the back of my head and my left ear was unreal. I had the sensation in my body that I was on a bungee jump 24hrs of the day, I was being pushed, pulled and thrown all over the place, my arms, face, anus, fingers and feet would twitch in unimaginable distress because my brain simply didn't know where my body was in time or indeed in space. I was in pure agony unable to sleep, nothing corrected the disorder, the stress and pressure this put me under pushed me to the brink of suicide once more.

In a desperate state Karina whisked me off down to Shaftsbury to live and be treated by a world class herbalist down there called Annette Montague-Thomas, and whilst she was kind and considered, expecting her to be able to treat my condition was in hindsight asking too much of her. But we connected on one very deep spiritual not clinical level, and even though that connection was for only a very brief moment in my mortal time; nevertheless it was an experience of merit and I will always be grateful for that.

I am the master of my own happiness, for its in my interests to live life to the full

Nevertheless, blood testing by this time had proven that I was indeed a very ill man and that my mitochondria had just about given up the fight. To such an extent that my private GP Dr Sarah Myhill was simply shocked when she received my results. It seemed that my body simply could no longer deal with all the toxins, contaminates and conjugates inside me, ATP production had just about shut down and by now I was hovering around the six and half / seven stone mark. She stepped in immediately and prescribed Vitamin B12 and Magnesium Sulphate injections in an attempt to re-energize me by lowering my overall toxin load on my failing body. Nevertheless the Lymes Disease started to take hold of me again because I was simply unable to tolerate any corrective medications due to the additional inflammation that the fall out toxins caused to my vestibular nerve and nervous systems. My only release by now was twice a week when I medicated at night with 0.5mg of clonazepam.

Even in my desperate state I made friends in the local community quite easily upon settling down in Shaftsbury. It was from there that I continued my desperate internet research at a local charitable operation called the 'Swans Trust'. That's where I met and connected with a Cornish photographer by the name of Dave Martin and I remain good friends with the 'Man in a Hat' to this day. They were very black days in Shaftsbury as I was driven to the brink of suicide almost every day, yet in that autumn all my research confirmed that I did have micro vascular syndrome i.e. an artery pressing on a nerve. Now to prove that I needed another MRI but this one had to be the best machine I could find, Dr Myhill came back with a facility in Winchester which she knew had a highly competent radiographer, *'hmmmn very rare I would say to find anyone with any degree of competency within the UK medical world'*.

My results came back and there it was an artery clearly in a place it shouldn't be. One week later I'm off to see another private consultant on the south coast and low and behold it's not the artery to blame for my problem it is of course me. Oh yes, the same old 'clap trap' I was clearly neurotic and my symptomology simply did not make sense or stand up to my shit for brains expert. I'd had enough now, if I'd had a gun I would have blown my bloody head off because I simply couldn't stand any longer what my body was putting me through.

In one last desperate throw of the dice I start looking online for a surgeon in Europe who had a proven track record in micro vascular decompression surgery. After ten mind numbing days of research with the most debilitating condition Dr Luc Dweale of AZ Saint Lucaz in Belgium pops up a true expert in this form of surgery. Two weeks later the guys operating on me I wake up after surgery to find him there leaning over me, 'Mr. Hardy I did the best I could do how are you?' I said, 'fine but the pulse was still there'. This guy is a good guy and he says to me 'hmmn we must give it time, but you have an artery which is running through your vestibular bundle and there is nothing I can do about that'. There was actually no improvement after the surgery and after a further six months of unmitigated suffering and further self-funded testing at Professor Herman Kingma's vestibular research facility in Maastricht it was concluded that a selective nurectomy of the superior vestibular nerve would be performed.

I am the master of my own happiness, for its in my interests to live life to the full

That basically means that the nerve will be sectioned or in layman's terms destroyed by cutting a big chunk of it away. So in March 2007 I'm back in AZ Saint Lucaz undergoing a second self funded neurosurgical procedure executed again by Dr Luc Dweale. As with the first procedure I awake and there he is by my side. He was really happy that I could move all my face muscles and with the way the procedure had gone.

The insult though slightly lower in magnitude, was still unfortunately there. I was distraught, both he and everyone I talked to said; 'give it time it will sort it's self out' but I knew however the situation had not been resolved.

'Bloody hell what had I done that was so wrong to deserve all this'? Why was I being punished like this I simply didn't feel that I could do any more?

Deep down however I knew that I some how had too, because I had to write about all the appalling medical experiences I'd had. To show that industry for what it is, an ignorant bastion of bullshit, incompetence, self preservation and greed. This book is part of that redress process for me, so now let's have a look at my decline and let's explore why things went so badly wrong, by reconfiguring my decline map with appropriate entries and then exploring that in following final few pages of this chapter.

But before that please take a look at the image on the next page which was taken during my last neurosurgical procedure which clearly shows My Psychiatric Artery insulting my vestibular nerve. Now the reason I'm showing this image in this book is because it's essential to note that if anyone is suffering with a chronic, yet currently undiagnosed illnesses or condition. You simply must NOT give up or give in to: 'the rogues, luddites and charlatans' or should I say lizards in third rate grey or navy blue pin striped suits' that do nothing but place the blame for your condition back onto you. You see, from my perspective I believe that it's a gross crime against humanity how our 'medical rogues' conduct themselves and an absolute scandal in terms of the sheer hell, despair and lengths that I had to go to simply to acquire scientific clinical diagnosis on my numerous chronic illness conditions. But the fact that I did that demonstrates that there are always answers to complex problems, all we ever need to find those answers is the right approach, the right people and the right skills set.

We all have that potential and because of that, we can always find the answers that we need if we're determined enough, brave enough and strong enough to see our search for answers through. I'm bloody livid about the way I've always been let down by the medical industry, I'm bloody livid about the amount of money I've had to spend to secure numerous clinical diagnosis whilst funding 'cretins' via my taxes who are only happy simply to write me and people like me off.

I am the master of my own happiness, for its in my interests to live life to the full

I cannot contain my rage and contempt at times towards this industry, because I'm constantly annoyed by the fact that:

- It wasn't my bloody job to do all the research.

- It wasn't my bloody job to educate highly paid 'cretins' in their own industry, whilst trying to acquire some form of relief from my own chronic illness impediments.

And

- I'm bloody annoyed that at every step of that process I was abused by 'cretins' with shit for brains.

Look it's as simple as this; **DO NOT** let any medical or clinical cretin write you off. Take no notice of any rubbish they talk about in terms of congenital conditions or the state of your psychology. Stay strong and believe me it's really okay to vent your spleen at them when you know they're failing you, as long as you stay committed to your self resolution task.

Because at the point that you secure your true scientific diagnosis you're ultimately able to prove that they are the 'cretins' that you've known them to be all along. So what if we have a congenital condition and we've lived with it for 5, 10, 20 or 50 years at the point as my case it moves into a psychiatric state then we need diagnosis and resolution not abuse from lizards with brains the size of a pea. The picture of my PSYCHIATRIC ARTERY running through my vestibular bundle on the previous page is a clear indication of just how our bodies at times are capable of getting it completely wrong long before we're in any form of rational or conscious state.

I am the master of my own health, for I take my quality of health seriously

Yet whilst the effects may not always be easy to detect, that shouldn't just mean that we're immediately written off as nutters or have to put up with 'clap trap and abuse' with no hope of effective diagnosis, treatment and resolution. Now let's have a look at my overall decline in health now and let's explore what really happened to me.

RAPHAEL'S LEGACY

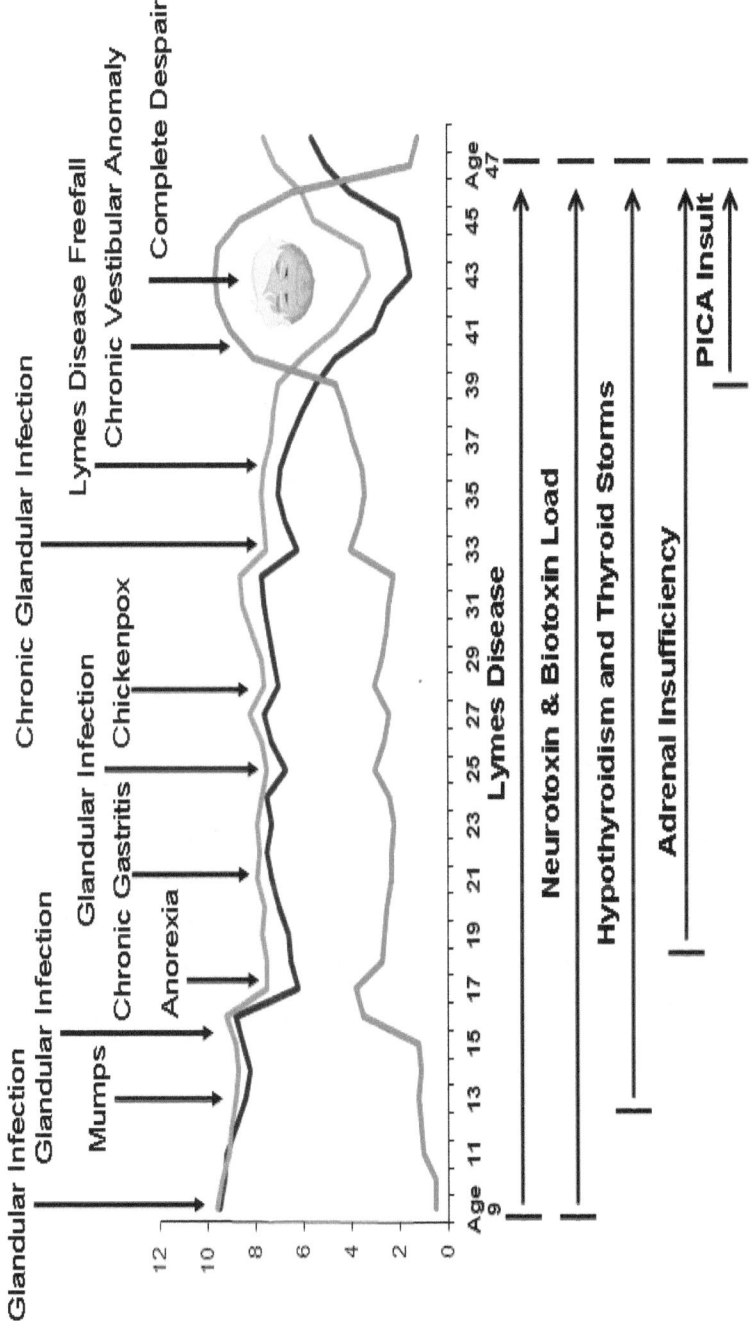

I am the master of my own health, for I take my quality of health seriously

- I contacted Lymes Disease at a very young age the impact of which was that it compromised my liver, my brain and my endocrine systems.

- My bodily systems were simply unable to cope with that untreated load and so over the years battling to solve my body's infection, my body simply burnt itself out.

- When exposed to even higher levels of Lymes Disease my limited defenses were simply overrun and my health simply went into freefall and I therefore moved very quickly into a rampant Lymes Diseased state and accompanying toxic body syndrome.

- This is a situation compounded still further by the chronic activation of an horrendous vascular vestibular insult which is completely poo poo'd until I'm able to prove its origin via self-funded imaging and neurosurgery.

Now the point I'm making is that if we had clinicians who were any good at their job they would hear our whispers and we their employers, would never have to deal with the screams of our disease. Instead they are devoid of any medical or personal common sense and therefore unable to compile objective clinical records.

So that by the time our bodies decline into a chronic diseased state the root cause of our disease on our records is hidden or masked by psychological inaccuracies or simply medical clap trap.

I am the master of my own happiness, for its in my interests to live life to the full

This book was written in 2008 and since my last neurosurgical procedure I've been abused still further on Harley Street etc, by so called medical experts, all of whom have ignored my condition through lack of firm data and placed the blame for my predicament directly back onto me. Whilst I've also been in discussions with several leading lights around the world, it's hard to see these days as our global economy turns down, just how I would secure the 30K+ needed to undergo effective resolution surgery albeit two cutting edge neurosurgeons are interested in my case.

But I'm a fighter and either my artery will rupture and I will be released from my suffering or I will get through this and prove that my medical abusers are the 'shameless incompetent cretins' that I've known them to be all along. I have nothing but respect for Dr Luc Dweale and his team at AZ Saint Lucaz, but there are not enough medical or clinical experts around and that's simply unacceptable in this the so called enlightened 21st century. It's simply unacceptable that we have to fight for our lives and quality of life whilst we fund an industry that is rotten to its core i.e. top down, bottom up. We cannot and should not as an evolved society accept any longer the shoddy service that we're currently forced to endure from the medical industry because its contrary to every other modern day industrial practice. It's simply impossible to defend this industry any longer because it's an industry:

- That is happy with underperformance.

- That is happy to continually write its customer base off.

- That is so locked in inertia that its own scientific base is at least one hundred years ahead of its front end service delivery.

I am the master of my own health, for I take my quality of health seriously

I'm personally not prepared to support of pay for this level of service anymore, I'm personally not prepared to fight for the preservation of this industry anymore. Because I've been party to all its failings over many many years and both it and the people who work in it sicken me to my very core. I simply cannot conceal my contempt of this industry and those who permeate every aspect of its being.

You see, we have a saying in West Cumbria that expresses succinctly our contempt of anyone and its 'I wouldn't piss on him/her if he/she was on fire'

Now that's a very graphic statement of contempt i.e. the person is detested to such a degree that you wouldn't even urinate on them to help extinguish flames engulfing them.

Well as ever, I will take that one stage further, such is my contempt of representatives from the medical industry that if I were to inadvertently stumble across one of them on fire, I'd certainly look for additional combustible material to help them on their way. I might even sell a few tickets if there was the opportunity to do so!

I am the master of my own happiness, for its in my interests to live life to the full

Personal Notes

I am the master of my own health, for I take my quality of health seriously

Personal Notes

I am the master of my own happiness, for its in my interests to live life to the full

Personal Notes

I am the master of my own health, for I take my quality of health seriously

Personal Notes

I am the master of my own happiness, for its in my interests to live life to the full

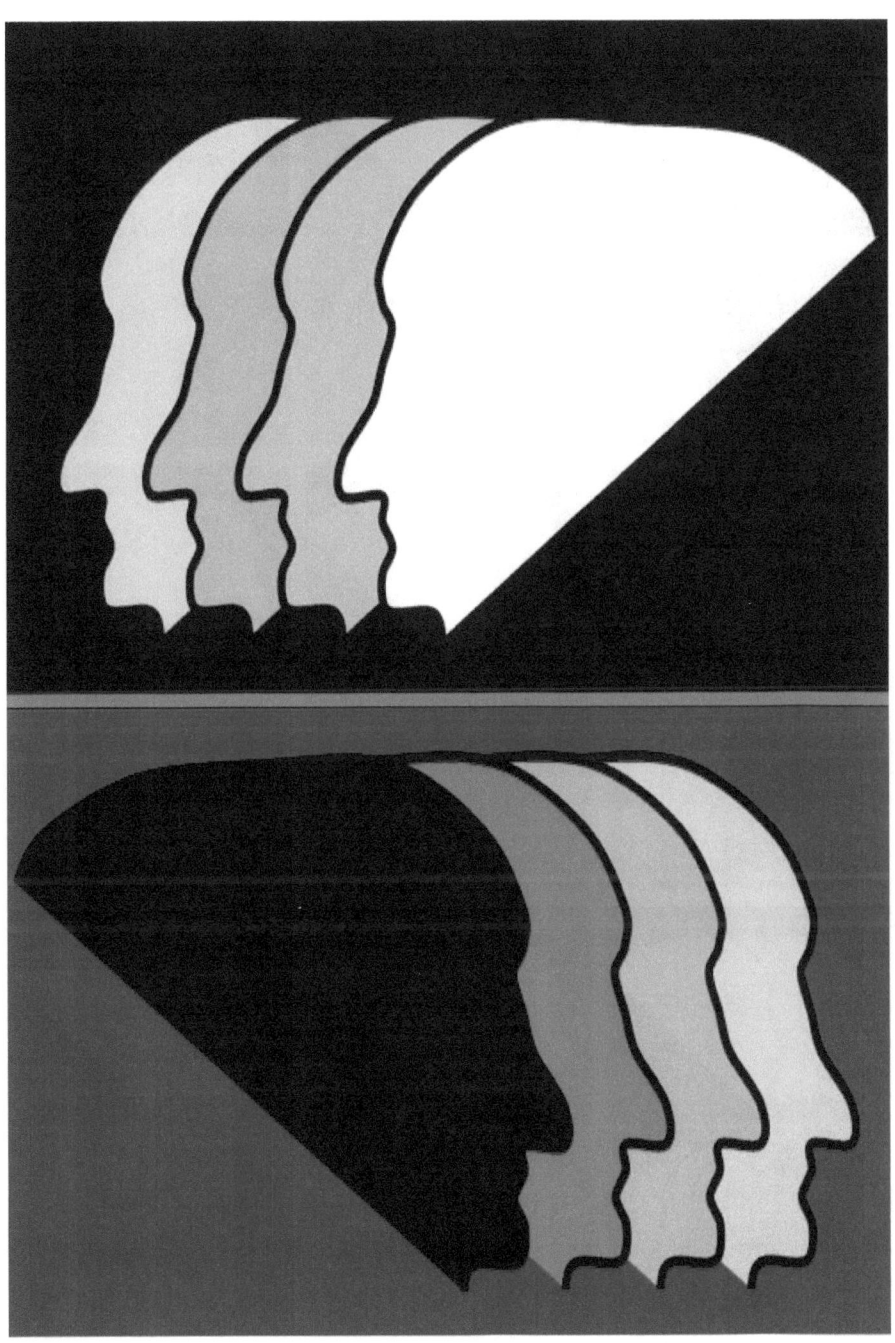

I am the master of my own health, for I take my quality of health seriously

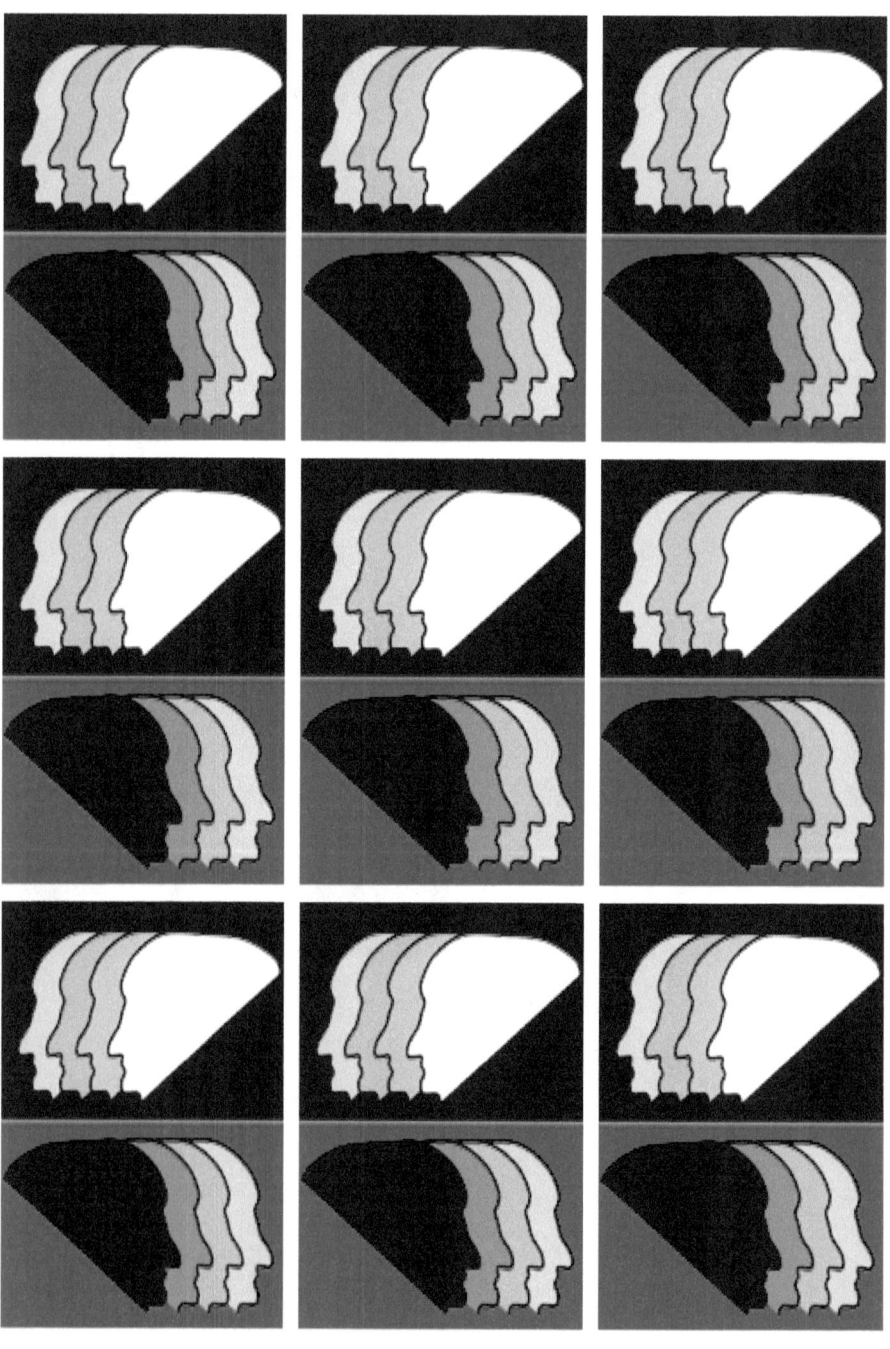

I am the master of my own happiness, for its in my interests to live life to the full

Psychological illness fact or fiction?

How frequent is it for patients' problems to be simply written off as nothing more than a deluded psychology? Well far more frequently than you may expect. You see, there is a prescriptive culture within the medical world which has a predisposition for looking to offload all the patients' problems back onto them. It's basically part of the overall clinical abuse model and its guiding principles are no more than:

- When in doubt just call your patients illness a psychological problem.

- When tests don't indicate a deviation from normal values, just call your patients' illnesses a psychological problem.

- When imaging doesn't show up any abnormalities just call your patients' illnesses a psychological problem.

- When you simply can't be bothered with your patients' perceived or preposterous symptoms just call their illness a psychological problem.

I am the master of my own health, for I take my quality of health seriously

But what is the truth and just what part does our psychology play in the bigger scheme of things when it comes to our health? Well first we need to understand that whilst we may be familiar with the term 'psychological illness' few of us know that the modern day originator of this scientific field was 'Wilhelm Wundt' who established the first psychology lab in Leipzig, Germany. Believing at the time that *properly* trained individuals should be able to *accurately* identify the mental processes that accompanied an individual's feelings, sensations, and thoughts. The emphasis here is upon *properly trained* individuals accurately identifying the processes that underpin the emotional predisposition of individuals in any given psychological state.

Now the development of this science didn't happen by chance, mankind in all its societies has battled throughout its entire documented history with the thorny issue of mental illness and insanity. That's why we in the United Kingdom still have such draconian measures as the 'Mental Health Act' where citizens can be sectioned and detained under said act for extended periods if they pose either a danger to others or more often than not simply a danger to themselves. Now there is absolutely no doubt that some individuals are insane, we see that in the likes of Shipman, Stalin, Hitler and Saddam Hussein.

The problem is there have been no major advances since time began to delineate between organic insanity and biologically insults that have the propensity to inflict insanity upon mankind. So we still have no way of knowing who's insane and who's simply biologically ill. I'm advocating therefore that the golden psychological card which is so readily used to explain the unexplainable illness i.e. there is a significant psychological component to your illness, is simply a complete red herring in the majority of chronic illnesses.

I am the master of my own happiness, for its in my interests to live life to the full

Those inaccurate value judgments simply have no clinical grounding upon which to base the assumptions of a psychological condition upon save for some cursory presenting symptoms.

Now it's that point of clinical evidence that I wish firstly to focus upon. You see; if you present yourself to a medic suspecting that you have let's say; possibly hypothyroidism. The first thing they will do is:

(a) Poo poo and ridicule you.

And then

(b) Perhaps agree reluctantly to give you a thyroid test.

They will then rattle on about how they couldn't possibly give you a trial of low dose thyroid medication until your tests results come back and prove that you do indeed have an issue with your thyroid. Yet the same medical practitioner within 5 minutes of another consultation will conclude with NO clinical data that you are indeed suffering from a psychological condition and therein he or she will feel eminently comfortable to prescribe anyone of a line of toxic psychiatric substances. It seems to me incredulous in the 21st century, that some unqualified cretin can make such sweeping statements about the condition of someone's psychology. More so when we realise that we pay these rogues insane salaries for the little that they do. Affording them great status to comply with the values and defining principles of the Hippocratic Oath. But my question is; do they deliver greatness for the greatness we bestow upon them? Well they're certainly paid insane salaries and afforded great status but very few of them have ever actually signed up to any form of; Hippocratic Oath. Furthermore it's fair to suggest that many of them don't actually know what the original Oath actually says despite the fact that they frequently hide behind it.

I am the master of my own health, for I take my quality of health seriously

I actually look at that point further in the chapter Hippocratic Oath Or Merely Hypocritical Froth focusing upon specifically all the medical illusions that we as a society are sold.

Nevertheless I'm going to labour my point here of psychological postulation over scientific rationale, by asking this:

- If I have an abscess inside my mouth accompanied by intolerable pain do I have an abscess and intolerable pain?

Or

- Do I have a psychological problem which is manifesting the symptoms of pain?

Well clearly it's the first bullet point not the latter unless that is you're employed in the medical world. You see, in the medical world seeing is not always believing whereas in the presence of no rationale, believing is always right. It is that preoccupation with self importance and unqualified value judgments that continues to blight our medical records and destroy our lives.

But what if I substitute abscess for undetectable anomaly generating misery and great pain that flawed tests and investigations are unable to detect. What do I have then?

- Do I have an undetectable anomaly which is causing misery and pain?

Or

- Do I have a deep seated psychological problem that is manifesting symptoms of misery and pain?

I am the master of my own happiness, for its in my interests to live life to the full

Well of course it's the latter in terms of medical rationale because; the very fact that my problem cannot be found means that it simply doesn't exist. It must therefore be a manifestation of my fragile psychology which requires no further input from them. Is it any wonder that I regard these rogues as the lowest form of life?

It's clearly apparent to me now that in bog standard, tricky or complex medical investigation situations we the patients are always to a greater extent perceived to be the responsible party for the clinical problem we're experiencing because as mere mortals we have such fragile psychologies. Surely though this situation is truly insane, how can this industry say on one hand that, unless their outdated investigation techniques are able to detect a problem then it simply doesn't exist whilst in the same breath assign clinical labels to patients with the shallowest to zero investigations of their case?

I do not argue or disagree with the fact that our psychology plays a very big part in the way we cope with, or handle our difficulties. But it is not the root cause of all mans hidden or seemingly translucent diseases and I therefore repudiate the waving of the psychological cause golden card by cretins within the medical industry.

If our psychology was the root cause of the majority of illnesses then we would be able to see for ourselves the advances in the treatment of psychological conditions over the past hundred years. Because the money we spend on this aspect of medical care via so called research and residential care etc, is simply insane. The reality to my primary postulation is quite stark and I say that because the medical industry is having a laugh. Nothing much has changed in the diagnosis and treatment of these conditions despite the oceans of scientific papers that have been written.

I am the master of my own health, for I take my quality of health seriously

There have been no major breakthroughs in clinical analysis, qualification or treatments of psychological conditions save for commercially sponsored indoctrination and use of debatably successful drugs. Now if anyone who has been put on those drugs has improved, all I can say is good for you, but for the majority of us who didn't need them in our body to solve our health condition, then I would respectfully suggest that they are:

- Dangerous

Or

- Complete waste of bloody time.

Yet the medical world's view remains without any validity that all illness derives from an emotional or mental state and that physical illness if it cannot be pinpointed simply doesn't exist. But surely these are the views of yesterday's men, the sorts who questioned the validity of;

- The shape of the earth.

- The purpose of the sun.

- The make-up of the moon.

- The relevance of the stars

They are the views of men who dared not seek to discover if the world was flat or round and who shouted heresy if a man sort to postulated different thoughts or articulated and challenged perceived truths.

I am the master of my own happiness, for its in my interests to live life to the full

The very fact that this approach happens almost by default in clinical surgeries throughout the UK, simply validates my position that the medical world is seemingly still stuck in the dark ages, ignorant and despite its protestations, doesn't really care. Were they motor mechanics with the same approach to problems these people would be simply unemployable or even in jail e.g.

- 'I'm sorry Mr. Hardy but I couldn't find anything wrong with your car, but incidentally have you ever tried counselling, sometimes it really does help?'

Or what about this favourite one;

- 'Yes I hear what you say Mr. Hardy but that is just a sensation of knocking at the front of your car, I'm the expert here I can't find any signs of knocking so perhaps its more of a psychological issue than you think, how's your sex life by the way?'

Two months later the engine in my car implodes;

- 'Oh well these things just happen sometimes Mr. Hardy, I've checked your notes and it would appear that your tyres and exhaust were fine when you were last in here, now you're clearly agitated so I'm going to suggest that there seems more to this than just an engine in your car, do you think you need to see a psychiatrist?'

I am the master of my own health, for I take my quality of health seriously

- 'Answer, no I don't think I should see a psychiatrist you bull shitting waste of space, I was in here not so long ago and I told you that there was something seriously wrong with my engine and all you did was check my bloody tyre pressure and exhaust mounting. Now I'm back here today with a damaged engine and I'm asking you this, are you a bloody mechanic mate or simply a mechanic on your great grandmothers side of your family because your technical and professional capabilities are shoddy to say the least?'

The thing is if this happened in real life we would be straight to trading standards but when it comes to the medical industry we're all very guilty of not being prepared to take those bastards on. The public at large would be shocked if they knew just how little psychological or psychiatric training non specialists in that field actually undergo before they're let loose on us.

I liken their understanding of psychological or psychiatry to that of the fat clever bastard who we've perhaps sat next to as lovers of football in the football stands all around our country. You know the one I mean. From beginning to end he hurls his abuse and yet he's probably never played the beautiful game. Yet he's somehow deluded himself into thinking that he's some kind of football guru.

Well, the truth is that the average medic you will ever encounter has little to no training in either psychological or matters of psychiatry and as such are the least qualified of clinicians to prescribe conditions of that nature to you or about you. Yet they have bought into ignorant schools of thought which date way back to the 1920's.

I am the master of my own happiness, for its in my interests to live life to the full

Outdated schools of thought that postulated that we, as individuals, are responsible for all our own thoughts and our perceptions on life and that we all have demons and un-reconciled issues deep within us that frequently manifest themselves as illness. Today that belief is still perpetuated by our ignorant medics as a way of offloading the cause of a tricky problem back onto the shoulders of its originator simply because they know that they can do that.

So much so that you can bet your last £10 that if you encounter any extended or unexplainable medical issue at any point in your life, that the psychological postulations or dogma that will be rolled out or recorded on your medical records will be a derivative of some unqualified cretins understanding of:

- Personality Psychology – This specialist area looks at the various elements that make up individual personalities and includes Freud's structural model of personality as an example of a protagonist of this field.

However at the point a qualified psychologist is brought onto your case I can guarantee you that Personality Psychology which has already been used by medical ignoramuses as ammunition against you will be almost entirely dropped in favour of:

- Clinical Psychology Investigations – This specialty area is focused on the assessment, diagnosis, and treatment of mental disorders.

I am the master of my own health, for I take my quality of health seriously

However the study of psychology has moved on tremendously since its conception and there are now many widely differing schools of thought and differing approaches to this challenging subject including:

- Cognitive Psychology - This specialist area is the study of human thought processes and cognitions, including topics such as attention, memory, perception, decision-making, problem solving, and language acquisition.

- Abnormal Psychology - This specialty area is focused on research and treatment of a variety of mental disorders and is linked to psychotherapy and clinical psychology.

- Social Psychology - This specialist area is a discipline that uses scientific methods to study social influence, social perception, and social interaction. Social psychology studies diverse subjects including group behaviour, social perception, leadership, nonverbal behaviour, conformity, aggression, and prejudice.

- Comparative Psychology - This specialist area is the branch of psychology concerned with the study of animal behaviour, believing that the study of animal behaviour can lead to a deeper and broader understanding of human psychology.

- Forensic Psychology - This specialist area is an applied field focused on using psychological research and principles in the legal and criminal justice system.

I am the master of my own happiness, for its in my interests to live life to the full

- Industrial-Organizational Psychology - This specialist area uses psychological research to enhance work performance, select employee, improve product design, and enhance usability.

- Developmental Psychology - This specialist area is the branch of psychology that looks at human growth and development over the lifespan. Theories often focus on the development of cognitive abilities, morality, social functioning, identity, and other life areas.

- School Psychology - This specialist area is the branch of psychology that works within the educational system to help children with emotional, social, and academic issues.

- Biological Psychology - This approach is the only area of accessible psychology that studies how biological processes influence the mind and behaviour.

Ironically though; Biological Psychology will never be rolled out unless you've been through surgery, a crash or a smash. Yet this approach is the only area of accessible psychology that studies how biological processes influence the mind and behaviour. Now there's no getting away from it *Biological Psychology* is still light years away from where it should be by now but at least it's sort of heading in the right direction. The only problem is as ever when undergoing medical interventions, your future will depend entirely upon the training of the psychologist responsible for driving any biological investigations. You may well find that in most instances he or she just simply reverts back to or refers you to another Clinical Psychologist on the grounds of costs or insufficient evidence to warrant extensive testing.

I am the master of my own health, for I take my quality of health seriously

Throughout my darkest days I battled like a Spartan albeit a very ill Spartan to find the root cause of my illness and I was frequently told by medical representatives, 'no we're not testing you for this or for that'. Or 'we can't keep on testing for different things indefinitely Mr. Hardy you're simply going to have to understand that you have a psychiatric problem'.

Now there is absolutely no doubt that if we feel low it's difficult for us to feel happy until we shift our mind set. We see that day after day in the emotions and moods of ourselves and our kith and kin. It's simply preposterous to suggest to someone who is ill that if they change their mindset things somehow will resolve and they will feel better.

You see; life as we know is not like that, we are not like that, there are always impositions placed upon our bodies which make it impossible for us to feel happy simply as and when we choose to feel happy. The best we can ever hope to do is to recognise and accept that we have a part to play in that process yet understand that we do not always hold all the keys. So the question remains, is 'psychological illness real or simply a medical form of illness fiction?'

Well there's no doubt in my mind that there are many forms of psychological illness, but in the absence of firm biological data I cannot accept or agree that psychological illness is an illness in its own right. If the root course of a problem cannot be qualified then it MUST fall into the category of symptoms from an unknown disease. Therein there must be a concerted effort made to search out the origin of that disease and not simply to attempt to treat the symptoms with dangerous views, perceptions or drugs. Under no circumstance can an unknown disease be morally written off as an emotional or psychological illness because I would respectfully suggest that act in itself constitutes gross clinical malpractice.

I am the master of my own happiness, for its in my interests to live life to the full

I therefore advocate that anyone being written off by a medical representative, must document that incident via a formal communiqué to their practice in readiness for future legal action. It is only at the point we start bringing the medical industry to account, day after day that we will:

- Get the services we so desperately need.

And

- Weed out the 'luddites, rogues and charlatans' who shouldn't be in the industry in the first place.

I am the master of my own health, for I take my quality of health seriously

The global market place we live and work in is full of medics desperately looking to explore new boundaries. So if we don't have the quality home grown medics that we need who are prepared to accept that we're all part of the 21st century. Then I say, lets simply offload the; 'luddites, rogues and charlatans' to the unemployed wastelands where they belong and lets import brighter, fresher service support professionals as we would do with plumbers, builders, electricians and engineers.

You see; as a former sufferer of all that's wrong with our insidiously flawed medical model we simply don't have the time, money or resolve to bring the luddite bastions of our medical industry kicking and screaming into line with our modern needs, standards and expectations.

We need effective medical services now, not light years from now, but tomorrow, or at the very latest the early part of next week. What's more we can all play our part in bringing about change; help create a medical model that is technically competent, robust and able to meet ALL our needs. Start today, and let's hope that no one ever has to document the level of personal suffering that I've been forced to document and voice via *Raphael's Legacy* etc.

I am the master of my own happiness, for its in my interests to live life to the full

Personal Notes

I am the master of my own health, for I take my quality of health seriously

Personal Notes

I am the master of my own happiness, for its in my interests to live life to the full

I am the master of my own health, for I take my quality of health seriously

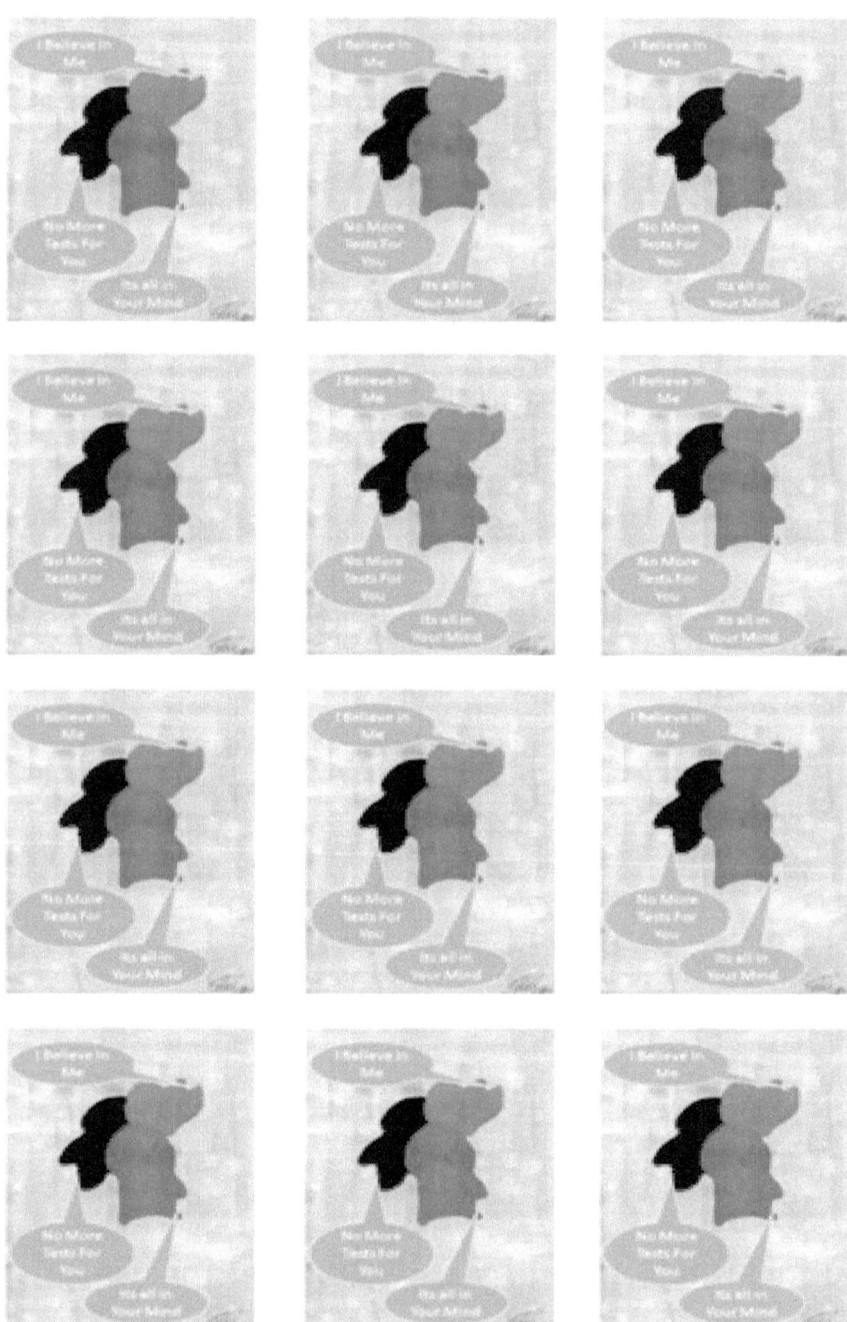

I am the master of my own happiness, for its in my interests to live life to the full

Hippocratic oath or merely hypocritical froth

One of the most laughable things I've found about the scum ridden corridors of the medical industry is that it is always blowing hot and cold. One minute its postulating higher ethical values and the preservation of life and the next minute it's refusing to treat patients on the grounds of:

- Cost
- Flawed diagnosis.
- Personal prejudices.
- Anything that's flavour of the month.

We've all read and heard about cases of people losing loved ones because a medic or series of medics simply couldn't be arsed to do the job they're paid to do. What may not be apparent however at the point a clinical case failure is brought to our attention is the sheer hell that the patients' family has had to work through in an attempt to seek redress for their loved one's injustice.

I am the master of my own health, for I take my quality of health seriously

But why is it so hard to seek redress for shoddy care, we put our lives in these peoples hands because we think that they know what they're doing. So when it's obvious they've screwed up surely they should just hold their hands up and come clean, in line with the principles of the Hippocratic Oath. That isn't, I would suggest, too much for us to ask of them is it? Well the truth is I'm afraid it is.

You see even when the medical industry or one of its representatives get it wrong they simply can't hold up their hands and say I or we got it wrong. They may even have known for some time that they have a weak member of staff in their midst who is or could be jeopardizing peoples lives, but it's not part of the industry's psyche to stand up and proactively address 'shit performance'. What invariably happens is that the old boys club kicks in and self preservation remains the order of the day.

How many times have you seen and heard news reports where a so called medical expert is simply spewing verbal diarrhea in defense of the indefensible. With either a semi self-humbling posture or an arrogant parental disposition where he or she will rattle on about how sorry they are, and how everyone had done their best for the patient but that this was just an isolated case. But the plain fact of the matter is that too many patients are dying who shouldn't be dying under the care of these shits and what's more; too many patients are being written off who should be living rewarding and happy lives.

I am the master of my own happiness, for its in my interests to live life to the full

Nevertheless; I'm confident however that as we begin to clear the debris from years of cover up after cover up we will find that there is no such thing as an isolated incident of failure of due diligence when we're in clinical care. I'm confident based upon my own personal experiences that we will unfortunately discover that it's an endemic theme of poor service delivery. Or in my granddads words; *'At the point you get ill son or are silly enough to get old, you're no longer a person son you're nothing more than a piece of meat on the chopping board of life son and no one really cares'*.

But what is the problem here? And why does this situation exist? Well the answer is simple; the Hippocratic Oath is a myth. Well that last line is not fair really because the Hippocratic Oath is not a myth and you can read a translated version of it later in this chapter if you wish. The real myth is that vast majority of those engaged in medical or clinical work have never signed onto and have never been compelled to sign up to a Hippocratic Oath to allow them to practice. Therein resides the myth, you see, the rogues that we encounter who talk about upholding its values are the very same rogues who by matter of course break all its principles daily. In essence we're being spun a line of thought which is a crude fabrication and not an ethical reality. This is because in truth, as far as we the patients are concerned the Hippocratic Oath simply doesn't exist. Medics simply do what's best for themselves and to hell with the patients in their care. So should we make our medical staff sign up to a modern Hippocratic Oath? Well in truth I don't' really care if they do or they don't, for an Oath is no more than a joke to me when its signed up to by self obsessed cretins and oafs. What I won't to see is:

- Deregulation of the industry.

- I want to see greater clinical accountability.

I am the master of my own health, for I take my quality of health seriously

- I want better training and greater clarity in the selection processes for anyone thinking of joining that industry.

- I want ease of access to all things medical without the clap trap, bullshit and the golden psychology card.

Only when we've moved this industry kicking and screaming into the 21st century can we rid ourselves once and for all of the pompous, arrogant and incompetent service delivery that has been up to now society's greatest medical disease e.g. the people who work within the industry. Just in case you're ever in a sticky situation with a medical representative where the individual is prescriptively using the Hippocratic Oath to validate something they're saying. I've enclosed both an old and a new example of the same to help you determine for yourself if that person actuality lives in entirety the principles enshrined within. On the next page is the oldest version or translation of the Hippocratic Oath that I could find on the web.

I am the master of my own happiness, for its in my interests to live life to the full

Older Version of the Oath

I swear by Apollo Physician and Asclepius and Hygieia and Panaceia and all the gods and goddesses, making them my witnesses, that I will fulfill according to my ability and judgment this oath and this covenant: To hold him who has taught me this art as equal to my parents and to live my life in partnership with him, and if he is in need of money to give him a share of mine, and to regard his offspring as equal to my brothers in male lineage and to teach them this art - if they desire to learn it - without fee and covenant; to give a share of precepts and oral instruction and all the other learning to my sons and to the sons of him who has instructed me and to pupils who have signed the covenant and have taken an oath according to the medical law, but no one else. I will apply dietetic measures for the benefit of the sick according to my ability and judgment; I will keep them from harm and injustice. I will neither give a deadly drug to anybody who asked for it, nor will I make a suggestion to this effect. Similarly I will not give to a woman an abortive remedy. In purity and holiness I will guard my life and my art. I will not use the knife, not even on sufferers from stone, but will withdraw in favour of such men as are engaged in this work. Whatever houses I may visit, I will come for the benefit of the sick, remaining free of all intentional injustice, of all mischief and in particular of sexual relations with both female and male persons, be they free or slaves. What I may see or hear in the course of the treatment or even outside of the treatment in regard to the life of men, which on no account one must spread abroad, I will keep to myself, holding such things shameful to be spoken about. If I fulfill this oath and do not violate it, may it be granted to me to enjoy life and art, being honoured with fame among all men for all time to come; if I transgress it and swear falsely, may the opposite of all this be my lot.

I am the master of my own health, for I take my quality of health seriously

Now here is a draft transcript of the only modern version I could find of the Hippocratic Declaration created for those passing through Imperial College School of Medicine. I'm unclear if this was ever adopted but it was complied I assume to focus the minds of the recently trained in terms of providing an honourable service……..yeah that right, where at?

Refined Version of the Oath

I solemnly promise that I will to the best of my ability serve humanity caring for the sick, promoting good health, and alleviating pain and suffering. I recognise that the practice of medicine is a privilege with which comes considerable responsibility and I will not abuse my position. I will practise medicine with integrity, humility, honesty, and compassion working with my fellow doctors and other colleagues to meet the needs of my patients. I shall never intentionally do or administer anything to the overall harm of my patients. I will not permit considerations of gender, race, religion, political affiliation, sexual orientation, nationality, or social standing to influence my duty of care. I will oppose policies in breach of human rights and will not participate in them. I will strive to change laws that are contrary to my profession's ethics and will work towards a fairer distribution of health resources. I will assist my patients to make informed decisions that coincide with their own values and beliefs and will uphold patient confidentiality. I will recognise the limits of my knowledge and seek to maintain and increase my understanding and skills throughout my professional life. I will acknowledge and try to remedy my own mistakes and honestly assess and respond to those of others. I will seek to promote the advancement of medical knowledge through teaching and research. I make this declaration solemnly, freely, and upon my honor.

I am the master of my own happiness, for its in my interests to live life to the full

Sweet eh? Fine fine words! But I wonder just how much of this froth and rubbish they'll actually manage or be willing to uphold once they're on the fat, greedy, pompous medical gravy train which is to be their life. Who knows, perhaps they will uphold it all with a bit of luck or then again perhaps they simply stick to the bits that make life easier for them. Perhaps I'm just too cynical now, but then again, I do have good cause. The fact of the matter is that I have a dreadful illness which could so easily have been prevented and a genetic condition which makes my life exceedingly difficult but I've never experienced the inspiring principle of the Hippocratic Oath applied to my case. You see, I've never ever wanted anything from this industry save for its representatives to be:

- Technically and clinically competent.

- Decent, honourable and true.

- Interested in solving problems instead of offloading my problems back onto me.

I would never have felt the need to be so disrespectful if I had any respect for this industry at all, but I've been on a treadmill for years now where I've tried to engage with, begged and even demanded from this industry and all to no avail. No matter where I go or who I see the answer is always the same, '*Yes I hear what you say Mr. Hardy but I'm afraid you're not listening, the only problem you have because I've read all your reports are the psychological problems in your head*'.

- Where are all the heroes?

- Where are our service delivery ethics that are enshrined in the Hippocratic Oath?

I am the master of my own health, for I take my quality of health seriously

- Why are we the hard working masses, paying so much to underwrite a privileged yet dysfunctional load of crap?

Well I have to say that there are few industries in the modern world today where governments tread so lightly, but this is one that our governments MUST get to grips with once and for all. Because this industry actually believes that both it and those who work in it are actually above due diligence and matters of personal well being and state supported clinical care.

But let's change that flawed perception Ladies and Gents and let's change that starting today, let's bring the bastards who fail us kicking and screaming into the reality that we ourselves are forced to live in every single day. Let's start wrecking the lives and careers of medical rogues if there is good cause or grounds of failure of due diligence can be proven. Because the people who wrecked my bloody life are still out there wrecking the lives of many more people right now.

Personal redress for the underperformance and failures in due diligence are the only way that we, the taxpaying public are ever going to be able to move the medical industry forward kicking and screaming into the modern world.

Therefore when a medic fails you, complain about his or her conduct and then sue them if needs must. When a medic fails a loved one of yours, complain about his or her conduct and then sue them if needs must. Let's collectively generate a real state of fear for these rogues for in doing so:

I am the master of my own happiness, for its in my interests to live life to the full

(a) We will bring about the changes that we need in terms of securing a world class holistic professional service delivery from this industry.

And

(b) We will generate a culture where protectionist old boys clubs are smashed completely by default and for good.

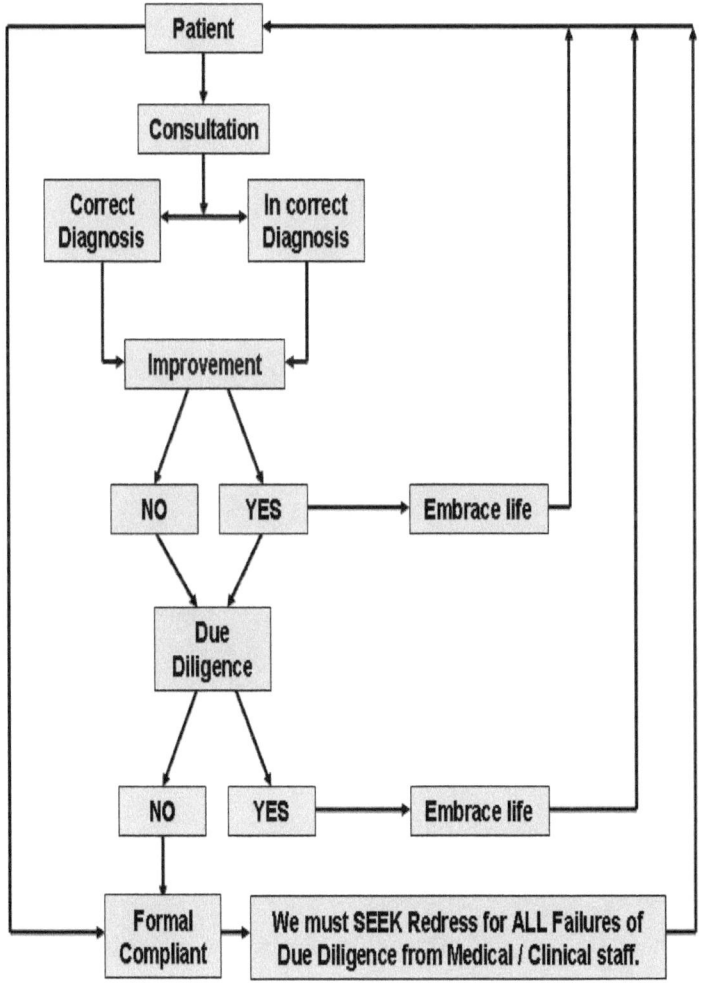

I am the master of my own health, for I take my quality of health seriously

If we all commit to this process, I'm looking forward too and optimistic that following generations will not need to suffer like we have, at the hands of cretins who secure great riches and status from working within the Devils own Institutions.

I am the master of my own happiness, for its in my interests to live life to the full

Personal Notes

I am the master of my own health, for I take my quality of health seriously

Personal Notes

I am the master of my own happiness, for its in my interests to live life to the full

I am the master of my own health, for I take my quality of health seriously

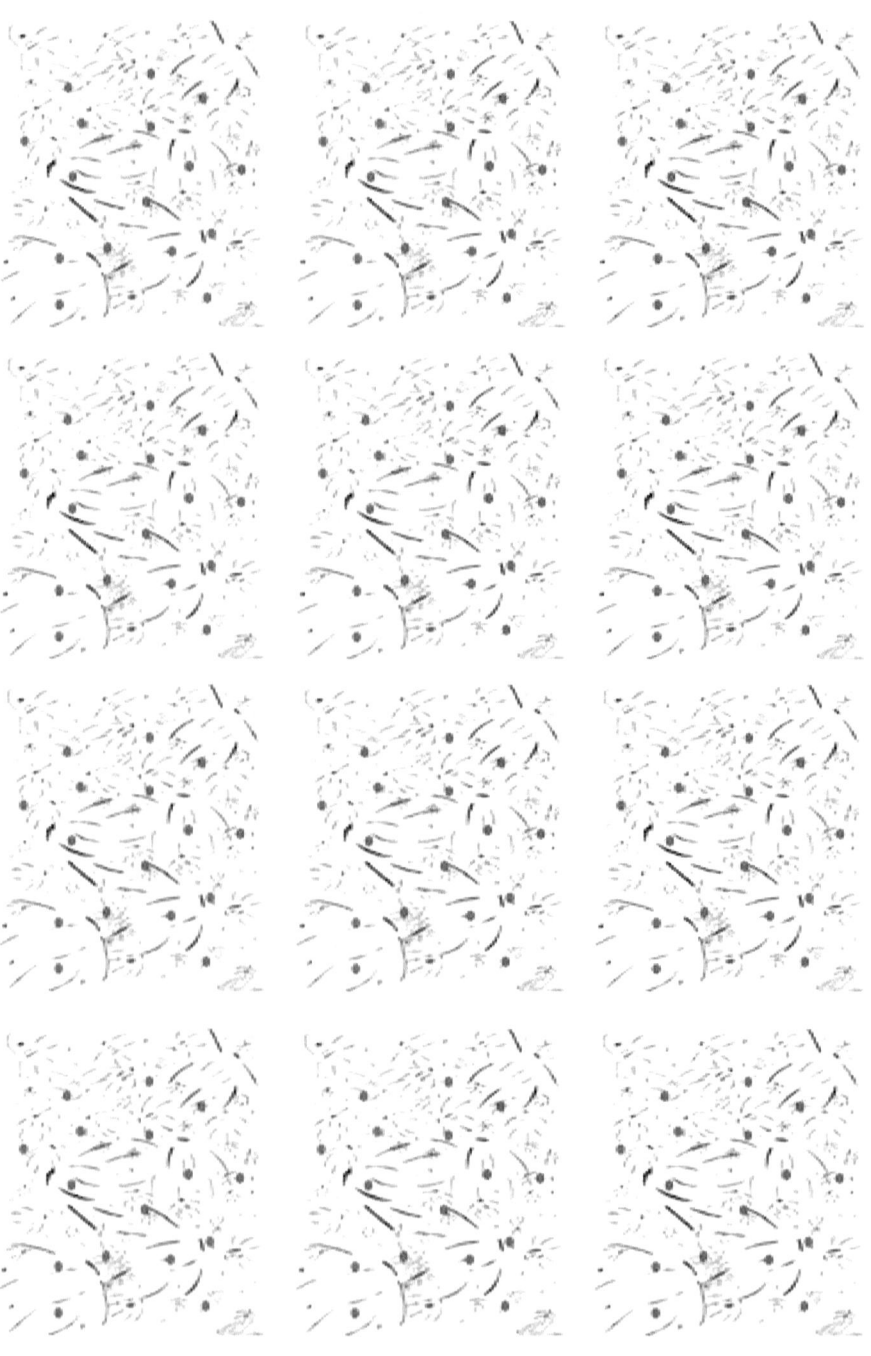

I am the master of my own happiness, for its in my interests to live life to the full

WHEN ALL ELSE FAILS TEST FOR LYMES DISEASE

Be scared, be very scared if you live in the Scottish Highlands, the Lake District, the Yorkshire moors, the New Forest, The Welsh Hills, The Peak District, The Cotswold's, Dartmoor or any British town or village. For there is a disease so deadly out there it can literally destroy your life in a matter of days not weeks! But this disease is not one that you've probably ever been warned about; because this is a disease that our government and our chief medical officers refuse to accept is a major problem or even here amongst us today. So deadly is this disease that it can be spread through sex, through food, through the placenta, through ticks, through midges, through mosquitoes and through wild animals and domesticated pets that have fleas. The disease that I refer to is no other than the life sapping, body destroying, Lymes Disease or its official name the Borrelia burgdorferi Bb spirochete. Typical Lymes Disease symptoms include:

1. Sudden unexplained skin rashes with a whitish centre.
2. Joint pain.
3. Joint swelling.
4. Stiff neck.
5. Unexplainable fatigue.
6. Flu-like symptoms.

I am the master of my own health, for I take my quality of health seriously

7. Frequent fevers and shivers.
8. Frequent sore throat.
9. Heart irregularities.
10. Depression & mood swings.
11. Digestion and stomach related problems.
12. Difficulty eating nausea or vomiting.
13. Muscle twitching or muscle cramps.
14. Indications of sinus infection.
15. Hypoglycemia.
16. Bell's palsy.
17. Carpal tunnel syndrome.
18. Vision problems.
19. No mobility in muscles or tendons.
20. Sensitivity to light and sound.
21. Cranial pain or symptom of pressure inside head.
22. Strange shivers up and down spine.
23. Dizziness unsteady on feet.
24. Seizures unexplained blackouts.

Typical Associated Neurological Problems include;

1. Manic–depression.
2. Short-term memory loss.
3. Poor concentration.
4. Slow mental processing.
5. Brain fog.
6. Sleep disturbances.
7. Hallucinations.

Lymes Disease the great pretender can also mimic;

1. Multiple sclerosis.
2. Anorexia nervosa.
3. Alzheimer's disease.
4. Parkinson's disease.
5. Bipolar depression & psychosis.
6. Hypothyroidism.
7. Fibromyalgia.
8. Guillain–Barré syndrome.
9. Cranial nerve disturbances.
10. Heart abnormalities.
11. Arthritis.
12. Gulf War syndrome.
13. Obsessive compulsive disorder (OCD).
14. Attention-deficit/hyperactivity disorder (ADHD).
15. Chronic fatigue and immune dysfunction syndrome (CFIDS).

Now I'm not going to dwell or delve too heavily into all the issues associated with Lymes Disease. But is important that we as a society sit up and tack notice of the fact that when we have a condition in our midst that is not responding to treatment, it is vitally important that we test patients for Lymes Disease. The reason being that I believe that bloody disease is wrecking too many lives is simply because its potential presence is not being considered or detected and instead people are just being fobbed off by clueless medics with diagnosis such as; ME, CFS, Depression, Stress, etc, etc, etc.

I am the master of my own health, for I take my quality of health seriously

The difficulty however that we all face if we are infected with this disease is that there is a lot of misreporting about this disease, where common dictum suggests that:

(a) It doesn't exist in the UK.

And

(b) If you do contact it which is highly unlikely or so the medical world would say, it can be cured with a few short weeks of antibiotics.

Both those statements are completely wrong, it is here and you can be infected very easily and as yet there is no effective one stop or fully ratified treatment process through to cure.

On top of that diagnosing Lymes Disease can be a very difficult task, which is why so many cases are missed, or patients are diagnosed with other illnesses entirely.

You will acquire no support from the NHS in your endeavours to be either tested or treated for this disease and so it's very important to note that if you believe you have this condition you must take the initiative and privately fund your own investigations.

However please note that whilst there are a number of laboratories used to try to detect Lyme Disease the vast majority are notoriously inaccurate, often producing "false negative" results, i.e. showing that a patient does not have Lyme Disease when in fact they do and I can certainly relate to that.

I am the master of my own happiness, for its in my interests to live life to the full

Way back in 1988 I tried to engage my GP with the spectre of Lymes and was immediately poo poo'd by him. So I went out and had the wrong lymes test performed privately *which cost me a lot of money at the time* and it came back negative. The very fact that it came back negatively threw my chances of recovery completely off line for a further 17years whereupon in desperation I had the correct form of the test performed resulting in the confirmation of ballistic levels of lymes.

So why are there so many false negatives? Well the reason for this is due to the fact that the Borrelia burgdorferi spirochete is so adept at evading both our immune cells and conventional bacterial detection methods. In laymen's terms it's just too darn difficult to be detected by the protection processes in our body and by normal clinical processes used to detect disease. Borrelia burgdorferi, does not have one single, static appearance or chemical signature, and is able to alter these in order to evade detection. In this way, Borrelia burgdorferi is therefore able to evade standard laboratory testing procedures and when you add the fact that there are over 250 known strains of Bb, it becomes obvious that this truly is one very elusive bacterium.

I am the master of my own health, for I take my quality of health seriously

It is not uncommon therefore for a patient to be highly infected by Lymes Disease only to repeatedly produce negative lab test results. You can see how these poor souls just like I was; get tarnished and written off by the medical world as neurotic and hence offloaded to the shit which is psychological and psychiatric intervention treatment regimes and zero treatment options designed specifically to address any underlying diseased states e.g. Lymes Disease. So then how are you going to make sure that if you have Bb that you:

(a) Identify it correctly?

And

(b) You identify it with the degree of speed you need?

Because

(c) It's important to note that every week wasted can add literally months onto the painful task of clearing this dreadful disease from your body.

Well you're going to have to either engage your clinical practice in the first instance or find some qualified person who can extract blood from you. You're then going have to contact the Bowen Research & Training Institute in North America and request their Bowen Q-RiBb test vials and transfer packaging etc. The term Q-RiBb stands for, Quantitative Rapid Identification of Borrelia Burgdorferi which is a relatively new test was developed by Jo Anne Whitaker, M.D. an international medical researcher and a Lymes disease patient herself. The method uses a fluorescent antibody technique on whole blood. As it is 'quantative' the test can determine the extent of infection and that is precisely why I

I am the master of my own happiness, for its in my interests to live life to the full

chose the test for myself. A preliminary report of the findings is provided to the patient within 24 hours of receiving their blood specimen and final report including digital photographs is issued a few days later. Now that's what I believe medical investigations should be all about i.e. rapid testing and rapid reporting coming together as one. The other great thing about this test is that the Q-RiBb is the only test that is unaffected by whether the patient is currently or recently has been taking antibiotics. The reason that is important is because as previously mentioned Bb can detect when it's under threat and can change its form or identity via masking hence evading all other screening processes. It cannot evade however this screening method, so if you do have lymes this test will prove it.

Let's take this situation one step further now, let's assume that you have had your results and you have tested negative for lymes via Q-RiBb, what do you do? Well you do all that you can do to find out what's really wrong with you because that's all anyone of us can ever do. Assuming that you agree with me that laying down and doing nothing is simply no way to live or be. You see I personally dislike names and handles that are thrown out and anchored onto patients by the medical industry e.g. she has OCD, he has ME, she has MS, he has IBS, he has Lymes Disease etc. There is far too much of this and not enough help for patients with these terrible conditions. The unfortunate truth however is that we can either choose to live with those handles and use then as our crutch or we can battle and fight for a better quality of life. In the greater schemes of things it doesn't matter which sits most comfortably with us because as individuals in our own right we each have the right to choose which path we'll follow in life and it really is as simple as that.

I am the master of my own health, for I take my quality of health seriously

Now if your tests are negative and you still choose to battle for a better quality of life then there is a stark reality that you're going to have to wise up to. You're never going to get the sort of help and support that you need from our fundamentally flawed NHS. I know its annoying that a terrorist bomber can get a blood transfusion to save his or her life and that a paedophile can have his coronary bypass performed regardless of the former suffering he's caused during his life. But that is the way of things and I know that it simply doesn't make sense that those 'deviants' can get what they want when they need it and yet no one either hears the suffering or pain of those amongst us infected with Lymes Disease. But that is precisely why we need detach completely from the hypocrisy of those who cite the Hippocratic Oath in order to moralize the actions they take.

By accepting and not allowing ourselves to get hung up on the way things truly are we actually empower ourselves. With that shift in perceptions we're able to accept that the NHS always fails the chronically ill and because of that we can never be let down by it ever again. It is only at the point that we begin to recover that we can begin to kick and scream out loud that our so called glorious NHS is nothing but a cash hungry dinosaur filled with brains the size of peas. But don't despair there is help out there and there are solutions to insurmountable problems to be found. All we need to do is be careful yet willing to explore the potential of alternative views on disease, the treatment of disease and our perception of living and life.

As a working class lad who fought tooth and nail for the NHS I never ever would have thought I would find myself saying that money is the only thing in clinical care that can move you out of the darkness and into the light. But if you are ill and wish to recover, I'm saying it loud and clear right now, you will need to read, to spend your own money and then spend and read some more.

There are no magic wands, no miracles or benevolent healers at hand; chronic illness recovery starts only when a proper diagnosis has been made and an effective treatment process undertaken. At that point and that point only can your unnecessary suffering start moving towards an end.

Nevertheless I always say this to anyone suffering from a chronic illness if you're not making any progress on the treatment regime that you're on, you've either had the wrong diagnosis or your treatment protocol is wrong. The only reason I can say that is because as you will read in the later chapter The Treatment Explorer, I've got a wardrobe full of treatment failure t-shirts.

However I'm not the sort of guy who will stick with a treatment if I feel it's false or an untruth; because my fervent belief is that for a return to health there must be a point when we finally get over the chronically ill pain and suffering hump. And if that isn't happening then the treatment isn't working and it's time to understand:

- Why not.

And

- What you need to do to move that situation on.

I am the master of my own health, for I take my quality of health seriously

There are many diseases out there responsible for chronic illness, some apparently treatable some not, all I can say is if I'd bought into the rubbish that I'd been sold for years, I wouldn't be writing this book now because I would never have made any form of recovery.

Nevertheless I've covered a Bb test result coming back negative, but what happens when it comes back positive. Well sadly it's not much different from above, you won't get the sort of help you need from the NHS. You're going to have to:

- Apply a multi pronged approach to ridding your body of as much of it as you can, including the neurotoxin load that it has produced.

- You're going to have to get you endocrine system working well again as well as your liver to ensure that you're able to remove the remnants of this disease from your body.

- Above all you're going to have to be strong, because the journey through to recovery is both difficult and possibly lifelong.

Personal Notes

I am the master of my own health, for I take my quality of health seriously

Personal Notes

I am the master of my own happiness, for its in my interests to live life to the full

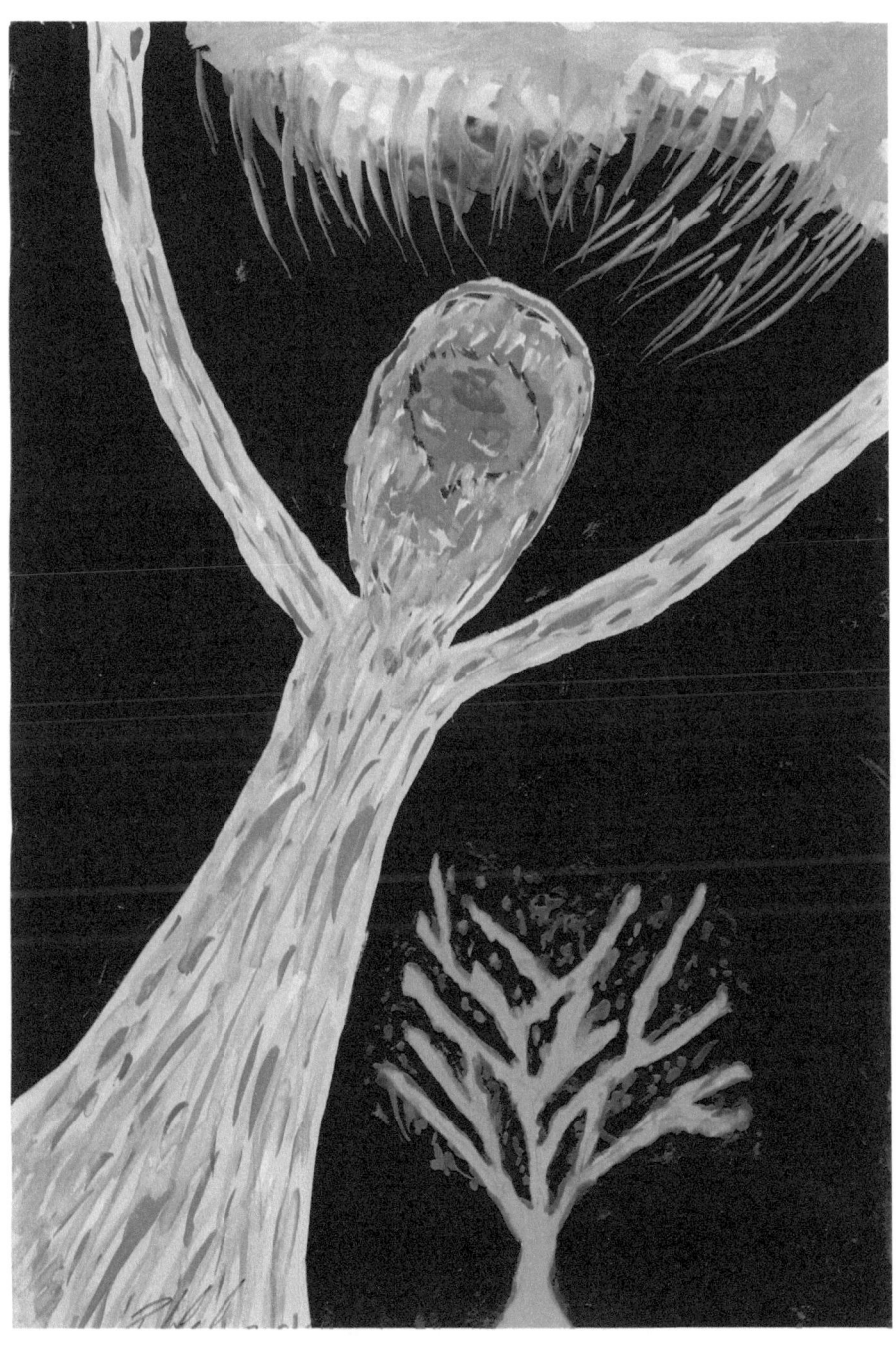

I am the master of my own health, for I take my quality of health seriously

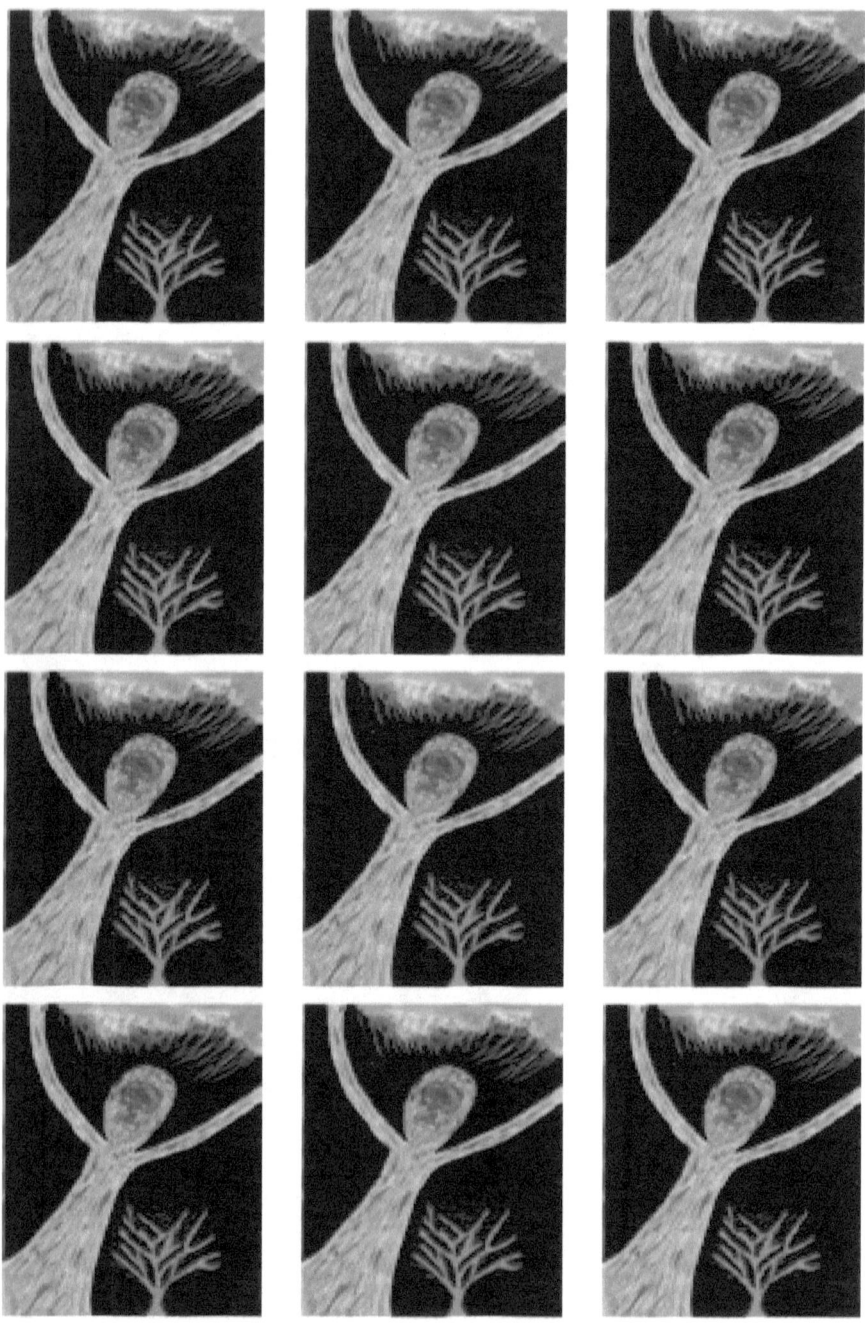

I am the master of my own happiness, for its in my interests to live life to the full

DEPRESSION EXPRESSION AND WHAT WE ALL NEED TO KNOW

Clinical depression is defined as a state of intense sadness, accompanied with the absence of pleasure or the ability to experience pleasure. Unfortunately many people mistakenly identify the feeling of being depressed as 'feeling sad for no reason' or 'having no motivation to do anything'. But clinical depression is more serious than normal depressed feelings, because it often leads to constant negative thinking and thoughts of escapism through either substance abuse or through self harm. It is precisely because of this populist misunderstanding, ignorance and society's intolerance of this disease that individuals suffering from this condition find themselves with nowhere to go. The most common feelings associated with clinical depression include:

- Feelings of overwhelming sadness and/or fear.

- Changing appetite and marked weight gain or loss.

- Disturbed sleep patterns, such as insomnia.

- Fatigue, mental or physical, also loss of energy.

- Feelings of guilt, hopelessness, loneliness and anxiety.

I am the master of my own health, for I take my quality of health seriously

- Trouble concentrating, keeping focus or making any form of decision.

- Recurrent suicidal thoughts or plans for committing suicide.

Despite depression being a simply appalling condition it's still regarded by society as a personal weakness. General perceptions are that it's not a diseased state but that it's something that weak people use to highlight their weakness. Therefore because it's not regarded as a diseased state those suffering from it are therefore not given the level of support or assistance that individuals with lesser but clearly more visible conditions get.

But why isn't this condition regarded as a disease? Well because the medical world has failed wholesale for millenniums to bottom out the root course of this condition. It doesn't matter whether a sufferer sees a GP, a psychologist, a psychiatrist, a counsellor, a herbalist, or a homeopath etc, it's always the same result. The symptoms are the primary point of interest and then the patient's background becomes the main focal point. All parties have different approaches, orthodox clinicians go for the soft options of sedation and detachment whereas alternatives clinicians attempt in the majority of instances to fight fire with fire taking the depressive condition head on.

Neither of those approaches work in the majority of instances because they don't actually try to determine what is really wrong with the patient. To me and having been through what I've been forced to endure, it's simply ridiculous that detailed testing is never carried out but completely understandable because:

I am the master of my own happiness, for its in my interests to live life to the full

- Depression expression suffers from historical prejudices.

And

- Our biological and diagnostic testing techniques are frankly outrageously poor.

What the entire medical and clinical world seem to be happy to ignore is that the human body is a unit which has a multitude of direct and indirect processes working day and night just to keep our bodies in balance. Because it's much easier for them to simply write their patients off than to commit to any relevant, detailed or protracted clinical investigations.

However what happens if any one of those processes in our bodies either becomes defective or more over we are born with defective processes in the first instance? Well its not rocket science is it? If we have defective processes we normally end up having problems and those problems nearly always present themselves as a diseased state. The impact of that can have dreadful consequences upon our lives and I cover the lifelong impact of scarlet fever and romantic fever upon my mum in the chapter Genetic Time Bombs.

Nevertheless, that's why I believe that depression expression, in the majority of instances, is not a psychological or mental health issue, it is nothing more than:

- A derivative or symptom of a diseased state.

- Placenta transferred derivatives of diseased states.

- A breakdown in generic body processes or process coding.

- Genetic abnormalities in generic body processes or process coding.

And only rarely;

- The manifestation of our perceived weak psychology.

I am the master of my own happiness, for its in my interests to live life to the full

If only we were prepared as a society to accept this postulation then we would be able to accept the need to find the root biological cause of depression and not always simply write it off as an emotional or mental illness. Once a root cause is scientifically determined we are better able to treat a condition effectively and hence remove it from our lives completely.

I can hear the howls or derision right now though, 'What is this guy talking about? We always identify the root cause of depression doesn't he understand just how incredibly difficult this condition is to treat?'

Well in truth I do, you see; there were many years where I would have eaten dog shit if I thought it would make me feel better so I certainly do know how difficult living and treating depression can be.

I also know that the only reason I freed myself from that life sapping condition is because I changed my perceptions and my views upon all its possible causes. Depression, if not caused by injury to the brain, is always the result of bodily process breakdown and I mean by that the breakdown of processes within the entire body and not just the brain.

When depressed its impossible to either contemplate or attempt to simply think or rest ourselves out of depression. This diseased state doesn't simply go away of its own accord and medication which compromises still further detoxing systems in our body is absolutely no solution at all.

I am the master of my own health, for I take my quality of health seriously

So what am I actually saying? Well what I'm saying is that we can't treat or medicate a condition if we don't really know what's wrong. But what we can do is shoot from the hip and think we know what's wrong and in doing so pump all sorts of shit into our body resulting in confused results at best and dangerous results at worst. That is unfortunately what happens across the board to the majority of us when we seek medical intervention for this terrible condition.

Now that's a very bold statement and what possible grounds can a plumber have to even dare to postulate such outrageous views? My answer is, nothing more than personal experience and an enquiring and problem solving mind, that's all.

You see, if we fail to enquire we fail in everything we do, because it is only through understanding the entire picture that we are able to fully understand the potential for risk and gain in anything we undertake or do.

My view is that in terms of depression treatment we've made very little progress in the past 2000 years and I believe that is purely because of our sociological attitude to this condition which is continuously preventing any evolution in our perceptions.

Now I was both a civil and mechanical engineer by profession prior to having to find ways through my health conditions. Working in those professions I was exposed to many applications, many environments and many ways of being. It also became obvious to me from a very young age that in all walks of life and work there are people with, 'can do mind sets', people with 'can't do mindsets' and people who 'simply don't give a damn'. Within those mindsets there are, the conscientious and the bodgers, the well trained and the chancers, the problem solvers and the problem makers, the perfectionists and the couldn't care lessers, the owners and the off loaders. There are mind sets who try to make situations far more difficult than they really are and mind sets that inappropriately make problems lighter than they really are. That is just the way it is in engineering, in science, in medicine and in life, etc. *It is the innate paradox of man that he has the ability to be simply brilliant whilst also retaining the ability to be a complete idiot and general waste of time that never fails to blow my mind.*

I am the master of my own health, for I take my quality of health seriously

But why should this paradox's have such a grave bearing upon depression? Well because at the point we buy into clubs or schools of thought or simply choose to conform we lose or chose to ignore our ability to think outside of the box. It is only the men who've chosen the hard route and thought out of the box who've have helped move all our sociological perceptions and expectations along since time began. They achieve that simply by shattering false illusions, generating new belief structures and challenging their peers to prove through science or by example that what they are saying and doing is wrong.

Now let me make it very clear here, I'm no guru, no eminently qualified man of science, I'm simply a guy with the ability to think out of the box and in that spirit I'm going to formulate a simple insight to underpin my root cause of depression views. Despite what many in the medical industry would postulate that it's impossible to draw analogies between the physical and the non physical. My considered retort is simply this; luddites why do you even aspire to work in a modern world when your minds are as closed and dark as the darkest of nights?

I am the master of my own happiness, for its in my interests to live life to the full

You see; if we have an open mind it is eminently possible to draw upon the scenario crossovers that exist in all forms of science and life. Note that when I previously referred to physical I was referring to living breathing life forms and when I refer to non physicals I refer to manufactured support tools, equipment or devices. The only delineations I make between the physical and non physical are spontaneous thought, feelings and pain, barring that; everything be it physical or non physical is conceived, lives and expires' end of story.

In fact there is a simple statistical tool which describes the process of sustainability and it's called the bath tub curve. In essence, it's a graph based upon statistical data which plots predictable life profiles. It doesn't qualify pain, thought or fear it just prescriptively maps the potential for burnout, failure or death.

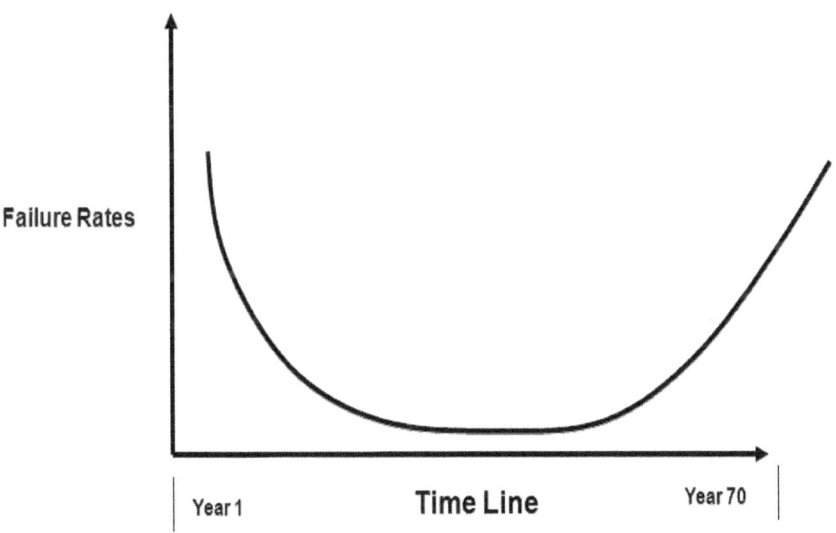

I am the master of my own health, for I take my quality of health seriously

As you can see there is potential for burnout, death or failure at a very early age but that burnout, death or failure drops off until in the human case it starts to climb again at about 60 years of age. It will continue climbing thereafter exponentially as the burnout, death or failure of this standard distribution graph so reliably predicts.

Now I've used that simple thought stimulating proposal to enable me to move onto my next point, so please don't get too hung up on it, simply try to bear with me for now. You see; in all walks of life there are comparisons and crossovers that can be drawn and so if we always remain open to those potentials we can always take givens from one situation and apply them where they've never worked or been used before. Such that even when the medical world argues that you can't compare the engineering science developed by man with the biological science that some qualify as divine, I will always argue from a higher place that you can and we must do so if we are ever to improve the lot of mankind. Because the people who cry heresy are not crying heresy for any go reason at all, save to protect themselves from having to do what they're paid to do anyway.

I am the master of my own happiness, for its in my interests to live life to the full

Nevertheless and moving that point on, most people are completely unaware of just how complex modern manufacturing techniques are and just how little room there is for error. All we ever see is the end product such as, the car, the watch, the sofa, the bed, the mobile phone, and the laptop etc, etc, etc. Yet these are all products of extremely complex manufacturing techniques.

Take even the simplest of manufacturing techniques; let's say for example, a chewing gum manufacturing facility or a porkpie manufacturing facility. Both require tremendous intellect and continuous intellectual investment to ensure that their product is fit for the market, meets all compliance criteria including, quality, legislative, commercial and financial investment criteria's. However in order to meet these givens in any process environment there are multitudes of process streams and because of that there is a need for a multitude of quality and compliance checks, each of which can be as easy or as complex as they need to be.

For the purpose of what I'm trying to explain, I've mapped a very simple manufacturing process with multiple process streams on the next page.

I am the master of my own health, for I take my quality of health seriously

BASIC MULTIPLE PROCESS MAP

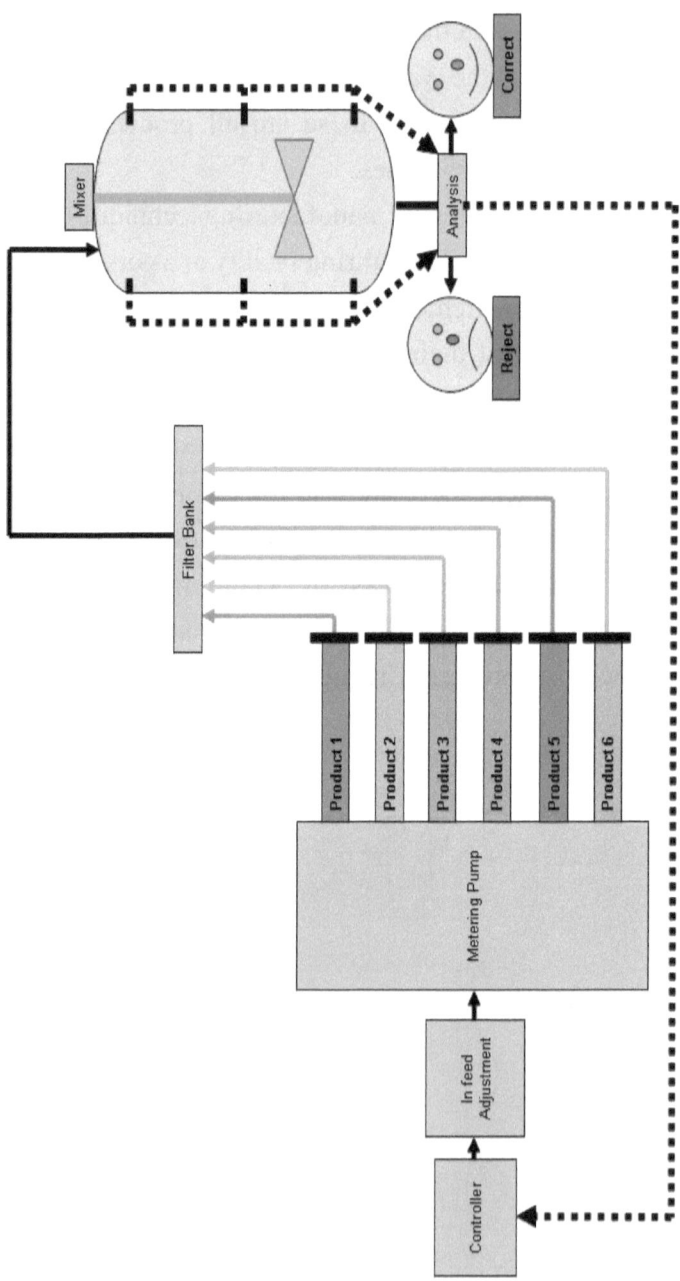

I am the master of my own happiness, for its in my interests to live life to the full

You will see that my basic manufacturing process consists of:

- A logic control processor.
- Bio feedback loops back to the logic control processor.
- An in feed adjustor.
- A pumping mechanism.
- Six different product process streams.
- A filtration unit.
- An agitator or mixer.
- A main reactor vessel.
- An outlet point with analyser.
- Two final product streams correct and reject.

Now if you or I were responsible for ensuring that this simple process ran correctly, there are a few mandatory things we would need to ensure that we had in place first.

- A thorough understanding of the process and what we were expected to do and achieve.
- Robust and properly maintained support equipment and access to suitably qualified repair personnel in the event of its breakdown or failure.

- Quality compliant process streams free from contamination or degradation.

- An ability to analyse effectively when the process has drifted out of acceptable parameters and the knowledge of how to bring it back into line.

- An ability to analyse fault data and to instinctively know which part of the process was to blame.

- An ability to think logically, laterally and rationally about any and all possible eventualities as and when they arise.

Apart from those key points the only remaining holistic essentials we might require are:

- A good work ethic and a desire to do the best that we possibly can do at any given time.

Now the reason that I mapped personality profiles earlier in this chapter is that I wish now to focus upon productivity and performance.

You see, the biggest impediment we all face as a society in achieving our goals is the impact of the people factor. The people factor can either impose great impositions upon us or simply inspire us beyond belief, but it is, I'm afraid to say the greatest of all intangibles simply because when all said and done it's frequently remains outside of our control.

I am the master of my own happiness, for its in my interests to live life to the full

As I've previously stated; I personally believe that anything and everything is possible when the right skills, the right people and the right approach are applied to any given problem or situation and that is the way I choose to live my life. But what matter my own personal beliefs if the people factor problem somehow keeps getting in the way as was the case with my own 30+ years of; inappropriate clinical and medical care. Nevertheless and for the purpose of discussion let's have a look at the people factor in terms of the manufacturing unit.

I am the master of my own health, for I take my quality of health seriously

So the chewing gum manufacturing process has begun to drift and the product is clearly out of specification. The net result is that everything that is being produced is now being rejected. The operations lead in charge simply can't be bothered because his shift is finishing soon, so he leaves the problem to the next shift later that afternoon. The new process controller thinks, shit this problem can only be the result of a problem with process stream number three, I've had this problem before and when I increased its flow rate the process corrected itself albeit very slowly. So he cranks up process stream number three, but the product still remains widely out of spec. In reality he doesn't really know what the problem is, he's just applying at best a calculated guess at what the problem may or may not be. Well what to do next? He's worked very hard trying to sort the problem out but his shift is over soon too.

Solution, he leaves a raft of notes about what he's done, how hard he's worked and then goes onto explain what he thinks needs to be done. Shift three comes in, its late at night, the lead process controller is tired and he can't really be that bothered so he basically shuts the process down and calls in the operational manager. The operational manager goes ballistic and starts lashing out verbally at anyone and everyone in his path. He or she says 'just get this process back on I don't care what you need to do just do it and do it right now'. So the lazy shift process controller simply takes the view, sod it if that's what he/she wants I'll just fire the process up again because I'm out of here soon and it takes five hours to fire the process back up and by then I'm off shift too.

But the process won't fire up again because the product has changed completely, its solidified everywhere and now the entire process stream is blocked. The result is that the process plant now requires a major strip down and large sections of it and components from the various in-feed process streams now need to be scrapped.

I am the master of my own happiness, for its in my interests to live life to the full

Believe me that is not a rare phenomenon, it's an endemic theme of manufacturing and life. When problems are not thought through correctly, when people are not fully committed or accountable then the end result is always unnecessary expenditure, trouble and strife. Or should I say unnecessary in the case of our own personal well being when engaging with representation from the medical or clinical worlds; unnecessary suffering, isolation and the real possibility of a loss of life.

Now of course it can be dangerous to think that we know all the answers, but no more dangerous I would suggest than to abstain from thinking at all. Root cause analysis, whilst sometimes painfully slow, is the only way we can make progress, because the lessons we learn frequently allow us to grow. My view is that it's just as dangerous in a manufacturing environment as it is in our own personal well being if we make value judgments based upon assumptions, prejudices whilst in an environment of fear. If we're not encouraged and rewarded to think laterally and carefully whilst remaining open to the possibility of new ideas then the end result will always be, stagnation and eventually tears because we stifle all our opportunities to grow.

Please take the time to allow these ideas to sink in and try to get a feel for my manufacturing process map. In the next section I'm going to draw some comparatives between effective and defective manufacturing and the current approaches to the analysis and treatment of depression.

I am the master of my own health, for I take my quality of health seriously

For the purpose of my comparative explanation, I've mapped the same manufacturing process but I've simply replaced manufacturing terminology with biophysical terminology. You will see that the map now consists of:

- A brain not a logic control processor
- Bio feedback loops back to the brain not back to a logic control processor.
- A liver not an 'in feed' adjustor.
- A heart not a metering pump.
- Six biological substances not just six different product process streams.
- A blood brain barrier not just a filtration unit.
- An activity stimulated circulation system not just an agitator or mixer.
- A body not a main reactor vessel.
- An outlet emotional/perceptional thought process not just a set point analyser.
- Two final product streams 'happy' and 'depression' not 'correct' and 'reject'

BASIC BODY PROCESS MAP

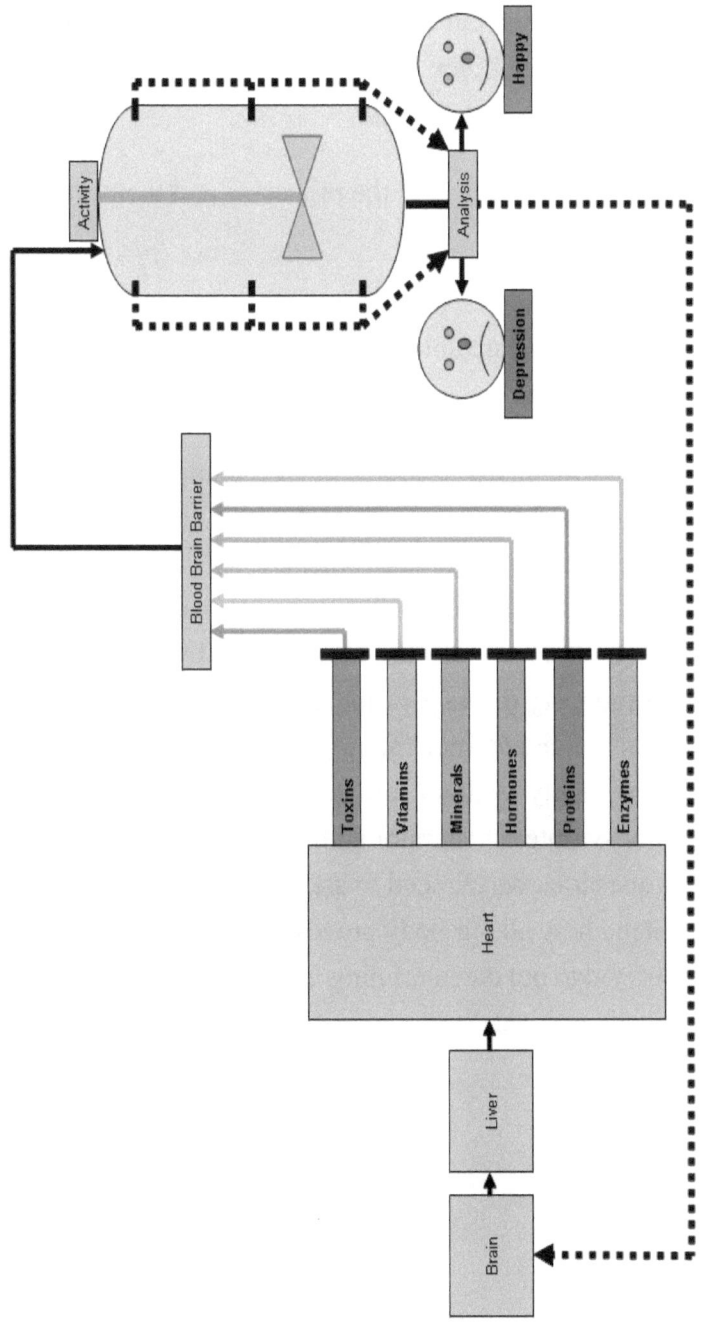

I am the master of my own health, for I take my quality of health seriously

The point I'm making with the revised process map is that there is no real difference between us and an artificially created manufacturing process stream. Take out our humanistic themes and we're both nothing more than a series of complex chemical processes interacting with each other. The key in both instances is:

- How we perceive the processes and their interactions.

And

- How we are able to read the information that is generated therein.

Let's look at the first example of the manufacturing facility, clearly the fault originated from a component within the process stream and then ignorance, incompetence, bad practice, call it what you will, made that original fault much worse than it needed to be. The point I'm making is no fault can be repaired until we fully understand the root cause of that fault. In the case of the depressive state, the medic traditionally makes a snap judgment about what he/she thinks is wrong with the patient invariably without any sound clinical data e.g. symptom addressing not symptom generator addressing data.

The questions we all need to ask here are, do these so called experts understand how all our body processes hang together? And is their training restricted to out dated training in matters of the mind or are they applying holistic rationale?

I am the master of my own happiness, for its in my interests to live life to the full

Well to answer those questions let's test the waters then. What happens when we present with a depressive state to a medic? Well, you may at best receive a thyroid blood test, but I will guarantee that when the results come back stating within normal values all further biological investigation will stop. You see, it doesn't matter that the criteria for that test is rubbish, which I cover later in the chapter about testing. The fact of the matter is; all further biological tests will STOP.

Now I personally don't think that snap judgments represent either effective process management or effective clinical management. In fact from a clinical perspective to me it amounts to gross clinical negligence and accompanying clinical abuse FULL STOP. Nevertheless as part of this clinical negligence and abuse loop your biological investigations will stop and thereafter you will have two choices only. Either to reject your medic's postulations or to go with his or her knee jerk treatment suggestion which in reality is based upon nothing more than:

- His or her dogma driven instincts.

- His or her reluctance to explore root cause analysis.

Or

- Hmmn I've come across this before and so here you go take these and see how you get on e.g. offered the obligatory anti-depressants.

Absolutely fine if you wish to spend a life racked with side effects and living in complete despair, but if you don't then perhaps we as individuals need to take more care. You see as far as I'm concerned the problem with taking drugs to try to fix symptoms is akin to replacing oil in our car engine with honey on a mere thought or anecdotal whim. Whilst both have similar characteristics i.e. sticky and gooey, they are in fact completely different things. But don't take my word for it ask anyone who's put oil on their toast or filled their car engine up with honey and see what sort of results they gained.

For our brains to work effectively there are a myriad of processes that must work in synergy, processes in organs, organs sending signals to other organs telling them to produce substances or equally sending signals to stop those substances from being produced. In fact we have small, dynamic manufacturing processes all over and through our body.

So let us be very clear on one thing here and that is that the process of emotional and mental well being does not simply start and finish with our brain. Our brain is merely a feeder upon the nutrients and energies that our body's in either a healthy or diseased state provide for it.

Let's look at it like this, when we go down with influenza and we feel depressed or low, are we feeling that way because we are mentally or emotionally low? Or are we experiencing the imposition of disease pressing down upon us which is making us feel mentally and emotionally low? Well I will bet that no one ever gives much thought to those two questions when they're suffering from influenza. Because in general we have the influenza and then just as quickly as we contracted it, we get over it and in time we begin to feel like our old selves. But what happens if we never feel like our old selves again after an influenza infection? Or what if from birth we've always felt like shit?

I am the master of my own happiness, for its in my interests to live life to the full

Well to me the answer is very simple, we're in a chronic diseased state, a DNA or placenta transferred diseased state, an ingested or sexually transmitted disease state anyone of which could be compromising our body's ability to function as it should and so we're simply unable to feel happy, contented or good about ourselves. When systems and processes within our body are in a diseased state or their performance is being adversely affected by a state of disease how on earth can we even think that we can feel healthy or normal? The body relies upon these functions to work in synergy and if they're not in synergy then the end result is just like the manufacturing example I gave earlier, we get an indication that there is a deviation from norm. Our body will start letting us know with lots of symptoms not least of all we may become suicidal in our depression expression.

So what if we have low grade viral, fungal or bacterial impositions, what if our assimilation processes, our bodies manufacturing process break down, what then? Surely we just go to our GP's and explain what's happening to us and they simply fix us because after all that's what they're paid to do. Wrong, wrong, wrong, wrong, wrong that's what we were brought up to think in our pill popping generation, the reality is that most medics haven't got a clue about basic diseased states let alone being receptive to help you recover from one. They merely look at our symptoms like the jack of all trades that they are and *'master of none'* and put two and two together and arrive at five.

For example, if a man keeps smashing his car against the back of his garage wall every time he tries to park it, do you just put a foam buffer on the back wall? Do you fix his brakes? Do you suggest that perhaps he needs a smaller car? Or do you suggest he has his eyes tested?

Now I don't know why the guy in the last example has such a problem with parking his car, I'm simply making the point that there could be one or a whole host of reasons why he can't park his car. But the sooner he finds out the root cause of the problem the sooner he can move on. However the probability of him moving on effectively from knee jerk reactions or assumptions I would suggest is actually very low.

You see it's eminently possible that anyone of the previous parking correction suggestions could address his problem. But it's equally possible that none of them would offer any solution at all. Because we may discover some way down the line that the guy:

(a) Never passed his test?

(b) Has a wooden leg?

(c) Needs a light installed in his garage

Or

(d) Needs his hair cut?

I am the master of my own happiness, for its in my interests to live life to the full

Do you get my point? Root cause analysis and only root cause analysis can possibly lift the lid on his parking problem. But one of the main reasons we don't have root cause analysis in terms of depressive expression is because the big pharmaceuticals have sold us all an illusion that they've created concoctions which actually solve that problem. The greatest proponents of this are those who've patented the familiar anti depressant classified as Selective Serotonin Reuptake Inhibitors or SSRI's. It would appear according to those manufacturers that the vast majority of depressive conditions lay firmly at the door of one single neurotransmitter which is of course Serotonin. And these drugs work by shutting some receptors down in your brain hence creating a situation where you're able to maintain artificially high levels of serotonin in the brain. So if you've got any form of depressive illness I can guarantee you that this form of medication will be imposed upon you immediately without any biological testing, because this holds the ultimate key to success in treating depression; or does it?

Well actually they don't and they don't because there are at least another five major neurotransmitters in the brain each of which play some part in our emotional expression so why is all the focus upon serotonin?

Simple of course, because the proponents of serotonin drugs have bagged and blagged the market and so what they have been postulating for years about the success rates of these drugs has now seeped into every aspect of the medical psyche and is literally perceived to be the only appropriate treatment approach when depression expression is suspected.

I am the master of my own health, for I take my quality of health seriously

What happens therefore if you take these drugs? Do you feel better if your serotonin levels now increase? Well I couldn't possibly say because they never made me feel one bit better.

Instead I developed chronic nausea, headaches, fuzzy thinking, nervousness, anxiety, dizziness, low libido, significant weight gain and an immediate increase in my suicidal depression expression. Actually what I developed was an increase in **ALL** the horrible symptoms that I was actually trying to get away from. Shit you may say 'that sounds scary'. Oh yes, believe me it was very scary and very depressing excuse the pun.

You see, all I wanted was to feel much better, instead I felt much worse and in fact I felt like absolute shit. But desperate to feel some little bit better I did the rounds on these bloody things, SSRI's, NASSA, TCAs etc, etc, etc, all with the same results, no improvement but a significant personal exasperation in the resulting magnification of **ALL** the original presenting symptoms and the additional imposition of newer even more debilitating symptoms. It gets even worse however, you see; the problem with taking these substances is that:

(a) You've now become a psychiatric patient.

And

(b) You're getting further away from identifying the originating disease responsible for your condition and presenting symptoms.

I am the master of my own happiness, for its in my interests to live life to the full

But that is the dilemma that the majority of people with depression find themselves in. So what is happening here? Why do people like me not get better on these drugs?

Well perhaps we never had a bloody serotonin deficiency in the first place; perhaps the neurotransmitter issue was never a major problem and our depression expression was merely a presenting response to dysfunction in other processes or the imposition of disease and disease generated toxins.

The truth is as I see it that perhaps these drugs are the best thing ever invented for some people but I've no way of judging that save from my own experiences. But just pay a visit to a depression expression forum and you'll discover that few either:

(a) Make much progress from taking them.

And

(b) The majority wish to get off them as soon as they can because of their unacceptable side effects.

However if they work for you then go for it, because I would never advocate that anyone should stop taking them if they truly want to and/or are gaining benefit from them.

I am the master of my own health, for I take my quality of health seriously

Nevertheless my personal belief is in using them we're simply back to the honey and crude oil in the engine situation again. We're back to people making snap judgments about what they think will work without any substantive biological investigation results to support that judgment. In essence we're back to our chums in the process manufacturing unit and the results in that example if you remember weren't that great.

You see if our body is being attacked by things like Lymes Disease or low grade Viruses, Funguses, Chlamydia, Candida or any one of a number of genetically, placenta or socially transferred diseases, toxins or organic anomalies. Of course we're going to feel ill, low, depressed and even suicidal. Why on earth wouldn't we? Our body clearly is being prevented from performing in a fashion which allows for optimum health.

I am the master of my own happiness, for its in my interests to live life to the full

It is at this point I feel the need to extinguish another insidious sociological false truth. How many times as a chronically ill person have you been told:

(a) There's nothing wrong with you.

And shortly after that being informed that:

(b) The body is a remarkable thing, always trying its best to heal and repair?

Implying that if you did have something wrong with you then your body is certainly doing its best to help you but your mind is preventing that good work happening. Well the next time anyone dares to say that to you, simply compose yourself, and look them straight in the eyes and say, 'fuck off and don't talk such bloody rubbish' If our bodies are that bloody clever, why do I feel so ill and why do mortals:

- Develop cancers which are contrary to everything the body needs?

Before;

- Eventually dying from some or all of our diseases!

Now the reason I feel so strongly about this point is because whilst I accept that the body has an abundance of program logic, I know full well that at the point our body is attacked, disrupted or compromised by a foreign logic, it responds just like a PC when attached by a worm virus. It completely loses the plot and is unable to repair itself. Those of us who've been struck down by chronic illness know precisely what it's like when everything we take either gives us a short term lift or plummets us into deeper despair. We know what it's like when our body scares the living daylights out of us every single day. We know what its like to feel that our body is constantly working against us and not for us. The plain and simple fact is that our bodily protective mechanisms in chronic illness states simply stop working completely, slow down or start producing the wrong formulas and substances which serve only to keep us in our chronic state. It is precisely those problems which prevent chronically ill people from making any real progress back to health or some degree of normality.

Yet at the point we address the underlying causes and remove toxins from our bodily systems, depression almost always becomes a thing of the past, save for low grade expression of the condition as we cleanse our body via purging over the ensuing weeks, months, years or perhaps even a life time. In a diseased state, bodily processes breakdown, incorrect volumes and expressions of chemical processes are the result. Mechanisms designed to filter and adjust flow become blocked and mechanisms designed to be selectively permeable become indiscriminately permeable. The net result of this is that we end up with a very sick body, with many differing and presenting symptoms, not least of which is an expression of depression.

I am the master of my own happiness, for its in my interests to live life to the full

If the body is invaded by a disease or an impediment to normal functioning, immediately our program logic kicks in and tries to fend off that or those insults. This results in a whole host of bodily disruptions and inevitable toxins production which pushes us into a marginal toxic bodily state. But what happens if for some reason the body despite its best efforts is unable to conquer this imposition and those insults and imposition start taking over and interfering with other processes and systems causing greater confusion in the body?

What if a byproduct of this imposition is the production of high levels of toxins which cause inflammation, death and destabilization of feedback loops and organs within the bodily functions and systems. All of which are designed to regulate the production and absorption of key, wellbeing enzymes, proteins and chemicals etc!

Well the answer is simple, the body simply breaks down, damage occurs and the probability of the body being able to repair itself becomes greatly reduced. What I'm really talking about here is, toxin overload, a severely compromised liver function, a breakdown in effective bodily production and repair processes, an imposition to the body and blood brain barrier and a circulating soup which is both highly toxic and of a non standard composition and invite you to once again have a look at the bodily biophysical process map again on the next page.

BASIC BODY PROCESS MAP

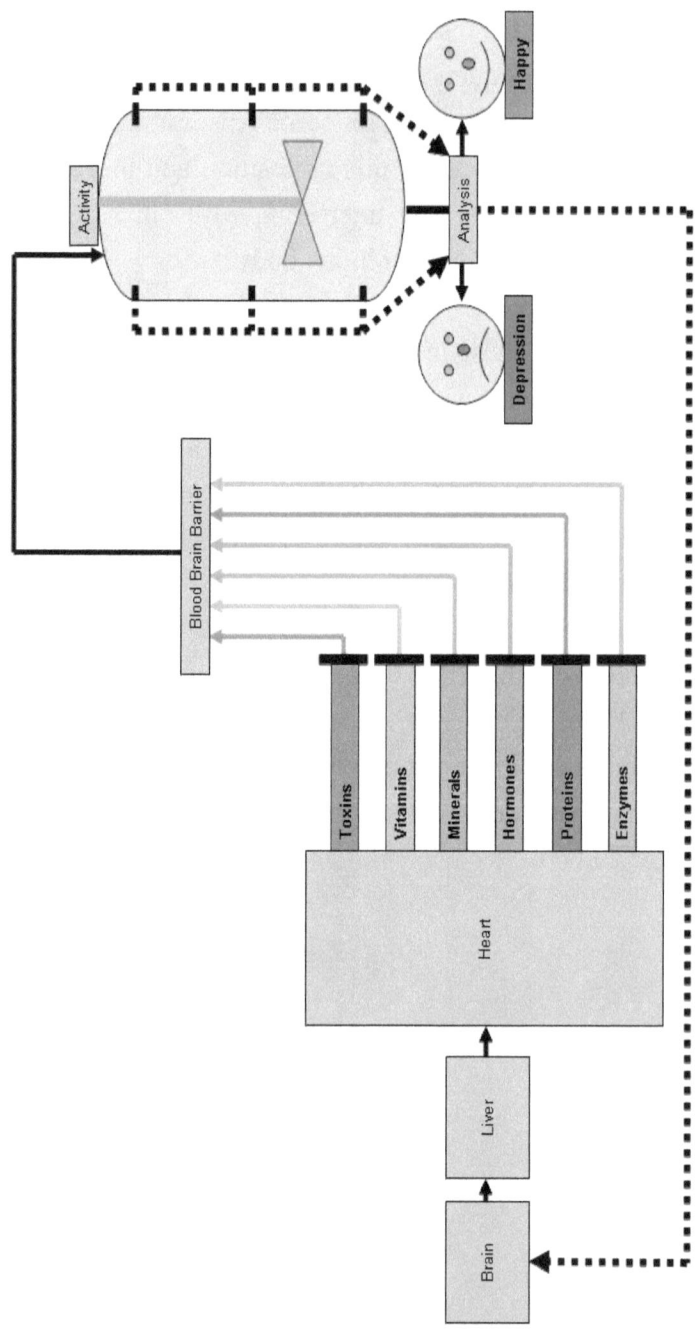

I am the master of my own happiness, for its in my interests to live life to the full

What I'm talking about is the successful formula for the presentation of deep depression and possibly suicidal depression. Now that's not rocket science is it? Neither is it to preposterous to be true. Well I'm afraid if you talk to anyone from the medical industry about this proposition they will immediately poo poo it and why? Well:

(a) They haven't got a clue.

And

(b) How dare you raise the spectre that you know what's going on in you; they're the expert, not you.

Okay so I covered the body's inability to recover and repair itself as a matter of course. Now I want to touch upon another area that really pisses me off. It's the area of disproportionate empathetic illness connection that we, who are chronically ill, frequently encounter. It's those silly people who try to apply and impose the recovery logic of their past shallow medical impositions upon us. Now reading this book it might be difficult to accept that I once was a very gentle man, a highly spiritual man because I'm the first to agree that there is a lot of liver anger or cathartic cleansing coming through in the theme of this book. Nevertheless I was funnily enough a *very* spiritual man once upon a time and because of that I met and knew lots of people on their own unique spiritual paths. Some used it as a crutch, others used it as a point of social contact, some used it to explain away their idiosyncratic flaws, some used it as a foundation for growth and some were quite simply charlatans and frauds.

The reason I'm covering the so called enlightened dimension is because to some who are chronically ill, perhaps as their condition declines, their only points of contact will be with those of so-called an enlightened inclination.

You see, we all need someone to talk to and to feel that there is a reason and a season for everything, that's just the way it is. Even the biggest unbelievers amongst us will cry out to their God at the point another man holds a gun to their head. But there is a real danger lurking in the midst of the spiritually enlightened brigade. There is a culture of acceptance, of assigning conditions to some form of spiritual lesson, of not fighting the condition but letting it beat you. If I had £10's for every time some 'so called enlighten dude' said to me 'give it up to the universe Baz you're choosing to suffer and struggle' I would be driving a brand new Porsche not relying upon public transport.

I am the master of my own happiness, for its in my interests to live life to the full

The give it up to the universe thing is absolute bloody rubbish and what's worse is that its invariably offered to you from a platform of projected great understanding when in reality there is little understanding at all.

Let me tell you where I am on this sort of shit, I would frequently say to my best friend John, there must be a reason for this pal and yet his pragmatic West Cumbrian reply was always this, 'perhaps not Baz, perhaps shit just happens and you're just getting more than your fair share of the shit marra'. Now John was not a spiritual sort of guy he was just a very decent and honourable guy of that there was never any doubt. His reply was as pragmatic as he'd been blessed in living his life. But when I postulated my view to members of the spiritual brigade their retort was frequently, 'let go of your ego Baz, your choosing to suffer, just give it up to the universe etc, etc, etc'. Now the reason that still rankles me even to this day is that I knew those people more than they thought I did and I could see their hypocrisies deep within. Soft music, candles, joss sticks, beans and lentils but give them the slightest problem and their whole world came tumbling in around the shallow façade they'd built for themselves. Yet there they were listening but not hearing my despair, quoting verbatim extracts from anyone of a number of inspirational ways of being books that they'd just read, telling me I must do something and then by subtle innuendo placing the blame for my condition back onto me. It's simply preposterous to think that if we do nothing we will have:

(a) Completed one of our karmic challenges.

And

(c) That perhaps our condition will sort itself out if it's truly meant to be.

I am the master of my own health, for I take my quality of health seriously

What if we solve the problem ourselves surely we've solved the karmic challenge and won't need to do it again. Also in solving the problem we've given our body the sort of help and support that it needed or needs. Look, if I have chronic toothache:

- Do I have chronic toothache?

Or

- Is that a karmic lesson?

If I give my chronic toothache up to the universe, does the universe hear me and does it take my pain away? Well the answers are:

- Of course I have a toothache be that of a karmic or physical nature who really cares?

But

- Sitting and waiting for something to happen from a divine perspective is not going to take my pain away.

My tooth needs dental intervention, be that an extraction or repair and when I'm feeling much better I can consider the karmic scheme of things whilst taking better care of my teeth. Now look the point I've caustically emphasized here is, if anyone ever says to you give your condition up to the universe or you're choosing to suffer from depression, look them straight in the eyes and tell them to 'fuck right off'.

I am the master of my own happiness, for its in my interests to live life to the full

The road to depression expression diagnosis and recovery can be tortuous and slow, but at the point we begin to accept the bigger scheme of things, that's the very same point we begin to regroup our perceptions and thoughts. We begin to understand the complexity of depression, the many systems and issues that we need to address simply to enable ourselves to be completely depression free. I couldn't possibly cover all the complex components of depression in this book including, toxins, disease, hormones, inflammation and histamines etc, but I hope my insights and perceptions have at least simulated your own thoughts.

I am the master of my own health, for I take my quality of health seriously

Before I sign this chapter off let me leave you with one final thought in terms of my differing views on the expression of depression. You see; when I was a young guy growing up in the small town of Whitehaven, there was an expression that was used in a matter of fact sort of way and that was; every time we were greeted with a bright full moon. People would look to the sky and jokingly say; 'Bloody hell, the 'A ward' and 'police station' will be full tonight marra' and what's more they were frequently right. The same families, every time there was a bright full moon, would be involved in some sort of ruckus, the same guys would be done for drunk and disorderly matters and the same guys would be lifted and carted off to the local psychiatric 'A ward'. Because time after time the same people would experience subtle changes in their personality every time we had a full moon.

Big joke eh! People were referred to as wolf men and satirized all their lives. When in reality it was no joke and the reason why it was no joke is because those changes in their personalities were completely outside of their rational control. All of them I suggest had some form of DNA, placenta transferred, ingested or sexually transmitted parasitical, viral or fungal infestation which meant every twenty eight days they experienced an event known simply as hatching. You see there are no coincidences in terms of emotive reactions and depressive expression during full moons etc.

Those actions are the result of increased toxin loads brought about by parasitical hatchings which are always in tune with our moon's cycle. I know from personal experience only too well how those hatching cycles can affect us, because that's the approximate cycle of Lymes Disease etc. So you see, there are so many things that can exert a depressive expression upon us, which means that the key to our well being must always be to simply note and record our body's expression of disease.

I am the master of my own happiness, for its in my interests to live life to the full

For over time we're then able to profile our disease, hence removing all the delusions and illusions that we've allowed ourselves to buy into, by simply using my process logic map below as an aide-memoir.

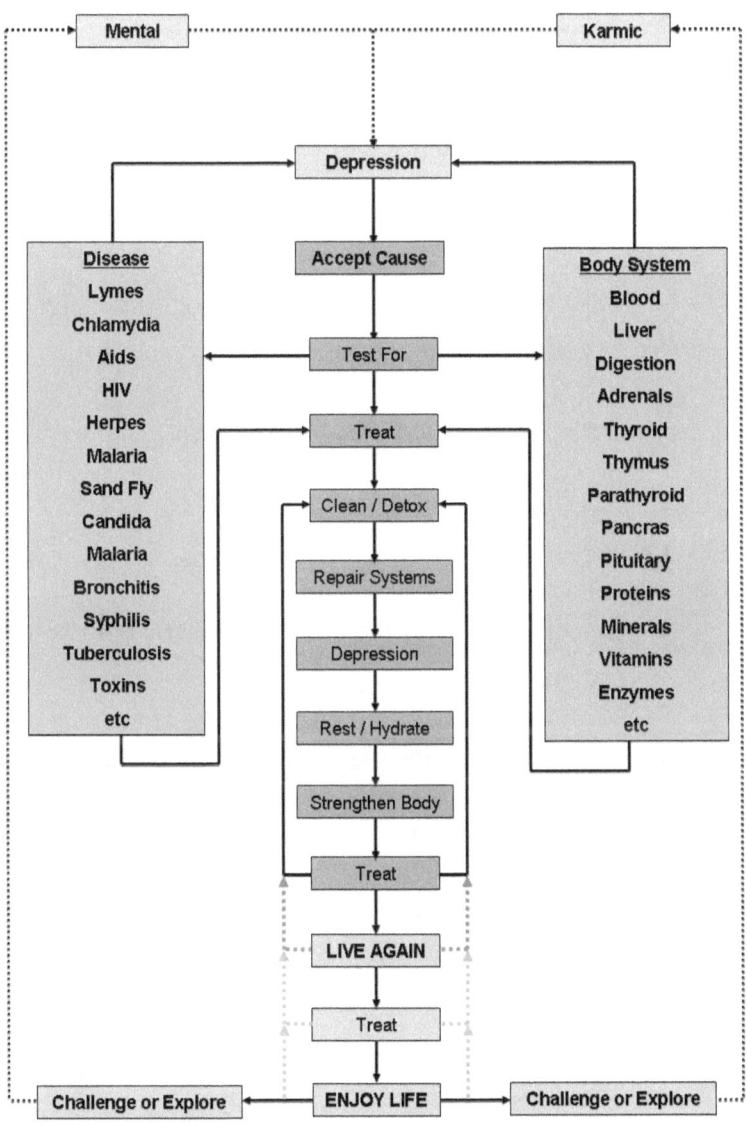

Does a man move into depression expression because of the state of his mind or is he pushed into depression expression because of the state of his body? – YOUR CHOICE !

I am the master of my own health, for I take my quality of health seriously

With reference to this simple process logic map it's important that you take control of all your diseased state expressions and if one of those expressions is that of depression, then your choices are:

- Accept the spiritual suggestions of giving your problem up to the universe.

- Accept the diagnosis offered by your medics.

- Determine how you're going to follow their advice.

- Take the medications and suggestions they offer and stick to that treatment regime.

- Accept all eventualities from any and all course of actions that you take.

Or

- Reject the words of wisdom offered by your spiritual associates.

- Reject the diagnosis offered by your medics.

- Explore the potential of multiple impositions.

- Commit to taking complete ownership of your pursuit of well being.

- Accept all eventualities from any and all course of actions that you take.

Personal Notes

I am the master of my own health, for I take my quality of health seriously

Personal Notes

I am the master of my own happiness, for its in my interests to live life to the full

Personal Notes

I am the master of my own health, for I take my quality of health seriously

Personal Notes

I am the master of my own happiness, for its in my interests to live life to the full

I am the master of my own health, for I take my quality of health seriously

I am the master of my own happiness, for its in my interests to live life to the full

STOP STRESSING ABOUT STRESS!

Stress appears to be simply everywhere, every time you talk to someone they tell you how stressed they're feeling, stressed about work, the wife, the husband, the girlfriend, the boyfriend, the kids, their finances and so on. 'Stress' seems to be an everyday part of life. Stress; what a great word if you're a medic, you can write so many things off as being stress related. 'You're suffering from stress Mr. Hardy'

- *Patient*: 'Blimey am I? That sounds dreadful is it treatable?'

- *Medic*: 'Hmmn well it depends upon what you mean by treatable'

- *Patient*: 'Shit, tell me, what is this stress when it's at home then because it sounds a bit serious?'

- *Medic*: 'Hmmn well that's the $60.000.00 question isn't it?'

- *Patient*: 'Er…. is it? Okay let me ask you then the $60.000.00 question, what is stress?'

- *Medic*: 'Hmmn, well you see Mr. Hardy no one actually knows what stress is'.

I am the master of my own health, for I take my quality of health seriously

- **Patient**: 'Er….. sorry no one actually knows what stress is and yet you're telling me I've got it, you're having a bloody laugh mate aren't you? How on earth can you say I have something when no one knows what the hell it is?'

The medic at that point then loads his or her Mr, Mrs or Ms. Pompous, Nasty or Arrogant head on:

- **Medic**: 'Look just take it from me Mr. Hardy, you're suffering from stress and I should know because I've seen it so many times in people like you!'

So let me ask, how many of you have encountered that line of clap trap? How many of you have spoken to or consulted a so called expert about a stress related issue and found that you've never been given a straight answer? That there was an undercurrent postulated that perhaps your personality was somehow contributing and even generating its manifestation.

I am the master of my own happiness, for its in my interests to live life to the full

Yet the funny thing is its so simple to define stress, it really is, so are you ready for this? If so, then take a deep breath, relax and prepare yourself to be suitably unimpressed. Stress is the generic name used to identify the physical and emotional symptoms of adrenal fatigue or in worse case scenarios adrenal burnout. Got that? It sort of roles of the keyboard so I'm going to type that little ditty again, *Stress is the generic name used to identify the physical and emotional symptoms of adrenal fatigue or in worse case scenarios adrenal burnout.* That's right, you haven't got some terrible and incurable disease, you're not insane, you haven't had a nervous breakdown and you're not a neurotic waste of space.

You're normal; you're a potentially fully functioning mortal who unfortunately for some reason is experiencing the very real and terribly debilitating symptoms of adrenal fatigue or in worse case scenarios, adrenal burnout. Stress is, and be under no grandiose illusion nothing more than that. It is an eminently recoverable issue with your adrenals and that is it in a nut shell.

Phew that was an easy chapter to put together eh? We've qualified what stress is so I guess I can move onto my next chapter? Hmmmn if dealing with stress was as simple as understanding its root cause how simple life would be, but life is not simple at all! You see; I've sold you a line of thought about the root cause of stress, but now I need to qualify what on earth the adrenals are or you're none the wiser.

The adrenals are just two little walnut sized organs that sit on top of our kidneys on either side. They are responsible for producing a whole host of lovely life giving hormones not least of which include: Adrenaline, DHEA and Cortisol. Now don't worry if this sounds confusing or too technical because to help simplify the myth of stress generation I've knocked up some sketches to explain the issues I'm about to cover.

I am the master of my own health, for I take my quality of health seriously

So what am I talking about when I refer to the adrenals? Well I'm referring to two critical organs within the endocrine system. 'Blimey' I can hear you say, 'what on earth is the endocrine system? This is starting to get difficult to follow'. Well just hang on and don't worry, the muddy water will clear very soon; just go with me for now yeah, because the endocrine system is just an aspect of our central nervous system. Our adrenals job is to perform a vital aspect of our nervous system. When we are in a state of adrenal fatigue or burnout and our adrenals are unable to perform well this is often the point where ignorant medics colloquially describe your presenting condition as nothing more than, 'stress or 'you've had a nervous breakdown'. Out will come the SSRI's and you will be written off without any further investigations.

However for anyone wishing to recover from nervous system fatigue or burnout it's important to understand just what the nervous system is. You see, our nervous system is basically made up of two major systems, the sympathetic and the parasympathetic nervous systems which are commonly called the autonomic nervous system. These systems work in balance with each other and directly or indirectly affect almost every structure in our body including our: heart rate, blood pressure, lumbar function, kidneys, blood vessels, stomach and intestines. The parasympathetic aspect of our autonomic nervous system has mainly a relaxing function whereas the sympathetic aspect is the key to our successful survival as far back in days of yore i.e. when we needed the ability to cope in a world when everything either wanted to eat, shag or kill us. Our autonomic nervous system is most important in two situations: emergency situations that cause fear and require us to 'fight' or take 'flight' *sympathetic*, and none emergency situations that allow us to 'rest' and 'digest' *parasympathetic*. Our autonomic nervous system also acts in 'normal' situations to maintain normal internal functions and works with the somatic nervous system i.e. the systems which allow us to relax and sleep.

'Hang on, hang on, stop right there, I can hear you say, where is this going there's been lots of words about lots of things and yet the adrenal stress thing hasn't been mentioned yet'. Relax yeah, all in good time, you'll fire up your sympathetic nervous system if you're not careful and then you'll get yourself too agitated to read on. If that were to happen you won't want to finish this explanation just as it's getting to the most interesting and eye opening part for you. So in order to keep you onboard I'm going to move this on quickly now.

Let's put you in a stressful situation and let's see what happens to you? Well actually let's not because you don't need the hassle. Okay so let me make it easier; let me tell you what happens to you when you're in a stressful situation. Well what happens is that immediately your body's sympathetic nervous system kicks in and reacts in time old fashion to signals it's receiving from your thoughts about the potential danger you feel you're in.

You immediately get the fluttering butterflies in your stomach and start to feel a bit panicky; the bronchial tubes in your lungs widen to give you more oxygen so you start to hyperventilate and may even become light headed. Also blood is sent in greater volumes to your brain whilst your skin and internal organs get less and that sort of unnerves you. Your body's muscles tighten up around the shoulders, neck and your head and your heart meanwhile feels as if it's in your mouth, but your mouth feels parched.

Did I miss anything? Er…. no I don't think so unless you're also one of the many that also experiences a need to evacuate your bowel or bladder or both together when you're feeling a little stressed!

Okay, that my friend is normal stress reactions covered, and that my friend is something that was once a very close companion of mine. But let's not call it stress from now on lets call it what it really is: 'endocrine hyperactivity and or adrenal insufficiency'. It's not a mental health issue; it's not a personal weakness, but a real physiological condition which can push us all beyond our own personal points of mortal endurance.

Now it's sort of easy to understand why this condition has been ignored by the medical world and sort of dropped wholesale in the mental health world. This is because its symptoms can have profound emotional implications and what's more, mainstream endocrinologists don't accept grey areas of disease such as subtle insufficiency. More importantly as I've discussed already, mainstream medicine is simply happy to treat symptoms and is therefore not in the least bit interested or concerned about identifying the underlying cause of a condition. However whilst I can understand the historical incompetence's that generated this situation, I'm simply not prepared to accept this approach and appalling level of technical expertise from highly paid public sector workers in the 21st century because its quite simply an outrageous situation.

So I'm going to explain adrenal insufficiency to you now in I hope an engaging and simplistic fashion, but before I do that I would like to have a look at the two sketches I did way back in 2003 when trying to understand what was happening to me. I deliberately haven't updated them, save for giving them a title because I wanted you to try to connect with where I was then. They are as raw today as the day I put them together and yet when I put them together in my desperate state, absolutely no one said to me, 'Yes I see now Baz what you've just described makes sense I've got it, what you're actually suffering from is adrenal insufficiency mate'.

No what I got was clap trap and rubbish, what I got were responses like these:

- 'Well he must be bipolar if he can do things like that whilst depressed and claiming to be stressed'

Or

- 'He can't be that depressed or he wouldn't be able to do things like that'

Or

- 'He's obviously just an attention seeking neurotic'

I also got a lot of mental health crap, I got a lot of:

- 'Sort yourself out crap'
- 'Why don't you just connect with nature crap'
- 'Hey I really can't be bothered with you mate crap'

Anyway, enough already, just have a look at the next two flow diagrams and see if you can relate to them and then I will begin to break down the adrenal insufficiency mystery for you, bit by bit......

RAPHAEL'S LEGACY

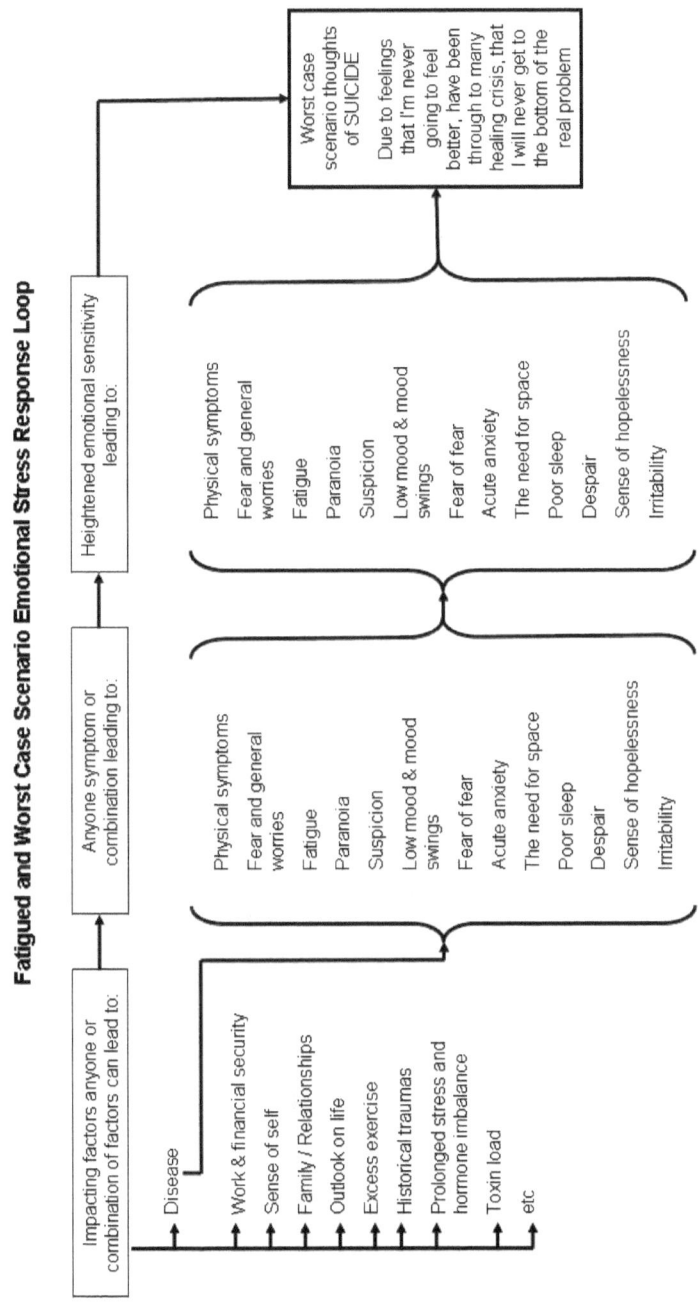

I am the master of my own health, for I take my quality of health seriously

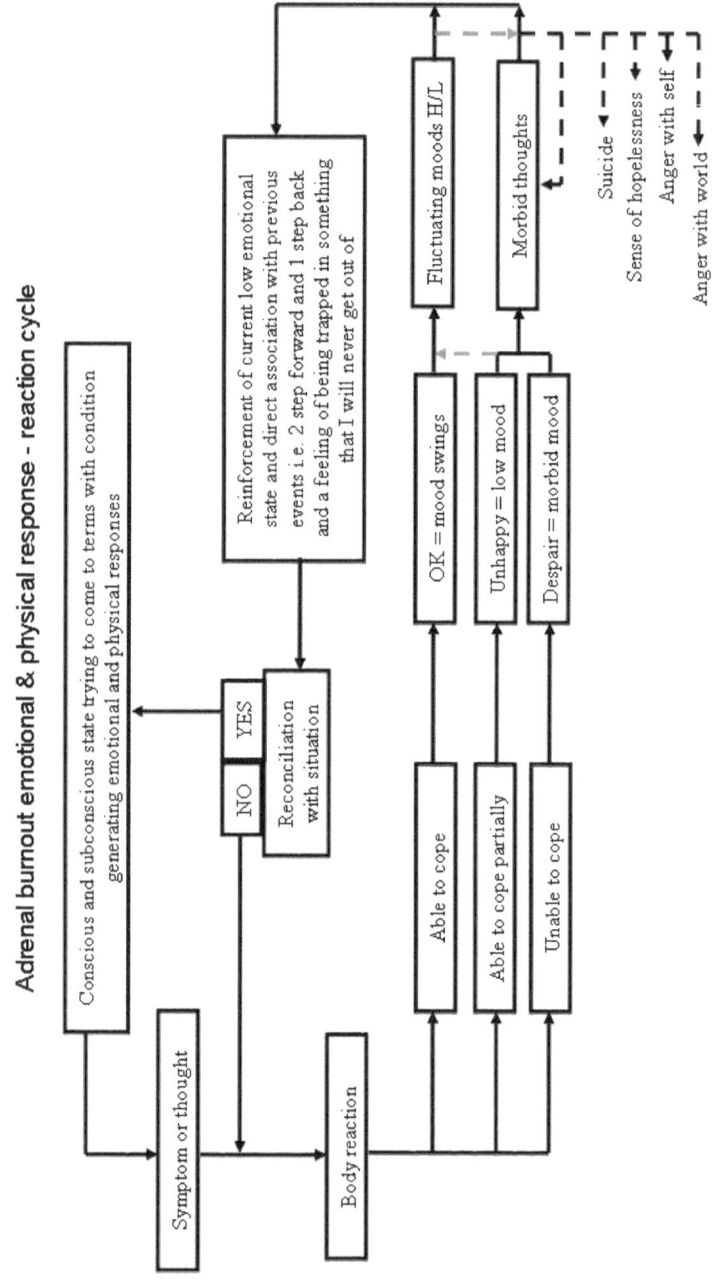

I am the master of my own happiness, for its in my interests to live life to the full

So why was I experiencing such terrible and life debilitating symptoms when suffering from adrenal insufficiency? Well to understand that we must first explore the endocrine system, its major components and what they do inside our body.

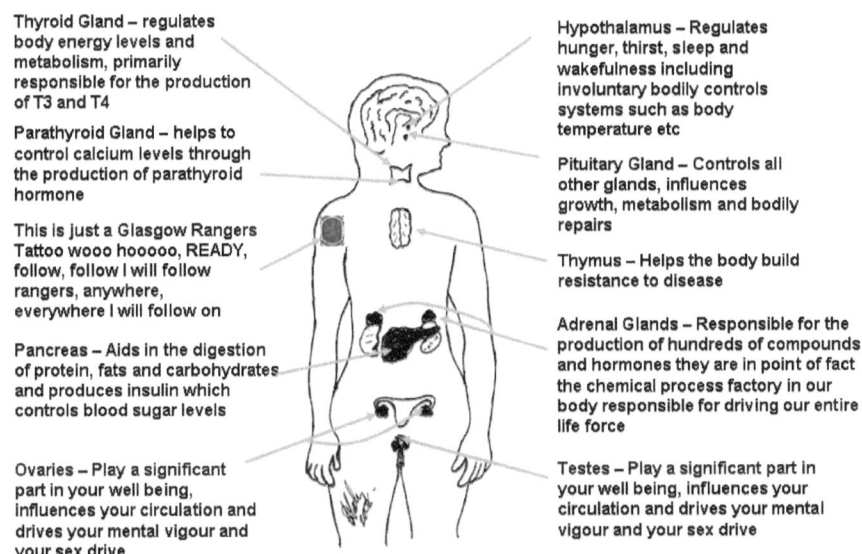

Is a man responsible for all his thoughts or is he at the mercy of his body? - Your choice

As you can see, the endocrine system in our bodies is simply a series of organs. However, what you can't see yet is that within those organs there is a hierarchy of process initiators and inhibitors via feedback loops within the body. To me there is no difference between that process and any modern manufacturing situation i.e. when things are right the process runs smoothly and the results are good, when things are not right the process does not run smoothly and the results are not so good.

I am the master of my own health, for I take my quality of health seriously

All we need to do to is connect with that reality and to substitute results that are good for 'happy' and results that are not so good for 'depression'. So as discussed earlier when our endocrine or autonomic nervous system is running normally, five main things happen in our body via our sympathetic nervous system when we're scared, in danger or feeling threatened.

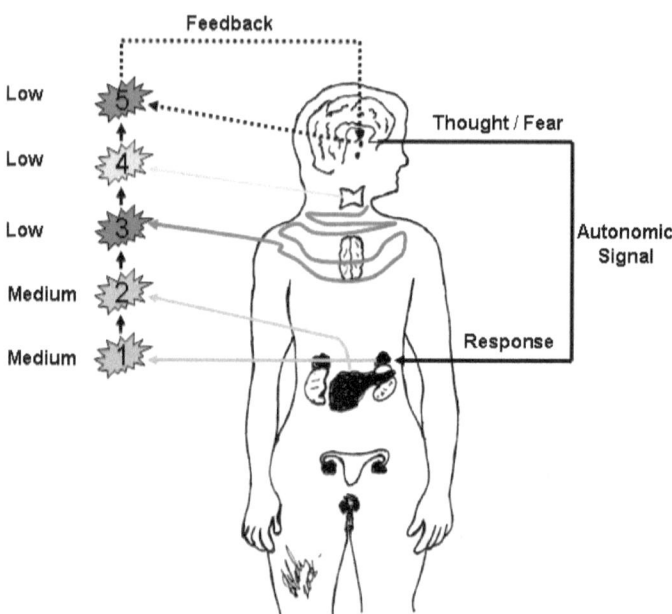

**Is a man responsible for all his thoughts or is he at the mercy of his body? –
Your choice**

An incident happens which shocks or threatens us; a boo, a car horn or a bumpy flight, it doesn't really matter. At the point the shock hits, a message is sent from your hypothalamus to your adrenals and they immediately pump out low volume adrenaline, that's the butter fly sensation you feel in your stomach. Now if you remember, I said that our autonomic system is still primed to work like it did way back in days of yore when it was at the forefront of our ultimate survival capabilities, i.e.

I am the master of my own happiness, for its in my interests to live life to the full

something is going to eat me, shag me, kill me, I need to get away etc. Our adrenalines primary function is to propel us clear of danger i.e. 'flight'. Shortly after the adrenaline surge has hit, it is shut off and cortisol is pumped from the adrenals. Cortisol is a fantastic substance; it is the staff of life, without cortisol we simply die. It is cortisol that gives us the courage to turn and fight, to get out of bed in the morning, to recover from illness, it is in essence, the elixir of life, the only hormone that allows man to adapt and cope with anything. Sounds too good to be true, er…..not really, it is fantastic stuff, but as with anything too much of it is no good for anyone.

So that's biological response one (1) taken care of and its reactive level is medium in a healthy body. At the point cortisol is released, a message is sent to the pancreas which encourages it to release insulin into the blood stream. That's to also energise the body and it is also a medium response in a healthy body. So we now have response two (2) covered yeah? The body's muscles begin to tighten in preparation for activity and in a healthy body that's a low response and covers biological response number three (3). Response number four (4) then kicks in and it too is low, it's the thyroid producing T3 and T4 hormones to support and energise our metabolic rate. The danger may have simply passed by now and we think via response number five (5), 'bloody hell or phew'. Then continue along as normal not giving the incident much thought.

In essence our body then simply settles down and we're able to continue business as normal, working, gardening, relaxing, reading, watching the TV etc. We know that we are in a healthy state when this very normal bodily function takes place and it has absolutely no impact upon us or indeed our overall quality of life. When we move into a diseased state however it is I'm afraid to say a very different proposition, our quality of life falls, our sense of self is diminished and our moods are

I am the master of my own health, for I take my quality of health seriously

frequently turbulent to say the least. We can quickly move into endocrine hyperactively when our body is under attack, which results in insufficiency and more often than not we begin to experience symptoms of depression expression.

We Are Always Off Colour When We Move Into A Diseased State!

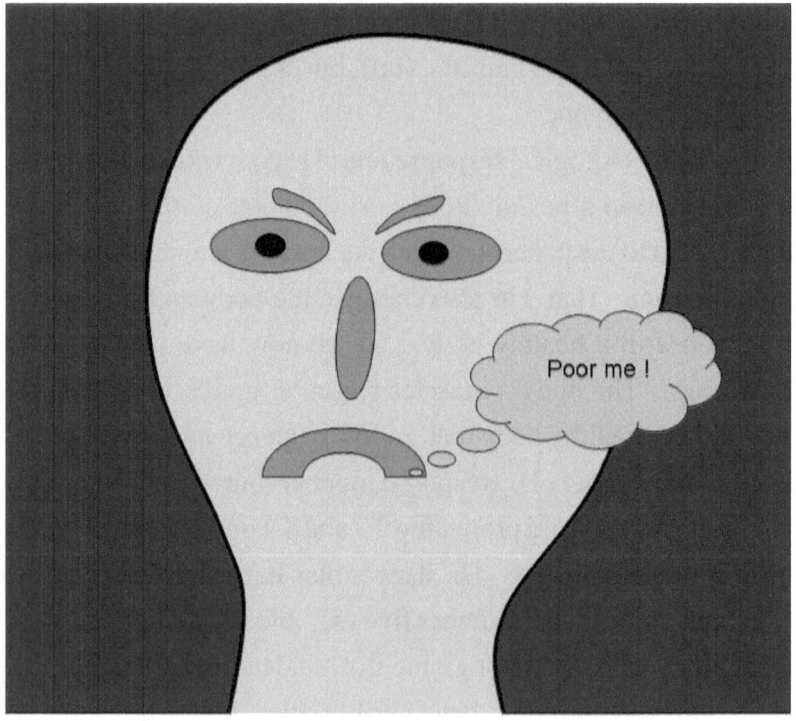

Take a very good look at this face, the colour of this face and the expression it carries with such pain, being stressed out of your body and mind is no joke at all and not in the least bit served well by luddite medic's who can only prescribe SSRI's or mental health act incarcerations.

I am the master of my own happiness, for its in my interests to live life to the full

When we move into a diseased state or are moving into adrenal fatigue, our responses, whilst following the same pattern, taken on considerably different magnitudes. Values in our 1 to 5 biological responses change and we find that: *Response 1* now results in 'higher 'amounts of adrenalin and cortisol being pumped out. *Response 2* now results in 'medium' amounts of insulin but this may oscillate between 'medium and high' levels of insulin being pumped out which can push us into a, 'Hypoglycemic state' *Response 3* now results in 'medium' muscle tension, it may stay longer or it may be more noticeable. *Response 4* now results in 'great' demands being exerted upon the thyroid and as such it may not be able to meet all the demands placed upon it, changes to body temperature occur and unexplainable pains. *Response 5* now results in 'conscious awareness' of the problem and we start to become preoccupied with the condition.

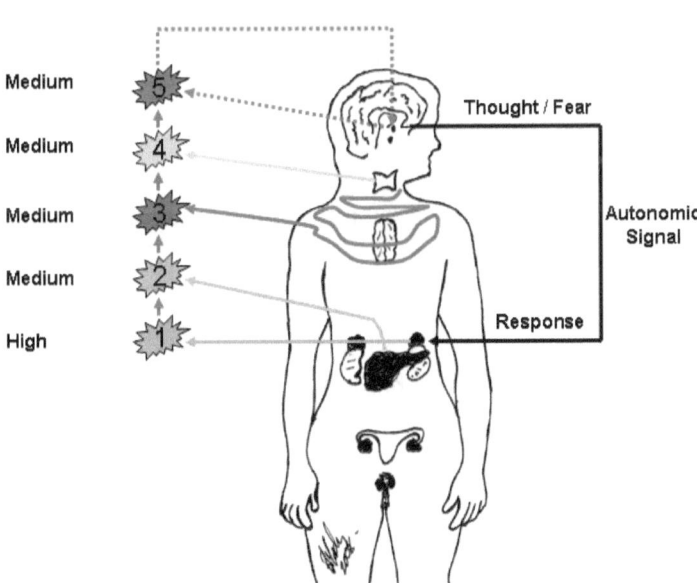

Your Endocrine Chronic Fear Cycle Simplified

Is a man responsible for all his thoughts or is he at the mercy of his body? – Your choice

I am the master of my own health, for I take my quality of health seriously

It's important that I cover Hypoglycemia at this point because its presentation can have very profound effects upon our quality of life and sense of well being. People who suffer from 'glycaemia' related conditions can either be hypoglycemic or hyperglycemic. When we move into a hypoglycemic state we can suffer from a number of serious symptoms including comas etc. The best way to minimise these symptoms is to follow a straight forward hypoglycemic diet. A hypoglycemic person should avoid sugary foods & never miss a meal if possible. If you do miss a meal this can make blood sugar levels decrease and so symptoms will start and all this puts an every increasing strain upon your endocrine system. The best solution for a hypoglycemic is to have a personalized diet which will ensure your blood sugar levels are kept at the right levels and serious symptoms can be avoided. This is not a cure for Hypoglycemia it is merely a necessary addendum to help you optimize your health by lowering the physical stress expression being imposed upon your compromised endocrine system. Symptoms of Hypoglycemia include:

- Being constantly hungry or tired.

- Highly irritable for no good reason?

- Feeling depressed even though you have no obvious reason to feel down?

- Suffering from insomnia, where you often lay awake night after night unable to get your racing mind to calm down.

- Feeling as if you're a slave to the constant cravings you have for potato chips, soft drinks and sweets.

I am the master of my own happiness, for its in my interests to live life to the full

When we move into a 'deeper' diseased state or we move towards adrenal burnout, our responses, whilst following the same pattern, taken on considerably different magnitudes. Values in 1 to 5 biological responses change and we find that: *Response 1* now results in 'high' amounts of adrenalin and 'low' amounts of cortisol being pumped out and so the fear factor increases but our ability to cope reduces significantly. *Response 2* now results in dramatic oscillation between 'medium and high levels' of insulin being pumped out and we find ourselves in a constant hypoglycemic state. *Response 3* now results in 'high' muscle tension; it may be a permanent impediment causing tension headaches, stiff neck and lack of mobility in general. *Response 4* now results in 'dramatic' demands being exerted upon the thyroid and the thyroid may move into a hypothyroid state simply unable to produce the hormones we need to regulate our body metabolism. *Response 5* now results in a vulnerable, depressed, anxious and confused state with racing thoughts, and we think we've gone insane.

It is generally at this point that we force ourselves to either see a GP or an alternative practitioner because living in our body is becoming a very difficult proposition to deal with. Only those who have ever experienced this appalling physical situation truly understand the sheer torment that mortality can be. It is a dire situation simply lacking in any rationale where your body can completely eclipse all your former beliefs and sense of who you are, as it pushes you beyond your own personal levels of endurance. It's the point where you're possibly written of as a neurotic, a depressive or simply someone with a weak psychology, when in reality you're merely in a state of adrenal insufficiency.

Your Endocrine Burn Out Cycle Simplified

Level	Stage
High	5 — Thought / Fear
Low	4
High	3
Medium	2
Low	1

Thought / Fear → Autonomic Signal → Response

**Is a man responsible for all his thoughts or is he at the mercy of his body? –
Your choice**

I am the master of my own happiness, for its in my interests to live life to the full

Now I'm going to use that stupid 'kop out' word again, I'm going to use the word, 'stress' and why am I using it? Well because I want you to digest what I've been postulating. Then I would like you to decide for yourself if you have 'stress' or you have an expression of, 'endocrine hyperactivity or adrenal insufficiency'. With 'stress' you have an incurable enigma, with an expression of 'endocrine hyperactivity or adrenal insufficiency' you have an insight into perhaps what's going on in your body. If you agree that you could have 'endocrine hyperactivity or adrenal insufficiency' then give yourself a big hug. Because you've reached a point where you can begin the process of self ownership of the problem and a significant improvement in your quality of life is possible.

If you disagree with what I've just postulated, then give yourself a big hug also for being strong enough to live by your own beliefs and I wish you well on your forward journey. But please STOP READING this chapter and book right now it's simply not for you, but hey that's cool!

However if you're interested in moving into better health than turn to the next page but please do spare a kind thought for all of those readers you now leave behind.

I am the master of my own health, for I take my quality of health seriously

Assuming that you've concluded that you do have some form of 'endocrine hyperactivity or adrenal insufficiency, then relax and above all don't get too excited. There are many many issues that can cause those symptoms and just thinking you have the problem simply isn't good enough. You need to test, to test and then test again as I outline in my chapter on, Depression, you see you don't have any condition unless you can prove it. There are so many things that move you into a endocrine hyperactivity or adrenal insufficiency and you will make no recovery by just treating those systems. You need to find out why you've moved into that state and treat according to disease findings, not symptom expression.

Now that situation is slightly complicated as I've already discussed because the medical world is simply not interested in root cause analysis. There is also the other major problem when experiencing endocrine hyperactivity or adrenal insufficiency, the medical world only recognises three endocrine conditions, Healthy, Cushing Disease and Addison's Disease. So if you start approaching medics about endocrine hyperactivity or adrenal insufficiency you will be simply ridiculed.

But why would you be ridiculed by the medical world over endocrine hyperactivity or adrenal insufficiency? Well because endocrinologists and mainstream medics only understand excess cortisol and very low cortisol; they simply do not accept endocrine hyperactivity or adrenal insufficiency as a real physical problem.

I am the master of my own happiness, for its in my interests to live life to the full

So what is high cortisol? Is that what you may experience in adrenal fatigue? Er…no it's not actually. In medical terms excess cortisol is classified as Cushing's disease. This is a hormonal disorder caused by a non-cancerous pituitary tumor that produces large amounts of adrenocorticotropin (ACTH) for an extended period. The excess ACTH causes the body to produce extra cortisol, the symptoms of which include excessive weight gain, fatigue, and purplish stretch marks on the abdomen, thighs, and breasts.

So why would my high cortisol levels not be detected? Well it would be like comparing the height of mount Everest with Skidaw in the lake district, both are very high mountains but they are as different in height as chalk and cheese are in texture.

Okay but surely my low levels of cortisol in the burn out stage would be picked up? Er…..no they wouldn't I'm afraid! Low level cortisol is where the body has stopped producing cortisol completely and so it's not a case of cortisol being low as in adrenal insufficiency it's a case of there being no cortisol at all and in that situation Addison's disease is diagnosed. That is an illness in which the adrenal glands stop producing hormones that are important for certain bodily functions. The most common cause of Addison's disease is an autoimmune disease. Other causes of Addison's disease include tuberculosis and chronic infection. Common symptoms of Addison's disease include chronic fatigue, muscle weakness, and loss of appetite. Addison's disease, though incurable, is a condition that can be treated and controlled with medication.

'Hang on, hang on I can here you say that's precisely what I have, why am I not diagnosed with Addison's disease and treated'? Well the answer is very few people are ever treated for this condition; you really do need to be at death's door before this condition is treated seriously and even then patients are frequently messed around with poor medication and poor clinical management of their condition. This is so depressing isn't it? How do decent people with serious issues stemming from an endocrine hyperactivity or adrenal insufficiency issue move forward?

Well the answer is, they privately fund a twenty four hour saliva stress index profile, which is able to determine precisely where their adrenal function really is. If your adrenals are functioning well, than your circadian rhythm should be normal, i.e. your cortisol levels should be in keeping with normal circadian rhythm expectations as indicated on the first graph on the next but one page. Normal circadian rhythm consists of rising levels of cortisol from midnight until 'six am' where it should hold for an hour or so. This is essential because it is this rise in cortisol that enables us to get out of bed and cope with whatever the day has to offer. Our cortisol levels continue to fall during the rest of the day until by 'ten pm' our cortisol levels should have reached their lowest production levels. This reduction in cortisol level reduces autonomic stimuli and therefore allows us to relax and sleep.

You can see a dramatic change in cortisol production levels when the endocrine system is in an abnormal state with the red line in the second graph running much flatter but higher than normal levels, indicating high levels of cortisol. The green line running much flatter and lower than normal levels indicating low levels of cortisol production. But what do these changes mean? Well because our adrenals are responsible for so many diverse functions, their fall into an abnormal state has profound effects upon our body and sense of wellbeing.

I am the master of my own happiness, for its in my interests to live life to the full

When excess cortisol is present we may feel wired, unable to relax, paranoid, angry depressed and unable to sleep because of racing thoughts and whilst this lack of sleep causes fatigue, we're simply unable to knock our body off to enable us to sleep no matter what we try. That's why people in this state often turn to drugs and alcohol etc, as a means of escape, but the reality is that in pursuing that route further complications arise.

Conversely when low levels of cortisol are present, we're unable to cope, we may have a heightened sense of anxiety and depression due to high levels of DHEA, but equally we maybe fatigued beyond endurance because we're simply too tired to relax, cope or sleep. Experiencing endocrine hyperactivity or adrenal insufficiency is a very challenging experience but let me be brutally honest, no amount of reflexology, SSRI's, happy clappy thoughts of higher things will alleviate its symptom matic expression. Why you may ask? Well because those simplistic approaches are nothing more than like flapping your hands and expecting to fly. Anyone who tells you anything different to that is a complete charlatan and business sales, self motivated, compulsive liar.

I am the master of my own health, for I take my quality of health seriously

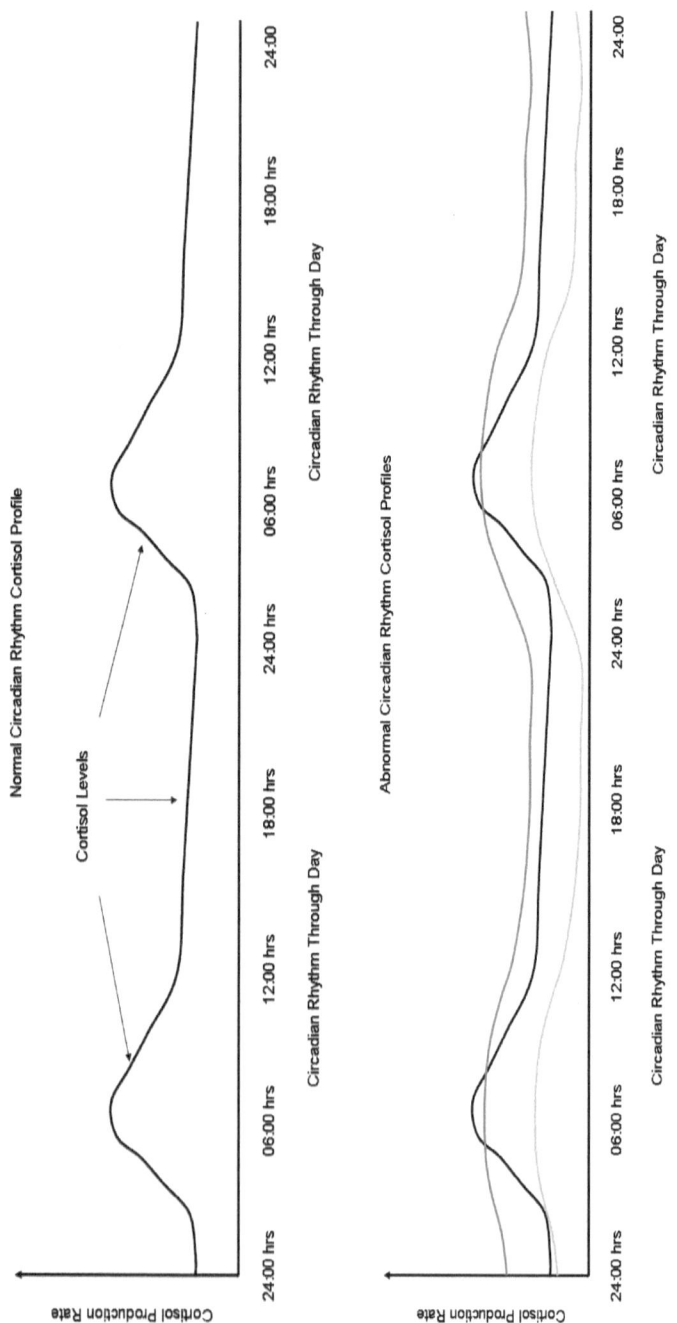

I am the master of my own happiness, for its in my interests to live life to the full

Now I can just hear you screaming, 'enough already, just what do I do to recover from this condition? Well I'm afraid there are no quick fixes, and furthermore the process of recovery can be challenging because there are so many contributory factors to be considered however your starting point must be:

1. A shift in perceptions to enable you to understand precisely what's happening to you and to your body.

2. Testing to find the root cause of your conditions.

3. Putting a holistic treatment protocol in place designed to help you recover and to help you with that process, I've developed my recover mapping approach, which is on the next page.

I am the master of my own health, for I take my quality of health seriously

Staying in control of your situation requires nothing more than a structured approach to what you're trying to achieve.

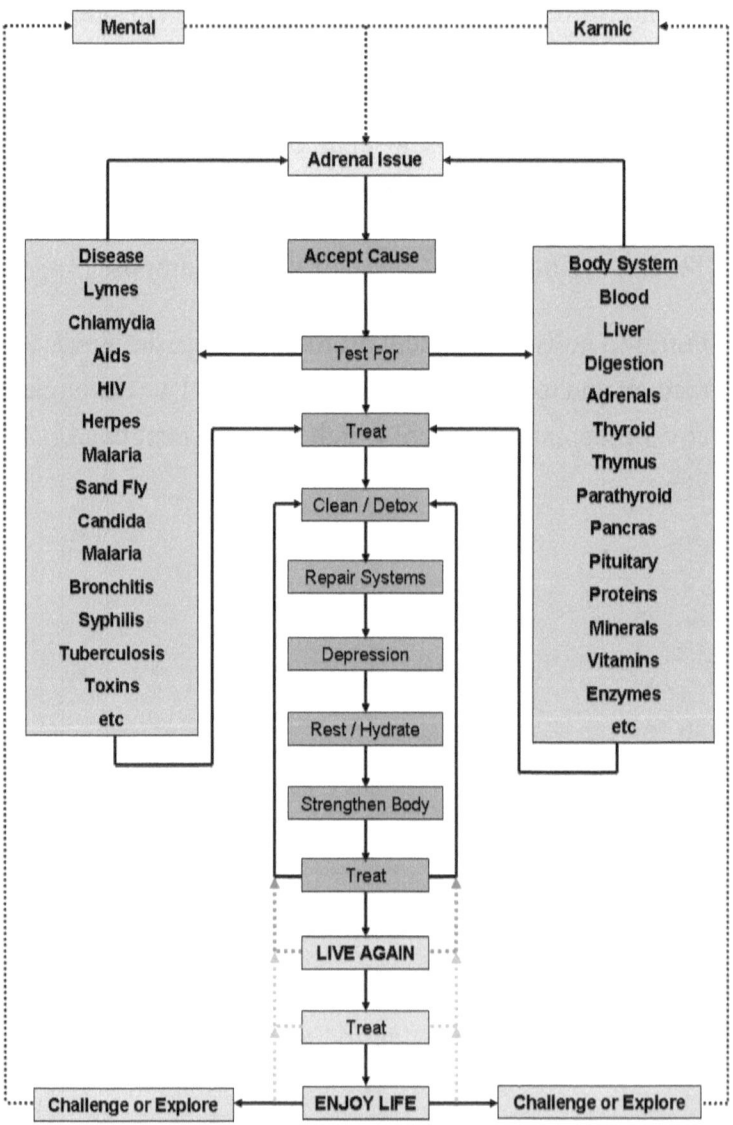

Does a man move into a faulty adrenal expression because of the state of his mind or is he pushed into that expression because of the state of his body? – YOUR CHOICE !

I am the master of my own happiness, for its in my interests to live life to the full

Let me re-cap on what our sympathetic and the parasympathetic nervous systems are in relation to bodily support functions.

Your Endocrine System Simplified

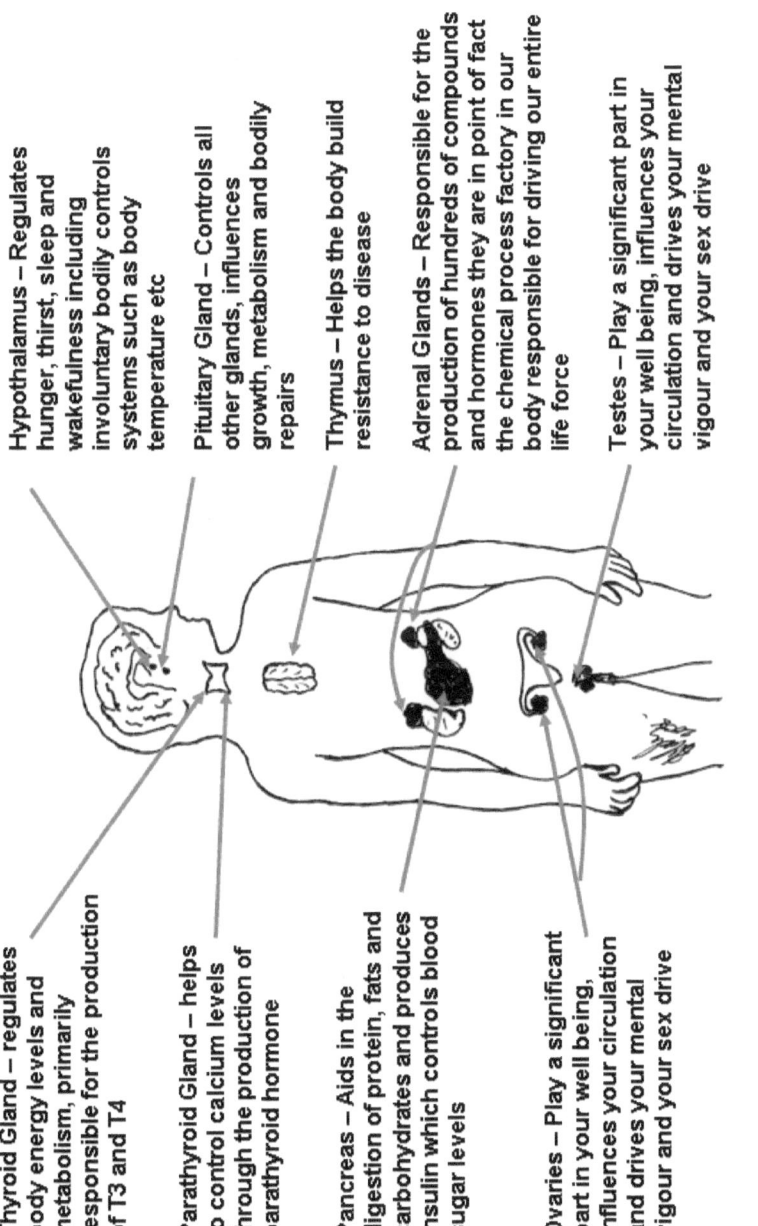

Thyroid Gland – regulates body energy levels and metabolism, primarily responsible for the production of T3 and T4

Parathyroid Gland – helps to control calcium levels through the production of parathyroid hormone

Pancreas – Aids in the digestion of protein, fats and carbohydrates and produces insulin which controls blood sugar levels

Ovaries – Play a significant part in your well being, influences your circulation and drives your mental vigour and your sex drive

Hypothalamus – Regulates hunger, thirst, sleep and wakefulness including involuntary bodily controls systems such as body temperature etc

Pituitary Gland – Controls all other glands, influences growth, metabolism and bodily repairs

Thymus – Helps the body build resistance to disease

Adrenal Glands – Responsible for the production of hundreds of compounds and hormones they are in point of fact the chemical process factory in our body responsible for driving our entire life force

Testes – Play a significant part in your well being, influences your circulation and drives your mental vigour and your sex drive

Is a man responsible for all his thoughts or is he at the mercy of his body? - Your choice

I am the master of my own health, for I take my quality of health seriously

Personal Notes

I am the master of my own happiness, for its in my interests to live life to the full

Personal Notes

I am the master of my own health, for I take my quality of health seriously

Personal Notes

I am the master of my own happiness, for its in my interests to live life to the full

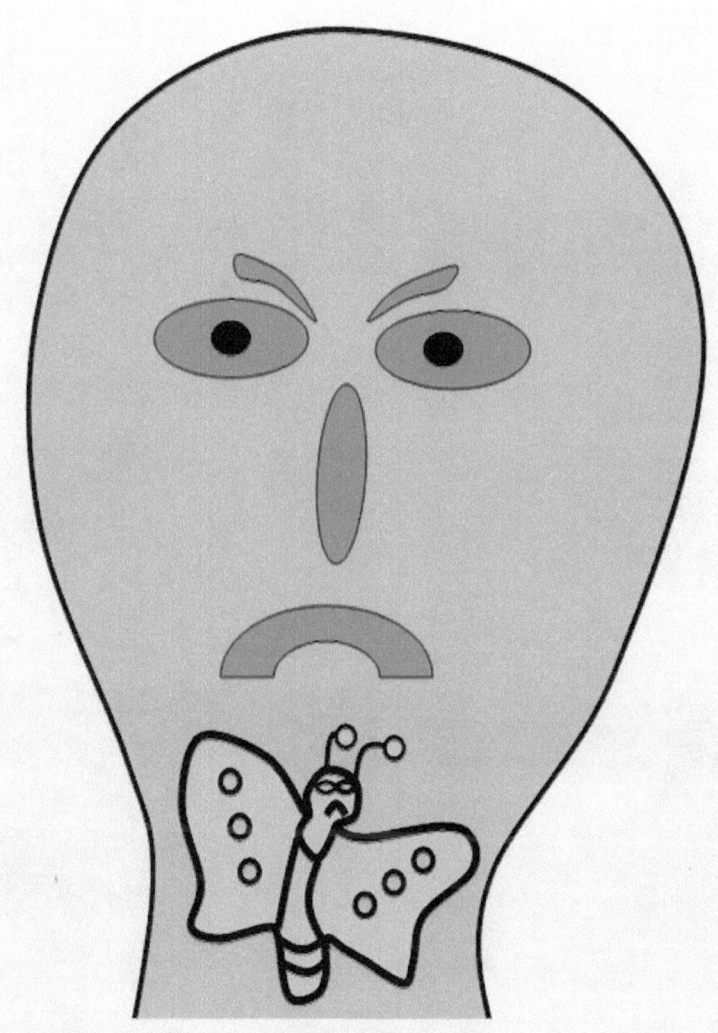

Mood Swings
Tiredness
Lifeless Hair   Depression
Fluid Retention   Feeling cold   Mental Slowing
Weight Gain or Loss   Aches & Pains

I am the master of my own health, for I take my quality of health seriously

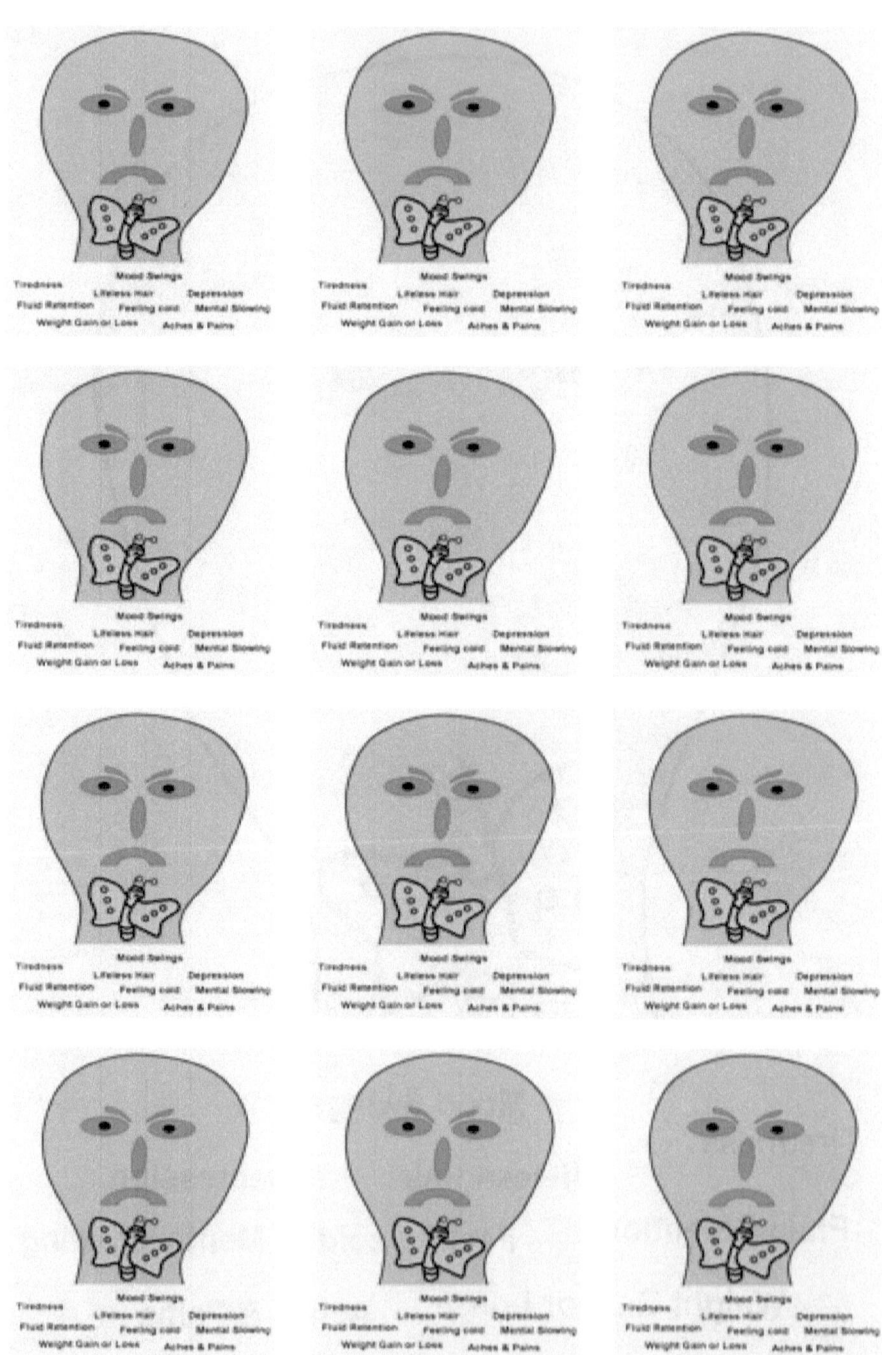

I am the master of my own happiness, for its in my interests to live life to the full

COULD OUR THYROID HOLD THE KEY?

During the early part of this millennium when my body and world were falling apart and I was being clinically abused on a daily basis, I spent tens of thousands of hours on the web searching for clues. I simply couldn't get my head around why there was so much ignorance, incompetence and reticence within the medical world to help me. It was like I was trapped in a sick horrible film, being forced to go round the same loop day after day. This was not a 'Bill Murray *Groundhog Day'* situation though, because that film's story line was all about acceptance, release, renewal and love. My groundhog days were all about abandonment, abuse, ignorance, it was a time of great learning, of great despair and a time of no rewards for a lot of personal courage and effort. Day after day I desperately tried to unravel the sheer misery of my condition, I did the spiritual cleansing and psychotherapy on one level yet I still believed that there must be a physical answer somewhere out there on another level.

I am the master of my own health, for I take my quality of health seriously

I researched and researched with absolutely no support from any one and found to my horror many times that the internet is at best fast food intellect and at worse fast food salmonella. There is so much information on the web, but not all that information originates from good hearts, *I will leave that point there for now because I pick it up again later in my look at the internet.* All I will say is, don't believe everything you read on the web, because some of it is certainly from fraudulent sources.

Anyway, some of my linear, lateral and abstract symptomology searches sort of arrived at a possible crossover i.e. the butterfly connection or the possibility that I had Hypothyroidism.

This is where I must raise a very important point. As a society we're brought up to think that the cause of illness has one point and one point only and at the point we discover that causal point then we are able medicate and to make a full recovery. So when we see, hear or read about someone making a successful recovery from a condition and their condition sort of replicates the symptomology we're experiencing we automatically think wooo hooo, I have the answer!

Wrong, wrong, wrong, wrong, wrong, that model works well with bog standard conditions such as influenzas where symptomology can be effectively treated, but it does not work at all well with complex bodily breakdown issues presenting as illness. The reason I say that is because during the course of chronic illness a whole range of related and non related biological processes and systems may have been adversely affected or damaged. Those systems and processes by necessity must also be supported, nurtured and somehow given a kick start to enable whole body health. There is also the real possibility that the symptomology you're attempting to treat is nothing more than a higher or lower level presentation generated by a hitherto undiscovered state of disease in your body.

I am the master of my own happiness, for its in my interests to live life to the full

The reason I've sort of laboured that point is because when I was at a very low point in my life, I like so many people, read Diane Holmes book 'Tears Behind Closed Doors'. The book is an autobiographical and moving account of the medical ignorance she endured with undiagnosed Hypothyroidism. Similarly, the book also has a tenacious campaigning and informing theme, in support of the recognition of people suffering from this condition.

The combination of this passionate presentation on life, pain, love, research and championing for a cause, rightly generates an understandable cult status and following in some circles for both the book and its author Diane Holmes. Now I've never met Diane, although I was fortunate enough to speak to her one day on the phone and she did seem to be a lovely compassionate lady. I have to say though that whilst her book is extremely informing, its weakness in my opinion is the fact that it has the propensity to generate almost obsessive belief in one single cause of illness i.e. the thyroid. That from my own personal experiences at the time I explored the thyroid connection is almost dangerous. I must state here that my previous statement is not to imply that either Diane or the theme of her book are postulating dangerous lines of approach for she merely states the obvious including; the absurdity, pomposity and ignorance of the clinical world time after time.

Nevertheless, the simple fact of the matter is that we all love a great success over adversity story and Diane Holmes' recovery was simply all that and more. She certainly suffered but through adversity and belief she some how managed not only to make a remarkable recovery but to also document her story and then go on to campaign for greater awareness and support of her condition.

I am the master of my own health, for I take my quality of health seriously

Never forget however that 'Tears Behind Closed Doors' was Diane Holmes' story and not yours, it is not a manuscript for wellness, it provides like many books *my own included* simple milestones and pointers along the way to your own unique recovery. You see if only all of us who had been chronically ill were able to recover fully and quickly through a single point diagnosis, then life would be so blissful. Life is not blissful though and because life is not blissful it's imperative that we as a society are not lured into thinking that we can repair our bodies using the same single point diagnosis formula that worked for someone else.

You see; I've been one of the unfortunates trying to recover my health thinking that because my body was indicating issues pertaining to hypothyroidism etc, which at long last I'd had found the answer to my prayers. After months of treatment my condition didn't recover and because of that I don't want anyone else to ever feel the level of despair that I felt when incorrect treatment after treatment did not improve my health.

Unlike Diane Holmes, I was never blessed with unequivocal bodily reassurance that my health issue had been solved. That's why I believe that when we are chronically ill we must explore every avenue and all possibilities. In essence we must rule nothing out and pencil everything in. Equally we must be able to understand when something is either working or not. If it's working then great, and if it's not, then its time to explore your condition and test for root causes again.

I was fortunate that I read 'Tears Behind Closed Doors' and I recommend that book to anyone concerned about thyroid conditions. I was also fortunate that I met Dr Gordon Skinner and Dr Barry Durant Peatfield personally during the time I was exploring hypothyroidism and hypoadrenalism. Because both guys' provided great care, humour and generosity, but more than that they were simply forward thinking clinical pioneers, not afraid to rock all the populist bull shitter's clinical boats.

I am the master of my own happiness, for its in my interests to live life to the full

And whilst neither of those guys directly helped me to solve my problem they did nevertheless help me to understand the bigger picture of chronic health matter.

One of the best books I've ever read on this subject is by Dr Skinner and it's the (Diagnosis and Management of Hypothyroidism) published through (Louise Lorne publications, 22 Alecester Road, Birmingham B13 8BE). To meet Dr Skinner was a treat, to read his book even years later is to connect with his wicked sense of humour, his great fun for life, people and of course golf and football. Both he and Dr Peatfield will remain forever in my memories as gentlemen of the highest order without any shadow of a doubt. Both champions of conceptual health management, both catalysts in the development of my own holistic approach to health i.e. 'read the signs, remove your prejudices and explore the potentials before you, for no man has all the answers, but he may know a man who holds a few'.

Anyway, back to the theme of this chapter our thyroid role in illness. So what is hypothyroidism? Well it's a very serious condition that debilitates life greatly and can even kill if not picked up in time. Hypothyroidism means that the thyroid gland does not make enough thyroxine, a clinical presentation of which is often referred to as an underactive thyroid. This presenting condition causes many of our body's functions to either slow down or stop completely.

I am the master of my own health, for I take my quality of health seriously

In contrast, if you have hyperthyroidism, you make too much Thyroxine and that presenting condition causes many of our body's functions to speed up.

What are the symptoms of hypothyroidism then? Well basically because all our bodily process systems rely to some extent upon the supply of thyroxine, when it's not made available in sufficient quantities every process and system in our body begins to 'slow down' and the symptoms that commonly occur include:

- Tiredness.
- Weight gain or loss.
- Constipation.
- Aches, pains in every part of body.
- Feeling cold.
- Dry skin.
- Lifeless hair.
- Fluid retention.
- Mental slowing.
- Depression.
- Mood swings and anxiety.

I am the master of my own happiness, for its in my interests to live life to the full

Less common symptoms include:

- A hoarse voice.
- Irregular or heavy menstrual periods in women.
- Infertility.
- Loss of sex drive.
- Carpal tunnel syndrome.
- Memory loss.
- Confusion.
- Dementia in the elderly.

I am the master of my own health, for I take my quality of health seriously

Now all these symptoms can be caused by other conditions however, and so sometimes the diagnosis of hypothyroidism is not as straightforward as one may think. Symptoms usually develop slowly over time and gradually become worse over months or years as the level of thyroxine in the body steadily falls. It's understandable therefore that hypothyroidism can often be missed by the medical world whilst paradoxically often being seen as the root cause of so many diseased states by the chattering health concerned masses.

However as bad as suffering from undiagnosed hypothyroidism is, I believe you must consider yourself extremely lucky if you're able to recover from being chronically ill if you; place all your clinical intervention hopes at the door of one clinical interventionist theme. If you suspect your thyroid is becoming sluggish or hyper, it's important to find out why before you start medicating. Because if it's your adrenals that are the actual problem then you might just find that you end up in a significantly worse state of health than the one you're trying to eradicate.

Similarly, if you have some form of biological imposition that's impeding your body systems from working as they would choose to do so, then simply treating the higher level symptoms may achieve nothing more than aid in the propagation of a condition, when in reality you need to get on top of and hopefully remove.

My fervent belief is that only when your root cause analysis has been fully bottomed out and you're able to both instigate and validate the effectiveness of a treatment approach are you truly on the path to a better quality of life.

I am the master of my own happiness, for its in my interests to live life to the full

Now I'm not simply saying test, qualify and determine what's wrong with you just for the sheer hell of it. I know only too well that when we're suffering all we want is to get over the hump and get back to some form of meaningful life.

But I've encountered far too many people who are prepared to accept handles like, CFS, ME and Hypothyroidism who actually don't get well at all. Simply because they are not addressing the root cause of their problem, which in some instances can originate from multiple conditions.

Now I'm not a hard man with insensitive or overtly dogmatic views, I'm merely a pragmatist and a sufferer who's been through far too many mills. However I realise now at my ripe old age that only if we are prepared to put the work in ourselves, can we ever hope to reap our just rewards.

You see, any so called expert I put my faith in can say I have many things wrong with me. But if he or she can't treat me or make me feel better I'm not really interested in any rubbish they have to say.

Because at the end of the day their words are as empty as my life is without: wellness, happiness, peace and love. Therefore we owe it to ourselves to connect with our bodies when we're chronically ill, and only when our body informs us that we're making a healthy recovery should we accept despite our cross over symptoms that our diagnosis is right.

So whilst it's true that the starting point of every journey begins with the first step, I would nevertheless urge anyone suffering from a chronic illness condition to take that first step carefully. To compile as much information as they can before taking that first step and under no circumstance simply accept a treatment protocol on the basis that it sounds plausible or has worked for a hero or maybe a close friend of yours.

I am the master of my own health, for I take my quality of health seriously

The return to optimum health is a process or evolution in the midst of iteration. Rule nothing out and pencil everything in, test, qualify and if the treatments not working then stop what you're doing and rethink your situation over again. The optimum health process map on the next page has been created to guide you through that process, so please connect with it and your desires for a better quality, because there's nothing complicated about having optimum health save for the chronically ill require it errrrrrrrrrr…………right now.

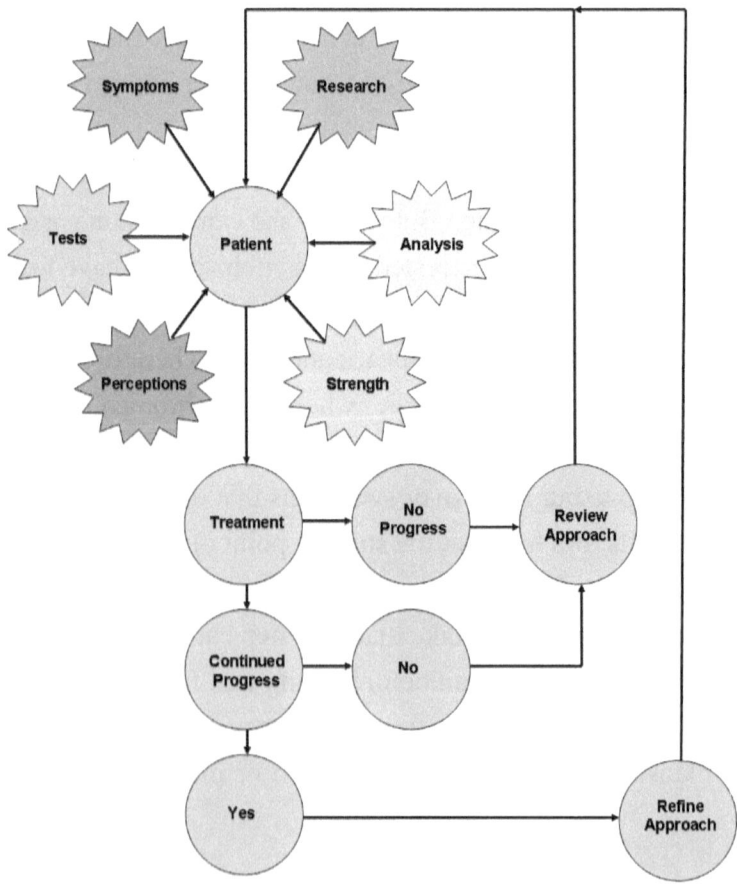

The return of optimum health, requires nothing more than optimum clarity of intent

I am the master of my own happiness, for its in my interests to live life to the full

Personal Notes

I am the master of my own health, for I take my quality of health seriously

Personal Notes

I am the master of my own happiness, for its in my interests to live life to the full

Personal Notes

I am the master of my own health, for I take my quality of health seriously

Personal Notes

I am the master of my own happiness, for its in my interests to live life to the full

I am the master of my own health, for I take my quality of health seriously

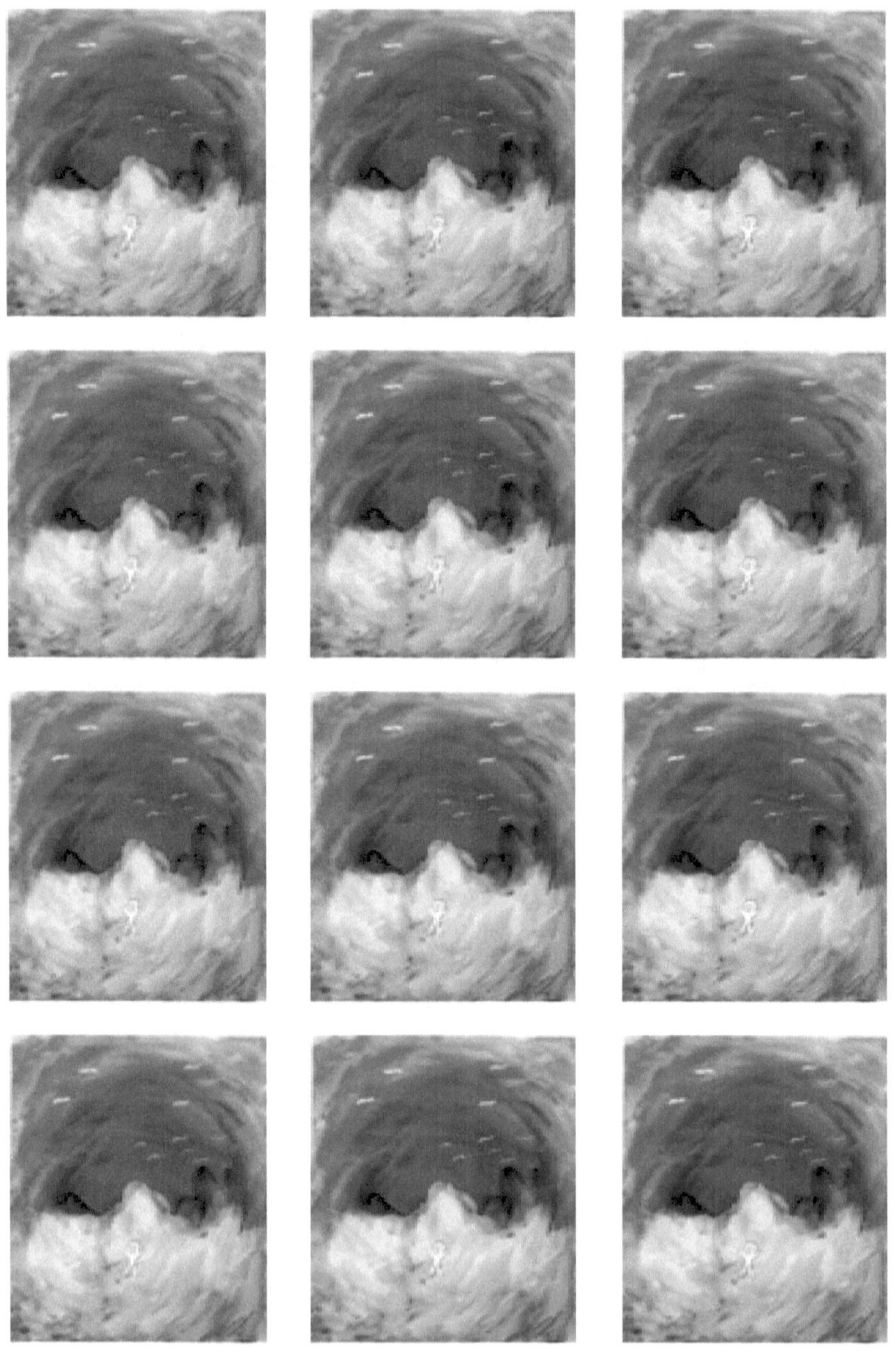

I am the master of my own happiness, for its in my interests to live life to the full

FIBROMYALGIA IS NOT JUST A PAIN

What is fibromyalgia? Well prior to being diagnosed with Lymes Disease I thought that I had it because fibromyalgia is a chronic condition that causes pain all over the body and I had that in excess. The condition in general manifests as intense and unrelenting pain that affects bands of tissue that connect bone to bone whilst directly and indirectly generating;

- Widespread pain.

- Fatigue.

- Depression.

- Extreme sensitivity to pain.

- Muscles stiffness.

- Tendons and ligaments.

The name fibromyalgia comes from the Latin word 'fibro' meaning fibrous tissues *tendons, ligaments*, 'my' meaning muscles, and 'algia' meaning pain. Fibromyalgia used to be known as fibrositis, which literally means inflammation of the muscles and soft tissue. The condition was renamed fibromyalgia however after some studies found that there was no inflammation, or nerve injury. 'Hmmn no damage, absolute bloody rubbish' however that medical non experiencing conclusion was probably drawn by some numpty simply propelling their career.

The problem is that despite current medical dogma surrounding what this condition is and what this condition isn't, you can bet your entire bank account that at the point your body dips into fibromyalgia symptomology. The medical world will fail you, will write you off and label you as a neurotic. What's more there will be rounds of clap trap talked about sleep cycles, psychological predispositions and treatment options as puerile as treating a severed leg with a band aid.

What there will not be is unequivocal diagnostic or validated scientific rationale applied to your presenting symptoms, simply because the medical world continues to bark up the wrong trees with conditions of this nature. You see, main stream treatment of fibromyalgia is geared toward improving the quality of sleep and reducing pain by the suppression of the sufferer's symptoms but not solving the overall problem. Instead medications that boost your body's level of serotonin and norepinephrine neurotransmitters may be the only thing prescribed in low doses on the premise that they modulate sleep, pain, and immune system functions examples of which include:

- Amitriptyline.

- Cyclobenzaprine.

- Cymbalta.

I am the master of my own happiness, for its in my interests to live life to the full

At no point will you be tested for any underlying disease, nor will your clinical care team be in the slightest bit interested in exploring the potential of disease. Simply because fibromyalgia is incurable and is nothing more than a psychologically driven condition or at least that's current medical dogma prescriptively dictates.

But is fibromyalgia an incurable and psychologically driven condition? Well it might be if the medical industry were able to prove both statements but the stark answer is, they can't.

Therefore fibromyalgia is only classified as an incurable and psychologically driven condition because the medical industry has been unable to identify its root cause and therein lies the problem.

At the point that the medical industry can't prove the root cause of a condition, then the condition simply doesn't exist except for the handle it's given and the generic prequalification status that is assigned to it i.e. name: Fibromyalgia, originator of disease: a psychologically driven condition, end of story full stop.

But people with this condition endure almost insufferable pain, because they're unable to rest, to exercise, or do anything remotely normal and quite frankly it is pain beyond any other form of pain. It's unrelenting, it's the last thing a sufferer remembers before they fall asleep (if they're lucky enough to get some sleeps) and it's the first thing that greets them upon awakening.

I am the master of my own health, for I take my quality of health seriously

It saps the life force from people, it lowers their emotions, restricts their capabilities and horizons; it is without any shadow of a doubt hell on earth. So the questions all Fibromyalgia sufferers need to ask themselves are:

(a) 'Am I prepared to accept this diagnosis?'

And

(b) 'Am I prepared to endure this level of suffering without support or recovery?'

If the answers to those two simple questions are yes and yes, then you may as well stop reading this chapter and resign yourself to your fate, but if you're not prepared to accept that position then carry on reading and good for you.

I am the master of my own happiness, for its in my interests to live life to the full

So; having concluded that you're not prepared to accept your current diagnosis and prognosis then you're at least open to the potential of recovery. And when we are open to the potentials of recovery our energies are expansive not restrictive. With that mind set, anything and everything is possible and your road to understanding of the potential of recovery has just begun.

So now let's just take this a lit bit further. What other sorts of symptoms may we experience with fibromyalgia? Well we may experience:

- Facial pain, often as a result of neck, shoulder, or jaw muscle stiffness.

- Tingling, numbness, prickling, or burning sensations in your hands and feet *paresthesia.*

- Dry eyes, skin, or mouth.

- Irritable bowel syndrome.

- Painful testicles.

- Temperature control problems.

- Unusually painful menstruation cycles.

- Distorted or changes in vision.

- Noise sensitivity.

- Foggy, muggy thinking and forgetfulness.

- Anxiety.

- Depression.

So having already read some of the earlier chapters in this book let me ask you this, are there any alarm bells ringing for you in terms of synergistic health connections between fibromyalgia and:

- Lymes Disease?

- Adrenal insufficiency?

- Neurotoxin / biotoxin load?

- Hypothyroidism?

Well there should be because there can be absolutely no doubt that fibromyalgia is nothing more than presenting symptomology of a diseased state. It's not some incurable psychologically driven condition, its real, and it's the result of your body being under attack by some form of biological assailant which is having a profound effect upon your body's recovery and building blocks.

The only challenge you face now is accepting that position after years of suffering, after years and years of many unsuccessful treatments and after years of being told that it was you who was ultimately responsible for your condition.

I am the master of my own happiness, for its in my interests to live life to the full

You see; the psychological damage of unrelenting suffering and highly opinionated yet spectacularly unsuccessful treatment approaches erodes our ability at times to think out of the box. Partners, lovers, clinicians and colleagues have all written us off, they've all bought into the orthodox false truth and so at the point you begin to challenge their perceptions of your condition that is the very same point that you will unintentionally alienate yourself further. Simply because people just love to assign everything and everyone into nice neat little boxes, and they simply hate it and us if we dare to change their view of anything or anyone that they've previously assigned a view upon. That's just the way it is I'm afraid so all you can do is accept it and allow yourself to move on.

Now there is no point talking to any ignorant medic about anything I'm postulating here because that will expend high levels of your emotional, physical and spiritual resolve that you quite simply don't have at your disposal when battling with your symptoms. What you need to do is sit back, stay open, commit to your own personal research and decide if you're going to take your clinical investigation up to another level. If you decide to take that route, then you will need to look for:

- Bacteria impositions.
- Fungal impositions.
- Viral impositions.

Then you will need to;

- Qualify your mitochondrial function.
- Qualify your neuro / biotoxin load.
- Prepare yourself for the options that lay before you.

I am the master of my own happiness, for its in my interests to live life to the full

You see, it's all well and good to have a diagnosis postulated, but until we have the entire picture, it's impossible to qualify which is the originator and which is indicator of any of our chronic health expressions.

Effective treatment requires root cause analysis, anything less than that simply results in potential escalation or at best palliation without ultimate resolution of a presenting disease state expression.

Fibromyalgia is an eminently resolvable condition when the focus of attention in its treatment moves as far away from the suppression of symptoms and moves closer to removing its originators and cleaning and repairing our bodily systems. Because disease eradication and not simply symptom addressing must remain at all times your one and only goal.

To improve you must subject your bodily functions to responsible clinical investigations, you must accept that there are organic and biological agents at work and you must focus your attention upon finding out what they are and how you will transform your body from that diseased state. Accept and understand that simply root cause analysis and nothing more will help you heal yourself and your healing process has already begun.

Word of caution always work with professional supervision, do not embark upon anything you don't fully understand, keep both your heart and your mind open and for sure you'll find the answer to your fibromyalgia expression. Thereafter you can bin that name because the truth of the matter when all said and done is that fibromyalgia in whatever part that it's played in your life. Was really nothing more, than a medically manufactured condition designed only to absolve the incompetent of any sense of responsibility in relation to their failure of due diligence towards you in your care. Now how perverse is that when all said and done in terms of ethically amoral conduct.

I am the master of my own health, for I take my quality of health seriously

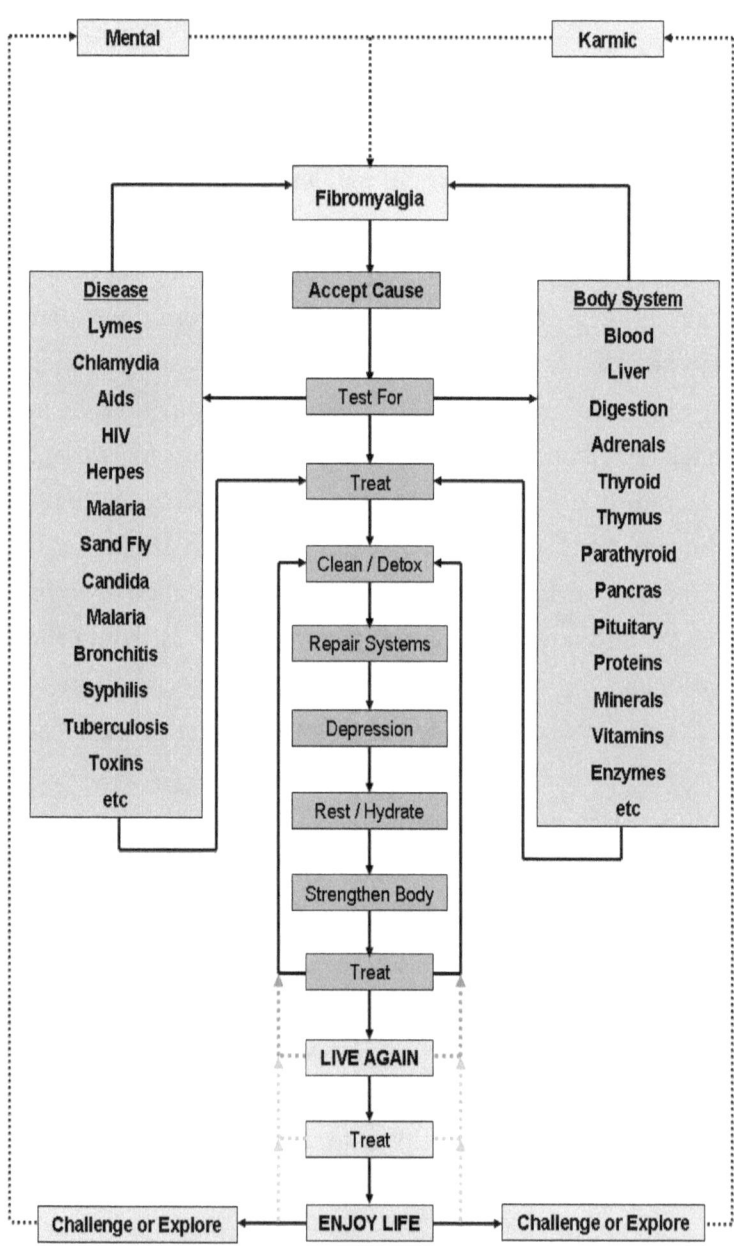

Does a man move into a Fibromyalgia state because of the state of his mind or is he pushed into that Fibromyalgia state because of the state of his body? – YOUR CHOICE !

I am the master of my own happiness, for its in my interests to live life to the full

Personal Notes

I am the master of my own health, for I take my quality of health seriously

Personal Notes

I am the master of my own happiness, for its in my interests to live life to the full

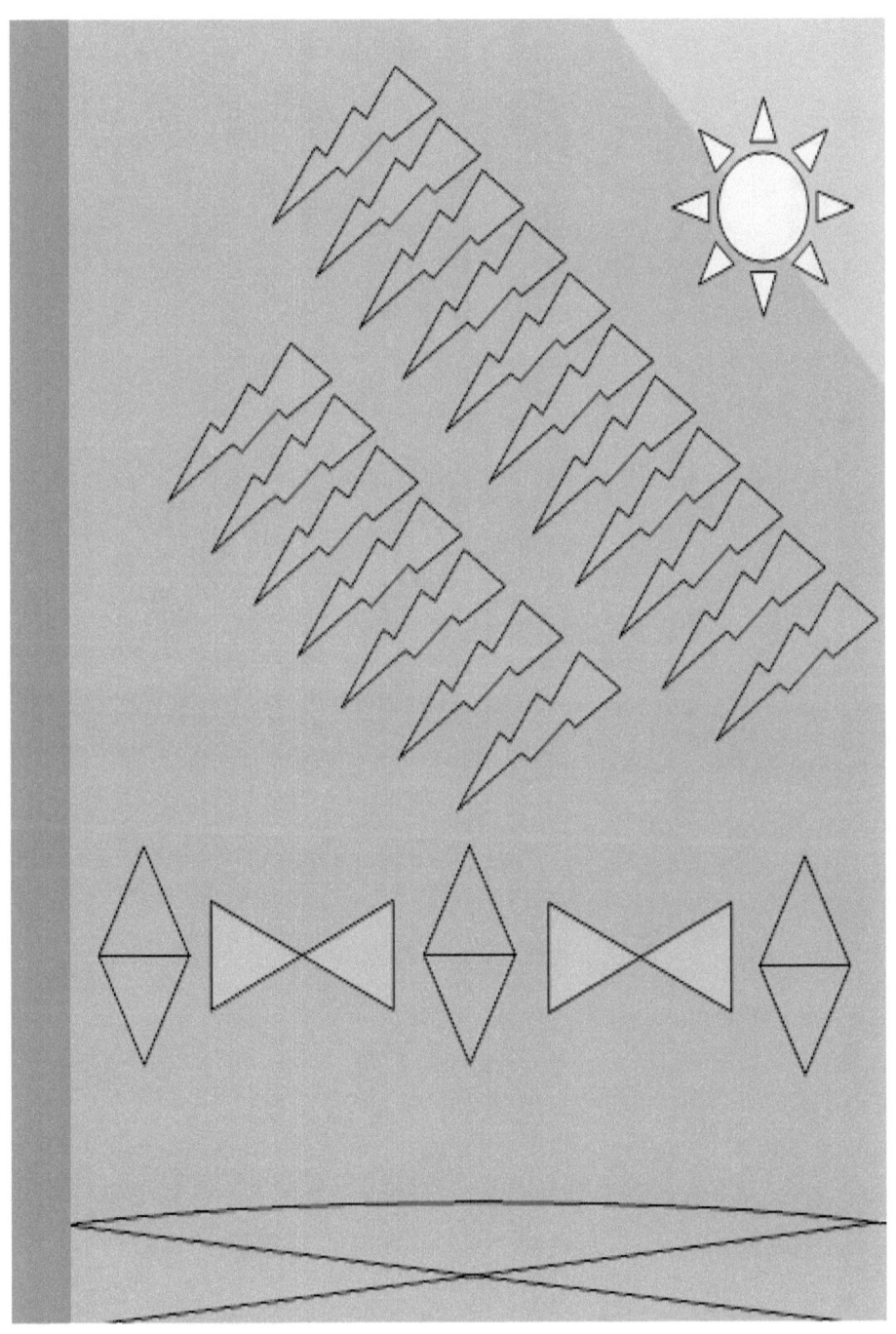

I am the master of my own health, for I take my quality of health seriously

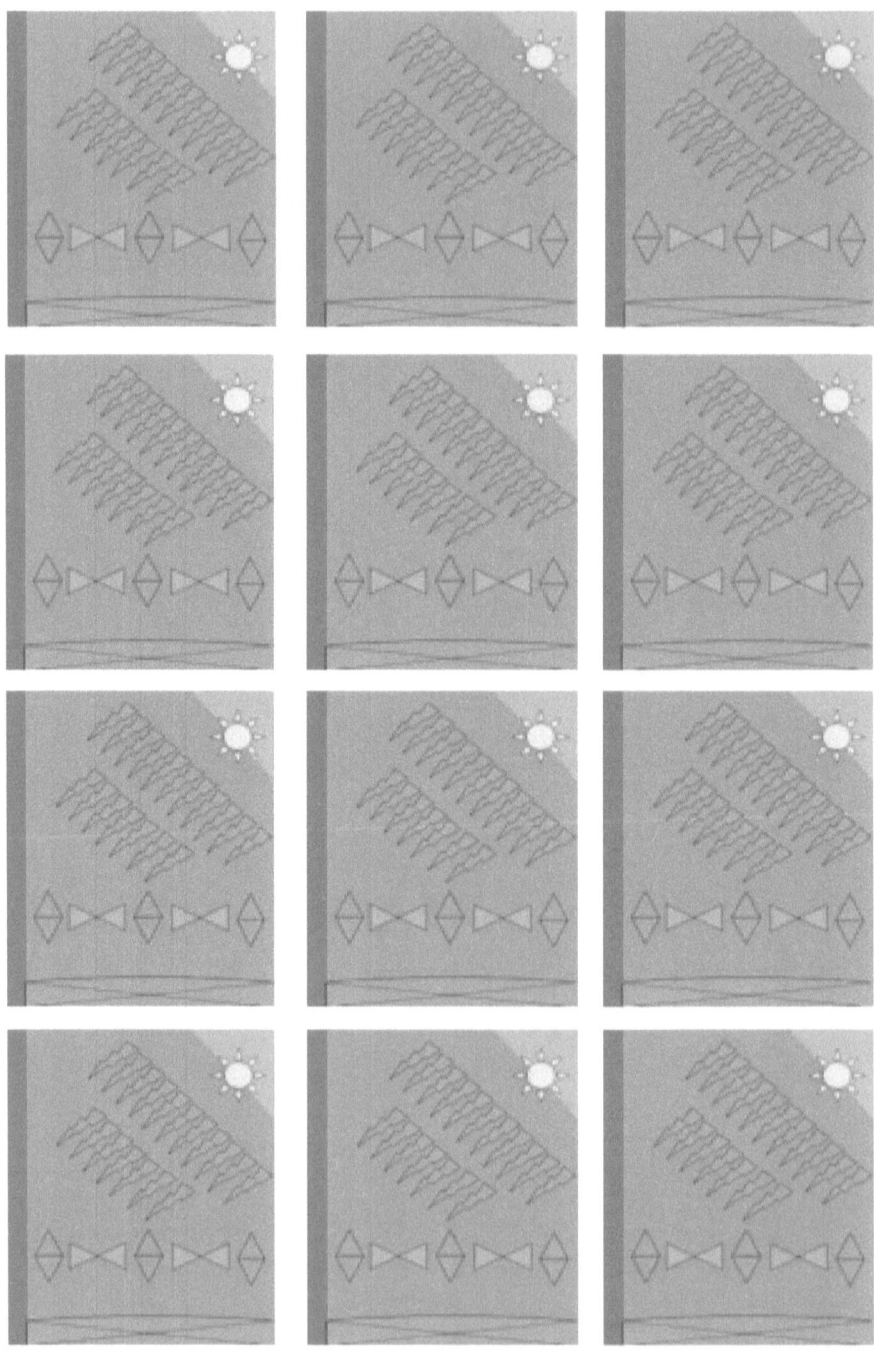

I am the master of my own happiness, for its in my interests to live life to the full

ME, CFS & PVFS: ILLNESS OR SIMPLY NAMES?

Do you know I've lost count of the number of people I've met through my life who have either been diagnosed or written off by the medical world using medical colloquialisms such as: ME, CFS or PVFS. So what are ME, CFS or PVFS? Well ME is Myalgic Encephalopathy, CFS is Chronic Fatigue Syndrome and PVFS is Post Viral Fatigue Syndrome or to put it bluntly they are generic names used to describe an undiagnosed condition that's main presenting symptom is fatigue.

The funny thing is that some people actually like these illness handles, they actually thrive on being physically compromised yet part of a mysterious illness group. Talk to most people diagnosed with any of these conditions and they will inform you immediately that they have an;

- Incurable condition.
- That no one understands them.
- That no one helps them etc, etc, etc.

But at the point you start a line of dialogue which even gently touches upon exploring root cause analysis etc, they immediately become defensive. It's like even though they make great play about how:

- Chronically ill they are.

- Weary they are of their life.

- No one understands them etc.

They appear too actually like being part of their mysterious ME, CFS or PVFS club. Now is that in part due to the elitist status that their condition has acquired due to the high profile celebrities who've succumbed to these spurious presenting conditions? Or in other words:

- Is it because they have allowed themselves to be fooled into the belief that their condition is beyond resolution?

- Is it because they are closed as individuals to abstract thought processes?

Or

- Do their presenting symptoms interfere with receptive thought processing?

Well I'm not really in a position to qualify any of those from a clinical perspective, but I do know that there is a degree of sociological receptivity given to these conditions which is not given to other generically similar presenting symptoms given to other conditions.

I am the master of my own happiness, for its in my interests to live life to the full

You see if someone is diagnosed with ME, CFS or PVFS, it is immediately perceived by the wider public as a clean condition, an acceptable condition a; 'O dear me I'm sorry to hear that' condition. But if the same symptoms are diagnosed as stress or depression then it's immediately perceived as a dirty disease by the wider public, it quickly becomes a; 'give yourself a shake' condition etc.

So it's understandable that being ill with ME, CFS or PVFS, whilst difficult, is not as sociologically alienating as other forms of illness, and in that may be the root cause for people with these conditions to just accept that they have an incurable condition. But hang on here, apart from the fatigue issue, what are the centralistic presenting symptoms of ME, CFS and PVFS? Well, common symptoms of ME / CFS / PVFS also include:

- Muscle and joint pain, muscle cramps and twitching.

- Fatigue that lasts more than 24 hours after exercise or exertion.

- Forgetfulness, memory loss, confusion, or poor concentration.

- Sleep disturbances - feeling tired, un-rested or trouble sleeping.

- Flu-like symptoms.

- Palpitations, chest pains.

- Sweating, rapid changes in body temperature.

- Feeling faint or problems with balance.

I am the master of my own health, for I take my quality of health seriously

- Painful glands in your neck, armpits or groins.

- A sore throat, horse voice, frequently losing of voice.

- Headaches, pains in head, pains in eyes.

- Feeling sick, low appetite, changes to sensory taste.

- Mood swings, depression, anxiety, fear and phobias.

Well forgive me if I sound a little too harsh, brash or even far too cynical here but come on, there is no great mystery to these conditions. Patients with these conditions are expressing all the classic symptomology of:

- A body under attack by biological agents.

- A body unable to fight that attack.

- A body unable to offload the debris from that invasion.

- A body in a toxic state.

Yet if you ask anyone suffering from ME, CFS or PVFS about the tests they've had to validate their diagnosis most will say none, whilst the remaining may indicate that blood tests were performed at some point in the far distant past which indicated an issue with their blood count.

I am the master of my own happiness, for its in my interests to live life to the full

But I would suspect because I've got hundreds of clinical blood tests t-shirts of shame that any such blood tests have probably been nothing more than a White Blood Cell Count *WBC* performed during a Full Body Count *FBC*. Full Blood Counts *FBC*, are requested for a wide variety of reasons but normally resulting from a patient presenting with illness.

Just so you know; counts that continue to rise or fall to abnormal levels indicate that the condition is getting worse, whereas counts that return to normal indicate improvement. An elevated number of white blood cells is called leukocytosis and this can result from bacterial infections, inflammation, leukaemia, trauma, or stress. A WBC count of $11.0-17.0 \times 10^9/L$ cells would be considered mild to moderate leukocytosis. Whereas a decreased WBC count is called leucopenia and this too can result from many different situations, such as chemotherapy, radiation therapy, or diseases of the immune system etc. A count of $3.0-5.0 \times 10^9/L$ cells would be considered mild leukopenia.

Now it's quite normal for someone presenting with ME / CFS / PVFS symptoms to have issues with their WBC, but then again why wouldn't they? They are in a diseased state! However, what never happens are requests for further clinical investigations to determine the root cause of deviations to their WBC. You see in almost every instance the softest option is just to qualify those initial deviations as viral impediments.

I am the master of my own health, for I take my quality of health seriously

In doing so, the patient can be successfully dispatched from any further clinical intervention under the premise that:

- It's a virus and hence can't be treated.

- It will resolve itself in time if the patient rests and addresses all outstanding psychological issues in their life.

- If it doesn't resolve itself then we can just assign it with a name e.g. ME/CFS/PVFS.

Now it is completely understandable that some individuals swallow that clap trap hook line and sinker and that they then go onto wear their condition as some sort of armband of unity. Because if they didn't they would be unable to justify their inability to recover. But the very fact that they buy into this sort of socially defendable, moralistic or even spiritual suffering identity is the very same reason why they are unable to recover.

You see, resting a damaged tooth, a broken leg or broken or shattered hand will not resolve those problems, neither will exploring any spurious psychological links associated with the manifestation of those problems. The only solutions are intervention i.e. rectification and stabilization of the damaged tissue etc, and perhaps a closer look at the social catalysts where appropriate which played a part in the conditions propagation in the first instance.

Likewise with ME, CFS and PVFS we know that patients with these conditions have an issue with their WBC, but resting and psychological intervention has no substantive clinical basis from which to postulate that it is the correct approach to achieve a full recovery. Therefore ME, CFS and PVFS sufferers need to look at:

I am the master of my own happiness, for its in my interests to live life to the full

- What is causing their condition?

- What impact that has upon their bodily functions?

- What they need to do to repair their body?

I advocate that being open to root cause analysis and committed to a formalised yet holistic approach to whole disease state irradiation and whole body recovery is the only way forward. That is the only way that we can achieve a life free of disease and a life free of disease relapse. But to acquire that state of being what we need is a:

1. Shift in our disease state perceptions.

2. Desire to identify our originators of disease.

3. Desire to remove all cellular detoxing impediments.

4. Desire to qualify appropriate treatment protocols.

5. Desire to strengthen all our bodily systems vitality.

6. Desire to pursue wellness at all cost.

I am the master of my own health, for I take my quality of health seriously

I myself have been through the most appalling levels of chronic fatigue and to this day, I have no idea how I managed from my pain filled bed to continue to research and search for a way forward. I guess I did so because:

- I had no option.
- I had been written off.
- No one was going to help me.
- No one was interested in exploring a new way of thinking for me.

Because;

- No one actually cared whether I lived or died.

However I cared then and I care now, to me it's simply immoral that people are written off with diseases that they're eminently able to recover from. So whilst I'm happy to concede that I have no part to play in the lives of those individuals who choose not to explore options outside of the box. I nevertheless believe that I do have a part to play in the lives of those individuals who are desperately seeking answers yet for whatever reason are unable to make the sort of progress they need.

I am the master of my own happiness, for its in my interests to live life to the full

As I've stated before, I am no guru, no clinician, I'm just a regular guy with a passion for life and I want that passion for life to be in everyone's life, because you know what? We're all worth it!

So for those of you looking for answers to ME, CFS or PVFS I advocate that the process of recovery is straight forward, you must:

- Change your perceptions.

- Test and qualify your diseased state.

- Connect with your body to understand the signs and symptoms you're experiencing.

- Accommodate your body's recovery processes in all that you do.

Ownership offers freedom from isolation, desolation and rhetoric prescribed as nothing more than a bluff to hide shallow clinical understanding. The choice you need to make is self ownership or abstinence and no matter which choice you make, be fully prepared to walk your talk.

I am the master of my own health, for I take my quality of health seriously

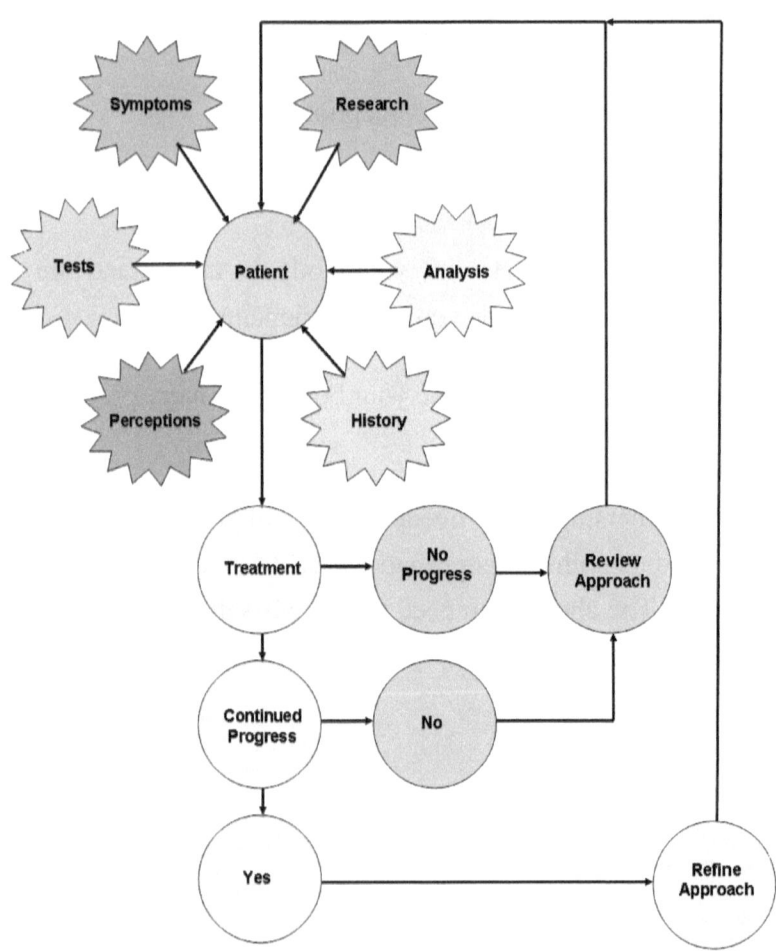

I am the master of my own happiness, for its in my interests to live life to the full

Personal Notes

I am the master of my own health, for I take my quality of health seriously

Personal Notes

I am the master of my own happiness, for its in my interests to live life to the full

Personal Notes

I am the master of my own health, for I take my quality of health seriously

Personal Notes

I am the master of my own happiness, for its in my interests to live life to the full

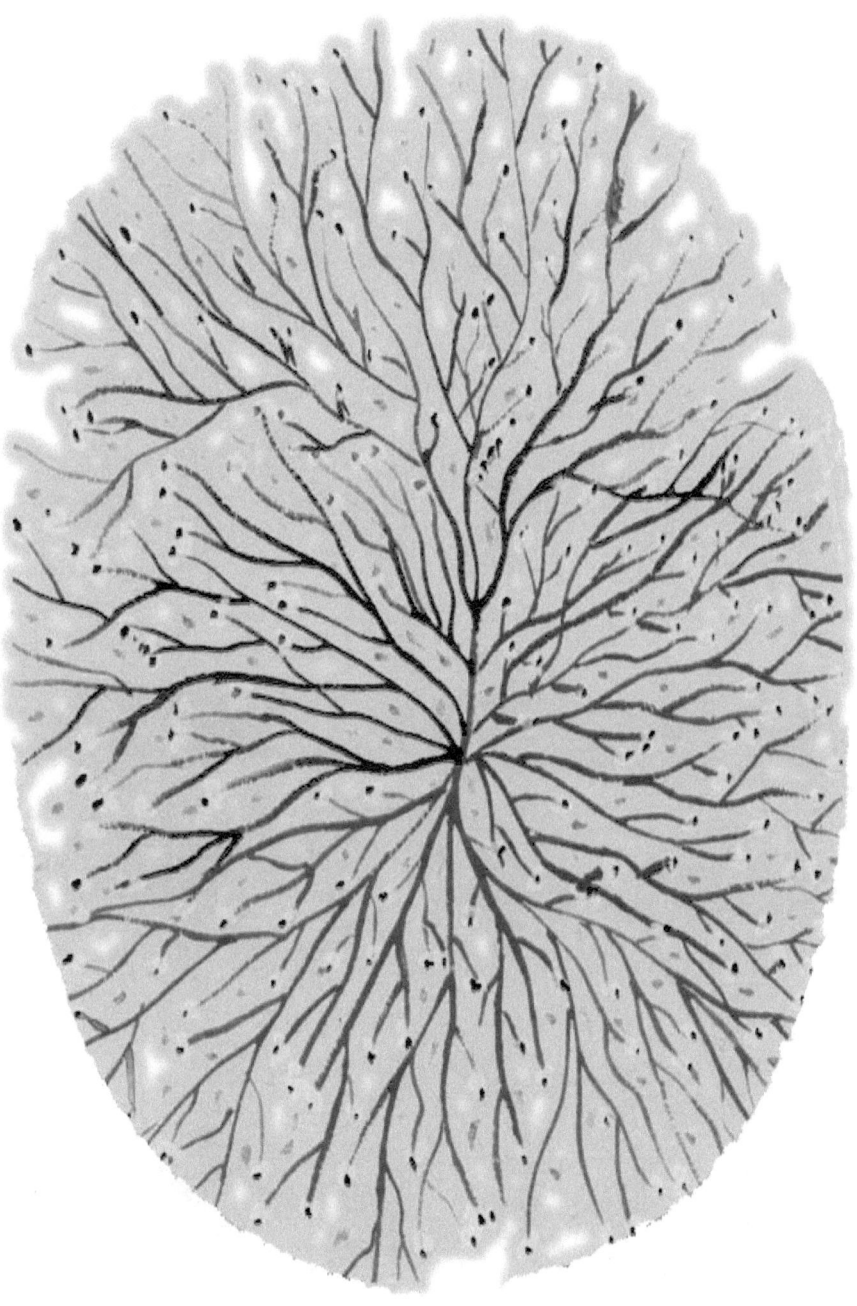

I am the master of my own health, for I take my quality of health seriously

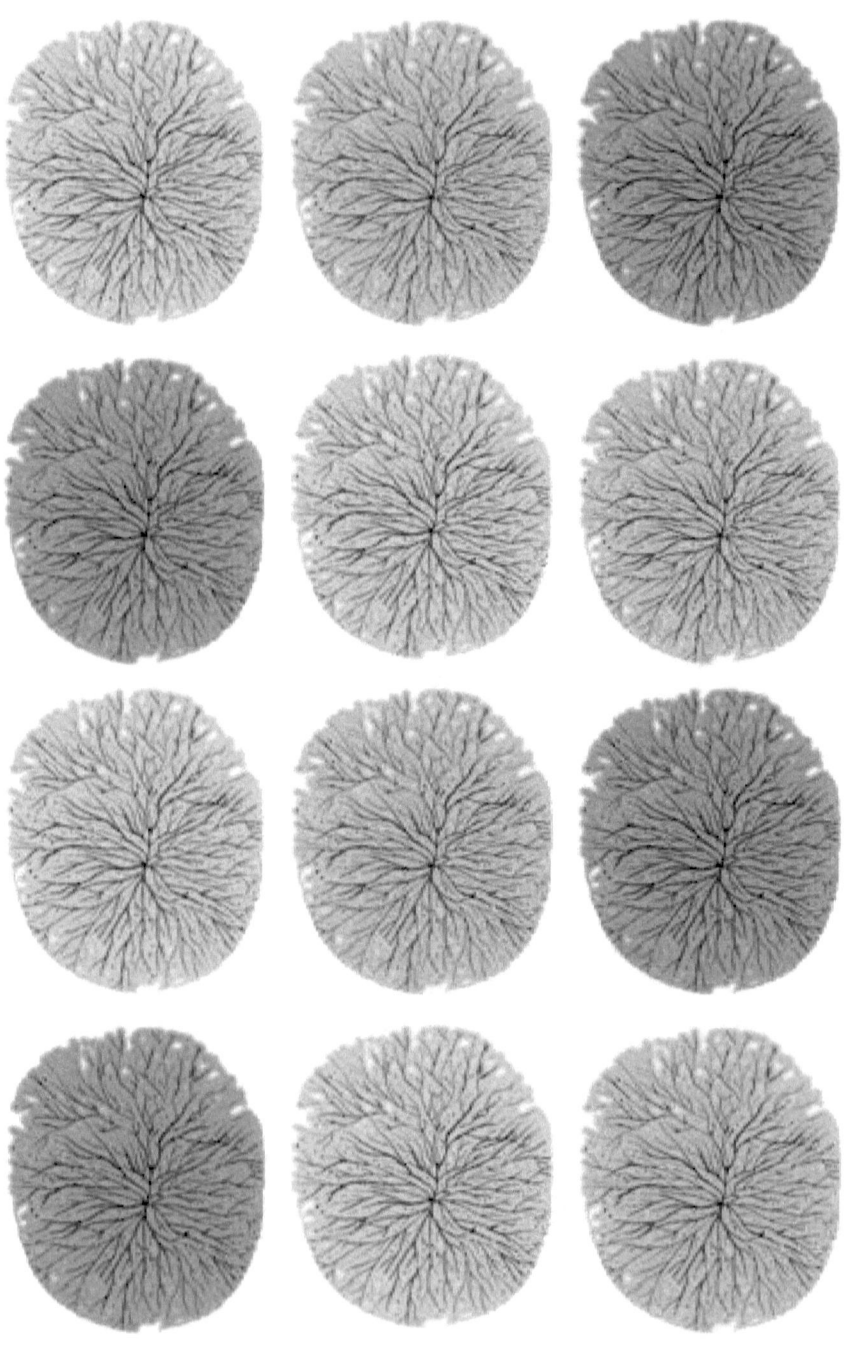

I am the master of my own happiness, for its in my interests to live life to the full

Passionate, Obsession, Addicted or Driven Life Force

Throughout my life I've struggled with the words; Passionate, Obsession and Addicted, because whilst all can have positive connotations equally they all can have negative connotations when either misunderstood or counterproductive to what society dictates is an acceptable standard. So let's have a look at those words and then explore how they are bastardized by society.

- Passionate; 'capable of revealing or characterized by intense emotion'.

- Obsession; 'state of persistent idea or impulse'.

- Addicted; 'person devoted to something'.

From a very young age I realised that I had the potential to be passionate, obsessive and even addictive. Yet in the most part the prejudices that surrounded me qualified those traits as negative and self destructive traits and not at all helpful, controlled or informed states. A formative, yet negative neuro-linguistic programming culture which meant that at the point I moved into a chronic diseased state and became chronically obsessive I bought into albeit only on one level, all the negative clap trap I'd been spun about obsession etc.

Now there can be nothing worse than living in a body when your mind is in a chronic obsessive state because that mind set takes you to places where you really shouldn't have to go at all. It's a place where destructive and counterproductive thoughts all but drive you insane. Those thoughts can range from self harm, to; chronic fear, physical detachment, delusion, thoughts of harming others and a raft of thoughts which are both irrational and counterproductive to acceptable standards in terms of quality of life. Chronic obsession can consume and destroy any and all sense of reality and whilst in a chronic obsessive state we are at the mercy of all our obsessive thoughts which in the most part are completely without validity or rationale.

Now the reason I jumped straight to the obsessive state is because I believe that we all need to soften our views on what constitutes Passionate, Obsessive and Addicted mind sets, because I believe all three states are one in the same. To change our perceptions however, we first must view all three with equal polarity. In doing so we can begin to understand the part they all play in the mortal process of stimulation, progression, stagnation and/or degeneration and any point in our lives.

I am the master of my own happiness, for its in my interests to live life to the full

Some of our greatest and worst role models have their roots based firmly in a personal predisposition towards intense emotions. They believe and believed with passion and are or were not afraid to air their views. It is that predisposition that seems to set them apart from their kin. Interestingly passionate individuals have the potential to both stimulate and antagonize populist beliefs with equal equity. Yet it is the shift in perceptions generated by passionate individuals that either causes buy-in to change or stimulates rejection which by default brings about paradoxical change.

But what you may ask has passion to do with obsession or addiction? Well I would argue that passion without obsessive or addictive traits doesn't really exist. In fact I would go as far as to say that all three dispositions are nothing more than derivations of a Driven Life Force (DLF). But DLF should not be confused with Divine Life Forces because the former is physical presence where as the later is spiritual higher presence.

I believe that it is the driven life force within us all that we need to understand because at the point we understand the generators and markers of DLF then perhaps we can begin to understand the subtle delineation between positive and negative manifestation of DLF. Or should I say the positive and negative presentations of Passionate, Obsessive and Addicted mind states.

You see; we are all nothing more than a complex mix of water, carbon and chemicals and yet it is that soup and its formulation that makes us the people we think we are. Some of us may feel inferior, troubled or even superior at any time or point in our life. But the bottom line at the end of the day is that our perception of who we are, is nothing more than a projection derived from the soup we either inherit or we've somehow managed to manipulate or corrupt during our passage through

I am the master of my own health, for I take my quality of health seriously

life. I argue that it is the constitution or subtle changes to the generators and markers of DLF that enables us to be both accepted and acceptable to society as a whole or alienate ourselves wholesale. DLF by default generates presence, it orchestrates great change, it challenges perceptions whilst retaining at its very core the self preservation which is that most unique facet that underwrites us all and the one thing that eventually generates the most conflict.

There is no issue for me in terms of the major components of DLF they are of course Passionate, Obsessive and Addicted mind sets. Therefore I believe that whoever has the constituent generators and marker of visible DLF will automatically demonstrate either in illness or good health; Passionate, Obsessive and Addictive mind sets.

Now whilst I accept the potential for everyone to have some degree of DLF presentation, I'm nevertheless of the opinion that active DLF is seen only in the minority and not the majority. I also believe its needs to be that way otherwise cohabiting on a global scale in a soup rich with DLF mind sets would be very challenging to say the very least.

For it is DLF mind sets that challenge and change the world we live in and be under no illusion about that, simply because DFL's view the components of life in more detail than their peers. Therein they push themselves harder than their peers; they are less prepared to go with the flow than their peers. Alarmingly at times however they present greater fluidity in the linear magnitude of their positive and negative DLF mind state and statements of intent.

I am the master of my own happiness, for its in my interests to live life to the full

DLF's are energized individuals so that when we explore DLF mind sets its clear that;

- A lazy man can never be a DLF because his very acceptance and preposition to being lazy indicates that passion and a passionate mind set are missing from him. It's simply impossible to be passionate about being lazy no matter what anyone says because to be passionate requires tremendous energy in mind and body. Therefore if a man has that and not simply using words then it's impossible for him to be lazy.

- Equally obsession requires tremendous energy; therefore those of a more sedate mind set are probably devoid of obsessive generators and marker because it's impossible to be sedentary amidst the stimulation of obsession.

- Addiction on the other hand has both a passive and active component to it; nevertheless I argue that to fall into an addictive mind set there must first be either an active enquiring or a generally unsettled mind, which is the primary drive I would respectfully suggest of a DLF in all its presentations.

DLF mind sets are extremely active and energized individuals; and I argue that it is that energetic expression of intent that manifests in both positive and negative expression in a DLF. Let me give you two diametrically opposite examples of DLF;

- Margaret Thatcher and Adolph Hitler clearly had intense DLF, they both had great presence, both had great passion, both had great obsessions, both demonstrated addictive personalities towards power, both had the ability to engage the populous and yet both had the potential of demonstrating gross cruelty which was seemingly justifiable in their minds whilst amassing great personal wealth at others expense. This I would suggest is negative DLF.

- Alfred Einstein and Isambard Kingdom Brunel clearly had intense DLF, they both had great presence, both had great passion, both had great obsessions, both demonstrated addictive personalities, both had the ability to engage the populous and both had the potential to endure great personal sacrifice in pursuit of their ideals. This I would suggest is positive DLF.

The problem some may argue is that both the negative and positive DLF's that I've just presented are nothing more than subjective derivatives of my own personal prejudices. Well that is the very point I'm attempting to make.

I am the master of my own happiness, for its in my interests to live life to the full

You see in the vast majority of instances where society expresses a view on Passionate, Obsessive and/or Addicted mind states, those subsequent assessments are always from points of personal prejudices and not from holistic clinical assessment.

It's very obvious to me that in differing times and differing situations both Margaret Thatcher and Adolph Hitler would have been devoid of any real power and actually considered lunatics and despicable mortals because of their propensity towards negative DLF. But they weren't at the most important time in their own personal history and that's what's really most important. Because perceptions are transient, subjective and frequently in tune with similar opportunist mind sets.

You see negative DFL's frequently have the ability to self propel their views by connecting with and manipulating the age old problem of collective acceptance of the unacceptable for fear of alienation or reprisal and/or buy-in to jingoistic zealous dogma from self interested DLF's. It is only at the point that they lose that connective populist alignment that the dynamic and perception of who they are, what they say and what they stand for is subject to; differing cognitive analysis.

Now I've sort of laboured that point because it is an important point in that I argue that what constitutes acceptable mind traits today may not always be deemed acceptable tomorrow and visa versa. In that our perceptions of who we are and the traits that we align ourselves to; do not have any other significance save for presenting themselves through the DLF that is unique to our body state at any given moment in time.

We may well have a clearly defined sense of our personality or mind state traits by the time we're in our mid teens etc. But in reality none of us truly know what the generators and markers of our DLF actually are. Because of that its therefore possible; to buy-in to formative neuro-linguistic programming perceptions of our DLF which can be counterproductive when for whatever reason our DLF moves further into either a positive or negative presentation of our understanding of what we believe is our base presenting DLF state. The result of that is we either big ourselves up or write ourselves off or we try to hide from what we're experiencing or thinking and eventually buy-in to perceptions of who and what we are in the complete absence of clinical diagnosis. I know that from personal experience that at the point chronic long term illness brings us to our knees we don't really know who we are anymore and are vulnerable to believe anything postulated as being in our best interests.

Be under no illusion that at the point our DLF moves into a perceived negative state, society in general begins to perceive our DLF to be an expression of some form of psychiatric condition. Now whilst that may be true in some instances I would argue that negative DLF is nothing more than an expression of imbalance in the soup that underpins normalized DFL states. Therefore I argue that we cannot correct that DLF expression with self beasting, simplistic or puerile drug treatment approaches. The only way to correct that is to analyse and determine the underlying causes of the deviations to our DLF.

You see, I frequently read about fallen stars and people who have been written off as having addictive and obsessive personalities and at one point in my life I bought into that perception myself. But I don't believe in that anymore because I believe that all mind states and cravings etc, are nothing more than impositions or deficiencies being imposed either directly or indirectly upon the soup that underpins our DLF.

I am the master of my own happiness, for its in my interests to live life to the full

We cannot ingest or be exposed to poisons or diseased states without them having a direct impact upon our DLF. Therefore when our DLF moves in a significant direction its imperative that we understand why that is, but we can only do that if we accept that DLF normalization can only be achieved through whole body view determination.

I simply don't accept now that negative DLF's in whatever presentation they take form e.g. obsessive compulsive disorder, sexual deviancy, drugs, obesity, violent conduct or alcohol etc, are based purely upon inherited mind states or predispositions. I believe the root of all those conditions lay in the soup that underpins normalized DLF's. If that soup is genetically corrupted in the first instance and/or we are exposed to factors that contribute to the disruption to concentrations of generators and markers to normalized DLF's then extremes of DLF expression is obviously going to be the ultimate outcome.

I therefore believe that it's time to stop all self beasting, all the poor me bullshit that we frequently allow ourselves to believe e.g. 'O my this was this and my that was that and that's why I am like I am etc'. But I say that only because I once allowed myself to believe all that crap and the fact of the matter is that in that mind set we only hold ourselves back.

There are many many things that move our DLF's from one extreme to another not least of which is life itself. But if we are ever to be in a positive DLF state it's important to note that positive DLF's cannot be found in medication or substance ingestion unless we've identified in the first instance the actual root cause.

You see; the bodily soups that underpin our very existence are responsible for all our perceptions and sense of reality. For it's that given and that given alone which drives all our focus and clarity of mind.

I am the master of my own health, for I take my quality of health seriously

That being said, we cannot possibly move from a functioning individual into someone racked by chronic DFL unless some form of corruption has played a part in the constitution of our DFL soup. When we stop viewing Passionate, Obsessive and Addicted mind sets in prejudiced, intransigent, single polarity values of positive and negative then we begin to understand who we are.

You see; a positive is of no use without a negative for we need both to ensure balance. Maintaining a balanced DLF however is a challenge because our DLF is always in a state of flux as the subtle changes to the constituents of our DLF soup ebb and flow. A balanced DLF is therefore by no means prescriptively set at some predefined intransigent position; it is as fluid as the universe we inhabit. The key however to individual and collective understanding of DLF is to accept the need to manage and not marginalize the concept and reality of the Driven Life Force that we all have the potential to hold.

We have a personal obligation if we wish to move to a healthy DLF to drive the determination of all DLF soup corrupting factors and not simply accept that there is nothing that we or anyone else can do to change an unhealthy DLF to a healthy DLF. The choice as ever remains firmly with us because we are the custodians of our DLF's. I accepted long ago that I'm a DLF, that's why I fought with all my might for better health, that's why I fight every single day of my life against ignorance of mind, body and soul. I have a DLF inside me which ensures that at all times I'm in touch and can access all my full potential.

I am the master of my own happiness, for its in my interests to live life to the full

Where are you now in terms of your DLF positioning? Well if you need help in determining that have a look through my simple DLF management tool below, who knows it could be the making of you.

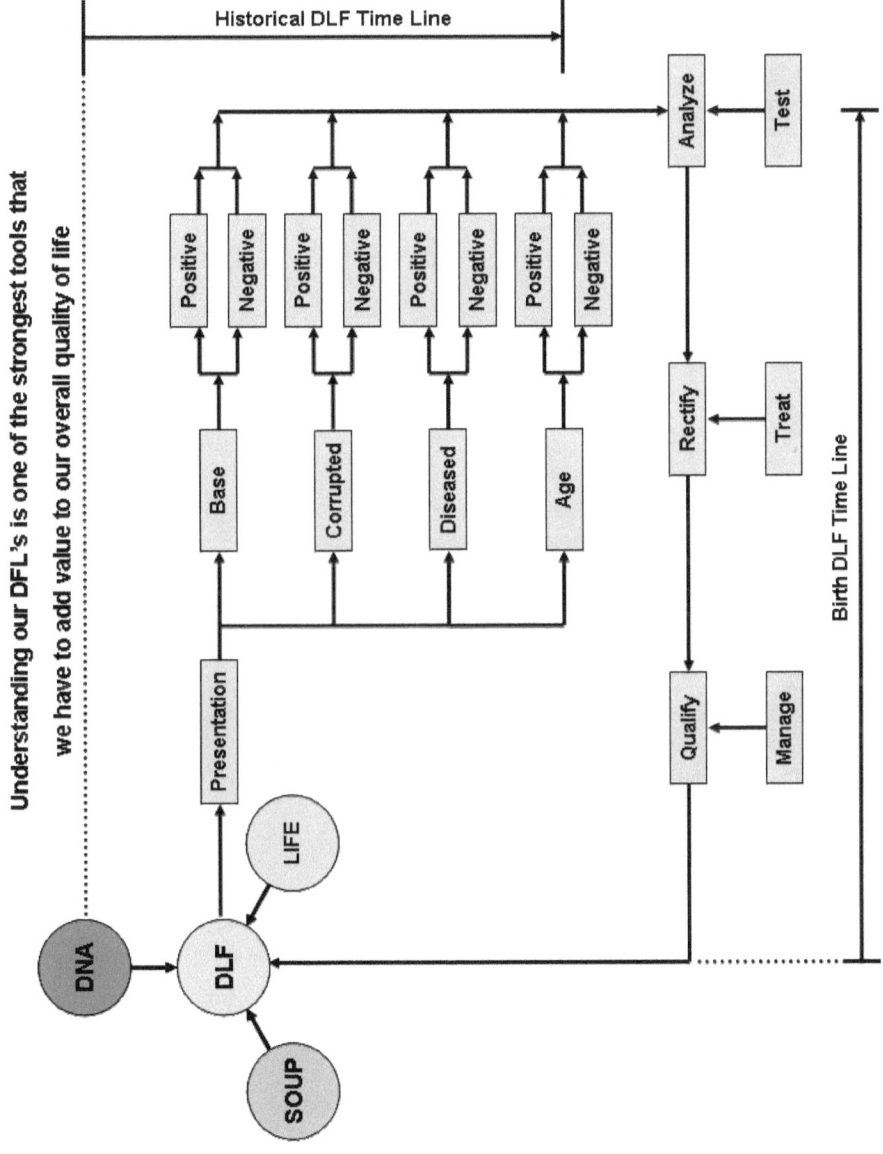

I am the master of my own health, for I take my quality of health seriously

Personal Notes

I am the master of my own happiness, for its in my interests to live life to the full

Personal Notes

I am the master of my own health, for I take my quality of health seriously

Personal Notes

I am the master of my own happiness, for its in my interests to live life to the full

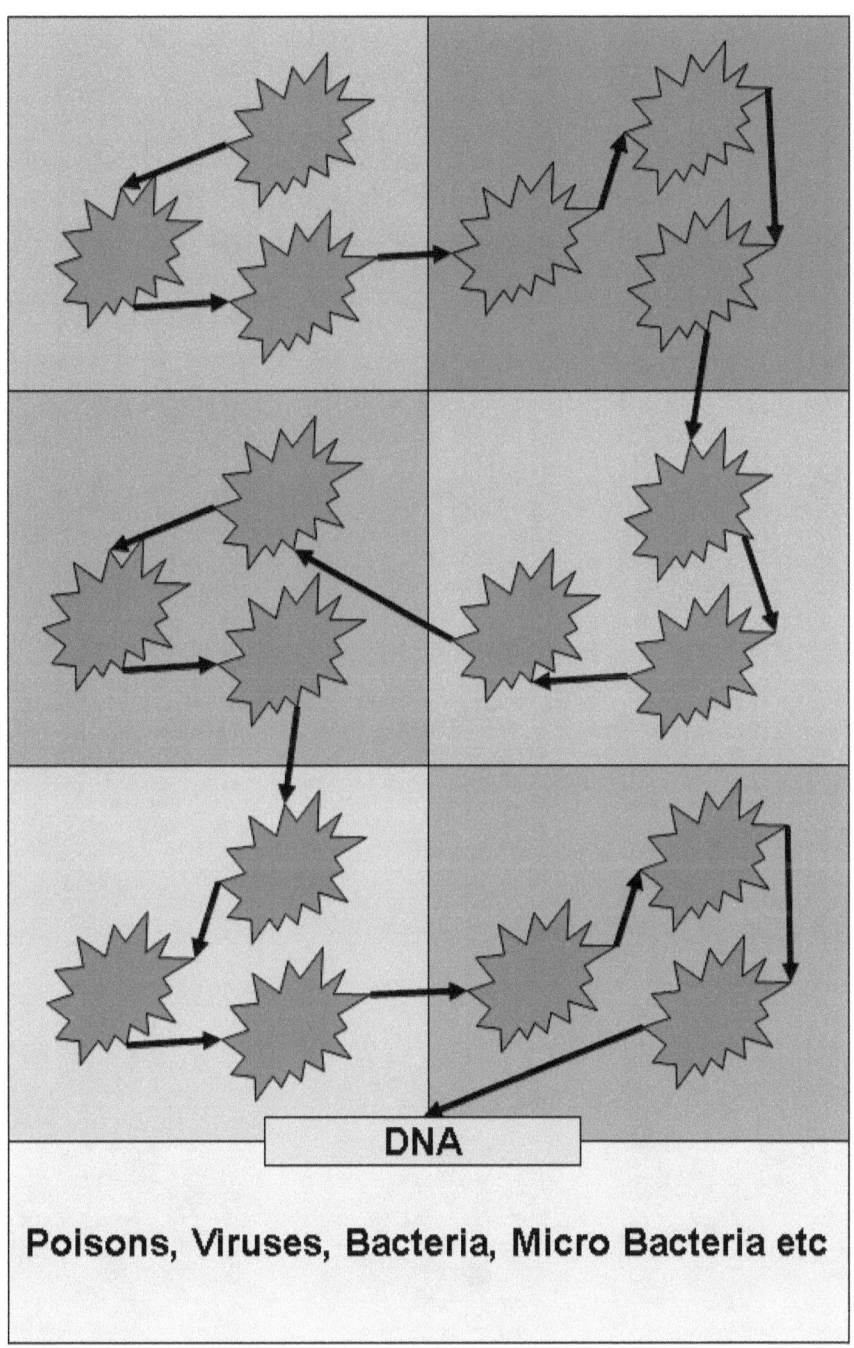

I am the master of my own health, for I take my quality of health seriously

302 RAPHAEL'S LEGACY

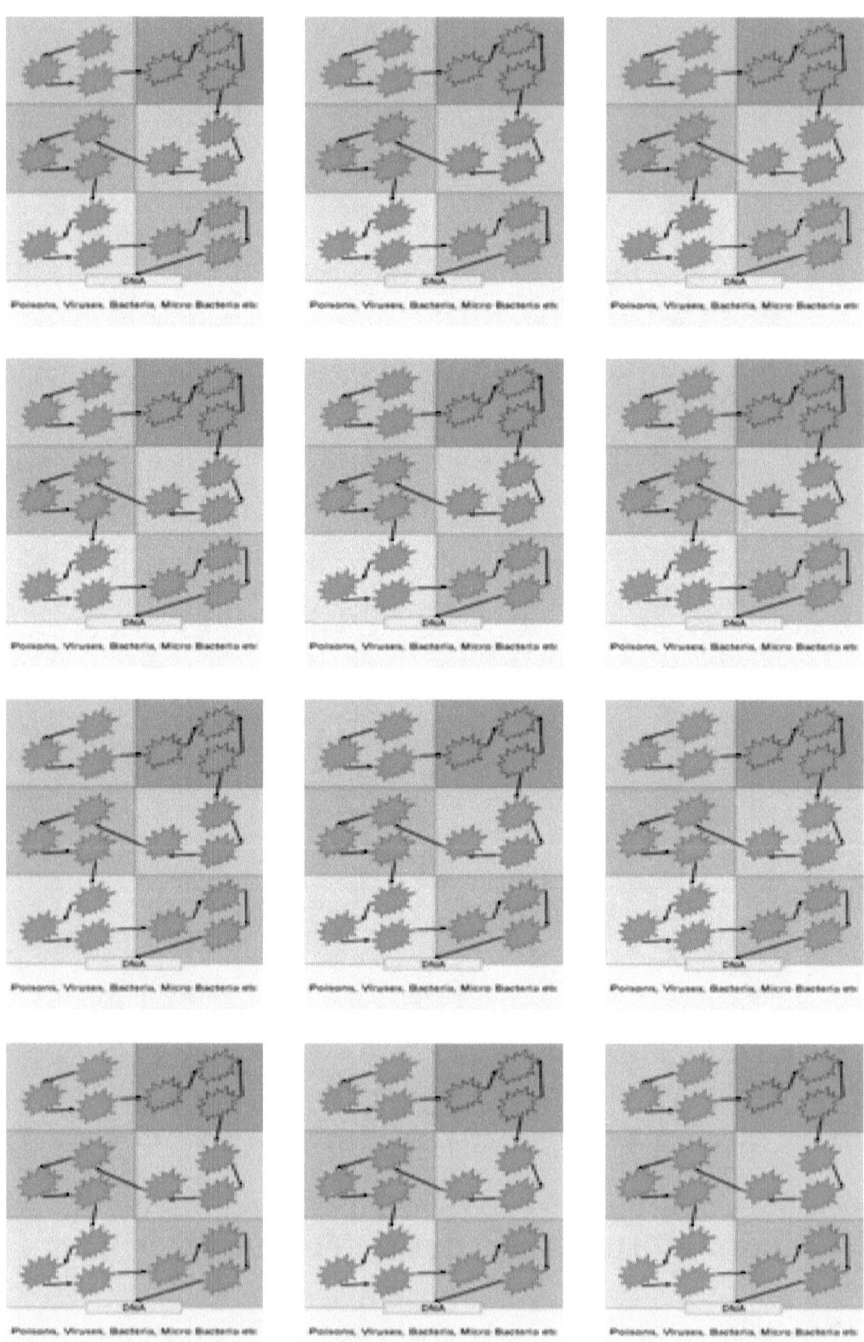

I am the master of my own happiness, for its in my interests to live life to the full

Our Invisible Time Bombs

Whilst I've explored conditions, perceptions and diseased states from a highly personalised view point and position in this book. I nevertheless believe that my pragmatic views originate from nothing more than an enquiring mind, stimulated by great personal suffering and learning. I have no great gifts to bring to the world, no great deeds to accomplish; save to try to acquire some grace and peace in this life for myself and to be brutally honest it really doesn't get any more complicated than that. You see; I personally don't believe, having suffered far too much that there is any great majesty in suffering. I believe as an evolved society we should have gotten through most of our unnecessary suffering by now. Yet if there is anything rewarding about chronic illness and suffering it is that we have time to revisit things that we once took for granted. In doing so, we afford ourselves the opportunity to explore our life and backgrounds from newer and more informed perspectives.

During the process towards my own personal recovery I looked at my mum, her background, her health conditions and the imposition that may have placed upon me. Not really what you would call an implicitly abstract case but certainly one that allowed me to shed more light upon her and the impact that genetics can have upon us all.

I am the master of my own health, for I take my quality of health seriously

My mum I'm informed was an extremely vivacious yet devout Roman Catholic, who had a zest for life complemented with a strong moral undercurrent. She loved people, animals, the outdoors and her favourite rugby team Whitehaven RLFC. She would frequently cycle hundreds of miles with her friends when not at work and help her dad in the garden taking much of his manual work. In fact nothing was a problem to her until she was struck down by two major illnesses in very quick succession. At 15 she was struck down by rheumatic fever only to sort of recover before being knocked for six at 16 with scarlet fever. My granddad, over the years I knew him, would frequently in his broad west Cumbrian dialect state, '*duz thou no marra, thee mother our Nancy was niver sham lass efter she ed scarlet end rumatic fever*'. He was indeed right, because from that point on:

- She would get tearful over silly things.

- She frequently had low moods.

- She would get tired quickly.

- She could sleep for England.

- Her thought processes were often confused.

- She was always cold.

- She always had pains in her joints.

I am the master of my own happiness, for its in my interests to live life to the full

By the time I was born and after much stress and much heartache my mum was already being treated with antidepressants and she'd already been written off as a nutter by her own family and my dad's callous and intolerant extended family. I spent all my childhood years removing and emptying buckets of urine from my parents' bedroom as my mum refused to leave her bed. Making her meals etc, and many, many times simply battling with her in floods of tears as I tried my level best to prevent her from committing or attempting to commit suicide whilst:

- My brother watched TV downstairs.

- My sister was in bed.

And more importantly whilst

- My dad simply lost himself in his horse racing or 4 pints of beer in kells legion or the red lion pub.

Such a life, such personal experiences at a tender age can be difficult to reconcile as we mature and I guess that's why I began doing so much work on myself at a very early stage in my life. The thing is, its only now that I've been through what I've been through that I'm able to totally forgive myself for any anger I had towards my childhood as well as any anger I had towards my mum for the dreadful childhood we had. I can't excuse either my brother or my father for their reluctance to engage or even to attempt to help or support my mum, but in reality I don't feel that I need to, they made their choices, that's just the way they are. It is however clear to me now that my mum has suffered greatly from social and clinical prejudices for the majority of her life.

I am the master of my own health, for I take my quality of health seriously

She's been through hell, medications, had electrodes placed on her head, injections, psychiatric incarcerations, operations and physical and emotional suffering beyond belief. But to her testament she's still with us in 2008, alive and kicking for all her might, a colossus in terms of those who have alienated her, insulated her and ridiculed her for a lifetime of undiagnosed suffering and pain.

It's only now that I understand that she never ever recovered from rheumatic or scarlet fever, that her body was constantly in a toxic state, that her detoxing capabilities and her ability to cope were as impoverished as her finances and her limited joys in life. It's actually very upsetting now to understand just what she was forced to endure and also very annoying that this should have been imposed upon my mum. All of her suffering and years of waste through nothing more than sheer medical ignorance and the sociological prejudices of her kith and kin.

Now the reason that I've covered my mum's predicament is because I believe that it's eminently possible that our health can be compromised at any time in our lives by a raft of unseen genetic time bombs. I refer of course to placenta transferred neurotoxins and low grade disease states; I refer to industrial chemicals and toxins trapped in our DNA. I refer to genetically damaged biological process systems and organs all of which constitute a variable and a ticking time bomb in our ultimate physiological state of wellbeing. Now the previous postulation is not as abstract, challenging or as ridiculous as it would first appear. You see in days of yore man discovered that if he planted his weakest fruits of the harvest, his harvest the following year was a disaster. However when he planted his finest fruits his harvest the year after that had vitality and there was food in abundance. In essence he was proving that vitality propagates vitality, whereas disease propagates deformity and living matter with a reduced vitality.

Well we as individuals in our own right are nothing more than the products of our parent's fruits, a product of their vitality or paradoxically a product of their diseased states and a myriad of other things. There has been some research on this matter specifically focusing upon the impact of holocaust experiences upon the lineage of survivors. But whilst results have concluded that biological systems have been impaired in the majority of instances, no global acceptance of hereditary impositions via such roots has been forthcoming as yet. A position I would suggest is more to do with medical prejudices and historical perceptions than it has to do with due consideration and clinical expressions of acceptable probabilities. But then again we know that the medical industry is the last remaining bastion of, antagonistic, for the sake of it and protectionist luddite men.

Unfortunately however, research into the imposition of historical toxic lifestyles, the industrial revolution, chemical warfare, chemical manufacturing and disease is negligible. Yet we know that all those variables killed our forefathers with impunity but not before their fruits were sown with other such contaminated souls in the creation of whole new generations. For instance, my modern industrial contamination lineage consists of coal mining, steel making, mustard gassing, textile manufacture, nuclear generation / reprocessing and chemical manufacture to name but a few. Now there is no way that you can convince me that the toxic cocktails that my family worked in, breathed in or were impregnated with before eventually killing them is not in some way playing a significant part in my life story. Simply because it's impossible for them not to be that's why I believe we need to stop simply living in the moment and start building smarter profiles when we become, because that's the only way we're ever going to get the full picture and put the stabbing in the dark approach to bed finally and for good.

I am the master of my own health, for I take my quality of health seriously

We know so little about the complexities of DNA toxic transfers, but we know that excess exposure to radiation and many forms of toxins be that, poisoning in low or high dosage, does effect and can damage a host's DNA. We know this because people die from such impositions it's as simple as that. Our DNA is nothing more than a blueprint from its previous owners and if their DNA was damaged, why shouldn't ours be equally damaged and prone to very subtle levels of developmental, repair and replication discrepancies which manifest at any point in our lives as subtle disease states?

I will take that one stage further. What if subtle issues with our DNA don't actually present themselves as a disease state later in life? But actually contribute to new disease states simply because the impositions placed upon our bodily functions, due to impediments in our DNA, render them weaker or less able to deal with the issues they're presented with. What if 'Barry Hardy' was born with historical mitochondria conjugates, which meant that my body's ability to detox at a cellular level was significantly compromised prior to point zero? Why then shouldn't I go on to develop serious and chronic health conditions? No matter what my body tries to do to fight off disease invaders, it's simply unable to offload the by-products of that battle and therein my body becomes toxic.

I hope you see where I'm coming from here, we all must have encountered chesty friends at school, kids who's summers were a nightmare due to hay fever etc, but neither us or they truly knew the origins of such impositions. Equally until we ourselves are presented with a health challenge we naturally believe that we were born healthy and that we've just sort of picked up a disease later in life. But my point is, unless we explore all avenues, all reasonable lines of research we have no idea what sorts of ticking time bombs lay deep within us. Because of that we may

I am the master of my own happiness, for its in my interests to live life to the full

never truly understand what it is that we really need to do to return us back to some form of quality of life once we've been struck down by a chronic illness.

I'm therefore advocating that lineage must be considered when exploring possible imposition sources to our health issues, but word of mouth and subjectivity in the detection process are simply not good enough.

We need to test and look for clues, for markers and for answers, because deep within us may just be the key that we've been looking for. That must be our starting point to recovery, the point we've prayed so hard for and I say that with all seriousness because I advocate that the legacy of more ignorant times may indeed still be wreaking havoc with the life forces trying to live in so called, more enlightened times.

To fully appreciate what I'm saying here we need to stop biologically living in the moment, we need to stop making snap shot biological value judgments, we need to accept and appreciate that we are the products of yesterday's men and women. We live in bodies that are nothing more than receptacles of historical DNA, the very same DNA that was malnourished and poisoned, generation, after generation, after generation. So the next time you get angry about the imposition your health places upon you, stop your thought process right there and take the time to connect with:

- Who you really are.

- What you really are.

And

- The suffering that your DNA experienced long before it manifested itself as you.

Simply because

- Your body may only be trying its best to deal with the fall-out imposed upon it by the historical damage imposed upon your historical DNA.

On a more personal note if there's any spark of delight I take from the formulation of this chapter it's that I realise and I'm fully content with the fact now that; with no birth children to my DNA my DNA and all that it is, is effectively over at the point I take my last breath…….yay.

Perhaps part of my battle to refine my Raphael Treatment Protocol (RTP) was nothing more than to arrive at that point, who knows, and furthermore, who save for me, really cares because in truth it was only my life path to walk anyway.

A Personal Closure

People often remark about the beauty of birth and then fail wholesale for a whole host of reasons to rejoice daily in the beauty of any given substance of birth. Similarly those very same people seem compelled to shy away from for the absoluteness that is our mortal passing, feeling it inappropriate to either discuss or explore the very essence of mortality. I've never had those problems, for I've always endeavoured to rejoice in the beauty of all the products of birth and am blessed enough to see our mortal finality as nothing more than blessed release from the pain we've endured for so long.

There is absolutely no sadness for me when a souls time is finally up, for I simply thank it and them for all that he, she, they were and for all that he, she, they aspired to be. At that point there is something deep inside me that allows me to let him, her, and them go to the place where their energy at that point needs to go and/or be. So I've shed very few tears over a blessed departure from mortality during my life, for I know that they all spent their time amongst us well and for that I feel nothing but unquestionable pride and admiration of and for them including the major part they played in my life.

It's important to note here that whilst I do not and never will shy away from the rigors of mortality, I'm tormented by its love, its finality and the great loss that it inevitably brings to us all. My belief is that when we connect in mortality we certainly learn to grow, but after that growth spurt we are often left with far too much time to reflect and participate in self flagellation based upon highly preventable regrets. That is I suspect one of the many frailties that we all encounter in being simply a mortal, maybe that's a life challenge that we all as mortals need to accept or at least try to conquer, but when all said and done who amongst us truly knows?

I am the master of my own happiness, for its in my interests to live life to the full

Personal Notes

I am the master of my own health, for I take my quality of health seriously

Personal Notes

I am the master of my own happiness, for its in my interests to live life to the full

I am the master of my own health, for I take my quality of health seriously

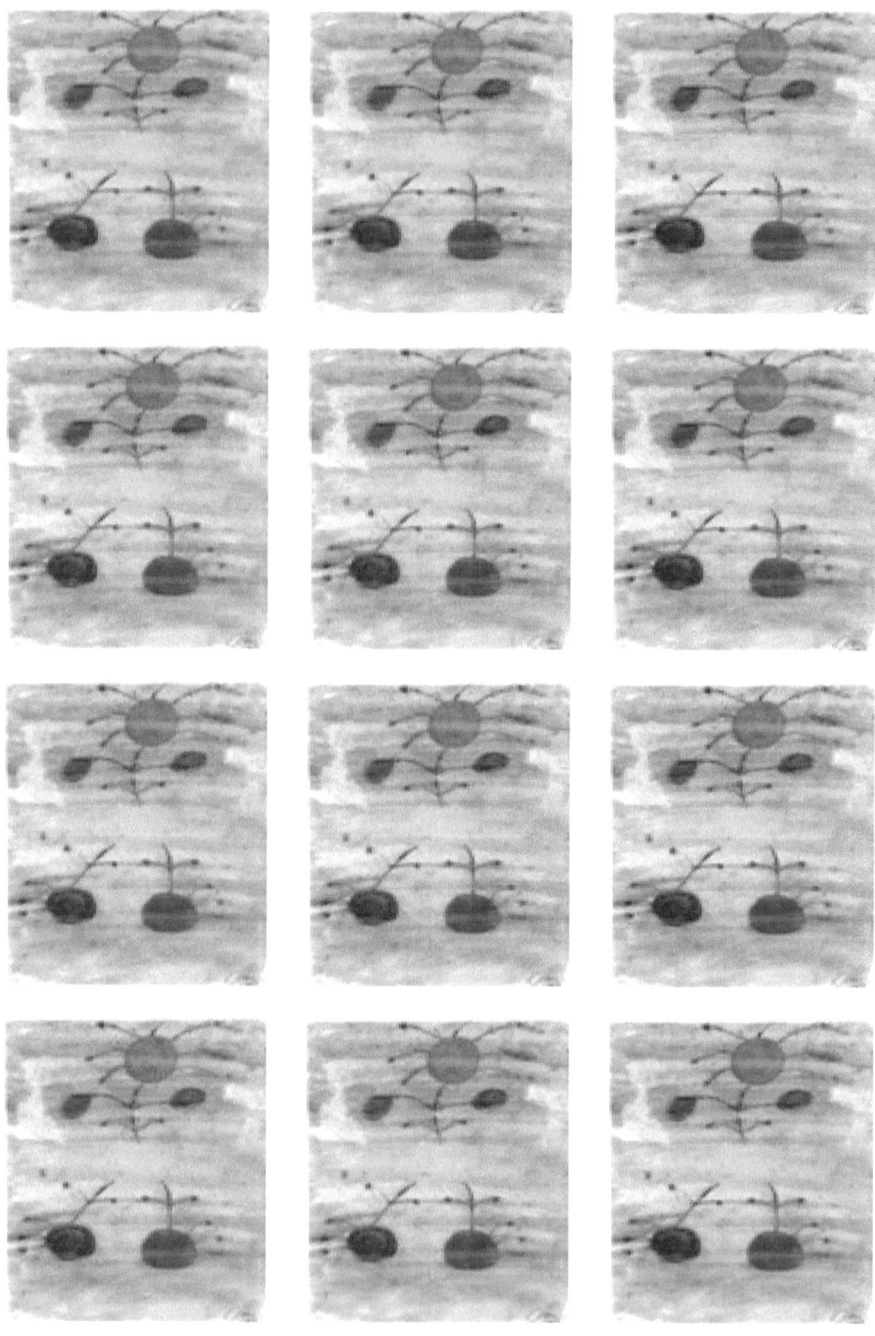

I am the master of my own happiness, for its in my interests to live life to the full

ARTHRITIS: THE GENETIC LINKS

There is nothing funny about arthritis save for the comical way that people refer to the condition e.g. *'our GP says that jims got bloody arthurritious now so he's told him to lose some weight and start jogging'*. Oh yes you can bet your last £10 that at the point some ignorant medic decides that you've got arthritis, their next statements will be 'lose some weight' and 'take up some exercise'. But the ironic thing is that the flawed diagnosis of arthritis only really creeps into the diagnosis when we've a bit of age about us. Very few of us are ever tested for this condition unless for some unexplained reason, our body's immune system goes into freefall and general arthritic symptoms are the main presenting symptoms. So as an opener let me give you three classic instances of clinical dismissal for the same presenting symptom:

- Young athlete goes to his GP complaining about a terrible pain in his knee, GP says: 'hmmn, stop running and take these e.g. anti-inflammatory tablets' Young guy says, 'Sorry I can't take them I've got chronic gastritis and those will make my condition worse' GP says 'hmmn stop exercising and see how you get on' End of consultation.

I am the master of my own health, for I take my quality of health seriously

- Young fat guy goes to see same GP complaining about a terrible pain in his knee, GP says: 'hmmn, you need to lose some weight and start taking more regular exercise'. Young guy says, 'Sorry I can't exercise man because I can hardly walk'. GP says, 'hmmn ok take these anti-inflammatory tablets for a month and see how you get on'. End of consultation.

- Middle aged guy goes to see same GP complaining about a terrible pain in his knee, GP says: 'hmmn, you need to lose some weight and start taking more regular exercise apart from that there's nothing I can do because you've got arthritis'. Guy says, 'Sorry I can't exercise man because I can hardly walk'. GP says, 'hmmn ok take these anti-inflammatory tablets for a month and see how you get on'. End of consultation.

Can you see the point I'm making? Do we really need to be paying our front line medics such outrageous salaries for that sort of non clinical appraisal? The thing is there is always an undercurrent of dogmatic, perceptions and a complete lack of empathy or desire to help the patient. A position compromised still further by the addition of secondary conditions or complications, via the only treatment option open i.e. stomach upset and/or further damage to the damaged knee through inappropriate exercise etc.

I am the master of my own happiness, for its in my interests to live life to the full

But what is Arthritis? Is it simply just pains in our joints or is there more to this condition than the majority of us realise? Well Arthritis is a chronic, progressive and disabling auto-immune disease affecting large sections of our population. It is an incredibly painful condition, can cause severe disability and ultimately affects a person's ability to carry out everyday tasks. The disease can progress very rapidly, causing swelling and damaging cartilage and bone around the joints. Any joint, muscle or tendon can be affected but it is commonly those physiological mechanisms directly related to hands, hips, shoulders, knees, feet and wrists that are at greatest risk. Furthermore Arthritis is a systemic, disease which means that it can affect the whole body and internal organs such as the lungs, heart and eyes. There are over 200 types of arthritis or musculoskeletal conditions, which are split into three classifications:

- Inflammatory arthritis such as rheumatoid arthritis, ankylosing spondylitis and gout.

- Non-inflammatory arthritis such as osteoarthritis, scoliosis and torn ligaments.

- Connective tissue disease such as lupus, sclerosis and Sjogren's syndrome.

Typical drugs used to treat arthritic conditions include;

- Cortisone.

- Ibuprofen.

- Indomethacin.

- Ketoprofen.

- Ketorolac.

- Mefenamic acid.

- Meloxicam.

All have differing success rates and all have associated side effects and potential complications, but none of them actually cure the disease. The best that they do is mask some of its main presenting symptoms, i.e. pain.

However it's only when you really start to examine this condition that you realise that the medical world, in terms of treatment and cure, simply hasn't got a clue. The industry rambles on endlessly about diet and exercise but seems resistant to any form of root cause analysis.

Time after time, international Arthritis research appears to show that whilst there are high instances of Arthritis in the developed world, in the undeveloped world the instances are quite low. But how can people in the undeveloped world be virtually free of this condition whilst we in the developed world appear to be tormented by this so called complex condition? Is it simply that we:

- Have the wrong diet?

- Don't get enough exercise?

- Simply a combination of the two?

- Or is there something still missing from the loop?

Well the picture is not as clear as it would first appear. This is because whilst there are clearly low instances of Arthritis in some areas of the undeveloped world. In other areas of the world where more ancient civilizations resided *which now forms part of our modernistic views of the developed world.* There is significant evidence to suggest that Arthritis was an endemic condition within those populations too.

You see, it has been discovered that amongst the indigenous population of North America, skeletons have been found dating back several thousand years which do show evidence of Arthritis. As a result of those findings there are some who have postulated that it is the presence of Arthritis in North America that potentially holds the key in terms of the manifestation of Arthritis in Europe. Citing perhaps some link to food groups, like potatoes and/or tobacco etc, for the manifestation of Arthritis in Europe that we now see.

But the only premise for that conclusion is that prior to the 1800's there was no detailed medical documentation of the condition in the British Isles or Europe. However, whilst the condition may not have been documented, we know from our own archeology that there is significant evidence to suggest high instances of cultural and non cultural Arthritis in the British Isles.

Therefore I simply don't believe the theory that indigenous foods from North America are responsible for the dispersal of Arthritis across Europe. I actually think it's all much simpler than that. I believe the problem is twofold, I believe it has both a gene pool DNA link accompanied by a genetic disease pool link. Both of which can be simply explained in the two points over the page:

I am the master of my own health, for I take my quality of health seriously

1. Malnutrition can certainly have an impact upon the way our bodies develop and respond to disease over time and there's absolutely no doubt that the indigenous peoples of North America and Europe experienced starvation and famine, generation after generation. I'm therefore happy to postulate that the initial Arthritic gene pool link is that of malnutrition. A bodily condition which disrupts compromises and/or destroys at very subtle levels, every process and system in the human body right down to our very DNA expression. It's no wonder then that offspring from populations subject to frequent malnutrition exhibit subtle changes in their DNA including their ability to retain and assimilate vital vitamins, mineral and other key process growth and repair essentials.

2. If we then add an external diseased state like lets say: Lymes Disease in the case of North America and Syphilis in the case of Europe. We then clearly have all the components needed to generated high levels of inflammation and bodily breakdown. Because we know that the eradication of spirochete disease is extraordinarily difficult to achieve because the disease has the propensity to lay dormant for years upon years before being re-energized. So my question is, why wouldn't these diseases be playing a major part in Arthritic complaints, well I believe that the only barriers to that suggestion is anything more complicated than this; it's the depth of ignorance that exists within our implicitly amoral medical and clinical institutions.

I am the master of my own happiness, for its in my interests to live life to the full

But how insane is this postulation? Well not really that insane at all because, for thousands of years the people of North America and Europe have battled famine, Lymes and Syphilis Disease because it wasn't until the introduction of penicillin as recent as the 1940's that mankind started winning some of the battles that we have with vicious bacteria.

However guys like Samuel Hahnemann as far back in 1810 where postulating new ways of thinking on matters of disease, cause and transfer in order to move us away from the barbarism that was the medical world in those days, so my views today are really just a play on his words then. *Hahnemann believed that the cause of disease is the disturbance to our life force and that disturbances in that force manifest themselves as specific symptoms. The Law of Susceptibility deals with the invasion of the body by diseases referred to as Miasms. These Miasms can be acquired acutely or they can be congenital or latent, until some negative experience or normal aging triggers their appearance as a symptom and then as disease.*

It is both our historical genetic malnutrition and genetic low grade diseased states that I believe are the fuels that constitute the presentation of Arthritis in our societies right now. The absence of Arthritis I believe in other ethnicities is down to nothing more than the presence of antibacterial and antimicrobial foods in their diet.

Now I know what I'm postulating here can be a little challenging because whilst we can relate to historical famines etc, it's difficult for any of us to relate to another man's disease let alone an historical, diseased state. Nevertheless the fact of the that matter is that both Lymes Disease and Syphilis are spirochete bacteria, both of which bring about a whole host of inflammatory conditions including degradation of cartilage, muscles and bone through systemic neurodegenerative processes. Both Lymes Disease and Syphilis have been with us for hundreds if not thousands of years and there is absolutely no reason at all why low grade gene pool expression of these diseases is not deep down inside us all. Sitting there just waiting for an opportunity to take hold of our bodies through ageing, bodily damage or simply on the background of a previous disease invasion.

Now hey as I've said many times I'm no clinician but you would have thought by now that someone in the medical industry would have put one and one together and come out with two. But they haven't and the consequence of that is that we as society are lead to believe that when we've been diagnosed with Arthritis we have;

- Some form of overly complex condition.

- That there is no cure for us and we must live with it.

And

- There's only the steroid and/or anti-inflammatory approach we can take.

Well I think the only thing that's complicated about Arthritis is the insidious impact that the untreated disease has upon our ability to live life as we would choose. I don't think we need to believe that living with the condition is all that we can choose to do. Neither do I believe that just popping in anti-inflammatory tablets to mask the condition is the right or most effective way to move forward. I simply don't believe what the medics have to say on this condition or recommend in terms of its treatment. I believe that if we wish not to be held to ransom by a condition we must detach from the prejudices that surround that condition and be prepared to research and explore it further. You don't have to be silly here all you need to be is receptive to a whole host of new ideas and perceptions. But if you're unable to do that then your only option is to stick with the current orthodox views that might or might not be working for you.

I am the master of my own health, for I take my quality of health seriously

Personally once I understood that the majority of medics that I elicited help from actually understood very little themselves. It became easy for me in that difficult position to accept that perhaps there's always more to explore about the originators of disease than a mere medic is willing to explore. My view now is:

- So what if you've been told you have arthritis, that doesn't prevent you from being tested privately to see if you have Lymes or any one of a hundred diseases!

- So what if you've been told you have arthritis, that doesn't prevent you from researching and exploring alternative treatments!

- So what if you've been told you have arthritis, that doesn't prevent you from trying under professional guidance a whole host of natural anti-bacterial, anti-viral and anti-inflammatory herbs!

But there is one thing for sure; if you let that disease expression take hold of your body by merely blocking its expression through high dose anti-inflammatory medications, then you will never be able to repair its damage. But then again it's your choice at the end of the day.

I am the master of my own happiness, for its in my interests to live life to the full

Personal Notes

I am the master of my own health, for I take my quality of health seriously

Personal Notes

I am the master of my own happiness, for its in my interests to live life to the full

I am the master of my own health, for I take my quality of health seriously

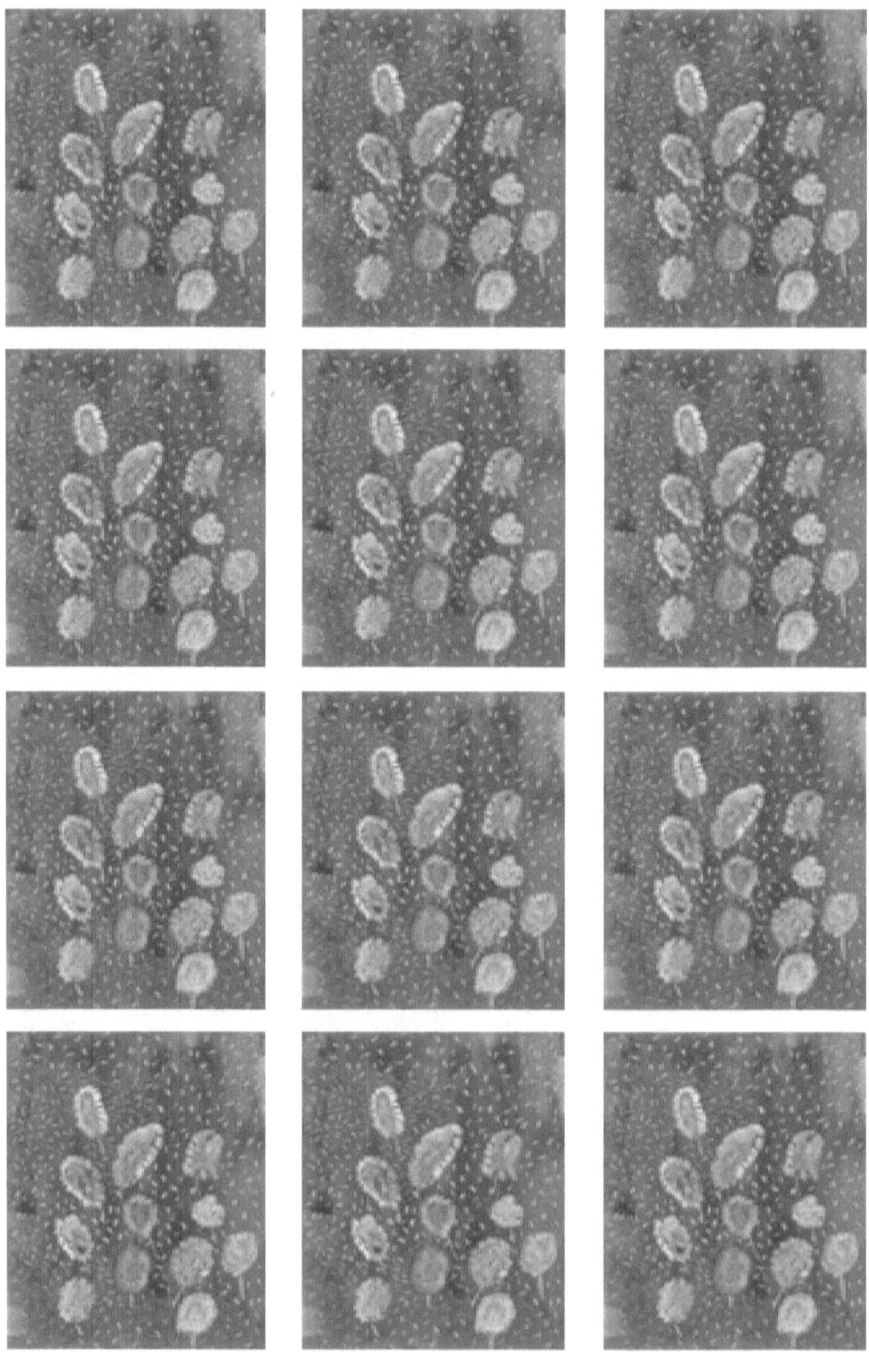

I am the master of my own happiness, for its in my interests to live life to the full

TOXIC BODY SYNDROME OR TBS

In pursuit of recovery from my chronic illnesses I was forced to look at illness from a completely different perspective to that which I was brain washed with as a child. Subsequently, my personal health struggles have proven to me:

(a) Just how insidiously corrupt that brain washing was.

And

(b) Just how appallingly ignorant our medics really are.

The simple fact of the matter is that:

(a) Few medics truly understand the dynamics of illness.

And

(b) Few are prepared to shift their perception of illness preferring instead to adhere to the medical clap trap they bought into as part of their so called medical training.

I am the master of my own health, for I take my quality of health seriously

Because of that it's very difficult when we're chronically ill to get any form of logical or scientific input from the medical industry full stop. Patients are written off at best and blamed at worst when presenting themselves to a medic with anything more than a cold, stomach bug or pain in the chest. It's like medics simply don't get illness at all, it's like illness is a great mystery to them which I struggle to comprehend really.

They don't seem to understand cause and effect, they don't seem to understand variable input dynamics and they don't understand basic physiology over and above basic anatomical understanding. In essence I've simply never come across an industry with such high levels of occupational ignorance towards the service it provides and for me that truly marks that industry as antediluvian *(old fashioned)* and as such no longer worthy of my respect.

Therefore when we are faced with chronic illness it's imperative that we take full ownership of our problem because it is the only sure fire way of making any progress. You see, chronic illness has many generators and we must understand that dynamic if we are to ever fully recover. Happily the majority of what we need to know as laymen in terms of illness is not rocket science either; its just common sense, body monitoring and holistic treatment management.

Now it may sound astonishing but it is eminently possible that the vast majority of chronic illness perpetuation and relapse results from nothing more grandiose than toxic body syndrome *TBS*. Now I can just hear the howls of derision from the medical world, *'You joker Hardy I've never heard such tosh; toxic body syndrome, away with you man you're talking through your arse'*. Well before you the non medical readers of this book all jump the gun too, just hang on before you too commit to that assessment to You see, were I a medic I might be able to talk through my arse, but I'm not; I'm like you a former sufferer of chronic disease,

I am the master of my own happiness, for its in my interests to live life to the full

therefore if you will bear with me I will explain TBS as a pragmatist and man of engineering science. TBS is a state of bodily function that prohibits optimum health because the regenerative processes and capabilities of the body are in a constant state of compromise. The very fact that a body is so compromised moves that body into a toxic bodily state, are you okay with that. You see; at the point we move into a toxic body state our expressions of disease always presents with 5 main features i.e.

1. Mood Swings.

2. Fatigue.

3. Pain.

4. Anxiety.

5. Depression.

Talk, live or read about anyone with a long term chronic illness and the key presenting features of that condition will be the above and it is that phenomenon that I'm now suggesting are predictable derivatives of TBS. The reason they are predictable is because they are classic expressions of disease resulting from the deviation of normal values of hormones, neurotoxins, funguses, viruses and bacteria within any given bodily state.

You see; when any irresolvable imposition is placed upon our body, it quickly moves into a toxic state due to the break down in our methylation and sulphanation processes and as such the classic and consistent expression of that toxic state are; Mood Swings, Fatigue, Pain, Anxiety and Depression.

I am the master of my own health, for I take my quality of health seriously

Now talk to a medic about TBS and he or she will simply poo poo it because:

(a) They are occupationally ignorant to disease generators.

And

(b) We are still light years away from having mainstream tests and/or a medical culture etc., in place capable of looking at illness with any degree of scientific clarity.

But the reality is; at the point we as individuals begin to look at our own illness with a degree of personal clarity we begin to understand what it is we must do to aid our recovery. What I'm suggesting here is that the linear progression of chronic illness through the standard hierarchy expression of; Mood Swings, Fatigue, Pain, Anxiety and Depression is nothing more than an expression of TBS. The key to understanding TBS is to accept that it is not bacteria, micro-organisms, viral infections and fungal infections that are the greatest impediments to optimum health. It is the derivatives of those impediments in the form of neuro and bio toxins that are the greatest long term hindrance to optimum health and the intrinsically linked failure and/or underperformance of our methylation and sulphanation processes. You see it is the toxic derivatives of diseased states that;

(a) Saturate our body during disease.

And

(b) That we are unable to expel that create the TBS state.

I am the master of my own happiness, for its in my interests to live life to the full

When our body however is under constant assault from neuro and bio toxins we are indeed in a state of TBS there can be no scientific argument against that. The real difficult aspect of this suggestion however; is getting to grips with the reality that in both high and low circulating TBS levels; the hierarchy expression of; Mood Swings, Fatigue, Pain, Anxiety and depression remains constant.

You see, such is the potency and potential corruptibility of TBS that our bodies are thrown out of balance very easily. Because of that it may be difficult initially or certainly prior to corrective intervention to determine whether a body is in a high or low circulating state of TBS or is simply being compromised by a high or low overall TBS load. The reason for that is that the neuro and bio toxins that underpin TBS are stored deep in body fat including the brain and it is only at the point that we begin the process of toxin removal that we begin to understand our TBS load.

TBS loading by default is unique to each individual because it's eminently possible to experience TBS from high levels of circulating toxins whilst having a relatively low overall TBS loading. The reason for that is because some of us are extremely poor at storing toxins in our body or creating additional body fat to store toxins there-in. The paradox to that is that some of us are very good at storing toxins in our body and generating additional fat to store those toxins. So that whilst there may be low circulating TBS, the originator of that circulating load can in some instances be a very high overall TBS load.

I am the master of my own health, for I take my quality of health seriously

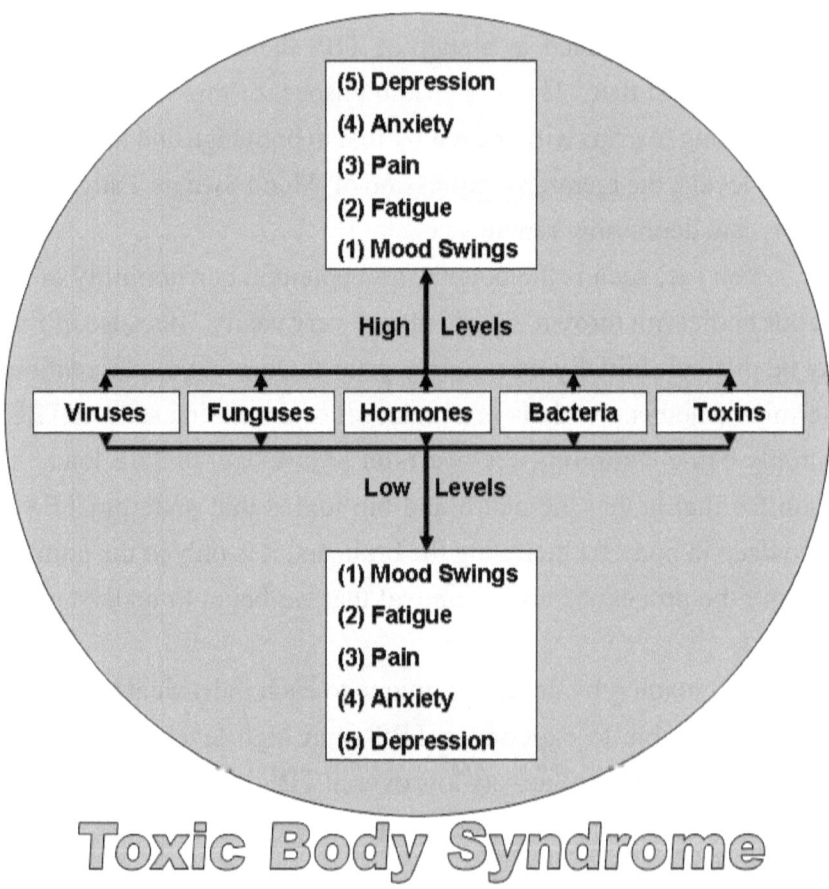

One of the main reasons that TBS is such a challenging condition is because:

>(a) Its presence is counter to all our former belief structures in terms of illness definition.

And because

(b) TBS in the most part exhibits symptoms in the form of central nervous system expressions which sociologically are always regarded as being of a psychiatric origin.

In that situation all ill informed TBS sufferers immediately fall into the trap of self blame and self doubt about what's actually going wrong or on in their bodies. A situation compromised still further by the fact that any medic they consult in relation to their symtomology expression invariably re-assigns the blame for their condition back onto them. Where in reality the dynamic is very simple:

(a) Low overall diseased state and low toxin load results in a balanced body state re: fig 1 below.

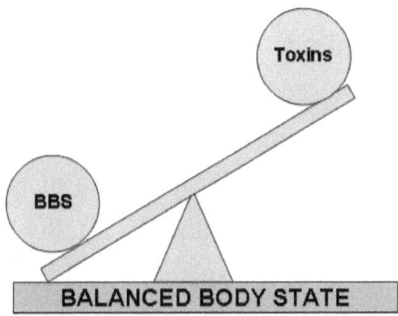

I am the master of my own health, for I take my quality of health seriously

Whereas

(b) A high overall diseased state and high toxin load results in a toxic body state re: fig 2 below.

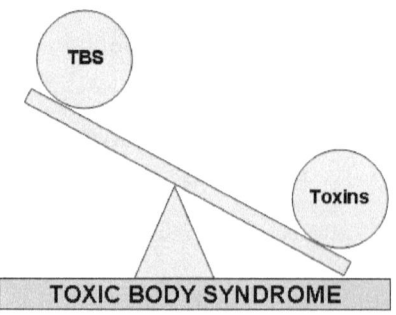

Now look I haven't just created a new acronym for the sake of it, the reason I'm bringing TBS to your attention is because actually its time that TBS was recognised. TBS is a chronic state of disease expression that is completely ignored by the medical industry and furthermore there is no effective mainstream or acceptable treatment option available to those suffering from TBS. Yet this state of bodily underperformance indiscriminately destroys lives and the quality of life and the real scary thing is that anyone of us can succumb to TBS at any point in our lives. Because whenever we move into a diseased state be that generated via a micro-organism, viral or fungal imposition and our sulphanation and methylation processes begin to falter. We potentially move into chronic TBS if our body is unable to deal or cope with the original imposition and/or its derivates e.g. toxin generation. The reason being that there is always potential for;

(a) Our cellular detox capabilities to stall completely.

(b) Our body's immune system to begin to deviate from norm.

And

(c) Our core TBS symptoms to cloud our actual clinical condition.

However be under no illusion that no matter what liver function analysis that you may have states; or how much detoxing you embark upon; TBS will be a present factor in chronic illness expression until the bodies overall TBS load is lowered or removed from the body completely. So then how do we initially test for TBS? Well you can't determine TBS via blood analysis you must undergo body fat biopsy and analysis, because that is where your TBS load resides. Okay; assuming that an excessive lipo-toxin load has been identified how do we lower it?

Well in truth and as yet I've not encountered a definitive protocol which eradicates this condition completely and believe me I've tried everything possible out there. However far infrared saunas certainly help to some degree and I'm sure that lipo-suction offers great potential, one of the areas of investigation however that I yet to personally undertake.

Nevertheless we all as individuals in our own right have to find a holistic range of techniques and protocols specifically designed to lower lipo-toxin loads which are not derivatives of ingestion detox and cleanse protocols. Because those are spectacularly unhelpful in terms of TBS eradication, simply because TBS is an insidious condition, dur to the fact it throws our entire body into a state of self destruct. When we're battling with TBS it can often feel as if everything we try to do to aid our recovery is continually disrupted by the influences of TBS.

I am the master of my own health, for I take my quality of health seriously

So it's not by chance that chronically ill individuals like myself move from lean muscle mass into surplus body fat generation we suffering from TBS. You see; I'm now one of those individuals who's bodily detox capabilities are so flawed that the only way my body can cope with my TBS load is to generate greater levels of body fat to encapsulate it in. The harder I work to lower my TBS load, the more toxins I release from their fat rich tomb and harder my body works to generate superfluous body fat to re-encapsulate my toxins in. The down side of that is:

(a) An increased risk of lipo diseased states.

And

(b) Every time I burn fat I'm thrown once again into intolerable TBS diseased state expression.

Nevertheless it's not all doom and gloom, my personal research and subsequent self testing in terms of lowering my own TBS expression has enabled me to enhance my own quality of life and so I'm confident that I will discover the optimum formula for lowering TBS expression in due course. For anyone diagnosed or experiencing TBS I say only this:

(a) Accept that you have a highly toxic soup trapped deep inside you.

And

(b) Do all that you can possibly do to eradicate that from you body.

But

I am the master of my own happiness, for its in my interests to live life to the full

(c) Under no circumstance embark upon any radical detox or dieting campaign for there is real danger if you do of you imposing an increased health risk upon your already fragile health state.

The road to TBS recovery starts with acceptance of the condition, followed only by an educated and holistic approach to lowering its insidious disease expression. Because the key to ultimate progression in anyone's pursuit of well-being is to understand that it is a toxic body that creates a toxic mind, not a toxic mind that creates a toxic body.

However at the point toxins are removed from the body, the mind clears, hopes rise and fullness in life can once more be ours to enjoy free of all unnecessary pain.

I am the master of my own health, for I take my quality of health seriously

Personal Notes

I am the master of my own happiness, for its in my interests to live life to the full

Personal Notes

I am the master of my own health, for I take my quality of health seriously

Personal Notes

I am the master of my own happiness, for its in my interests to live life to the full

The World Is My New Play Thing Yay

Yay...!	OMG !
Ur......!	Poor me !

Err..............phew maybe not.....!

I am the master of my own health, for I take my quality of health seriously

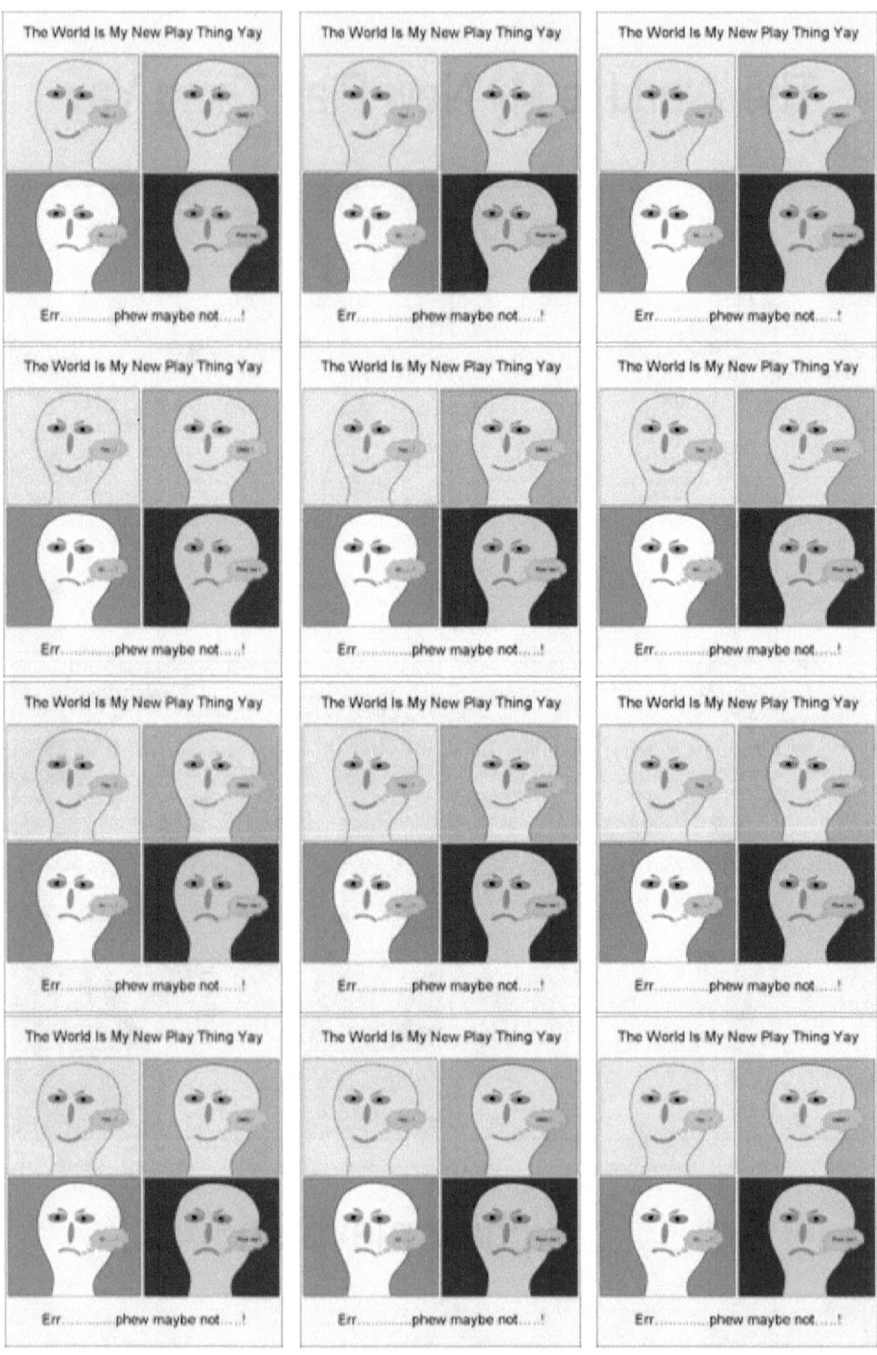

I am the master of my own happiness, for its in my interests to live life to the full

Expensive Illness Syndrome or EIS

One of the things that truly perplexes me in this life is the fact that whilst some men are born to travel and are continually committed to personal expansion others are simply content to vegetate in the comfort of well trodden paths and home. What's more there doesn't really seem to be any reliable tool out there that can prescriptively qualify which of those two groups any particular child will fall into at the point they embark upon their first worldly steps. All I know is that vegetating was never really for me and I always sort of gravitated towards individuals blessed with expansive personalities because that always better suited me. My slant on life was a complete paradox to that of my parents and siblings, so I guess it must have just been the way I was born to be, but who knows?.

Times have changed however since I was lad, because it's possible now to be a vegitator by persuasion whilst paradoxically acquiring ease of access to international travel opportunities in any given geographical location or time zone. You see, it's no longer the preserve of simply expansive personalities to travel around the world; anyone can do it now if they have the money, because in essence the fear in broadening horizons has been removed due to the corporate phenomenon that is globalization.

I am the master of my own health, for I take my quality of health seriously

Today it's difficult to tell whether we're in Cumbria, Paris, London or Katmandu because the planets high streets are the same where ever we go and communication technology is now so readily available that, people go off on so called expeditions whilst texting and emailing loved ones during every step of their journey.

These days travel doesn't seem to be about personal development and social integration, it seems to be more about having a blast in a different place whilst expecting to have access to all the creature comforts we take for granted at home. As a society, we in the west are guilty of collectively destroying the very essence of travel through ignorance of thought, mind and deed.

We've somehow allowed ourselves to slip into the mind set that we have a right to do and go wherever we want to go. And in that mind set we've somehow deluded ourselves as a society into thinking there is no difference between Cumbria, Paris, London or Katmandu but there is and it is that very fact which often results in the creation of preventable yet very expensive illnesses.

Now let me be very clear here, I do not have any problem with people wishing to explore new horizons, but I have a real problem with those who are not prepared and do not prepare themselves for the challenges that lay before them on their travels. I'm not talking here about obligatory vaccinations etc, I'm talking about accepting during your travels that you're not at home and as such you need look after your body in a completely different fashion. When we travel I firmly believe that we must be completely aware of the new environment we've proactively sort to place ourselves directly in. The insect dangers, the microorganism dangers, the hygiene dangers and geographical perceptions on life dangers, all of which I would respectfully suggest we disregard or dumb down at our peril.

I am the master of my own happiness, for its in my interests to live life to the full

I believe it's an essential part of our personal development to travel and to grow through that enlightening process. But I've encountered too many people who came back from a once in a life time experience chronically ill and/or chronically disabled. Simply because they didn't cross T's and dot I's prior to and during that once in a life time experience.

The real shame of which is that when they return back to the UK there's very little holistic medical intervention open to them. So be under no illusion that if you jet off to some far away destination and you pick up along the way some form of mysterious disease impediment. You can bet your last £10 that when you present yourself to your GP you will receive little to zero empathetic support for anyone one of them, save for perhaps the obligatory 'ME' handle etc.

You see, I have The Hospital for Tropical Diseases (HTD) in London 'bugger off' t-shirt BIG TIME, in fact I have two of them amongst my many abuse t-shirts hanging up with all my skeletons. So despite what you may think, there is very little help for Joe public if he or she picks up some form of internationally transmitted disease and because of that we all must look at international travel far more pragmatically than most of us would ordinarily choose to do so.

We have no God given right to travel anywhere in reality nor should we ever lure ourselves into the false perception that good medical insurance and few precautionary vaccinations are the secret to effective international travel. Be under no illusion, chronic disabling life sapping conditions can be picked up in far distant lands from a whole range of sources including through, water, food, sex and insects to name but a few.

I am the master of my own health, for I take my quality of health seriously

That being said I believe now that it's imperative prior to committing to sorting out the financing and visa arrangements of our trip that we take two steps back.

I advocate the first step back, because I would suggest that prior to any humanitarian of adventure driven international travel that the first thing we need to understand is, precisely how our body is functioning. The second step back I would suggest must focus upon, what naturopathic treatment options etc, are open to us prior to, during and after our adventure that will ensure that our immune system is currently and remains functioning effectively. When we've bottomed those two points out then of course we should have the obligatory vaccinations etc, if we decide to, whilst ensuring that we've bottomed the rest of our travel arrangements out effectively.

'So what you're saying Baz is that before international travel I should attend a well woman or well man clinic and have a MOT'? Er….well it's very understandable that you should think that's what I'm saying and whilst the MOT is a very good thing to have. But to be honest and indeed laboring a point what I'm actually advocating is far greater intrusion than a basic MOT.

I am the master of my own happiness, for its in my interests to live life to the full

What I'm actually advocating prior to any international travel is that you undergo detailed blood analysis of your Mitochondria. You see, there really is only one way to determine how well your bodily functions are performing and that's to investigate your capabilities at a cellular level. If you have normal Mitochondria function then it's reasonable to suggest that your body is:

(a) Adept at detoxing your body.

And

(b) There is no major underlying disease state ready to jump out on you should your body be challenged by a further disease state impediment during your travels.

If you have abnormal Mitochondria function however, then it's reasonable to suggest that your body is:

(a) Struggling to detox your body effectively.

And

(b) There may already be an underlying low grade disease state which may significantly compromise your immune systems ability to deal with additional disease state impediment picked up during your travels.

I am the master of my own health, for I take my quality of health seriously

Now the price of full blood Mitochondria function analysis may cost you anywhere between, £190-£250 but I would respectfully suggest that it's probably the most important thing anyone should do prior to international travel. Because at the point you have your results, not only do you fully understand how your body's functioning, but you also have a bench mark of your state of well being at your disposal for future reference.

Whether you proceed ahead with your travel upon receipt of your results is entirely up to you, but whatever you decide you will have a reference point which may prove invaluable should you then incur some form of disease state further down the line.

Now in relation to the second step back where I referred to naturopathic treatment options etc, I did so because I believe given my experiences with Lymes Disease that its essential at all time that we energize our body and do all that we can to keep any potential disease load to a minimum. No more so than when we are in far distant lands, where our body may be under attack on many many fronts every hour of the day. But when I refer to naturopathic options I'm not talking here about rattling with supplements etc, I'm talking here about simple unobtrusive things that we can do such as:

- Eating antimicrobial foods such as garlic etc, daily.

- Taking small amounts of organic sulfur weekly.

- Taking 1 or 2 drops daily of potent immune system enhancers' such as Samento, Cumunda and/or Grapefruit extract etc.

I am the master of my own happiness, for its in my interests to live life to the full

I believe that it's easy to accommodate the above into our daily regime, and what's more the cost and/or the storage requirements even in limited availability offer no significant impediment to a successful trip.

My experiences and the experiences of close associates would indicate that international travel can be extremely uplifting, but it also can have a very profound impact upon our quality of life if we don't take responsibility for our well-being seriously. If we fail to appreciate fully the potential for disease during and upon our return from international travels then we're in real danger of creating and hence imposing upon ourselves a very expensive state of illness. Expensive in terms of:

- You've paid to take yourself to a place of potential disease state imposition.

- Your health may become significantly compromised by your actions.

- Your general quality of life may become significantly compromised.

- Your career might simply fall apart as your health and your ability to cope become significantly challenged by the diseased state you've imposed upon yourself.

My take on international travel is, go for it if that's what you truly desire, but under no circumstance do so to the detriment to your own unique state of well being. Now the reason that I've put this chapter in here before the next chapter is because I wanted to set the scene to something that may happen to you if you're unfortunate to pick up a travel induced disease. You see, if you return from a trip aboard either with or go onto develop some for of disease state, you may find that all your attempts to find resolution through testing simply fall upon stony ground. Please spare yourself those distressing experiences by above all taking your travel responsibilities as seriously as you can.

I am the master of my own happiness, for its in my interests to live life to the full

Personal Notes

I am the master of my own health, for I take my quality of health seriously

Personal Notes

I am the master of my own happiness, for its in my interests to live life to the full

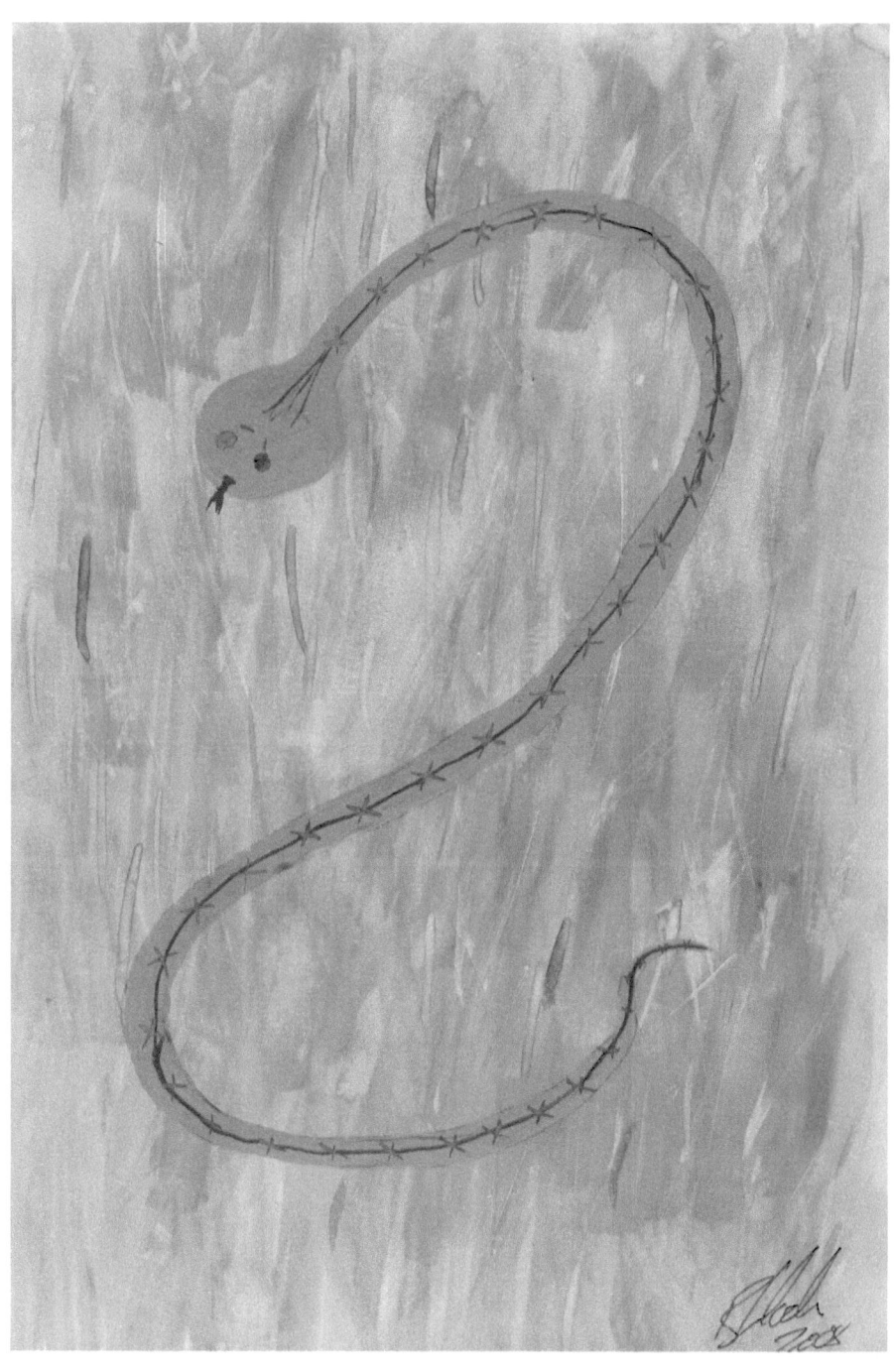

I am the master of my own health, for I take my quality of health seriously

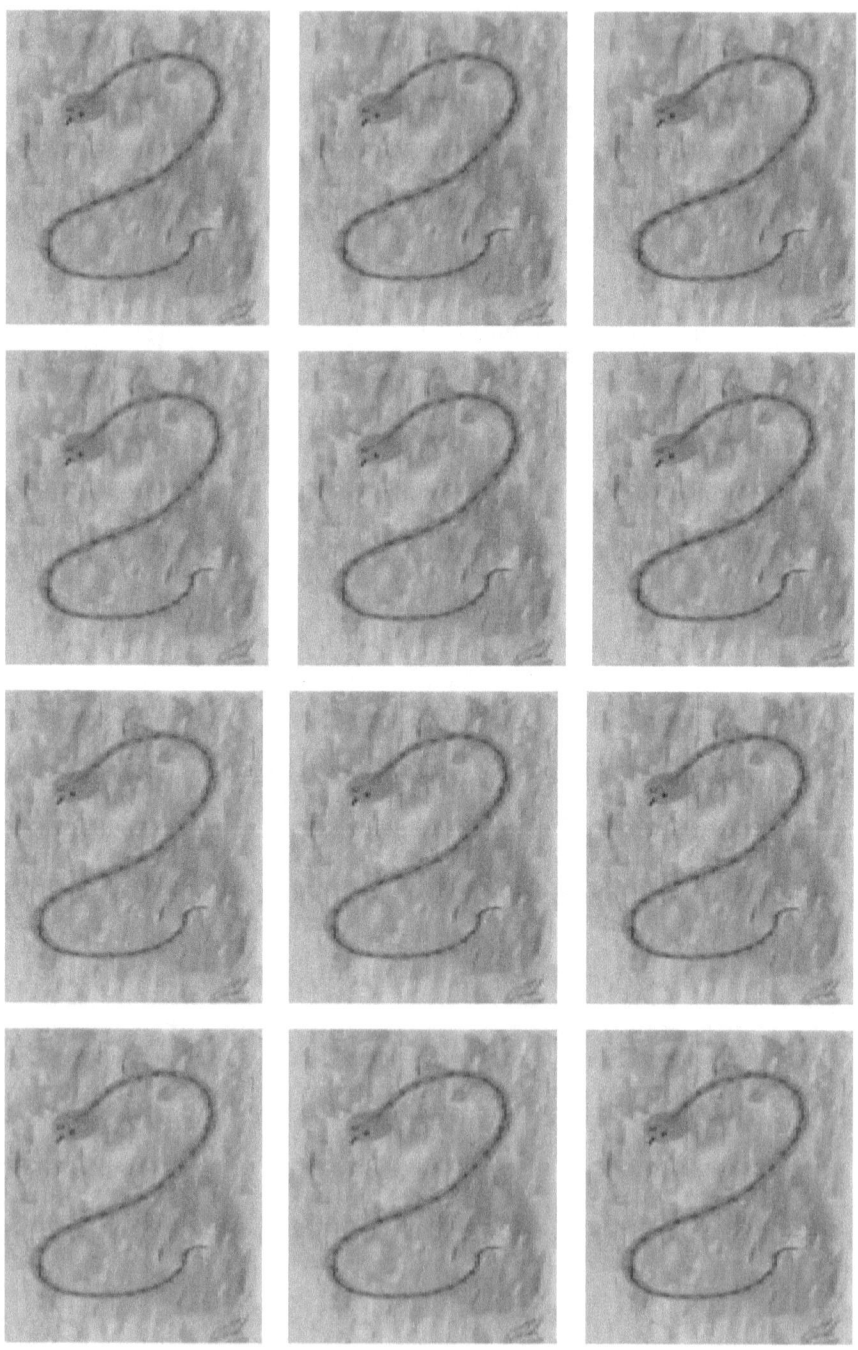

I am the master of my own happiness, for its in my interests to live life to the full

When testing has no sanity!

It's fair to say that some of us really go through the mill several times before our illness is finally diagnosed, yet at the point we're diagnosed we then hopefully via an effective treatment regime, can begin to make a substantive recovery from our presenting conditions. Sadly however, some of us actually never recover and that's primarily due to two reasons:

- Our condition is terminal.

- Or analytical sciences and clinical investigations are simply unable to detect a problem.

Ironically, during my baron chronic illness resolution days, whilst I was failed wholesale by UK analytical sciences and clinical investigations, I was diagnosed as terminally ill in the USA. How strange is that?

Well not that strange really when you scratch the surface of analytical sciences and clinical investigations in the UK. You see, the vast majority of tests, machines, and imaging devices that we have in the UK are not state of the art as the industry or our government would like us to believe. They're actually state of the ark. It's not until you actually analyse the state of that medical service sector that you find out just how bad things really are.

A situation compounded further by the front end medical cretins who request investigations and then either play a part or choose to abstain from interpolating any subsequent results objectively leaving us as the sufferer bemused.

I really don't think there can be anything worse than having a major health impediment and yet because of out dated and fundamentally flawed analytical sciences and clinical investigations no one can find anything wrong with you. At that point despite your intense suffering you're simply written off as a neurotic and the most alarming thing is that there is no difference either between the NHS and the private sector.

Time after time I've paid for very expensive consultations and tests and time after time some pompous, greedy, ignorant 'medical rogue' has said to me, 'actually there's nothing wrong with you your tests are normal Mr. Hardy' Followed by, 'have you considered psychiatric help?'

Equally in the NHS I've been abused in far too many situations by 'medical rogues' saying, 'Mr. Hardy there's absolutely nothing wrong with you it's all in your head' and their other favourite line, 'Mr. Hardy we can't keep on testing you why can't you just accept that you have a mental health issue?'

It is primarily because of all the rubbish and abuse I've had to endure that I advocate that we must take control of this situation. How dare some talentless, badly trained yet public sector worker say that the NHS can't keep testing me or anyone of us? I've / we've funded their bloody training, I / we've funded their bloody life styles and some of us have battled to preserve their bloody rotten industry from the ravages of Thatcherism. Boy do those 'charlatans' really make me angry.

I am the master of my own happiness, for its in my interests to live life to the full

You see, I really don't give a hoot if the NHS has to perform a thousand bloody tests upon me to find out what's wrong with me, that's what it's there for and therefore that's what it needs to do. Or it could certainly begin in the name of greater efficiencies, to look at the amount of money it's wasting on fundamentally flawed analytical sciences and clinical investigations and start bring its house in order.

Because if some clerical or 'clinical rogue' is assigning limits to the level of care that I can have from the NHS, then I for one now say let's have voluntary contributions to the NHS. Why should I a potential high earner pay ridiculous amounts of money to underwrite an industry that doesn't want to underwrite me when I need it? Yet it throws billions away on consultant's salaries and treats any chancer who decides to pop over to the UK for treatment.

Now hey I would never in a million years have thought that this working class lad from Woodhouse would ever have held such views towards the NHS. But having been exposed head on to all its woeful underperformance, ignorance and incompetence for years, I'm happy to voice my harsh views now. My belief now is that we need to bring this entire rotten industry crashing to its knees. So that as a nation we're able to build a clinical care service sector that is thorough, competitive; inspirational and world class and let's ditch the clap trap and rubbish of the past.

I am the master of my own health, for I take my quality of health seriously

The problem with that vision is that the people who have suffered most from its shoddy service are unfortunately the ones with the lowest vitality, presence or voice. So before any of its victims can commit to campaigning for change they need to get well for only then can they hope to bring about change. But be under no illusion that dynamic changes quickly at the point our health returns. Unfortunately the road to recovery can be lonely, long and unrewarding at times and so until we reach our desired destination, its best for all chronically ill patients to focus solely upon regaining their health and leave the clinical reform campaign to better times.

Prior to our return to health however, let me give you a flavour of what happens in the normal psyche when we're experiencing a health condition and require analytical sciences and/or clinical investigations. We immediately make either a big or small deal of the fact that our condition is going to be subject to further scrutiny. Some of us may be worried that something dreadful may be found, whilst others may simply be happy if something could be found to enable us to be treated, recover and move on. I've always come from the school of thought, 'I hope they can find something so that I could move on'. I've never subscribed to worrying about there being something dreadfully wrong with me, because I only ever wanted solutions. I knew for years that I had something seriously wrong with me; I just didn't know what it was. If we don't know what's wrong with us then we can't ever hope to recover and in poor health, recovery must be our sole interest if we wish to regain some form of quality of life. Therefore we must commit to testing and analytical investigations and when the results come through, we must do our level best to acknowledge them and deal with them as appropriately as we're able to or at the very least, see fit.

I am the master of my own happiness, for its in my interests to live life to the full

So let's play the cycle through now, our test results come back and they're always in the standard form of:

- (a) Your tests are normal.

- (b) Hmmn, there is a slight problem but that might just be congenital.

- (c) You have bla bla bla bla.

- (d) You need to make an appointment to discuss your results.

Now to understand the ramifications of that feedback we need to look at the two generic psyches I discussed earlier i.e. big or small deal propensity. So let's look at the big deal psyche first:

(a) Results normal = maybe happy deep down and prepared to take whatever the medical representative says in terms of treatments etc., but may ham it up a bit when speaking to colleagues, family and friends.

(b) Result might be a congenital issue = may be worried deep down yet prepared to take whatever the medical representative says in terms of treatments etc. Might however blow the condition completely out of proportion and will certainly ham it up a bit when speaking to colleagues, family and friends.

(c) Result you have bla bla = may be extremely worried and also might blow the condition completely out of proportion until reassured by the medic, but will certainly ham it up a lot when speaking to colleagues, family and friends.

(d) Result you need a follow up appointment = extremely worried and will blow the condition completely out of proportion, because that brings the drama they crave into their life. As long as it's a safe and controllable drama that's fine, should it however not be a safe drama then they will start off being publicly very brave and then simply implode putting tremendous pressure on anyone in close proximity.

I am the master of my own happiness, for its in my interests to live life to the full

So let's look at the small deal psyche now:

(a) Results normal = maybe confused deep down but prepared to take to some extent whatever the medical representative says.

(b) Result might be a congenital issue = may be worried but certainly interested in the result more from a clinical perspective than a sensationalist perspective.

(c) Result you have bla bla = may be worried but happy that there is something to discuss, but will need answers.

(d) Result you need a follow up appointment = worried until they understand what's wrong with them, but once they know they just get their heads down with it and are normally stronger than the people around them, who sometimes fall to pieces.

I am the master of my own health, for I take my quality of health seriously

Now look it doesn't really matter what personality type you fall into. The key to returning to optimum health is ensuring that you're either prepared to be driven or you're prepared to drive the situation. Either way your focus must be upon achieving optimum health, because if you're not experiencing optimum health then you need to understand why; assuming that is that optimum health is your real goal. I've postulated that we must all examine if optimum health is our real goal, and I raise that challenging point because whilst some people will say optimum health is their goal. You only have to talk or listen to them to understand that they are indeed lost or closed to the potential of optimum health. That is because some people really do like being ill, because in being ill they:

- Have the crutch they need.

- Don't need to compete.

- Can offload all their personal issues at the door of their illness or disease.

I am the master of my own happiness, for its in my interests to live life to the full

Now there is absolutely no crime in that, save to say, if a man does not wish to help himself, then perhaps help is not what he needs. You see there are no secrets to optimum health save for a desire to have optimum health, yet within that expectation and desire there are many levels of acceptance and abstinence. Only we as individuals have the sole right to make the value judgments that best meet our desires and needs.

My personal expectations have always been to secure a quality of life that is free from physical impediments and diseased states. Because of that I've mapped a holistic yet pragmatic approach to this process on the next page, now whilst it may initially look complex when you first see it. Just take time to follow some of the evolution and iteration loops from your own perspective and you'll find that it caters precisely for whichever mind set you are.

I am the master of my own health, for I take my quality of health seriously

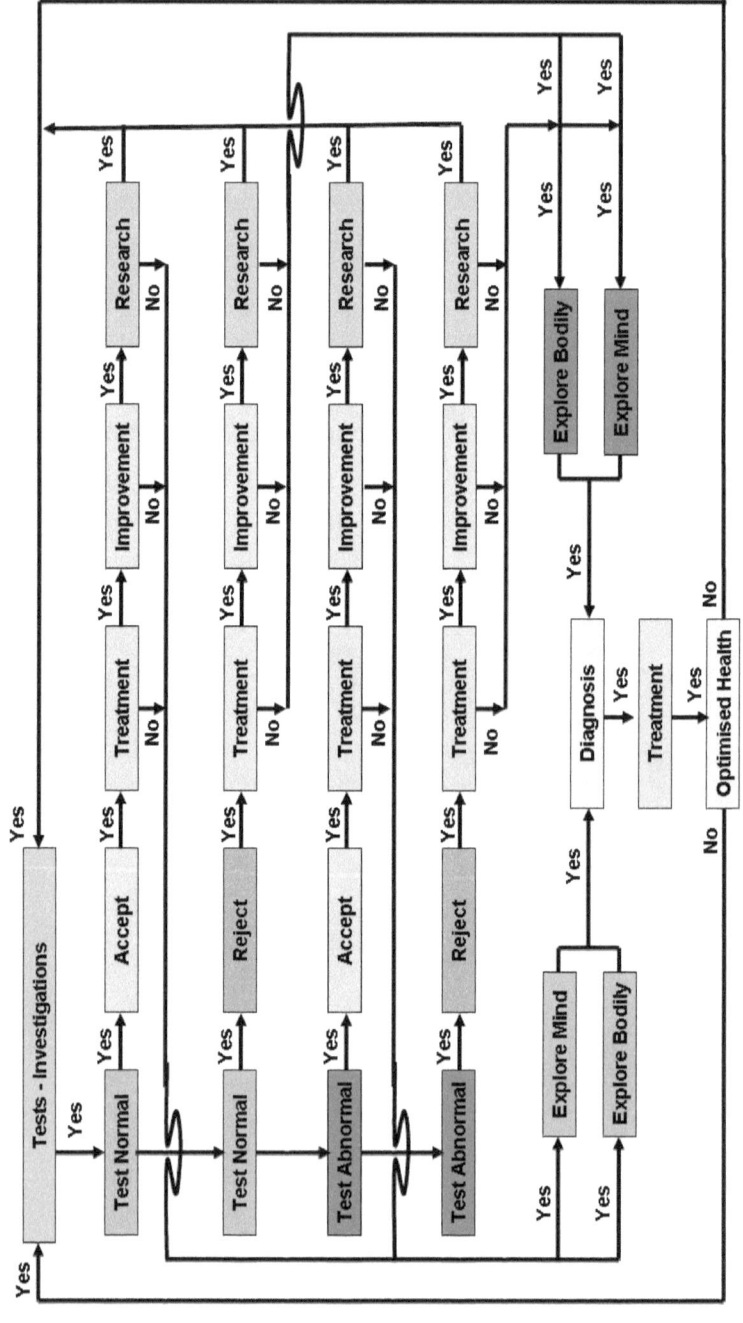

The only secret to having good health is ones personal determination to have good health

I am the master of my own happiness, for its in my interests to live life to the full

During my pre-diagnostic state my only abstinences were to reject wholesale any and all forms of clap trap or ignorantly manufactured dogma articulated to distract me from my goal. I advocate only this that in the pursuit of optimum health we all must accept that we alone are the responsible party for driving the process of recovery through diagnosis. For without our input, there is no other form of input worthy of comment and therefore no reasonable probability of making any form of sustainable recovery.

Yet whilst that is, or can be, a very difficult path for some of us to walk alone, in reality it's the only path that delivers access to clarity, understanding, effective treatment and recovery. It is by default however; a process of two stages, the first stage is the stage where we are in essence ignorant and unable to make progress because we rely completely upon false testing, consultations and investigations which have little if any merit. I've mapped that process for you on the next page, because once we understand all the loops in the process, it is no longer a mystery and can indeed become that defining point from which we all move forward.

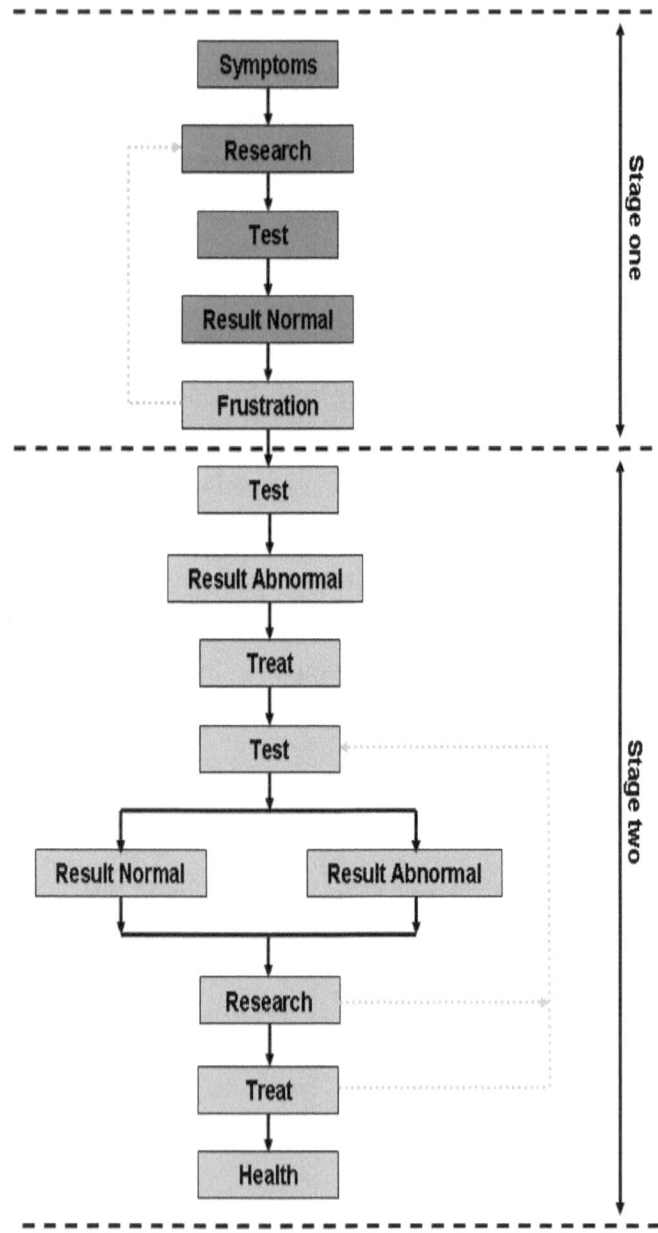

Ignore the doubters who say you can't keep on testing you can and you must

I am the master of my own happiness, for its in my interests to live life to the full

The second stage is where we take ownership of the intellect responsibility for substantiating our underlying condition or conditions. It is the point that we start unravelling our health mysteries, that remarkable point where we see the medical industry and those who support it for what and who they really are.

Both stages are incredibly difficult because they are both encountered when we have lower than normal vitality. Stage one will invariably consist of a 90% - 10% NHS and private involvement whereas 'stage two' will be the complete opposite i.e. 10% - 90% NHS and private involvement.

Therefore there are significant cost implications required of those attempting to return to a position of optimum health. Some of that money will be wasted and some of it will be money well spent. There is no right or wrong course of action to take, all we can ever be is true to ourselves and whilst we can't beat the obscene and perverse nature of the medical industry. We can get better through our own efforts and eventually realise our dreams if only we're prepared to drive the testing and analysis until a reflective diagnosis has been achieved. In my particular situation stage one of my investigation process consisted of nothing more than the following fundamentally flawed investigations below:

- 3 Liver enzyme tests.
- 3 Thyroid tests.
- 1 MRI.
- 1 CT.
- 1 X-ray investigation.

I am the master of my own health, for I take my quality of health seriously

The conclusions drawn from them were that I was fine and had nothing wrong with me except for mental health issues, time and time again. Whereas my stage two self funded investigations included:

- 5 MRI's.
- 2 MRA's.
- 4 CAT scans.
- 2 CT's.
- 60+ blood tests and bodily function analysis, tests and examinations.
- 9 Caloric Tests.
- 3 Hearing Tests.
- 9 ENG Tests.
- Two Neurosurgical procedures.
- 180+ clinical consultations all around the world plus travel and accommodation.
- Plus thousands of hours research on the internet long before cheap broad band, etc.
- In summation personal traceable costs in excess of 300K.

The result of my tenacity in the face of unbelievable odds was that I was eventually diagnosed with:

- Chronic late stage Lymes Disease.

- Chronic mitochondria failure.

- Chronic liver disease.

- Chronic adrenal insufficiency.

- And an extremely rare genetic yet organic anomaly resulting in a Posterior Inferior Cerebella Artery insulting my vestibular bundle and brain stem left side. *Note this condition still imposes great suffering upon me every minute of every day and that's why just putting my thoughts onto paper is such an almighty affair.*

Now look, the point I'm making is that there are far too many issues surrounding our poor medical investigation model and too many issues surrounding outdated machines and devices being postulated as state of the art diagnostic tools. How many of us actually know until we are faced with horrendous medical conditions just how bad the equipment and techniques used to analyse our bodies truly are through-out the nhs because if we did I'm sure our own dogs of war would be unleashed.

I am the master of my own health, for I take my quality of health seriously

How many of us have been for an MRI scan and been told that everything is normal, when in reality the MRI scanner being used is:

- Badly designed and maintained?

- Outdated and malfunctioning?

- An expensive piece of scrap metal?

- Operated by people who don't give a shit.

Now we all know the difference between top and low end motoring in terms of performance etc, but very few of us know that the same is the case in the medical industry. You see, in the push to kid us all into thinking our health is safe in their hands, NHS trusts all around the country installed sub standard equipment which in the majority of instances are nothing more than token gestures in terms of world class clinical investigation tools. The differences are so wide in terms of performing basic functions that it's like giving one man a set of binoculars and another an electron microscope to analyse the same bacteria, now that would be simply ridiculous wouldn't it?

Well the truth is, the state of our nation's clinical diagnostic tools is not simply ridiculous, it's actually a disgrace and we the front end users or mugs are the ones paying the highest price. We're sent for diagnostic investigations, the results come back normal and the result of that is, no further line of investigation undertaken despite the fact that your condition may continue to decline.

I am the master of my own happiness, for its in my interests to live life to the full

Simply because a shit piece of equipment operated by people who don't give a shit has indicating that you have no problem or in point of fact is unable to detect the problem you have. Now I sincerely hope that my observations through suffering and personal wasted expense has set off some alarm bells deep within you because those alarm bells need to resonate with us all as a society each and every day because we need this resolved not next year or next month I would respectfully suggest but tomorrow and it must happen before lunch time at the very latest.

Because I advocate that when and where there is evidence to suggest that the instruments, techniques, systems and protocols used to support clinical investigations are incapable of investigating with the degree of enquiry that we need, then we need to:

- Challenge the results.

- Find suitable systems etc, which can perform to the level and standard of integrity that we require.

You see, I'm no solo foot soldier here, millions of us are being written off every year by fundamentally flawed medical investigations, consultations and tests. So if you truly desire optimum health, you're going to have to fight for it with all your intellect, strength and might. You're going to have to:

- Ignore the personal and clinical prejudices that you encounter.

- You're going to have to spend money that you may not have.

- You're going to have to prove your condition yourself.

Because if you think for one moment that the state, the NHS or our private medical health circus will resolve anything more than a superficial health impediment then your sadly mistaken because they won't. Only you can drive this stage two part of your pursuit of disease expression reflective diagnosis, because in reality there really only is you who truly gives a damn. So to help keep you upbeat and focused during that process I've mapped a very simple process approach plan for you below.

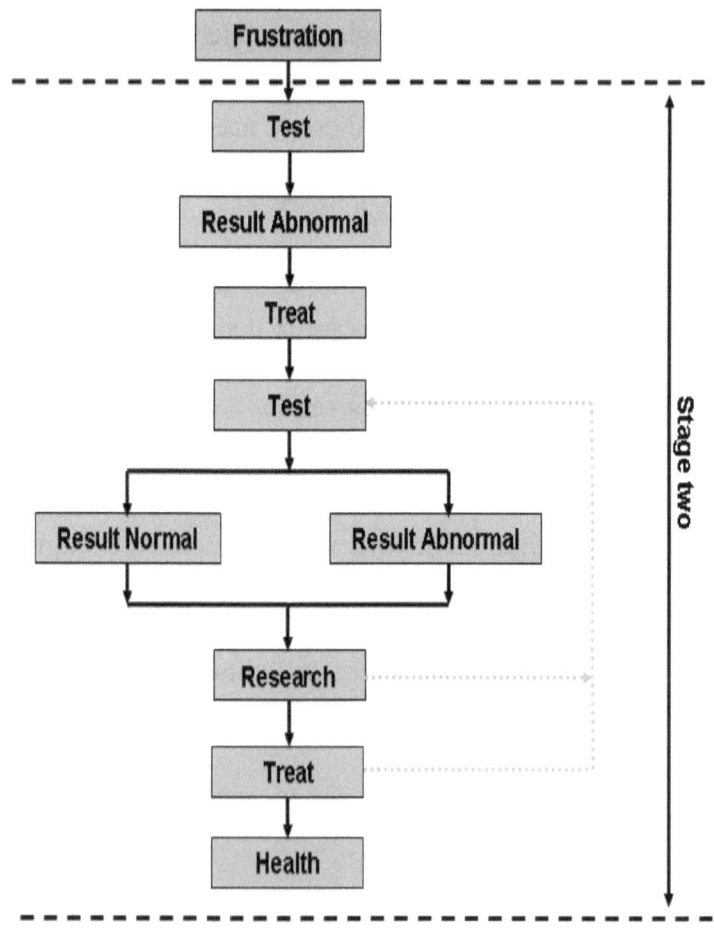

Ignore the doubters who say you can't keep on testing you can and you must

I am the master of my own happiness, for its in my interests to live life to the full

So that when you're at the other end of your health recovery campaign you can then speak from a platform of assurance, confidence and righteousness. You can challenge the integrity of those who failed you, ignored or abused you, because at that point you're more than an equal for anyone who would choose to play games with you because you're able to ask with assurance:

- Why are we as a nation wasting so much money on fundamentally flawed tests etc., whilst writing people off with impunity?

- Why are some of us, with a desire to be well, having to self research, self fund and self acquire best in class medical and clinical investigations outside the UK?

- Where is the medical establishment when we need it?

- Who within our current appalling medical service sector ranks can dare to defend this level of clinical and administrated incompetence?

I am the master of my own health, for I take my quality of health seriously

There really is only one way to ensure that you get through your health predicaments and that is to take control of your stage two process whilst ensuring you stay in total control of your entire health optimisation process re: below.

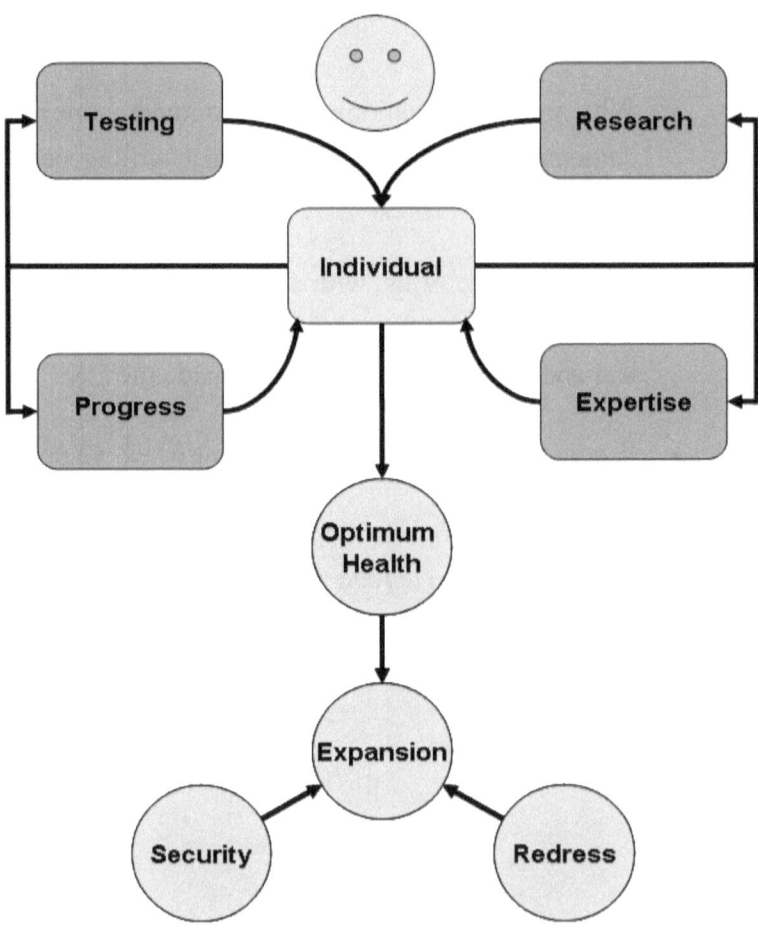

Taking Individual Control of All Health Related Processes

I am the master of my own happiness, for its in my interests to live life to the full

Personal Notes

I am the master of my own health, for I take my quality of health seriously

Personal Notes

I am the master of my own happiness, for its in my interests to live life to the full

Personal Notes

I am the master of my own health, for I take my quality of health seriously

Personal Notes

I am the master of my own happiness, for its in my interests to live life to the full

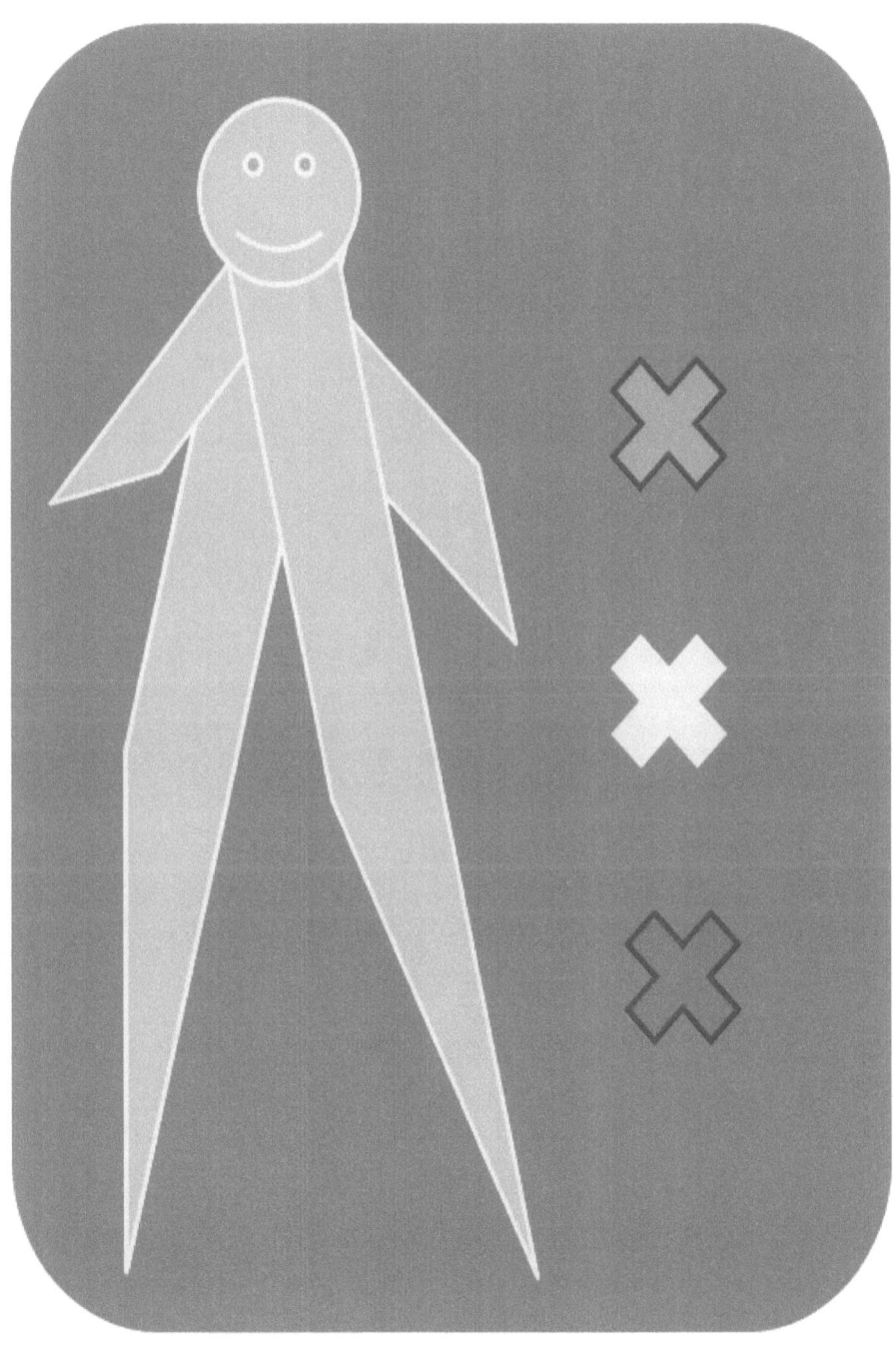

I am the master of my own health, for I take my quality of health seriously

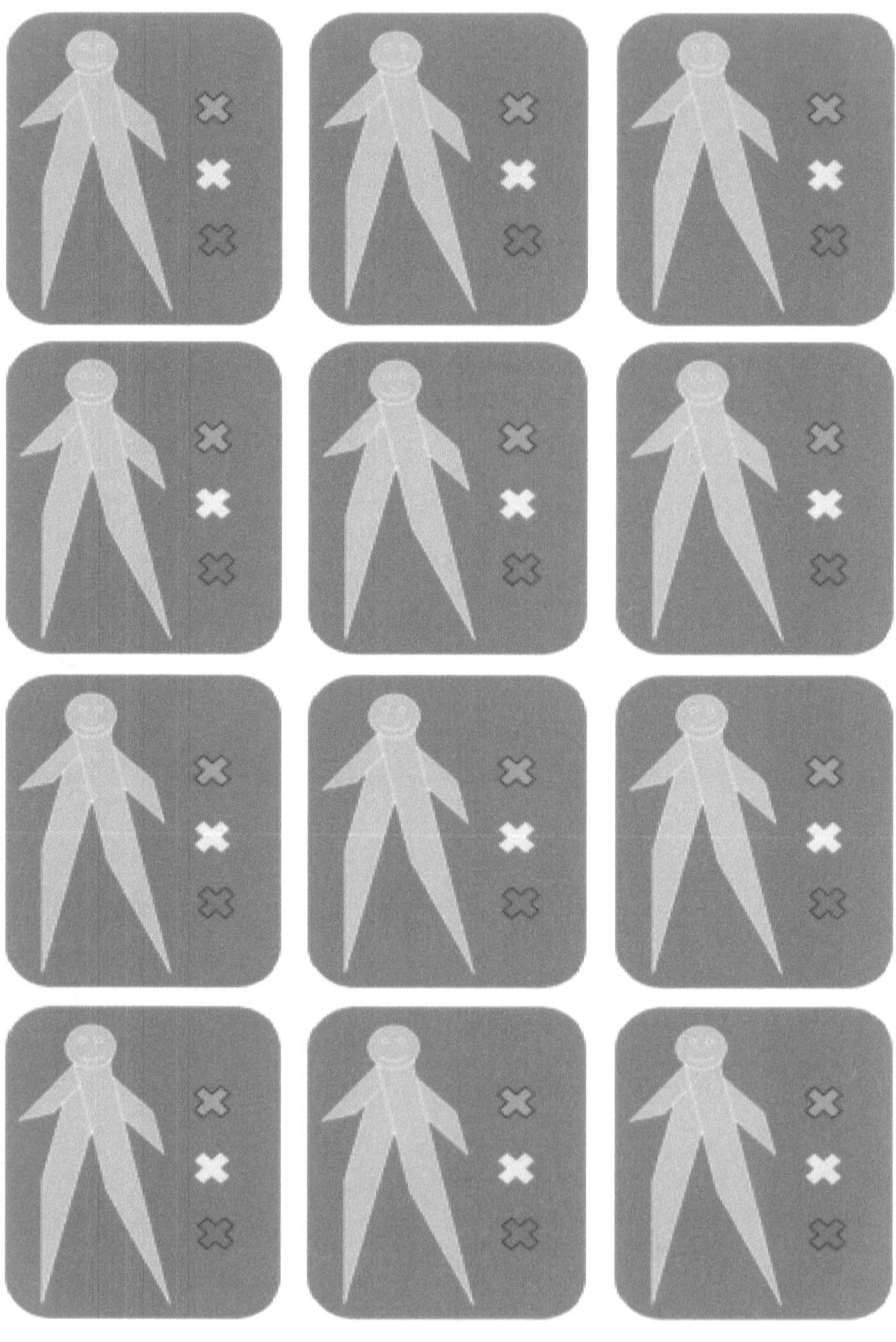

I am the master of my own happiness, for its in my interests to live life to the full

ANALYTICAL TESTING OPTIONS

I've made great play throughout this book of the need for effective testing and re-testing if necessary, to enable effective diagnosis of underlying diseased states. Yet whilst those tests can take many forms including: imaging and bodywork. I believe that the key to identifying the root cause of any chronic condition begins with effective blood and biochemical marker analysis. The clinic that I used for my detailed blood analysis via my private GP Dr. Sarah Myhill referrals was 'Biolab Medical Unit UK'.

Biolab Medical Unit is a; medical referral laboratory specializing in nutritional and environmental medicine which is located in the heart of the West End of London. They are a nutritional biochemistry laboratory measuring vitamin and mineral levels, toxic metals, other biochemical levels that are related to the availability of vitamins, minerals and other nutrients. They have an extensive range of profiles for assessing the effects of twenty-first century lifestyles on our bodies and are dedicated to assisting doctor's sort out their patients' problems in a way that does not rely on drugs as a first line of treatment. Biolab apply modern scientific laboratory analytical methods to establish what imbalances there are in the bodies of those who are suffering ill-health or non-optimum health, so that these imbalances may be addressed via nutritional and non-drug means, with the aim of achieving good health or, at least, improving the quality of life and minimizing suffering.

I am the master of my own health, for I take my quality of health seriously

I would therefore suggest that it's worth visiting their website at www.biolab.co.uk/ for a more detailed overview of their services, staff and publications etc. However please note that Biolab Medical Unit (UK) is a referral unit and will only perform tests requested by practitioners registered with;

- The General Medical Council.

- The General Dental Council.

- The General Osteopathic Council.

- The General Chiropractic Council.

All test reports will be sent to your practitioner as Biolab will not enter into direct discussions with you about your results, although they are happy to discuss their findings in relation to your tests with your practitioner.

It's important to note that I have absolutely no commercial, professional or personal arrangement with Biolab Medical Unit or any other analytical service provider. Furthermore those services providers will be completely unaware of my personal use of their services or my recommendation of their services. I would nevertheless strongly urge any individual suffering from a chronic health condition and wishing to undergo private blood investigations etc., to discuss their case with their medical/clinical service provider and request that they enter into discussions with respective analytical service providers such as Biolab. But be under no illusion that you may find that an uphill battle because medics in general traditionally poo poo anything that deviates from their own

I am the master of my own happiness, for its in my interests to live life to the full

ignorant perspectives. If that is the outcome of your discussions then you have only three choices open to you:

(a) Stay with your current service provider.

(b) Secure more appropriate service support.

Or

(c) Give up completely on life.

Ultimately as the masters of our own health and happiness we must make the choices we feel are best for us and in that we must be prepared to stand or fall, live or die by the choices we choose to make.

I am the master of my own health, for I take my quality of health seriously

Personal Notes

I am the master of my own happiness, for its in my interests to live life to the full

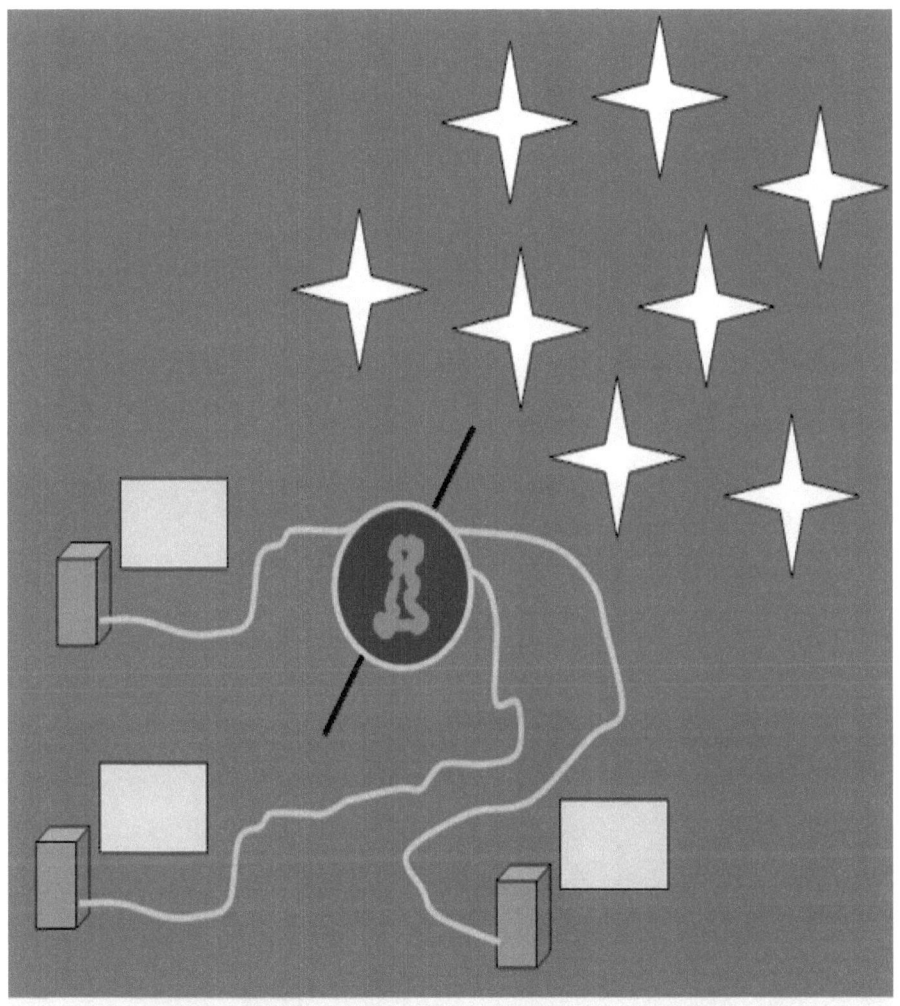

I am the master of my own health, for I take my quality of health seriously

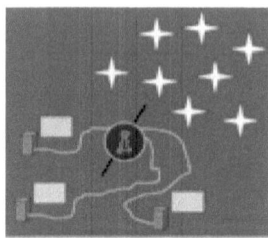 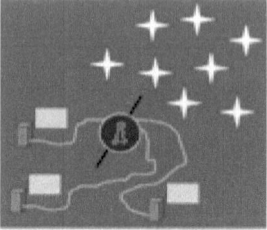 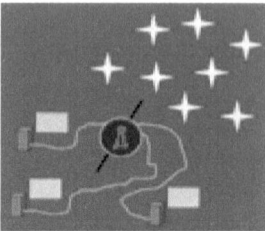
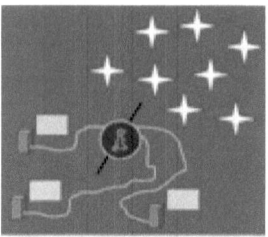 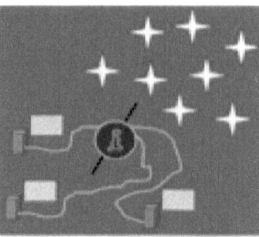 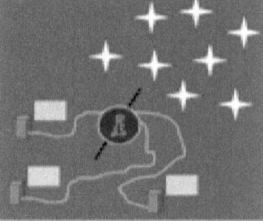
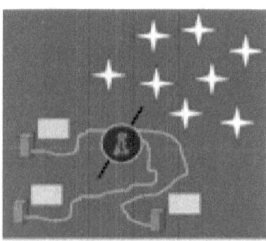 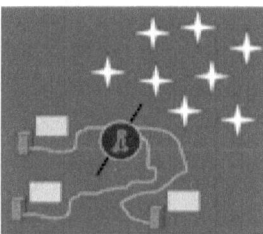 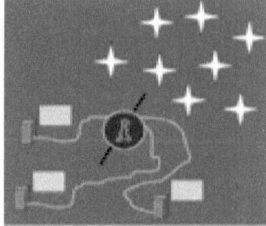
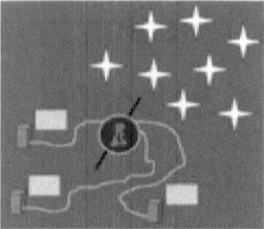 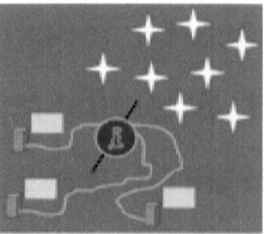 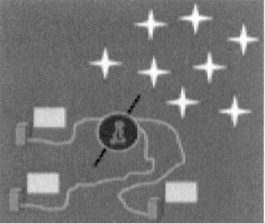

I am the master of my own happiness, for its in my interests to live life to the full

Last night the internet saved my life

You know, despite the heartache, suffering, pain and ignorance I've endured because of my chronic health issues. I am indeed fortunate to have been born at a time when the world's knowledge is so readily at everyman's disposal and more than that, the majority of it is free. The World Wide Web has simply transformed all our lives and whilst some aspects of it encourage self indulgence and create opportunities to corrupt or seek to gain advantage through deviant activities. It is nevertheless the most powerful tool that those seeking knowledge have ever had at their disposal since the beginning of modern times.

Had I been born and become ill at any point prior to the web's installation in our psyche, there is no doubt in my mind that I would be dead by now. The web enabled me to challenge not only my own personal perceptions but also those of the medical world who were failing me. From my bed the web afforded me ease of access to and hence understanding of all relevant issues relating to my physiology, endocrinology, neurology, toxicology, psychology and ultimately my diseased state pathology. It invigorated me, challenged me and misled me. Yet in the end it rewarded me with insight and for that I owe my life to our magnificent World Wide Web.

I am the master of my own health, for I take my quality of health seriously

Well actually the World Wide Web as we know it is just a platform of information. I actually owe my life to the men and women who felt the need to populate it with insight, with discussion but above all with endless possibilities. *'I'm hoping that you know what I mean yeah? So guess I've sort of put that one to bed quickly too as well eh? Time to move on, yet I can hear you asking yourself 'what was the point of creating a chapter just to say the web saved my life'?* Well the reason I wrote this chapter is an extremely valid point because it sort of puts my achievements in recovering from overwhelming and unsupported chronic health conditions into some kind of perspective.

As I've said many times in this book, I'm nothing special and will never claim to be anything other than a guy with a bit of intellect, a lot of tenacity and some very challenging or stimulating views and all that is depending upon where your personal slant on what I have to say takes you. But if I had a pound for every minute I'd spent researching, contacting and engaging with diseased state visionaries via the world wide web, I wouldn't need to worry about money or my personal finances for the rest of my life. You see we're not talking here about days, weeks, or months of research. We're talking about years of researching, contacting and engaging with scientist far clever than me. I'm talking about:

- Incredible personal expense, meeting up with scientist from all round the world.

- Self funding personal research.

- Self funding treatment protocols.

- We're talking about a level of commitment which I would even qualify myself unreservedly as obsessive.

I am the master of my own happiness, for its in my interests to live life to the full

Yet it had to be obsessive, it had to be full on, it had to be self-funded because I couldn't stand being in my body one moment longer than I needed to be and no one was going to do anything to help me. The World Wide Web was:

- My only tool.

- My only salvation.

- My only life line to sanity.

- It was the only mechanism that would eventually validate everything I'd ever said to anyone about any and all of my presenting chronic illness symptoms and conditions.

Now that sounds great eh? As and when we acquire a problem all we need to do is go online and hey presto, a bit of surfing and the problem is immediately solved. Er.......well no, its nowhere near as easy as that, the web is an inanimate oracle, its not a mind reader, if you don't know what you're looking for then you will never find an answer on the web. But you may well end up with either a headache or a degree of emotional stress if you fail to understand or get to grips with the first principles of internet searching.

To surf the web effectively you obviously need technological interfaces which enable adequate information access, speed and responsive search capabilities. Whilst current technologies include high speed broadband via fiber optic cable or wireless, who knows what tomorrows technology will bring. Nevertheless, it's safe to say that the faster you can access information, the faster you can move on if it either stimulates you or draws you down an information dead end.

I am the master of my own health, for I take my quality of health seriously

To find answers on the web you need to know what you're looking for, but to know what you're looking for you need to legitimise your own thought processes in the first place. In terms of a health condition that means qualifying what you think is wrong with you, then doing some abstract searches around that theme whilst noting points of interest that are derivatives of that search. The key is that any and all derivatives of your search may or may not have a direct synergistic link to your presenting conditions but they may open up a whole host of differing thoughts for you to explore.

Let me give you an example of what I mean, during the pre-diagnosis stage of my chronic Lymes Disease, I had the most appalling inter-cranial pressure i.e. pressure inside my head. Although I searched high and low for that symptomology I never came across any site or page that gave any indication of that particular symptom. That was until I stumbled across a page which was looking at cerebral spinal fluid movements and inflammation of the meninges. That page then indicated other pages of interest where disease was being cited as the actual cause for deviations to cerebral spinal fluid movement and inflammation of the meninges. At that point, I had my first insight into the possibility of creating a sense of pressure inside the cranium which would never be picked up by standard investigations or standard investigation techniques.

I am the master of my own happiness, for its in my interests to live life to the full

Now hey that finding didn't just happen in a day, in a week or in a month it took months and months of painfully slow and unrewarding searching. But it's a very good example of abstract links leading us onto a possible point of meaning i.e.

- I had pressure inside my head.

- I learned that the brain was bathed by a fluid *cerebral spinal fluid* in a sort of balloon *the meninges* that also has a long tube attached to it which ran down the entire length of the spine.

- These mechanisms could be affected and inflamed by disease.

- All I had to do was identify potential disease sources and then find a way of testing for their presence.

Now here is something that may or may not blow you away because I have no way of substantiating what I'm about to say. But after years of searching on the web I'm consciously aware now that the web will only divulge its mass of secrets when your karmic energy is in a zone to receive the missing links you're so desperately trying to find.

You can search day after day using similar phraseology a bit like a fisherman on the banks of a river and find or catch absolutely nothing. Then for no apparent reason the flow of information on one particular day is quite simply mind blowing to the extent that your understanding of the situation is propelled much further than your original expectations ever envisaged.

As I say, I have no way to validate that statement and I'm aware it could be challenged on many intellectual levels. But whether I'm right or whether I'm wrong it's irrelevant to me for a whole host of reasons. Because it's something I've experienced far too many times now to simply intellectualise its reality or likewise foolhardily ignore it. It's a real phenomenon and experience to me. So much so that when I'm searching on line now and making no progress, I accept that it's not the right time to progress with that search. So I simply leave my enquiry for another day. Time after time in recent years I've found that by letting things go and coming back to them on another day my searches become significantly more fruitful and are now a joy to behold. The World Wide Web is a truly marvelous thing most of the time but as with everything in life it too has a darker side.

Oh yes, let us never forget that there is a darker side to the World Wide Web, because it is also the playground of harpies or those from the darker side of life. They populate the web with:

- Misinformation.

- They postulate that they're something they're not.

- They infiltrate chat rooms and forums and lure people in whom they know are vulnerable.

So if I have any words of advice for people looking for health resolution issues on the web, I would say this:

- Join no forums.

- Stay clear of all self help groups.

- Stay clear of single illness websites.

I am the master of my own happiness, for its in my interests to live life to the full

Because the majority of misinformation that you will find on those sites will serve only to compound your endeavours' to find answers or improve.

You see; I learned the hard way that health forums etc were just the playgrounds of the sick of mind and the mindless sick. For me web forums play no part in exploring boundaries, no part in helping to change the way of things, the majority are simply there to provide a platform from which anyone can air their despairs.

Now look not all web forums are of the nature that I've just described, some are supportive, some are informative and some are a combination of both. But the majority are nothing more than misinforming, sycophantic, ego massaging dangers to society because within their midst sit some of the darkest of all living souls. People who perversely enjoy:

- Misinforming people.

- Stringing people along.

- Who delight in talking shit.

- Who relish the opportunity to build lines of dialogue with people they know they will never meet.

I am the master of my own health, for I take my quality of health seriously

All the best forums I'm lead to believe are policed to prevent the sick of mind from corrupting the integrity of the site. Ironically my identity was once checked without my knowledge by an associate link of one of the UK's thyroid sites. This is a bit scary because I must have been perceived as one of those cyber sicko's I've just mentioned as I pleaded for answers and described in my innocence the sheer despair and the hell I was in. So without labouringing the point, just be very careful on any self help site or forum, people are not always what they appear to be, in thought, in word or in deed. In fact there are people out there making lines of enquiries about you which in some instances are in breach of data protection.

The other main reason I detest such sites is because I've never received a relevant answer to any question I ever posted on a health related website. It's simply astonishing to me that there are millions of these sites all around the world and yet it doesn't matter which one you go onto or what illness it's actually focusing upon there are never any answers on them. Just clap trap, poor me stories and lots and lots of anecdotal misinformation. Let me give you a flavour of the sort of shit I encountered:

My Post: 'Hi my names Baz I have terrible pressure inside my head, my eyes feel like they will explode and I have chronic suicidal depression, has anyone come across this before?'

Posted Reply: 'Hi Baz, simon here, never heard of that but I have a pain in my left foot when I bend it and my chiropodists says perhaps I should change my shoes have you ever thought of that?'

I am the master of my own happiness, for its in my interests to live life to the full

Now hey I'm not joking here that is the sort of thing that happens on these sites. Plus there are the real numpties or sickos who reply with the same one line comment for every question posted i.e. someone posts a question about a pain they have in their left shoulder, the numpty or sicko has been sitting there waiting for a new question and then immediately reply's back with; 'have you tried coffee enemas?' No matter what the subject or what the question is posted, the reply from the numpty or sicko, 'have you tried coffee enemas?'

Now I'm not joking here this is for real every question posted; reply 'have you tried coffee enemas?' Now if it wasn't so sad it would be funny, but it isn't funny because someone is looking for answers and some numpty or sicko is simply connecting with them for connecting sake but in reality has absolutely nothing to say. You know its simply mind blowing to me that people are prepared to live like that, sending shit bloody emails to each other which are simply ridiculous e.g.

- *Posted email from sam:* 'Hey poppy; ruby says you had a bad day yesterday so I'm sending you a big snuggly, wuggly hug to make you feel better'

- *Posted reply from poppy:* 'Hey sam thanks for that I really need it, bug hug to you too babe'

- *Posted reply from sam:* 'No worries bade you're the best'

- *Posted buy-in from ruby:* 'Hi guys, its good that we're able to help each other with this big big love support, big hug to anyone who needs one today'

- ***Posted reply from poppy:*** 'Hey ruby same to you brave heart'

- ***Posted reply from sam:*** 'Hey ruby go for it! girl power'

I mean what has this got to do with a bloody ME site? What has this got to do with a Thyroid site? Or with any site designed to help promote insight into the complexities of chronic health conditions?

These sorts of people should all just stick to the 'let's waste our bloody life sites' and let the rest of us desperately trying to find answers to our problems get on with it without their puerile interference and chatter.

Now whilst some of the girl power merchants may cry 'foul' or 'you intolerant male pig' my answer is only this; I am not an intolerant male pig far from it, I just don't' do rubbish or forum trivia. Because I believe that if we wish to get well then we have to do all that we can to realise that goal. Equally if we want to wallow in self pity and slap the backs of fellow mind sets then we may as well give up all hope of wellness because either clearly that's beyond us or we don't really want it anyway.

My choice is knowledge, my choice is the pursuit of optimum health, if I had time for trivia, if I had time for 'clap trap' then I would simply choose to live my life that way. But I don't, so until then I'll leave that shallow way of existing to others who prefer that way of life, whilst proclaiming loud and clear 'long live the glorious, free '**World Wide Web**' Just be careful of the harpies and the trivia merchants who insidiously permeate every aspect of it. And on that very note I'd like to send out a: 'big snuggly wuggly hug to all the trivia email merchants out there in the hope that when you've grown up a bit and begun to live like true adults you'll realise the sincerity of my snuggly, wuggly intent'.

I am the master of my own happiness, for its in my interests to live life to the full

Personal Notes

I am the master of my own health, for I take my quality of health seriously

Personal Notes

I am the master of my own happiness, for its in my interests to live life to the full

I am the master of my own health, for I take my quality of health seriously

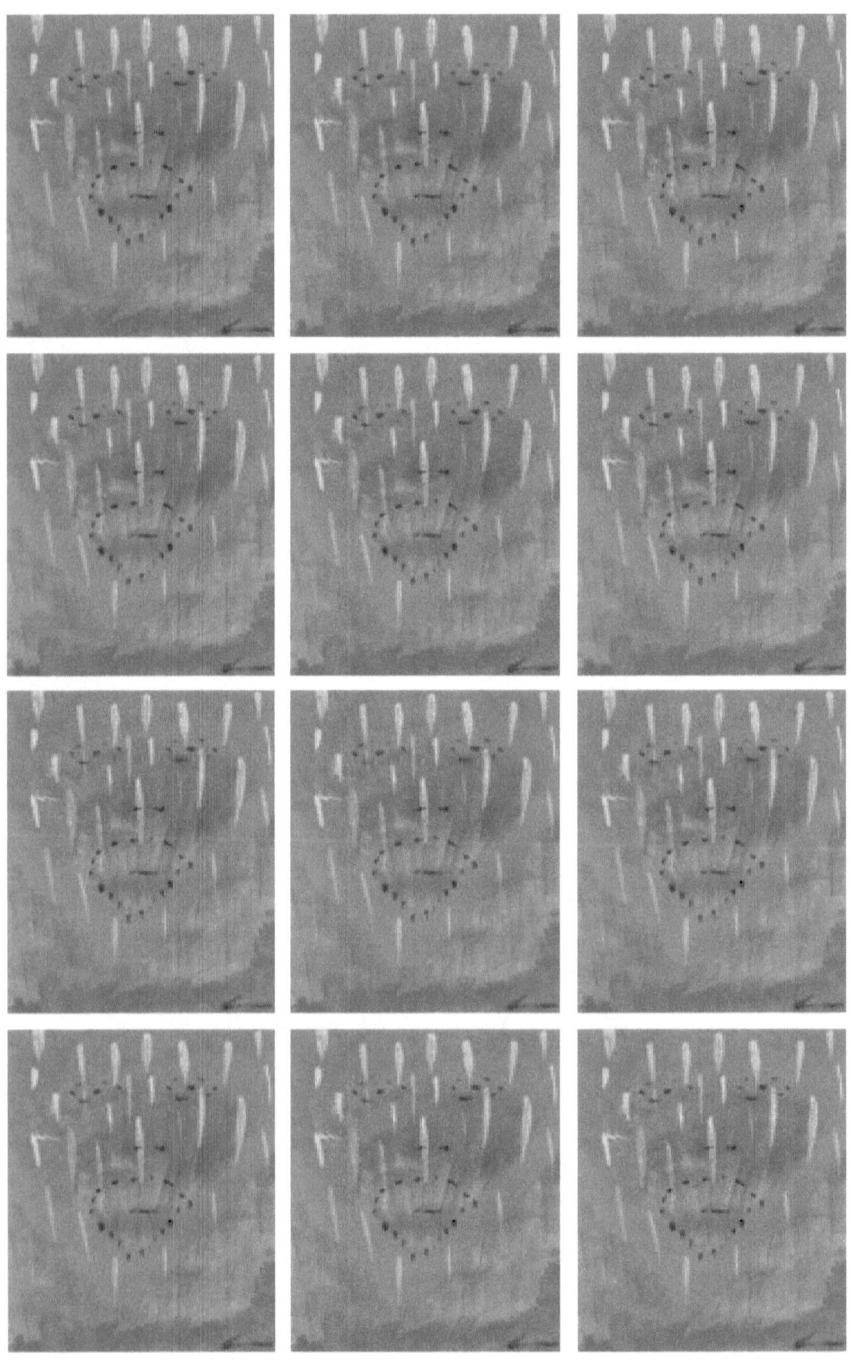

I am the master of my own happiness, for its in my interests to live life to the full

Spare Us All From The Numpties Of This World

You know if there is one thing that has really tested my patience in this life it's been the numpties that have imposed themselves and their agenda upon me and my life. But what you may ask are numpties? Well, they are in the most part plausible scoundrels interested only in their own perverse slant on life. In your company they will exchange niceties with you however when your back is turned they will tongue lash you with extraordinary bile simply because in reality that's all a numpty can bring themselves to do.

Numpties are the sort of people who somehow develop an illusionary view of their own intellect and/or intellectual capabilities. They appear to delight in ridiculing people and people's ideas and they create scenarios of intrigue and false spin just for the sake of it.

One may think reading this that there appears to be no difference between being a numpty and Machiavellianist. Well there most certainly is, you see; to be a Machiavellianist ones needs to have a modicum of intellect where as to be a numpty all you need to have is a degree of dysfunctional self belief in your own intellect and capabilities. The real difference however between a numpty and a Machiavellianist is that whereas a Machiavellianist works hard to heighten and/or safeguard their perceived station in life.

I am the master of my own health, for I take my quality of health seriously

A numpty is too thick to understand the delineations of station and intellect in life and therefore they always presume that they hold the higher intellectual ground and status on any issue that stimulates their interests. What's more; numpties come in all shapes and sizes, authors, lawyers, plumbers, GP's, window cleaners, engineers, dentists, road sweepers etc, it really doesn't matter, however if you're born a numpty you're always a numpty and that's just the way it is.

Okay well I've read what you have to say Baz and whether I believe you or not on this why should we need to be spared of numpties? Well the reason we all need to be spared of numpties is because they are all guilty of the same troublesome things. They will all misrepresent the truth of a point of view when ever they can, no numpty will ever put their neck on the line for anyone else, but all numpties will plant seeds of doubt when and wherever they can. It is for those reasons that we all need to be spared from the imposition of numpties in our life.

The problem is as I've suggested, numpties are very plausible initially, they appear to be friendly, they appear to be understanding and they appear to be approachable. It's only at the point that you begin to truly hear what a numpty has to say that you begin to understand how divisive a numpty can be. Because whilst a numpty may have lots to say, you can bet your last ten quid that if you ask them to validate or justify anything they've just said, they will immediately become defensive, aggressive or even just close the conversation down. There will always be an excuse why they cannot help you or participate in anything you request of them. They will always make their excuses and leave a situation at the point they think they're going to be asked to participate in something and not lead a line of approach or conversation.

That's just the way that numpties are, and that's why we all need to be spared from the intrusion of numpties in our lives. You see numpties in reality contribute absolutely nothing positive to any of our lives; their active participation in our lives is only to allow them to spew their own puerile garbage that they've convinced themselves is true.

A numpty will very rarely take the time to understand anyone at a humanistic level, because they're far too busy creating their perverse perception of everyone they meet, deep inside their head. So that when you do anything or say anything from your own personal experiences or beliefs that they themselves either don't or can't understand! They will completely misrepresent what you've said, and they will denigrate you behind your back to anyone prepared to give them the time of day.

A numpty will never hug you with sincerity, support you or say I believe in you, or even suggest that you should go for something that you truly believe in. Because to do that would propel them above the level of a numpty and they simply don't have the intelligence or integrity to bring that sort of rationale into play.

No a numpty will always sell you a myriad of negatives and then excuse themselves from your company with a childlike glee, because the only thing a numpty is interested in, is what is best or good for them. But why you may ask have I written this chapter and what on earth do numpties have to do with getting well?

Hmmmn are you ready for this? Well the biggest problem we all face in recovering from chronic illness is that we are all surrounded by bloody numpties. Because numpties are everywhere, and what's more they just love to spew their bile onto everything we mention, suggest or explore with them.

I am the master of my own health, for I take my quality of health seriously

They are the fountains of all knowledge or so they believe, but interestingly enough I've never met a numpty that's ever done, experienced or developed anything of any validity. But then again why would they, its far less taxing just to talk the garbage they talk because in doing that they spare themselves the effort of walking the walk.

Such is my utter contempt of numpties that I fantasize about having a air horn in my pocket and every time I hear a numpty go off on one I just pull it out of my pocket and set it off bellowing attention, attention evacuate the area, numpty on the loose.

Now excuse me if I've rattled on a bit here, but do you know what I think it's very liberating to get things like the numpty phenomenon off my chest. I think its just part of my overall perception on life and perhaps even a bit of karmic clearing. Either way I really want you the reader to be able to recognise these wastes of space from now on when you encounter them and I want you to visualise blasting your own imaginary air horn at them.

You see, I want anyone interested in helping themselves through a chronic illness predicament to accept that we don't need numpties in our lives, be they siblings, partners, lovers, work colleagues or so called friends. Because all that we need is strength of personality, sound clinical support and a bit of good luck from time to time.

As for the numpties, well they can all bugger off because there's enough pressure in this life without allowing ourselves to be brought down by what are complete wastes of space and absolute shits. However the good thing is that numpties are ever so easy to spot, and below are just a few of the opening lines that a numpty will open a conversation with, so just see if you can spot any numptyness in the people currently close to you e.g.

I am the master of my own happiness, for its in my interests to live life to the full

- I'm told that!
- They say that!
- If I had my way I would!
- Keep this to yourself but!
- I was gong to do that but!
- I don't know who she thinks she is but I could tell you!
- I remember him when he was only a!
- I'm not sure but they say that!
- You didn't here this from me but I've heard that he's!
- Who are you to say that to me I will tell you this!
- Well it's none of my business but!
- Correct me if I'm wrong but you told me that!
- Don't quote me on this but I've heard that he!
- I know what I would do if I were you!
- I can't speak for you but if I were you I would!
- Oh no I think you're wrong I would never have said that!
- OMG I have you heard about Baz, well I could always tell it was going to end in tears!

I am the master of my own health, for I take my quality of health seriously

Personal Notes

I am the master of my own happiness, for its in my interests to live life to the full

Personal Notes

I am the master of my own health, for I take my quality of health seriously

Personal Notes

I am the master of my own happiness, for its in my interests to live life to the full

I am the master of my own health, for I take my quality of health seriously

I am the master of my own happiness, for its in my interests to live life to the full

Pursuing wellbeing a treatment explorer

It was during the worst points in my illness when I discovered that orthodox medical clinicians seemed to be amongst the most technically ignorant so called professionals I'd ever encountered in my life. Nevertheless, there are some men and women of science on the fringe of that industry trying their level best to help people and to move the science of medicine along from the middle age culture that it remains to this day stuck in. The problem those guys face is that they are trying to change a culture that simply doesn't want to change. A position which invariably means that they are immediately referred to as quacks by their luddite medical peers, which means that being treated by them can become so much more difficult that it needs to be or should be.

Now hey I'm not saying that all pioneering clinicians are good guys because some are clearly not. I do however find it incredibly annoying to listen to incompetent orthodox clinicians rubbishing and or trying to dig dirt on people who are clinically committed to moving things forward. Whilst they themselves are responsible on a grandiose scale for legitimised medical genocide of the majority of people entrusted into their care. It is this macrobiotic and immutability of the medical industry that is really holding clinical treatment progress back. You see; here is an endemic culture of assumption within the medical industry

I am the master of my own health, for I take my quality of health seriously

which on the one hand prescribes as it sees fit, whilst on the other simply attacks and criticizes alternative approaches, based upon nothing than prejudices or personal understandings or assumptions. In the absence of clinical data they will cry foul, yet in the presence of flawed historical orthodox clinical data they will defend it to the hilt.

You only have to listen to, speak to, or be spoken to by an individual from the medical industry to appreciate just how technically incompetent they can be. How full of their own self importance they are and how intransigent they are to change and new ideas. Therefore is it any wonder then that the average clinician is reluctant to engage with new ideas, for to do so would immediately subject them to a level of scrutiny from their peers that they're simply not moralistically or intellectually able to defend?

It's for that reason and that reason only that we, as chronically ill people, must accept that when we engage in clinical dialogue with pioneers in the old fields of medical science, that both we and they are going to be ridiculed by any luddite we encounter along the way.

You see, medical pioneering history is littered with victims of the systemically hypocritical and undoubtedly fear based corrupt judicial medical culture that appears to be hell bent upon stifling innovation. Where a preoccupation with the intentions, integrities and intellects of pioneering individuals have been brought into question and careers have been wrecked simply because some deviants are hell-bent on preventing clinical progression. Yet in far too many instances perhaps even after the pioneers' death the validity of what they were saying is later and often proven to be true.

I would therefore suggest that there has to be something fundamentally wrong with this industry and our society when:

- A clinician trying to move the envelope of medical science and clinical care forward has a proportionally greater chance of being medically disciplined or struck off, than some incompetent practitioner who's well known by his peers as being negligent in all that he or she does.

You see, I have nothing but praise for the clinical practitioners that I've met who:

- Listen.

- Treat holistically.

- Are prepared to explore new ways of being.

You see; it's that approach and those sorts of people who will eventually change the lot of mankind for the better. Not the bullshitting cretins we encounter through our TV's or the pompous, arrogant, nasty, vindictive and incompetent rogues that we visit when we're in a state of disease. My chronic illness and the complete lack of clinical support at my disposal meant that I was forced to explore and self-fund many treatment protocols. That's why I feel it's only right that I document one or two of the treatments I explored if only to stimulate thought.

Pyrrole Disorder

Prior to my Lymes Disease diagnosis, I make no secret of the fact that I've suffered from chronic suicidal depression and suggest that there can't possibly be anything worse than depression when absolutely nothing helps to remove or suppress its symptoms. Such was my physiological and emotional despair that I felt I needed to explore Pyroluria, a genetic condition that exhibits a wide range of symptoms most of which I'd had in the past or was suffering from at the time I explored this condition including:

- Episode of psychosis and suicidal depression.
- Little or no dream recall.
- White spots on finger nails.
- Poor morning appetite +/- tendency to skip breakfast.
- Morning nausea.
- Pale skin +/- poor tanning +/- burn easy in sun.
- Sensitivity to bright light.
- Hypersensitive to loud noises.
- Reading difficulties (e.g. dyslexia).
- Poor ability to cope with stress.
- Mood swings or temper outbursts.

- Histrionic (dramatic).

- Argumentative/enjoy argument.

- Higher capability & alertness in the evening.

- Poor short term memory.

- Abnormal body fat distribution.

- Dry skin.

- Anxiousness.

- Significant growth after the age of sixteen.

Originally Pyroluria was known as malvaria which is a genetic abnormality in heamoglobin synthesis resulting in a deficiency of zinc and vitamin B6. People with pyroluria produce excess amounts of a by-product from hemoglobin synthesis, called OHHPL (hydroxyhemop pyrrolin-2-one). In these people an excess amount of pyrrole is found in the urine. Associated changes in fatty acid metabolism lead to low levels of arachidonicacid *an omega-6 fatty acid*. The presence of pyroluria can have a profound effect on mental and physical health and was first discovered in relation to schizophrenia. Now that's the science, here's the practicalities of the condition, you will not get tested or treated for Pyroluria on the NHS. You will need to test and pay privately via either hair or urine analysis should you decided to check for this condition. My only words of caution are that this condition is real and I tested positive for it, however;

- Finding a responsive service provider is difficult; I lost my temper and composure completely with the slow turn around in my results i.e. 8 weeks which is completely unacceptable when we are in a chronic state of suicidal expression through disease.

- I've subsequently discovered issues with my body's methylation cycle which makes treating pyroluria complicated and although I didn't know it at the time it certainly explains why my treatment of pyroluria failed.

- Advocating my recovery theme that symptoms are nothing more than the presentation of disease, I think it's important to undergo more detailed investigation before attempting to treat or stabilise pyroluria symptoms.

Exercise, yoga and meditation etc

Prior to my chronic health condition I was a highly active guy, running the high fells every weekend, whilst during the week comfortably running in excess of fifteen miles per day on the roads, cycling, weight training and all that after a hard day's work. One of the most important aspects of that regime was the mind and body work I completed after my physical exertion, because without relaxation and bodily cleansing I found my body simply didn't work or perform in a way that I expected of it and dare I say in my ignorance; demanded of it at times.

Yet some people never get this subtle recovery nuance, thinking that exercise in itself at whatever cost, is more than enough for a happy healthy life. However, if your body is in a diseased state or exhausted, then your bodily processes either slow down or give up the fight completely, at which point its easy for all of us to lose all sense of quality in life. Therefore, whilst exercise and relaxation are essential components of optimum health, I would nevertheless suggest that those suffering from chronic illness exercise with extreme caution. Because when our body is in a diseased or a fatigued state it simply:

- Stops producing the products required to assist with bodily repair or toxin detoxification.

And

- Stops producing the energies we need to support the basic demands of living a normal healthy life.

Therefore, anything that puts either an unnecessary or greater strain on those processes is not helpful. In fact it could actually begin to compromise any effort you make to try to recover from your chronic health condition.

You see, our bodies must be able to recover from any physical load we place upon them no matter how gentle or therapeutic an activity is perceived e.g. yoga. A failure to understand this basic principle will leave you feeling constantly fatigued and ill, which is not in your long term recovery interests at all.

Therefore despite populist agendas which state that, when we're chronically ill, pursuit of activities such as yoga are actually good for us, as some one who's been chronically ill myself, I must and do fervently disagree. My personal experiences dictate that in the majority of instances exercise of any predisposition is counter-productive to healing at best and quite dangerous at worst, until our bodies have begun, through proactive intervention, the process of invigorated self-healing. I therefore would urge anyone suffering or recovering from a chronic illness NOT to explore physical exercise in any way shape or form until that is their body is well enough to deal with such demands.

I am the master of my own health, for I take my quality of health seriously

Vitamins & Amino Acids

I don't think there is a vitamin, mineral, amino acid, superfood, glandular, herb or supplement that I haven't taken in the past thirty years. Such has been my devotion to the pursuit of wellness that numerous health food shop owners have actually known me by my first name and have even asked me in many instances for feedback on the rarer products I've tried. I've shipped products to the UK from all around the world and yet I've never found one single product or associated treatment protocol that did what its hype postulated it was capable of doing.

Now there are many reasons for that, but the fact of the matter is that if we decided to take supplements, then we must be able to determine when they are working and when they are causing rebound side effects. I've had simply hundreds of harrowing experiences on my road to recovery but the one that sticks clearly in my mind is my desperate attempts to stabilise my depression by attempting to adhere to the key principles of the 'Mood Cure'.

The Mood Cure is a protocol which postulates a comprehensive natural approach to stabilising moods through the ingestion of amino acids combined with a high-protein, healthy-fat, veggie-rich diet and other nutritional strategies. The key component of this protocol being, a four-part questionnaire designed to identify your mood type, therein once qualified mapping an appropriate treatment strategy designed to raise your mood. Now there is some legitimacy with some of the issues raised with this approach, but its biggest failing is that it attempts to treat symptomology and in my opinion completely ignores the root cause determination of disease.

It's for that reason that I advocate that approaching this protocol unsupervised is dangerous, for it's eminently possible to exacerbate your mood symptoms and find yourself in a deeper black hole. I've accelerated my thought processes beyond imagination, I've lowered my mood significantly, I've made myself hyper and I've made myself sombulant using products prescribed via the mood cure, yet I have no idea if that was because of my underlying disease state or not.

What I do know is that whilst The Mood Cure is very informing, it falls short of a holistic treatment protocol the reason being: it focuses almost entirely upon brain function with some in put about the adrenals, but ignores other possible origins of disease. That is it's failing as far as I'm concerned simply because it does not attempt to address holistically via scientific or clinical root cause analysis other disease states that can propagate shifts in our mood and/or lead to chronic depression expression at any point in our lives.

I am the master of my own health, for I take my quality of health seriously

Counselling

Having studied psychology for the best part of my adult life, there are not many counselling techniques that I've not studied, participated in or read about. The result of which is that I understand that it's very easy to either react and deny ownership of our emotions or drill down into them and analyse them to the far end of a fart. Safe to say that as a guy committed to my own development I underwent extensive personal counselling before my pre-diagnosed Lymes Disease which was driving me around the bend. Yet in all my dealings in this area I've only ever met two counsellors that I respected, because they were real people, they'd been through the mill themselves and yet they'd come through and out the other side.

The rest have been intellectual game playing cretins, complete bullshit merchants, hypocrites or charlatans of the highest order. So much so that I now advise anyone attending counselling to sit up and take note. If you're leaving a counselling session lower than you were before you went in, then the first thing you must do is cancel any further counselling session because it's not working or the counsellor hasn't got a clue. Either that or your organic diseased state is interfering with the process.

My view is as I've stated many times in this book, our thoughts are a product of our body's chemical process efficiencies. If something is affecting them, then our thoughts will not improve until we correct those processes. Anyone that's truly been through a major chronic emotional or depressive cycle will know that it's simply impossible to change your thoughts.

That is the major stumbling block that I have with counselling. I disagree that the mind can cure or resolve a chronic diseased state, but once the chronic diseased state has been tackled, then the mind can certainly help with a holistic recovery. So if you're thinking about attending counselling as a means of trying to recover from chronic illness, I would say think again and only do so if you're 100% sure that the origin of your symptoms are emotional and not simply diseased state generated emotional symptomology. But you'll only know that for sure once you've tested and ruled out organic disease in the first place.

My view is *'Our mind is the victim of our toxic bodily load, it does not self generate toxic emotions or toxic thoughts, our mind is as happy and free as a bird at the point that we address all our body's toxic load'*.

Hormone Replacement

When our bodies are under attack by illness or the sheer ferocity of life there is always the potential for our hormonal system to break down. When that happens we are presented with all sorts of physiological and emotional challenges which can be difficult at best and life sapping at worst. Facing that situation there is enough evidence to suggest that supplementation with small amounts of hormones and/or their precursors can be beneficial. Because of that I don't think there is a hormone or hormone precursor that I haven't taken in the past thirty years.

Now whilst I would never contest low dose supplementation of hormones and/or hormone precursors if an individual felt the need to do that, because I have received benefits from supplementing with low dose prednisolone, cortef and armour myself. I do through personal experience suggest that supplementing with pregnenolone, estrogens, (oestrogens) testosterone, DHEA and progesterone etc., should be avoided if at all possible. I say that simply because I've self supplemented with all the former hormones and to be honest it can be a very scary and unforgiving experience.

What's even more disturbing is that supplementing with low dose hormones and/or their precursors from my own personal experience actually exasperated my illness expressions. Therefore I would say to anyone interested in exploring supplementing with hormones and/or their precursors, take it very slowly, be sure of your research and above all; listen, monitor and record your physiological and emotional responses continuously. If you adhere to those simple guidelines you can ensure that at all times you're in total control.

I am the master of my own happiness, for its in my interests to live life to the full

Thyriod / Adrenals

For me the endocrine system plays a significant part in chronic illness and I was lucky because I met some very decent private clinicians as I battled to stabilise my well being. Whilst there is absolutely no doubt that supervised support of the adrenals and thyroid can certainly help some conditions. There are significant issues globally with the treatment of endocrine issues such as hypothyroidism and hypoadrenalism and it is certainly possible to treat those conditions to good effect.

However, support of the endocrine system is not the great panacea that some people have been lured into believing. Inspirational success stories like Diane Holmes and her book *'Tears Behind Closed Doors'* have created buy in to these conditions to the detriment of conclusive clinical investigations. When I was exploring hypothyroidism it was simply desperate reading online, people trying to emulate Diane by medicating with Thyroxine or Armour yet unable to make any progress.

It was only as I began to bottom out my own illnesses that I realised why that was. You see, whilst the thyroid might be underperforming it should not be simply taken for granted that all associated symptoms are directly attributable to thyroid malfunction. The key for me is, support your thyroid and adrenals if you feel you need to, but if you're not improving then you need to test for possible originating diseases because it may well be that it's the diseases that are challenging your endocrine system and not your endocrine systems that is in a diseased state.

I am the master of my own health, for I take my quality of health seriously

Massage & Heller Work

As a committed amateur sportsman I always understood the significant part that sports and remedial massage played in my physical performance both as a footballer and runner. It has to be one of the best ways there is to help push the debris of exercise out of your tissues and into your lymphatic system. During my chronic illness however I spent thousands of pounds on remedial massage, desperately trying to get some degree of flexibility again back into my legs, arms, back, shoulders and neck. All to no avail, my muscles would begin to lock up again in most instances before I'd even left the treatment room.

It's absolutely insane the number of medical personnel who wrote me off with stress and the number of clinicians who did the exact same thing as Lymes Disease destroyed, through neurotoxicity induced inflammation, all flexibility in my body. That is the point I need to make, if massage is unable to relax your muscles, ignore any comments about your body being in a state of stress, you must test and continue to test for originators of disease e.g. Lymes Disease etc, until you find your answer.

Because there is absolutely no way that your body can fail to respond to massage if you're simply suffering from stress in the form of adrenal insufficiency.

I am the master of my own happiness, for its in my interests to live life to the full

Samento

When I was diagnosed with Lymes Disease, samento was the first natural product that I was prescribed and it really did have a tremendous impact in terms of killing lymes. Samento's beneficial properties are mainly attributed to a group of actives called pentacyclic oxindole alkaloids (POA's) that act on the cellular immune system. In most Cat's Claw species, the presence of another group, the tetracyclic oxindole alkaloids (TOA's) greatly inhibits the action of the POA's yet Samento is certified to be 100% TOA free.

What does all that mean? Well it means that Samento is extremely potent, you only need to take small amounts of it to ensure that its antimicrobial effects kick in. Whilst that may sound great in the treatment of lymes, it is but equally its not. You see, the problem with Lymes Disease is that it disrupts lots of systems in the body ultimately disabling the bodies detoxing capabilities. This means that whilst you kill the Lymes Disease when taking samento, the probability is that your condition will not be significantly improved because the byproduct of that treatment regime is a ten fold increase in your mobile/circulating neurotoxin load.

In conclusion whilst Samento has a part to play if you choose to use it in your recovery from lymes. Simply supplementing with it will not bring about any form of recovery unless your detox capabilities are first enhanced and supported through your entire treatment protocol for life.

I am the master of my own health, for I take my quality of health seriously

Antibiotics

When herbal treatments didn't bring about the sort of recovery I needed from my Lymes Disease I explored orthodox medications such as antibiotics. Despite what you may read or be told that Lymes Disease can be cured with a short course of doxycycline, amoxicillin or minocycline, I'm clinically advising you now as a chronic lymes sufferer such statements are misleading and absurdly wrong wrong wrong. What they are capable of doing within days is to create a wide range of side effects including ototoxicity of the inner ear. That may mean nothing to you, but it should because it is irreversible damage to your inner ear and could result in you having to cope with rotary vertigo for the rest of your life as well as trying to cope with lymes.

My view is for chronic conditions such as Lymes Disease, stay as far away from antibiotics as you possibly can. There may be a place for them in other situations, but for chronic situations they're a complete waste of space.

I am the master of my own happiness, for its in my interests to live life to the full

Reiki & Spiritual Healing

Reiki is the name given to a system of natural healing which evolved in Japan from the experience and dedication of Dr Mikao Usui. He spent most of his life practicing and teaching Reiki. It is believed by many Reiki practitioners that it's possible to heal at any level of being, be that, physical, mental, emotional or spiritual.

Unfortunately, despite being a Reiki practitioner myself, it didn't help me, despite visiting more than a few practitioners in my pursuit of relief. Neither did spiritual healing; a situation which challenged me to my core since I had witnessed and believed in the spiritual dimension all my life. I was shocked that at my time of greatest need instead of the light forces coming in to help me it was only the dark forces that saw fit to attach themselves to me.

Now we can't be anything other than what we were born to be and I've been either cursed or blessed by the vast range and depths of powers and skills that I've experienced. All that I say on the matter of Reiki is stay open and if works for you then accept it, because if it works then as far as you should be concerned that's really okay in the greater scheme of things.

I am the master of my own health, for I take my quality of health seriously

Marshall Protocol

I tried this protocol when I was making no progress at all with my lymes treatment. The premise of the protocol is to block all inflammation process whilst killing all cellular microorganisms and bacteria's. The two hormones cited as drivers of the inflammatory process are Angiotensin II and the seco-steroid 1,25-dihydroxyvitamin-D. Blocking Angiotensin II apparently weakens immune evading bacteria to the point where they can be more easily killed, and reducing the 1,25-D makes it harder for the bacteria to slip in and out of the cells that they have infected. The angiotensin receptor blocker Olmesartan dosed approximately every six hours is used to block the Angiotensin II receptors in the inflamed tissue and small doses of Minocycline can then be ingested to finish the bacteria off. So does this treatment work? Well it certainly lowers inflammation but as far as improving health, well I'm not sure.

I didn't like the side effects of this protocol, I got to the point where I could hardly walk because of the lowering in blood pressure caused by the Olmesartan and I got very cheesed off with the vertigo cause by Minocycline.

Within a few weeks I didn't value the Marshall Protocol at all and I certainly didn't like the Marshall Protocol online culture. I would never recommend this treatment option to anyone but if people wish to explore it I would simply say to them; by all means go for it, but be careful whatever you do.

I am the master of my own happiness, for its in my interests to live life to the full

Mickel Therapy

I explored this treatment because there was a lot of hype around it at the time I was looking for answers. The main premise of the Mickel Therapy is Hypothalamitis. The therapy postulates that when 'infected' the hypothalamus thinks the body is under attack, so it will tell the body to produce chemicals to prepare muscles for fight or flight. That's a very long winded way of saying that your endocrine system is on full alert. The therapy revolves around you listening to your body and then telling it to calm down and in doing so your body starts to heal.

Well sorry not for me I'm afraid; there's no way on this green planet that anyone suffering from a chronic degenerative illness is going to recover from this therapy. But that's not to say that it doesn't have some validity, because there appears to be enough evidence to suggest that the therapy does work for individuals suffering from mild neurosis.

So if it works for them than I say great, but I would never recommend the therapy despite Dr David Mickel coming across on the surface to me as a thoroughly decent guy.

Homeopathy

With absolutely no faith in the medical industry I explored homeopathy because passed experiences had sort of indicated that it had some validity. Unfortunately I had prediagnosed Lymes Disease symptoms when I committed myself fully to this treatment approach and it simply failed my wholesale. My body was in a hypometabolic state which meant I reacted dreadfully to everything thing I ingested including all things homeopathic.

The result of which I have to say pushed me further into a diseased state as my adrenals etc., simply couldn't cope with the increased emotional load from its so called clearing fall out. I had many bad experiences with homeopaths and because of that I feel very strongly about some of their attitudes etc.

So if anyone from the homeopathic world ever says to you that the remedy is not responsible for the reaction your experiencing it's your body. Look them straight in the eye and ask them this, 'Did you or did you not give me a remedy' and they will naturally reply 'Yes' Your answer must then be, 'Well I took your remedy and that's why I feel like this, now can we please stop all the clap trap and bullshit, because I need some help'.

The reason that I've mentioned that is because there are some very talented homeopaths out there, but equally there are a lot of quacks and I even lived and allowed myself to be treated by a quack during the most dreadful period of and in my life. The quacks are both a danger to themselves and a danger to society and trust me on this I saw one or two full on quacks.

Anyway enough of that, so where do I sit in terms of homeopathic treatment? Well, my view is it can't clear or help anyone with a chronic bacterial, viral, fungal or neurotoxin load. But as the condition becomes more under control, then that's the point homeopathy comes into its own, supporting the patient though there coming to terms and letting go process and in my opinion nothing more.

I believe in the power of homeopathy when used in the right situation and prescribed by a first class homeopath. But when used in the wrong situation or prescribed by 'homeo-quacks' it's very, very dangerous and a complete waste of money and time.

CranioSacral

This therapy is a gentle, hands-on method of evaluating and enhancing the function of a physiological body system called the CranioSacral system. The CranioSacral system is comprised of the membranes and cerebrospinal fluid which form the fluid-filled sac around the core of the nervous system, surrounding, nourishing, and protecting the brain and spinal cord. Using a touch generally no heavier than the weight of a small coin, skilled practitioners can monitor this rhythm at key body areas to pinpoint the source of an obstruction or stress.

The problem with this treatment approach is that it's absolutely of no use when the body is in a diseased state such as with Lymes Disease. This is because the Lymes and its neurotoxin load just keep placing an exceptional amount of stress upon the body. Frequently I found that some CranioSacral practitioners were not able to accept that it was a disease and not me the patient who was preventing progress using this approach.

Moreover there's a practitioner whom I visited many times in the Lake District prior to my Lymes Disease diagnosis that I will gladly rip limb from limb if I ever meet him again for all the ignorant abuse he offloaded onto me. I can't believe that I paid some anal quack a lot of money, to weekly verbally abuse me about my personal psychology, citing that and it as the reason I was in such a desperate state.

Rife Technology

Desperate to get ontop of my Lymes Disease I purchased a Rife Machine from South Africa at a cost of £1800 pounds plus import duty of £250 pounds or so. The Rife machine was developed by Dr. Royal R. Rife in the 1930s and used a variable frequency, pulsed radio transmitter to produce mechanical resonance within the cells of the physical body. The Rife machine was, in its time, a pioneering front-runner for what today is the basis of energetic medicine. Rife discovered he could use specific electro-magnetic frequencies to kill a bacteria or viruses without causing damage to the surrounding tissue.

The portable rife machines of today also work on the principle of sympathetic resonance, which states that if there are two similar objects and one of them is vibrating, the other will begin to vibrate as well, even if they are not touching. In the same way that a sound wave can induce resonance in a crystal glass and ultra-sound can be used to destroy gall-stones.

Rife machines use sympathetic resonance to physically vibrate the cells of the parasite resulting in possible elimination. Now the reason I went for a rife machine over a Dr. Hulda Clark Zapper was because nothing I'd read or heard convinced me that that the Zapper was able to create anywhere near the breadths and depths of frequencies that the modern rife machines could.

So did and does the Rife machine work? Oh yes without any shadow of a doubt, the only problem is that it kills so much lymes and interrelated organisms that the herx reactions are extremely intense. When I first started using my Rife machine I was a very ill guy yet the results of using my Rife machine simply knocked me on my back as my body was swamped with neuro and bio toxins.

I am the master of my own health, for I take my quality of health seriously

It wasn't until I'd re-energized my detox capabilities that I was able to use my Rife machine with any degree of comfort.

The really good thing about the Rife machine when using it to treat Lymes is that the Lymes cannot change its form when under attack like it does with herbs and other treatment. Because the Rife Machine simply vibrates it to death whatever forms the damn disease chooses to adopt.

Would I recommend use of a Rife machine? Well yes I would but I think I would suggest that people buy one between them and take turns rather than forking out over 2k. It's a lot of money and whilst you'll have it for years, it does a lot of sitting around when not in use and I don't think that makes for a good investment because of the initial financial expense.

I am the master of my own happiness, for its in my interests to live life to the full

Detoxing & Blood Cleaning

There was a point in my health decline and numerous unsuccessful recovery treatment protocols that I tried many detox approaches and many blood cleaning approaches. So much so that when I look back now it's simply staggering because I never made any form of improvement for all the expense and suffering I endured. I now understand that attempting to detox via the various methods we read or see online, on TV or in magazines is simply not the right approach for chronically ill people.

You see, when we become infected with lymes or diseases of that nature, our livers and/or our overall detox capabilities are significantly damaged or compromised. That means that we move into a toxic body state because we're constantly being poisoned by the disease generated toxins that are constantly being circulating or laid down in the fat rich tissues of our body. Unfortunately the vast majority of so called detox experts don't fully understand how our body processes work beyond, the liver, gallbladder or pancreas if you're lucky.

They simply don't understand mitochondria blockage or the breakdown in methylation and sulfanation processes. They don't understand liver anger or herxing with any degree of acuity. All of them in general make ridiculous claims that after one week or one month detoxing on their regime you'll feel remarkably much better. When in fact you won't if you've got a chronic toxic body but there is a significant chance that you'll feel much worse.

My view is simply this; explore anything and everything you wish to explore in terms of detoxing, but do not under any circumstance undergo any form of rigorous detox regime if your suffering from a chronic illness. Because the price you'll pay is far greater than you could ever know i.e. significantly increased symptomology, increase fat gain around the middle despite claims to the contrary, greater fatigue, anger, depression and no improvement at all.

I am the master of my own happiness, for its in my interests to live life to the full

Shoemaker Neurotoxin Cleanse

This treatment protocol developed by Dr. Richie Shoemaker is based around the real phenomenon of biotoxins causing continuation of illness in the majority of chronically illness patients. The protocol advocates taking the medication Questran (cholestyramine) which is powder that acts like a sponge binding circulating toxins within the body to it. Questran is often prescribed to pull cholesterol out of people's bodies and is easy to ingest.

Now I tried this protocol because I believe in Toxic Body Syndrome *TBS* but unfortunately for me it didn't work at the time although I was only given a very short prescription of Questran from my GP. Nevertheless if anyone felt that they were experiencing TBS, I would certainly suggest that they read up on the Shoemaker protocol because there is great validity in lowering toxin loads in the chronically ill.

I am the master of my own health, for I take my quality of health seriously

Sauna Therapy

In an aid to help with detoxing I underwent years of wet sauna therapy and to be honest it did absolutely nothing for me. When I switched to a Far Infra Red sauna however the results were far more dramatic, so much so that I bought one and use one to this day. The infra red sauna is cheap to run, requires only a standard electrical plug point, its easy to sit in, stimulates a significant increase in sweat and toxin mobilization and I cannot recommend it highly enough.

Like all other conjunctive therapies though it needs to be treated with respect. When using a FIR we need to support our bodies with colloidal minerals and vitamins etc., we need to hydrate and we need to make sure that the sauna is kept clean and that we shower immediately upon leaving the sauna to ensure that we minimize re-assimilation of toxins.

In summation the difference between wet and FIR saunas is that the wet penetrates the skins surface and offers very little detox support. Where as the FIR penetrates deep into the body and mobilizes and pushes both fat and water soluble toxins out of your body and in essence reduces your overall toxic load.

Methylation

One of the areas of research that really stimulated my interest as I desperately tried to get on top of my neurotoxin load was the issue of our methylation process. Our methylation process is the primary driving force behind so many processes in our body's attempt to detox harmful substances. Effective 'markers' for methylation are:

(a) Whole blood histamine ref. levels 40-70 mcg/dL.

And

(b) Absolute Basophils ref. levels 30-50.

In terms of determining how effective our methylation processes, are elevated histamine and/or elevated basophils by default indicate undermethylation and that's not really good news. Methylation is involved in DNA synthesis, masking and unmasking of DNA detoxification, heavy mental detoxification, nerve myelination, carnitine and coenzyme Q 10 synthesis. Therefore it's essential if we are to have good health that we have an effective methylation process. But what can we do if our methylation processes are not working? Well current thinking is that we can kick start our methylation processes with the supplementation of precursors of the methylation process including:

- Folic Acid and Vitamin B12.

- Trimethylglycine (natural sugar beet source).

- Vitamin B6 (combination of Pyridoxine HCL and Pyridoxal 5 phosphate).

I am the master of my own health, for I take my quality of health seriously

- Choline (combination of Choline bitartrate and phosphatidyl choline).

- Taurine.

- Magnesium (Magnesium Glycinate).

- Zinc (Zinc Monomethionate).

- Copper (Copper Glycinate).

Now it would be fair to assume that by supporting our methylation process with those supplements that everything would sort of resolve itself and our methylation would recover. Well that would be the case if it was as simple as that but its not and it's not because some of us have dysfunctional methylation processes from birth. So much so that if we start pushing the methylation process over and above our bodily needs we can easily push ourselves into a much more dangerous state. As I've discussed earlier undermethylation can result in high histamine which can present as:

- Obsessive-compulsive tendencies.

- Oppositional-defiant disorder.

- Seasonal depression.

All of which are associated with low serotonin levels. If we push our methylation process to much though in an attempt to improve our detoxing capabilities we can drastically reduce our histamine levels. So what you may ask that's surely a good result isn't it?

Well in truth its most definitely not. You see, very quickly you could end up with suicidal depression amongst other things, because healthy levels of histamine are vital for so many functions in our bodies. That's why playing around un-supervised with our methylation process is unwise at best and extremely dangerous at worst; because with in a matter of days you may easily find that your thought processes are like those from another planet. In essence it's important to understand when pushing our methylation process the difference between histadelia and histadelics. So let me wrap up the biochemistry of high and low histamine so that you have a much clearer understanding of the point I'm trying to make, you see:

- Histadelia is a condition which is characterized by elevated serum levels of histamine and basophils processes similar symptoms to those covered early in pyroluria.

Whereas:

- Histadelics are people with low histamine and typical symptoms include under-achievement, more severe thought disorder and hallucinations, paranoid thoughts with less pronounced obsessions, suicidal depression, cyclic or suicidal depression, and anxiety.

Clearly therefore; when attempting to manipulate your methylation process, you must take that initiative onboard with great caution, because the dynamics of histamine balancing are extremely complex.

Now look, I've briefly covered a number of treatment options in this chapter but to be honest, I would say to anyone thinking of undergoing any form of treatment option. Before you commence your treatment option or protocol you must make sure that:

- You understand the science behind what you're doing.
- You are sure that it's the right approach for you.
- You have appropriate clinical support.
- You're going to be able to make the decisions you may need to make if at any point complications set in for you.

Above all things take NO notice of anecdotal evidence or retorts, including any passions expressed in this book. Because you must personally prove, validate and ratify everything you're about to undertake in your treatment approach, because your wellbeing and even your life depends upon it.

The bottom line at the end of the day is that your wellbeing and future happiness rests solely and at all times with you. So be honest and true to yourself and make sure that whatever route or options you take you remain always focused and in control.

But more than just that, I wish for you the best of luck and hopefully the return to that level of health and wellbeing that we all so richly deserve.

I am the master of my own happiness, for its in my interests to live life to the full

The key is to remember that the process of healing can be accelerated when we take control of effective root cause analysis etc, a dynamic clearly profiled in my pictorial healing times lines (a) and (b) and qualifying in (c) and (d) the dynamic of understanding whether you're on the correct treatment rationale for you or not.

You see; there are no great rewards for anyone in unnecessary suffering because it adds very little to our life at all. Therefore we must always listen to our body and our higher self and learn to understand the truth and/or substance of everything we hear, read, see or feel in our body as we pursue our quest of a greater and better quality of life. Without that personal commitment, there is no real potential for whole body healing, because the process of healing both begins and ends with our ability to self nurture, self solve and self support our bodies throughout our entire and overall healing process. Because in truth, we're the only ones who can give it our full and highly considered attention and that's because, invariably we're the only ones who truly care anyway.

I am the master of my own health, for I take my quality of health seriously

My Actual Healing Time Line
Time Line (a)

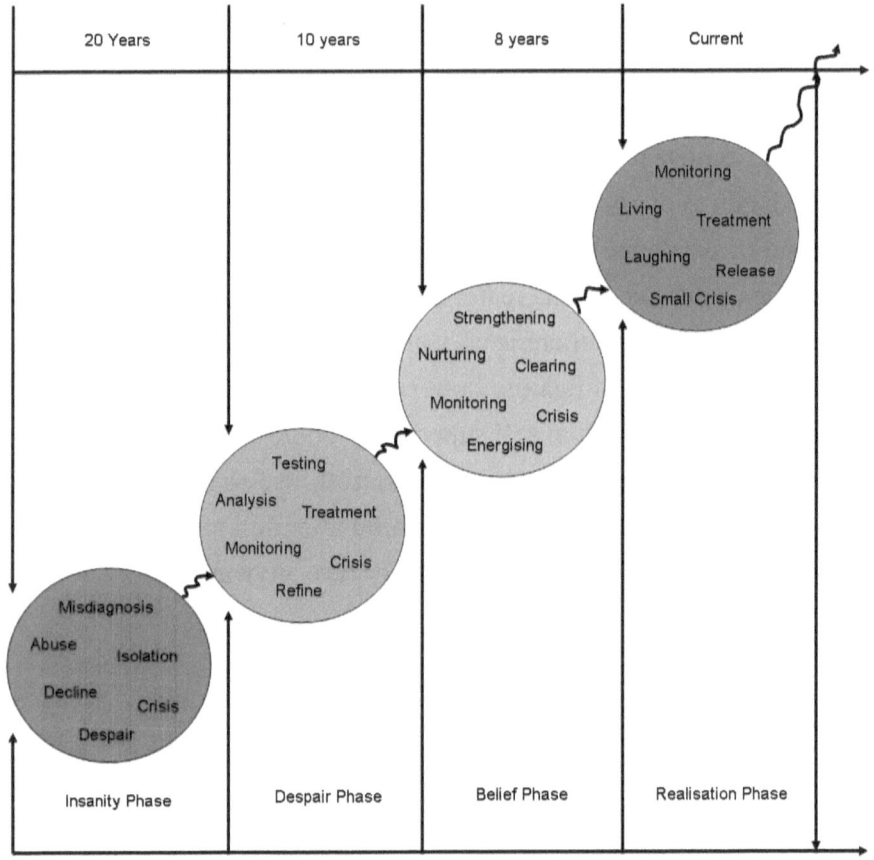

Time is only the great healer when our healing time is spent well

I am the master of my own happiness, for its in my interests to live life to the full

Possible Healing Time Line
Time Line (b)

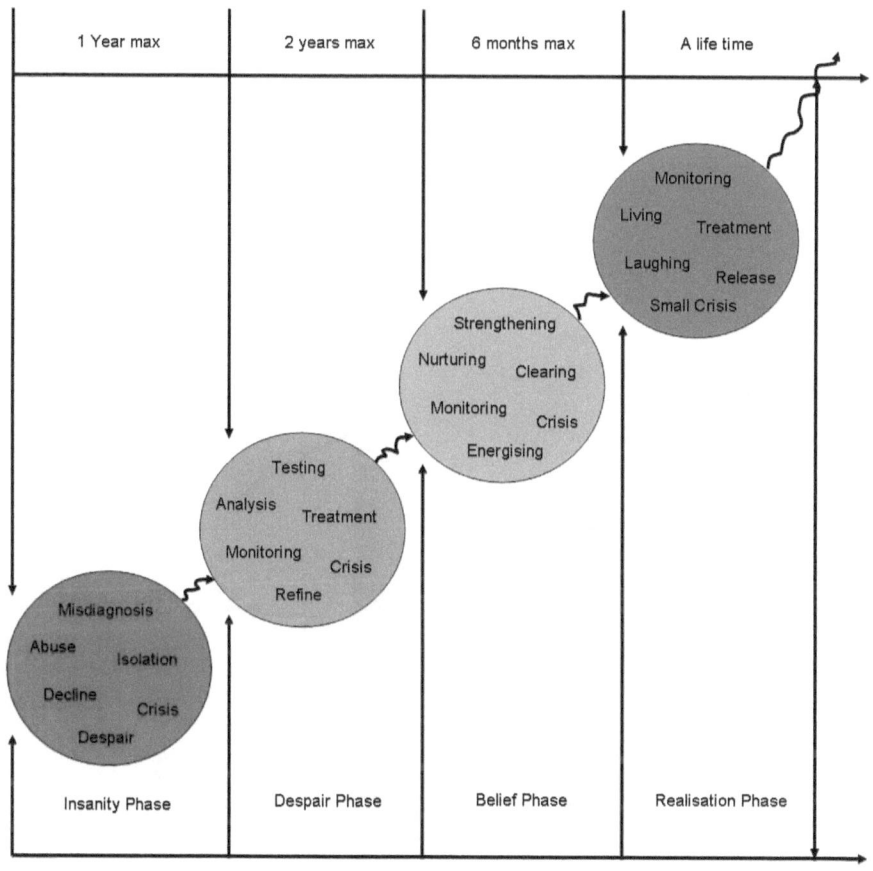

Time is only the great healer when our healing time is spent well

I am the master of my own health, for I take my quality of health seriously

Inappropriate Treatment Time Line 4U
Time Line (c)

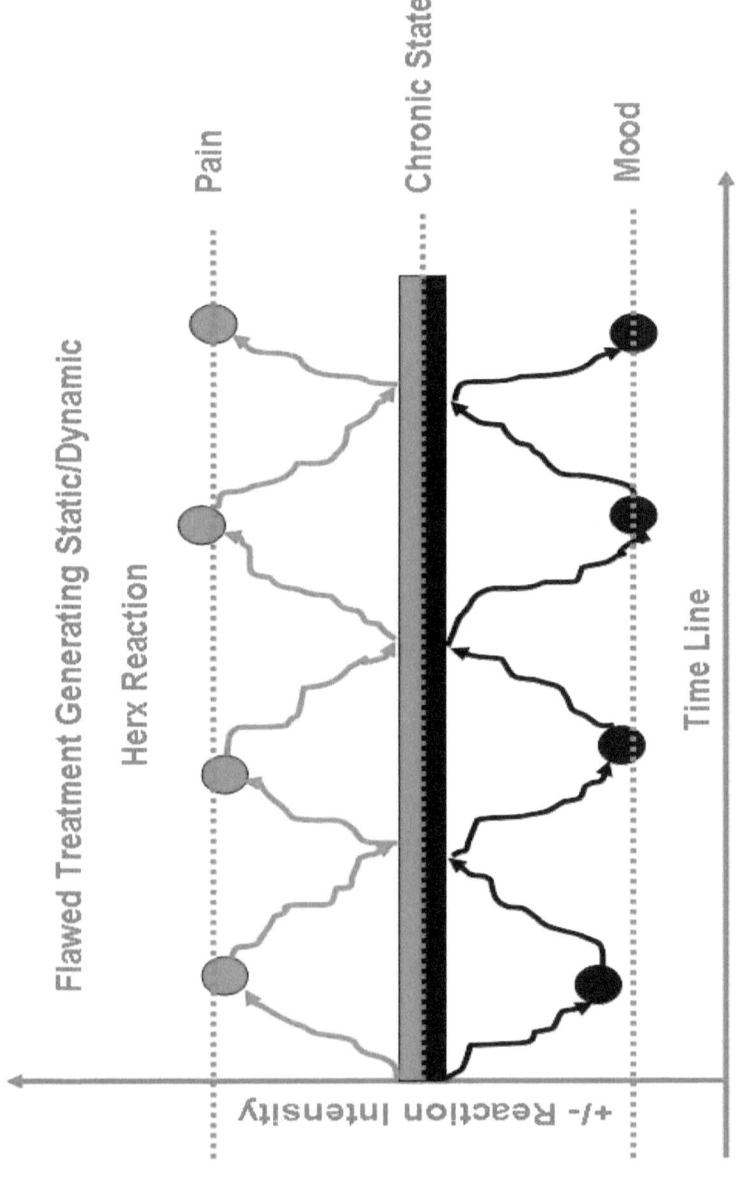

I am the master of my own happiness, for its in my interests to live life to the full

Correct Treatment Time Line 4U
Time Line (d)

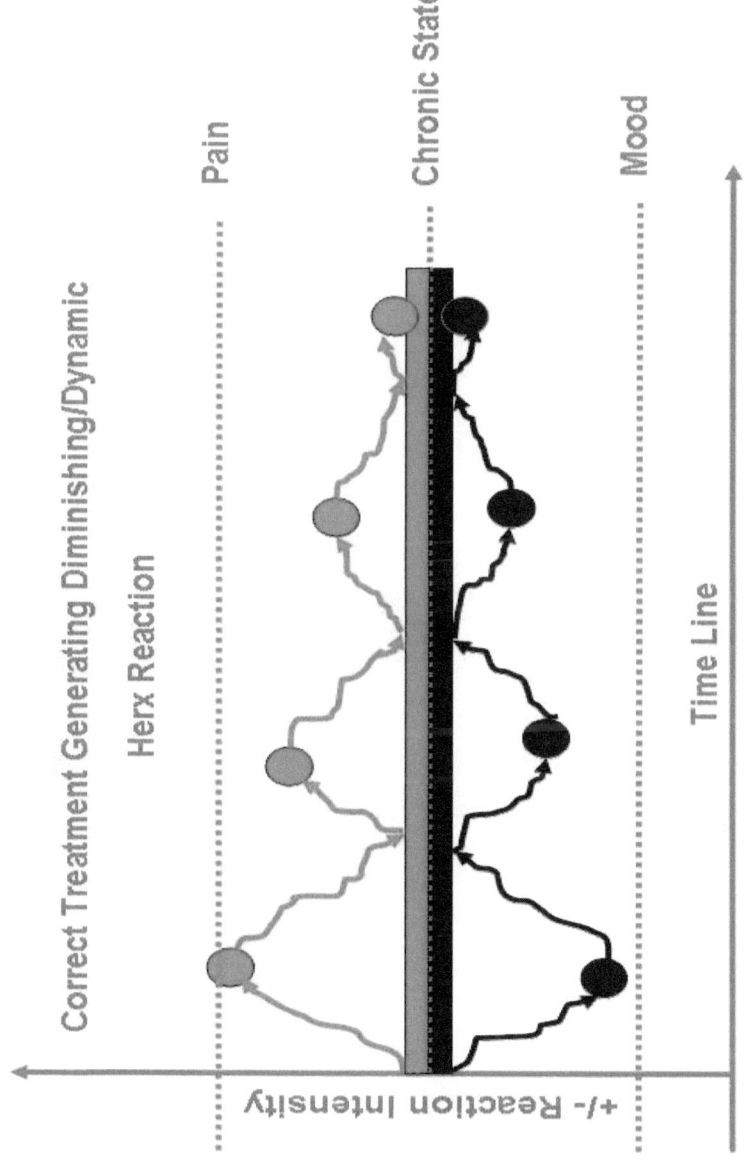

I am the master of my own health, for I take my quality of health seriously

Personal Notes

I am the master of my own happiness, for its in my interests to live life to the full

Personal Notes

I am the master of my own health, for I take my quality of health seriously

Personal Notes

I am the master of my own happiness, for its in my interests to live life to the full

Personal Notes

I am the master of my own health, for I take my quality of health seriously

Personal Notes

I am the master of my own happiness, for its in my interests to live life to the full

Personal Notes

I am the master of my own health, for I take my quality of health seriously

Personal Notes

I am the master of my own happiness, for its in my interests to live life to the full

Personal Notes

I am the master of my own health, for I take my quality of health seriously

Personal Notes

I am the master of my own happiness, for its in my interests to live life to the full

I am the master of my own health, for I take my quality of health seriously

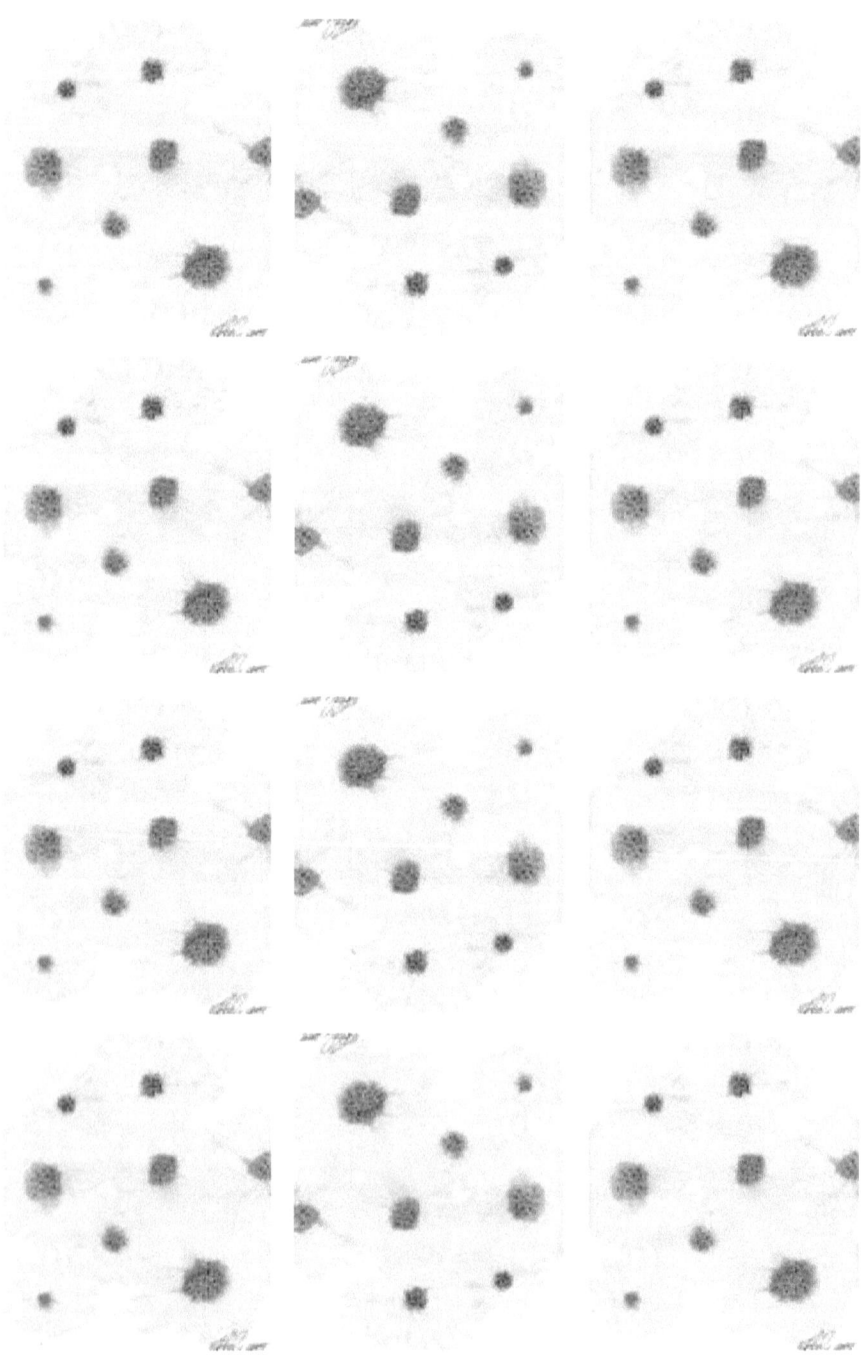

I am the master of my own happiness, for its in my interests to live life to the full

Treatment abroad - er....what?

I have to be very honest here; if anyone had said to me twenty years ago that I would undergo at some point in my life, private testing and surgery in Europe, I would have told them that they were insane. Because as a passionate socialist, whilst my local nuclear industry Thatcherites were revelling in her cruel dogma and turning a blind eye to everything she was doing in the country. I was out there lobbying central and local government on behalf of NHS etc. There wasn't a major city or political rally on behalf of the protection of the NHS that I didn't attend. I believed then that our NHS was indeed something worth fighting for and that a two tier health care model was morally reprehensible.

Well I still believe that a two tier health care model is reprehensible, however my views on the NHS have radically changed. I don't have anytime for the NHS now or the rogues that we employ within it. Our NHS is without any shadow of a doubt a complete shambolic disgrace, and in terms of our European colleagues our health care model is a very expensive and actually could also be described as a complete joke. Where it not for the fact the underperformance and shoddy care from a public sector facilitator cannot under any circumstance be laughed off because actually it's no laughing matter.

I am the master of my own health, for I take my quality of health seriously

We are paying the price in this country in terms of our health for the mistakes made by both the Tory and the Labour governments over many, many years. The biggest of those mistakes being:

1. UK plc never crushed the old boys clubs of the medical industry at the point of the NHS's conception, and we've spectacularly failed to do that since. The result of which is that we, the tax paying public don't even get a fifth rate service from those shits.

2. When Thatcher and her jingoistic, greedy sycophants began pulling the NHS down in the 1980's, they completely ignored clinical advice i.e. that in moving away from decentralized to centralized clinical care services there was great potential for the generation of a super bug phenomenon. Advocates who stood up and defended the decentralized model and in-house cleaning were all ridiculed on the back of the free market clap trap mantras of the time. But the result of those short term Thatcherite policies, as with most of the policies of that time, is that we the British public are still paying for those mistakes and likely to be paying for them for a hell of a long time. We have a chronic situation in Britain these days i.e. 'the MRSA super bug phenomenon etc' where our people might survive a surgical procedure but statistically there's a real probability that MRSA etc, will take them out.

I am the master of my own happiness, for its in my interests to live life to the full

For me it was because of the first point that I explored treatment aboard and not really the later, you see, I'd simply had enough of the shambolic pomposity that underpins our UK medical model.

I was tired of not being treated like an equal by people I felt were intellectual cretins. I was tired of making no progress because of the inertia and reticence that is an endemic theme of our health care model. Where everything is either the patients' fault or the culture of 'DSBL's' just grinds the patient into the ground.

Interestingly however it wasn't until I began to explore treatment abroad that the whole MRSA thing really came home to roost. Do you know our medical health care model is a complete disgrace; people aren't dying any where else in the developed world after surgery like they are in the UK. Our government and our shit for brains medical industry should hang their heads in shame, because the current surgical survival rate for patients in the UK is statistically catching up with mortality rates from the 18th century, now how much confidence does that engender in you?

It's not rocket science to suggest that there is something sadly wrong here with our medical model is it? And yet we as rational people have only two options open to us when we need some form of surgical intervention. We either stick with what we know is extremely poor, or we explore other possible treatment solutions. Well I advocate that if you have;

- The finances

And wish to;

- Move forward quickly

And want to

I am the master of my own health, for I take my quality of health seriously

- Be treated with respect and if you wish to survive your surgical procedure then you must explore any and all treatment options abroad.

Yes there are potentially language issues, yes there is always the possibility of something going wrong, yes you may be a long way from home, but in truth the only other option you have is to stick with what you've got.

Surgery abroad didn't solve my medical problem completely, but that was more to do with the complexity of my health condition than the medical service I received abroad. My experiences of being treated in a medical system in Europe was uplifting, its was informing, it was all that I once thought was mine by right from the UK medical model.

During my treatment abroad, I met highly qualified medical personnel who were decent, approachable and considered in all they did. Never once was I treated as if I was an intellectual cretin and never once did any member of any clinical department I ever saw demonstrate at any point that they felt they were some sort of earth god.

When it comes to our health there are many things that we must consider and many issues we must come to terms with. My only view on that is at the point I made all my considerations it became obvious to me that some of the issues I was being asked to come to terms with; were actually not clinical actualities in the majority of instances, they were merely fabrications generated through a reticence to help. I couldn't possibly know whether treatment abroad offers everyone the sort of solutions that I believe it potentially holds, all I say is look very closely at what we have in the UK and then allow yourself the opportunity to explore.

Of course there are many risks in exploring and undergoing treatment abroad and so I would urge anyone embarking upon that route to make sure that you cross all the T's and dot all the I's before you commit yourself 100%.

Never ever forget that not all healers are healers, never ever forget that no one offers to help you for nothing and never ever forget that some times, people are not at all, what they first may appear to be. Do not part with any cash until you know that your cash is safe, do not give out any personal information until you know that it is safe to give out that information and never be lured into discounted service provision because there are no bargain basement options when it comes down to world class medical care. My treatment abroad experiences were both world class and first class, so if you decide to go down that route I wish only the same for you.

On that very point I urge you to take care, but make your own value judgments and only allow yourself to move forward into a treatment environment when you are informed, comfortable and confident about any and all of your future clinical options and undertakings.

I am the master of my own health, for I take my quality of health seriously

Personal Notes

I am the master of my own happiness, for its in my interests to live life to the full

Personal Notes

I am the master of my own health, for I take my quality of health seriously

Personal Notes

I am the master of my own happiness, for its in my interests to live life to the full

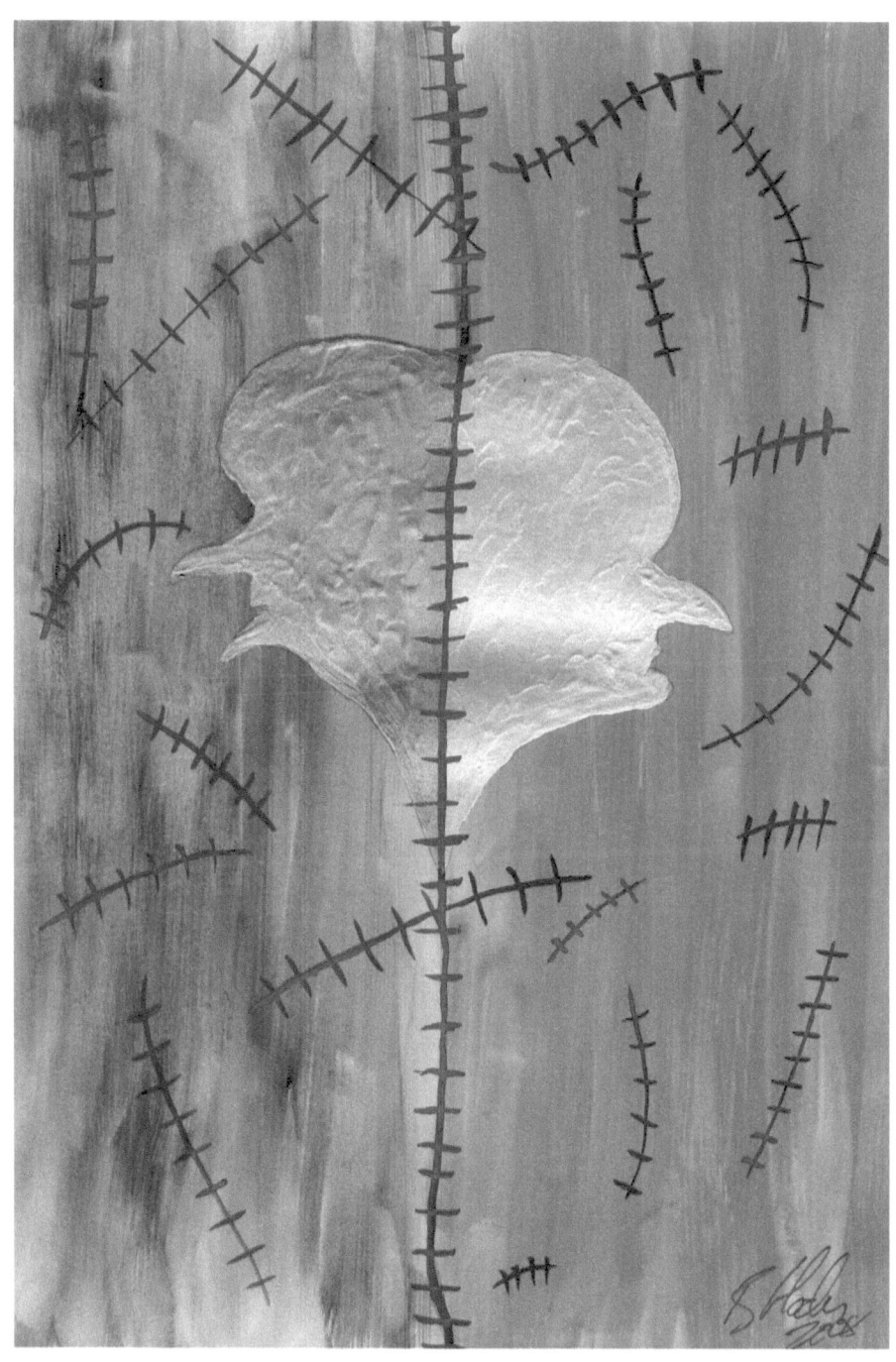

I am the master of my own health, for I take my quality of health seriously

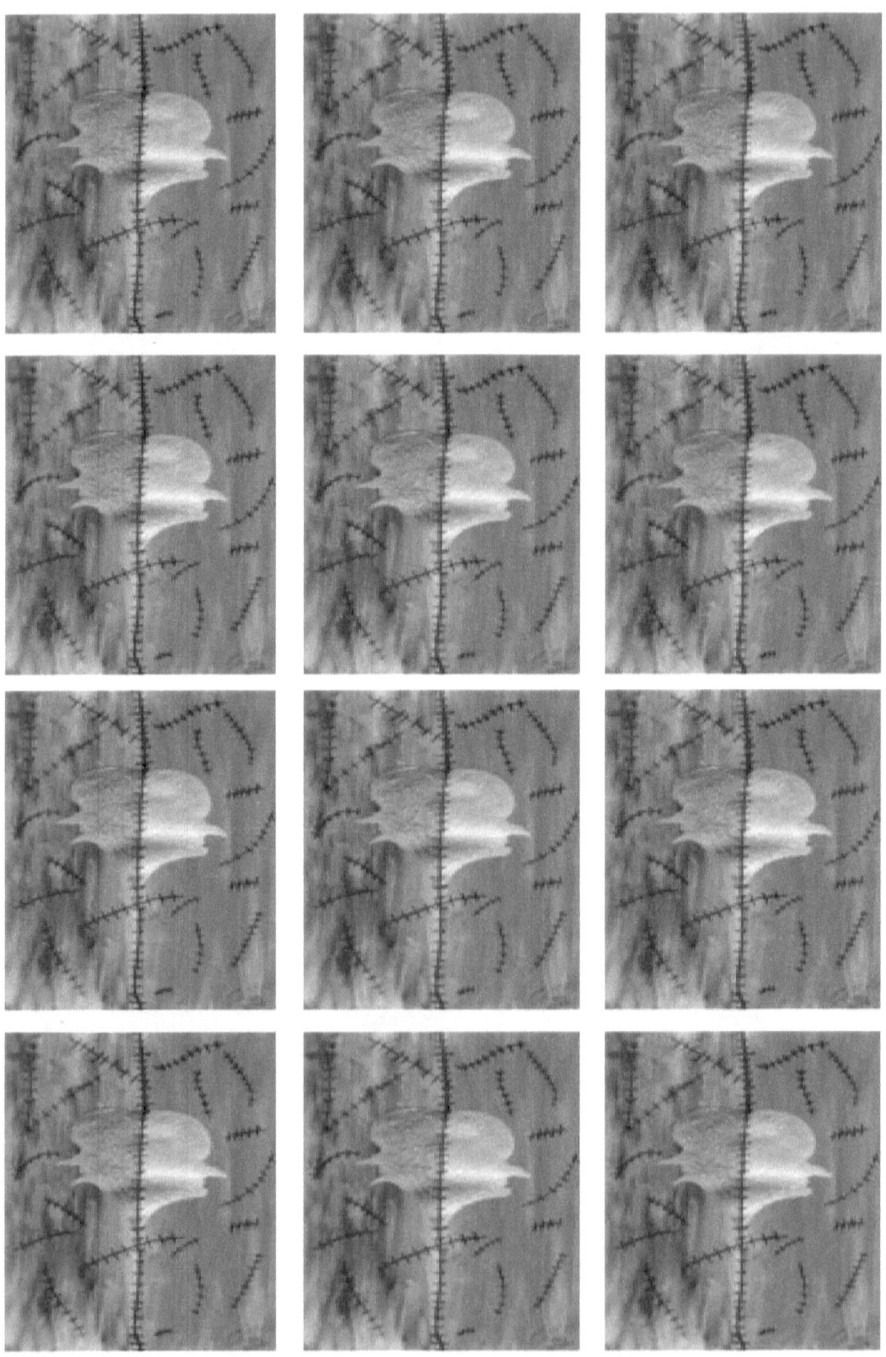

I am the master of my own happiness, for its in my interests to live life to the full

Insanity or Irony You Judge

Unless you've battled with something like an undiagnosed chronic health condition its difficult to understand just what extraordinary lengths we as mortals will go to just to find answers, treatment and/or rest. Believe me some of the lengths I went to looking back now are simply mind-blowing and if the majority of them hadn't been such dreadful experiences then they'd be considered hilarious, and that includes both orthodox and the not so orthodox approaches.

You know, you try to get answers from the medical industry, you try to find answers for yourself and you even try the best mystics you can find but there really are times when there are no answers to be had. That's when life becomes as lonely and terrible as mortality can possibly be. During my illness, I travelled tens of thousands of miles and I explained my symptoms and my case over and over again, in swanky clinics, gritty shit holes and even people's offices in garden sheds. During that time I got a lot of:

- Head nodding. ....
- Hmmn's.........
- I see's........

I am the master of my own health, for I take my quality of health seriously

What I never got was the one thing I was looking for, the answer to the illness that was crucifying me. I really don't know how I kept going at times, for even when I felt that it was the wrong thing to do or the wrong person to see, I did it and saw them just in case I was wrong and perhaps they would prove that to me. Time after time it was the same reply 'Hmmn Mr. Hardy your case is very complicated' to the extent that I've even said to some of them in the end:

- *'If you're even thinking of telling me that I've got a difficult case, you can stop right there. I know I've got a difficult case, that's why I'm here paying you a fortune just to sit there and nod your bloody head, if it was easy do you not think I would have solved it myself rather than coming here to see you, a so called bloody expert instead'.*

It's no wonder at times that some of them were rocked by my presence, but by that point I didn't give a hoot, I was weary of all of my conditions and even wearier of being turned over by money grabbing bandits and incompetent sods. Some of things I experienced were simply insane e.g.

1. I agreed in principle to pay one particular so called neurological expert an absolute fortune to be seen by him, his reply after the explanation of my case was; *'All I hear is words, but what is your problem?, you're talking about things that you can't possible have'*. I'd just sat and explained all my inter-cranial symptoms to the pompous bastard and he had the audacity to sit there in his third rate crumpled bloody grey suit and say that to me. I just looked him straight in the eye and said; *'Listen very carefully to me pal, if you're trying to play psychological games with me be very careful, because I don't play games when its much more satisfying simply to break the bloody neck of arseholes like you'*. The guy at that point got all flustered and immediately started to back track, but I just said; *'Yo dude; you can stop right there, this meeting is over! And don't even think of charging me for this rubbish because you wouldn't like it if I for any reason had to come back here to see you, okay?'*

2. I somehow managed to drive over to Newcastle to see another so called professor of neurology and after he'd gone through the same bog standard gait and cerebella checks I'd had countless times in the past he announced; *'Well dear boy there's nothing wrong with you that a course of anti depressants wouldn't cure'*. To which my reply was, *'Hang on a minute you're a neurologist not a psychiatrist and what about the pressure inside my head?* There was a brief moment of silence and then he said, *'Come come dear boy, you don't have any pressure inside your head you're only suggesting that you have pressure inside your head'*. *'Er……no I'm telling you I have pressure in my head so let me ask you this; what are you going to do to help take that away'*. His reply was, *'Nothing dear boy it's only a symptom it's not real you only think you have pressure inside your head'*. I was raging by now and not a little unwell so I said, *'Let me ask you this you fucking pompous fat twat, if I kick you in the balls which I'm very tempted to do right now, will you have a pain in your balls or just a symptom of pain in the balls?'* At which point the guy said; *'My word no one has ever spoken to me like that before'*. As I turned to leave the room, I looked back at him over my shoulder and said; *'Your luck has just run out dear boy, **do not** under any circumstance send me a bill for this fucking clap trap, okay dear boy?'*

I am the master of my own happiness, for its in my interests to live life to the full

Now it sounds as if I didn't pay my way as I sought the help I needed, but nothing could be further from the point. I notched up outrageous debts paying people who were supposed to be helping me, who were in reality only lining their own greedy pockets as I continued to suffer.

Like most processes however, there is a point of change, and I'd reached that point of change, I was extremely tired of living and I wasn't prepared to have my last few pounds mugged from me by some toffee nosed rogue filling his pockets on a Saturday morning on premises belonging to the NHS at my expense.

Nevertheless as I've said we'll try anything when we're desperate enough and I was desperate enough indeed so I even tried North American Drum therapy of all things with a head which felt fit to explode at one point. The therapy was conducted in the back room of a very lentils and beads charlatan, who went into great depth in terms of explaining to me just how good she was and then she danced around me banging a drum above my head for the best part of 30 minutes shouting out; *'Be gone dark energy be gone'*.

Well there was no change when she'd finished as I'm sure you're highly amused to discover, but in my despair I arranged to have four further treatments in the coming days of that week at £45 a session. However when I arrived for the final session I could tell she was all stressed out and she said she thought she was about to go down with a migraine because her boiler pilot light had just gone out and she couldn't get it back on.

I am the master of my own health, for I take my quality of health seriously

Can you believe that? My head was fit to explode with chronic Lymes Disease and yet I was paying some chancer £45 to bang a drum above my head to apparently clear away bad energy and yet she can't cope because of all things the pilot light on her boiler had just gone out? I just looked at her, smiled and said, *'Now that's very interesting my headache is still the same as its been for years but my pilot light has just this minute come back on and that's telling me that you're nothing but the charlatan that I've suspected you were all along'.*

She just looked at me gormlessly as I turned, put my jacket back on and headed for the door, she shouted out *'But but'* I just replied *'bang your drum pet for 5 or 10 minutes and I'm sure your headache will have gone by then and when it has give me a call and for £135 I'll give you the number of a very very good plumber who'll sort that pilot light out for you no bother'.*

All highly amusing hey, my west cumbrian repartee with the pompous git and the drum banging fraud? Well in reality it's not at all funny, because when we're in a state of desperation I personally think it's a disgrace that the world appears to be full of shits just sitting and waiting to rob us of our money. Nevertheless and as a sanity check I fully accept that during my life that I've been tortured and let down by my body in many ways that it's impossible to comprehend. But if I think about all the qualities I personally possess, the one that gives me the greats joy of all is not my passion, drive or tenacity in the face of incredulous odds, it's actually my incredible sense of humour which remains ever present even to this day.

I am the master of my own happiness, for its in my interests to live life to the full

Sometimes it's not at all easy to laugh at life or indeed laugh at ourselves and the situations or predicaments that we often find ourselves in. But if we can laugh at our own absurdity even for moment in the face of incredible or intense adversity, then I truly believe that we have a better chance of re-energizing ourselves because laughter always but always brings along with it almost instantaneous and momentary relief.

I am the master of my own health, for I take my quality of health seriously

Moving on, I think perhaps the most perverse issue that I became aware of whilst I desperately sought help from the medical/clinical industry was the: 'Dear Sir, I wonder if you would kindly see this man' and the, 'Dear Sir thank you for asking me to see this man' bloody medical/clinical bullocks and clap trap communiqués. Such was my great annoyance with this shit that I sort of created my own acronym after a while, *Dear Sir Bollocks Letters*, DSBL's. If you've ever experienced this crap you'll know what I mean i.e. 'Dear Sir I wrote several letters on your behalf but apparently you had the affront to die without infoming me, please note my bill for £350.00 is enclosed, payment conditions strictly within14 days'.

It's simply outrageous what goes on in the medical/clinical world, they spend more time putting together or dictating implicitly incorrect bullshit communiqués than they actually spend seeing or treating people either directly or indirectly in their care. Equally you can wait months to see a so called expert, but when you arrive for your appointment you find that it's not the expert who's going to see you now, its some bloody registrar who's clueless and nervous about everything. These people are playing with peoples lives and yet they simply don't get it. You attend these NHS or rip off private consultations and then you read the reply correspondence some weeks later that you've been CC'd into and its like what is this idiot on about? I didn't say any of that!

What's even more hilarious is that there's never even a hint of a positive suggestion or any form of potential resolution forthcoming from these communiqués, but there is always the obligatory reference to conjunctive counselling etc.

I am the master of my own happiness, for its in my interests to live life to the full

It really is a scandal, people are dying whilst these rogues write DSBL's to each other, letters that make no sense, letters that corrupt your files, letters for the sake of writing bloody letters. These people are a complete waste of space and an affront to everything decent. But it's worse than that, I remember seeing a so called expert on the south coast about my vestibular condition who then wrote a DSBL to my private GP. Suggesting that even though she was an expert in her field of medicine, it would perhaps is better if a saw someone whom she felt was more of an expert than her. Now hey some might read that and think 'hmmn very laudable' wrong, wrong, wrong, wrong, wrong. This person makes a living as a so called expert in her clinical field, so why couldn't she just pick up the phone and discuss my case with this other so called experts? Well because:

- (a) She didn't give a hoot about me or my suffering.

And

- (b) It was an opportunity for her to send some cash the way of one of her buddies, which is simply sickening really.

I am the master of my own health, for I take my quality of health seriously

But wait, it gets better; she finished her communiqué by saying whilst she was uncertain about the origin of my condition she would respectfully suggest that there was more than enough evidence to suggest that my condition could be more of psychological condition and not simply of organic origin. Brilliant eh? *'We are all experts but some of us are far more of an expert than others, and those of us who are not as expert as we think we are, can make if we choose too; expert assumptions about the origins of disease from a clinical perspective that we're not even qualified in, let alone expert enough to understand'.*

Sorry but there's more, when she sent her invoice out to me, there on the bottom of her invoice for £200 in bold was, *Note receipts will only be provided upon the forwarding of a stamp addressed envelope.* I really was tired of rogues like this by now so I personally wrote a DSBL back to her and advised her that I wouldn't be providing a stamp addressed envelope. Indeed I advised her that if she wished payment from me she would need to rethink her greed strategy quickly because I was certainly thinking of submitting her invoice to Trading Standards for closer scrutiny. The matter of my receipt was resolved quickly but I still submitted her invoice to the Trading Standards, screw her, the greedy, nasty, ignorant, pompous charlatan.

In another instance I had a private consultation in the north east with a little runt of a man, who conducted my entire private consultation with his door wide open. Time after time he just let rip into me and shouted at me as if I were a dog. It was the worst consultation I'd ever had and I remember coming out and being completely shell shocked by the whole thing. Within two or three days his invoice came and I thought screw you, I wrote out his cheque and attached it to a CC'd letter that I sent to the NHS trust where he was practicing making a formal complaint about his unacceptable conduct. Four days later the cheque was returned by his PA with a covering letter stating, in light of my dissatisfaction with the consultation, he'd decided not to charge me. I was very tempted to bill the poisoned dwarf for my travel expenses but I thought sod it, he's admitted liability for his impropriety, I have his DSBL on record and that was good enough for me.

I am the master of my own health, for I take my quality of health seriously

Around that time I had my second private MRI of the brain, and after six weeks I contacted the office of the consultant I'd seen to enquire where my results were. After days and days going around and around in circles they apparently managed to find my information but as yet he hadn't had time to analyse my results.

Can you believe that I'd paid £1150 for a private consultation and MRI and the so called highly recommended private clinician hadn't even looked at my films seven weeks after they'd been taken? A further two weeks after that I received a call from a very snotty clinical secretary saying, *'Nothing to worry about I had a watery cyst the size of a plum bottom left side of my brain but it had been concluded that it was a congenital condition and nothing to do with my presenting symptoms'*. My reply was; *'Well it wasn't on my last MRI'* to which her reply was, *'I can't comment on that you will need to speak to Mr. bla bla when he returns back from his six month sabbatical'*.

I was beginning to discover that there were no health workers with any decency, integrity, sensitivity or technical competence i.e. they don't give a hoot about anyone in their care and if a medic can't understand or doesn't know what a presenting image or symptom is than the best way to deal with it is to write it off as congenital.

What's simply staggering about this situation is that eighteen month later after extensive Lymes Disease treatment I asked during my third private MRI results discussion about the cyst. The guy just looked at me and said, *'What cyst'* to which I replied; *'The plum sized cyst bottom left side of my brain'*. His reply was, *'Oh that area there, it's probably nothing more than congenital discolouration nothing to be concerned about'*. I said;

I am the master of my own happiness, for its in my interests to live life to the full

'No no there was a cyst there eighteen months ago' to which he replied with utter contempt, *'If you say so but I'm telling you there's no evidence to suggest there was a cyst there in fact there's nothing wrong with you that perhaps some yoga, counselling or antidepressants wouldn't sort out'*.

How dare those fucking bastards think they can do and say what they like to us. Well they can I'm afraid to say simply because they're proactively encouraged to engage in such despicable conduct by their industrial luddite peers.

What's more and I have to say however, that some of the biggest jokers I ever saw where those 'clowns and deviants' that populate Harley Street, in total I saw 14 of them at a cost of over 9k for consultations, tests and MRI's etc. Never have I ever met such highly inflated egos working within an industry who are as fraudulent in all their dealings as the greedy, incompetent medical charlatans who buy themselves into the cash rich cows or rooms as they like to call them on Harley Street.

These people are the biggest rogues any mortal is ever likely to meet; they are all without exception, completely up their own arseholes and lacking in any form of human decency. I completely refuse to see them as anything other than they what are, the worst form of all mortal life forms, rogues masquerading as healers whilst lining their pocket through greed.

My advice these days to anyone suffering from a chronic condition is; do NOT go anyway near Harley Street, save your money and seek out true clinical excellence in Europe or any other part of the developed world. But please stay well clear of those horrible greedy fucking slime balls that prostitute their services in said locality.

I am the master of my own health, for I take my quality of health seriously

Now look, I couldn't possible go into all the things I encountered during my desperate, desperate years and don't think you would wish to read them anyway. What I will state is that it is safe to say that when we are ill or when we are desperate enough, nothing is beyond or should be beyond our explorations in search of wellness. The only points that I would make are; tread gently and pay no one who's opening line is I'm promising nothing.

You see; I've met hundreds of those charlatans and each and everyone them has mugged me with a smile of their face. My illness has changed me in so many ways, I've never liked bull-shitters or rogues and whilst I could sort of live with them before my illness. Today I'm extremely comfortable enough with myself to tell someone their talking bollocks if I think they are e.g. if I were to go to an Italian restaurant and ask the chef '*how good he/she was at preparing sea food linguini?*' and he or she replied, '*not bad but I'm making no promises*'. I would immediately think, *'Fuck that for a game of soldiers and tell him/her exactly what I thought of their reply and then leave to find a restaurant and chef who knew what the fuck they were doing'*.

Similarly we must take that approach when interacting with so called health workers. Because there are far too many rogues out there, making a living at the expense of people with chronic conditions in both orthodox and non orthodox applications. In fact the horrible bastards are everywhere these days. They charge you for your time as you give them your case history and they charge for all the materials they use on top of everything else, nothing is free and all you're ever seen as is; a simpleton or cash cow to them. Their favourite line is, 'Give it some time' when things for you are not getting any better.

I am the master of my own happiness, for its in my interests to live life to the full

But they never ever say, 'Look, I'm really sorry, but I'm not charging you anything for this appointment, because I haven't got a clue what's wrong with you and furthermore I don't know anyone whom I can recommend that you should see'. The plain fact of this unsavoury side of illness is that healers simply don't heal people, what they do is earn money and support livelihoods at the expense of the chronically ill. You will know if your healer is any good or not because your body will be the first to let you know.

Now this might sound strange or insane but believe me its true, the greatest and most powerful healer of all is the healer that resides deep within us. Let us never forget that, we can always heal ourselves if we choose to live our life with that sense of inner personal belief, all we need is the inner strength at times of low vitality to enable us to find the answers that we need. In a chronic illness state, no one is going to take sympathy upon you and give of their expertise for free, very few will be kind to you or have your best interests at heart.

The way to look at healers is no different from any other form of practitioner; they have a set of skills which they're charging you for on the open market, they are certainly doing you no favours. Therefore chronic ill health costs money and generates great income, so don't ever forget that it's a business not a moral or social service or responsibility.

Above all things, take care, and may you understand when you're in the presence of greatness our merely interacting with 'clowns' for the difference in service delivery should be immediately evident in your healers deeds and not in any bullshitting words or phrase that they may wish to cite or use.

I am the master of my own health, for I take my quality of health seriously

At my age now and with all my terrible experiences it's easy for me to lament upon that fact that life is certainly a very real and gigantic challenge for some of us complicated by default by the sheer volume of clinical/medical charlatans, idiots, slime balls, cretins and clowns that we unfortunately have to meet.

All I can say on that point is let's bring back capital punishment, and lets start hanging, beheading and flogging a medic every day 'again' until our message finally gets through their incredulous, think, insensitive and callus skins that we want;

- Accountability

- Decency

And

- Excellent from them in all their undertakings because that is not an aspiration in any way shape of form, it's actually a real and a deservedly righteous expectation.

I am the master of my own happiness, for its in my interests to live life to the full

Personal Notes

I am the master of my own health, for I take my quality of health seriously

Personal Notes

I am the master of my own happiness, for its in my interests to live life to the full

Personal Notes

I am the master of my own health, for I take my quality of health seriously

Personal Notes

I am the master of my own happiness, for its in my interests to live life to the full

I am the master of my own health, for I take my quality of health seriously

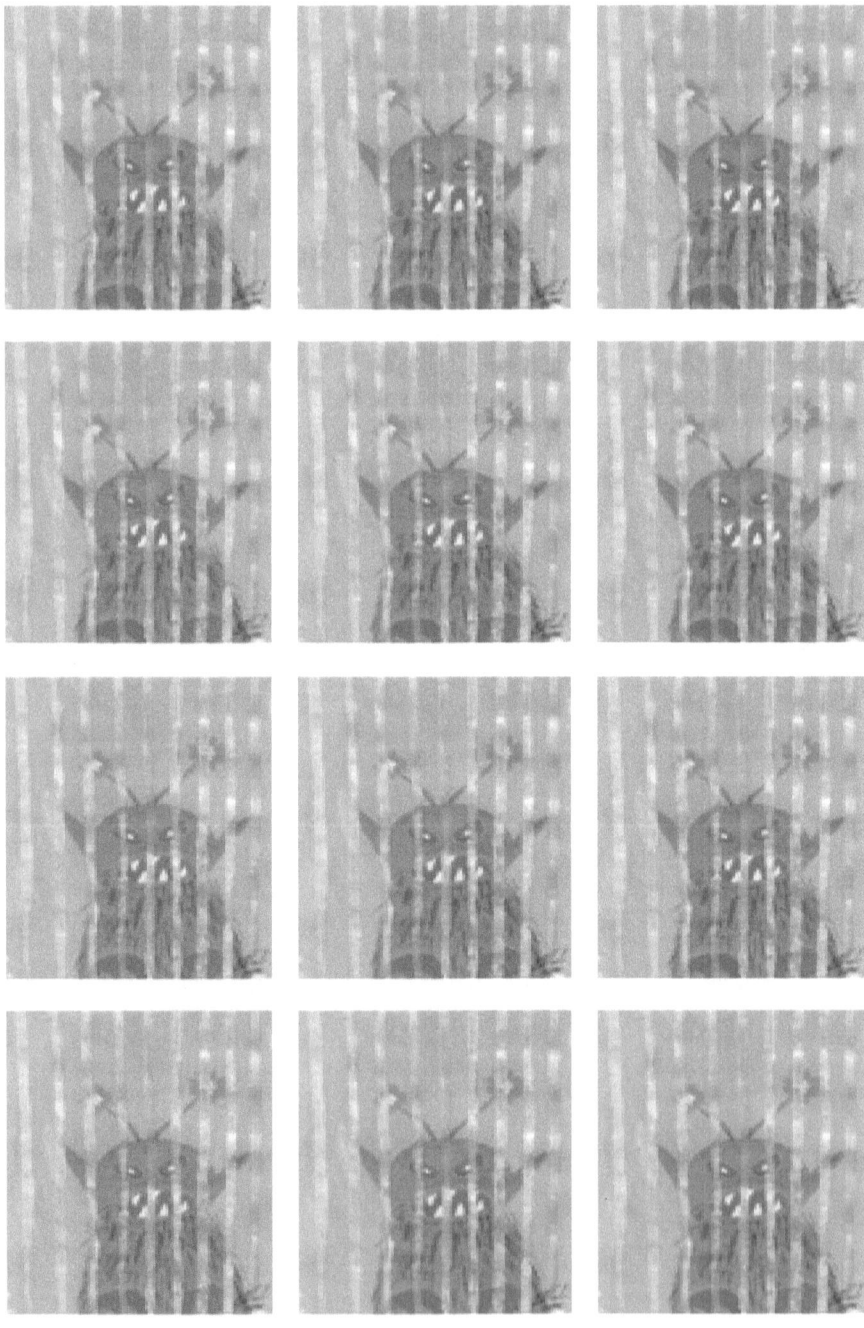

I am the master of my own happiness, for its in my interests to live life to the full

Fantasy punishments and mind anger released

You know I've encountered many many very special people in my life and I'm incredibly grateful for the interactions that I've had with them all. I've been blessed to meet fine tradesmen, carers, beggars, artists, clergymen, engineers, bus drivers, road sweepers, teachers, librarians, sportsmen etc., to name just a few. Each one special and unique in their own right, each one bringing something special to my life and yet I can count on one hand the medics I've met whom I would bestow the accolade of special upon.

Yet I make no secret of the fact that whilst I will be as gracious as circumstances dictate when interacting with members of the medical industry. I nevertheless have absolutely no respect for that industry or the views of those employed within it for unless I meet a medic who is able to speak or offer a service from a point of true expertise and I don't mean legitimized bullshit. Then I'm simply not interested in what any medic has to say, and I mean, I'm not interested in anything they have to say on health, politics or any major imposition on life.

I am the master of my own health, for I take my quality of health seriously

You see, as far as I'm concerned they are the lowest of all mortal forms of life. The way these people conduct themselves, fail and abuse people in their care is a scandal and disgrace and for that I'm adamant that for their crimes against humanity they must pay a very heavy price, be that in this life or the next I really don't care. Until that happens I think its fine to explore in your head exactly what you would do to the rogues who've abused and failed you if you ever got the chance to deliver your own unique and personal retributions.

Now whilst some may say: *'Oh dear it's important for our souls and our recovery that we must let go of hatred and anger towards others'*. My answer is simply this, *'Explore that position again when you're tormented by a toxic liver, a toxic body and when every system and organ in your body has been damaged by an insidious bacteria, when it all could have been so easily prevented'* and then I would urge you to simply think your belief structures over again.

You see I personally believe that it's actually extremely healthy and positive to exercise your liver and brain anger. To explore just how far your emotions take you and what you think is suitable, punishment or not, for the suffering you've endured. Who knows, the very fact that you're prepared to explore those thoughts whilst accepting them for what they are, may just be an essential component of your recovery and a vital process that must not be ignored.

With that point of view in focus, I've had some lovely despicable thoughts about what I would like to do to the rogues who failed me. I so desperately want them to feel the level of pain that they create and perpetuate for people like me every minute of every day of their career. I've had thoughts of rounding all medics and their families up and transferring them to great football stadiums around the country.

I am the master of my own happiness, for its in my interests to live life to the full

Where I would strap the medics into chairs and make them watch their loved ones being torn apart without mercy by Hyenas. Now obviously that would take some time because there's only so much a Hyena can eat at any given time but that's okay, the longer the suffering for all concerned the better as far as I'm now concerned. You may ask why I chose Hyenas not lions, tigers, wolfs or bears, well it's because of all the big carnivores the Hyena is in my opinion the cruelest of them all. They don't waste energy killing their victims they simply rip them apart limb from limb. I think being eaten alive and enduring unbelievable suffering before death is fine for the sort of people that I have in mind.

Now of course and after a few years naturally there wouldn't be any family or loved ones left to brutalize, so I would turn my attention directly to the medics. At which point I really would enjoy playing mind games with them torturing them day after day for years. I would inject them with all sorts of substances and break the odd one or two limbs. There would be no quarter given, no repose on grounds of mercy.

But I might allow the odd one of two to read a few books on psychology if they felt it would help them deal or cope with their physical and emotional pain. I would inject some with Lymes Disease, some with HIV, some with syphilis and some with a blend of all three. But before all of that I would revel in playing games with their head and simply talk infinitum about a whole host of things I was planning to do.

I am the master of my own health, for I take my quality of health seriously

The key in all my punishment regimes would be the generation of intolerable isolation, desolation and despair, creating a situation devoid of any humanistic sympathy or due diligence and care. In fact to replicate the culture that these rogues have rolled out on us for years, only in my regime there would be no 'DSBL's' written, no bullshit spoken and no postulation of care, my open and honest policy would be one of simple retribution and payback for the insidious lives that they'd lived.

Now I'm not sure if my anger towards the medical industry will ever subside but what matter that, all that I know is that I can't possibly allow my hatred of them to hold me back. I'm no longer their victim or some innocent that they can indiscriminately abuse, for I'm now 'Barry Hardy' the battle hardened medic hater who will delight in pursuing legal retribution and in due course regardless of whatever form or format that takes.

You see; I want everyone who's ever been chronically ill yet failed by the medical industry to realise and accept fully that they themselves were never to blame. In accepting that they, like me can exercise the demons that reside deep within us all after years of suffering. Because in accepting and not fighting our mind anger, I firmly believe that we're actually setting ourselves free. Simply because personal exploration as far as I'm concerned is nothing more than an intuitive expansive trait and if we choose to live in expansive state we very often leave our pain and suffering behind.

I am the master of my own happiness, for its in my interests to live life to the full

Now, let me make myself clear, I would never advocate actual violence against any medical service sector worker, rogues though they are by default. Nevertheless I certainly believe and therefore think that it's healthy and positive to accept and explore our brain and liver anger because it has a vital part to play in anyone's recovery.

My only footnote would be in closing this chapter is; go gentle into that vile place and never allow yourself to be completely consumed by your cruel thoughts, just accept them for what they are.

It really is okay to hate your medical abusers and accept that they are complete 'shits, cretins and clowns'. It's okay to hate their husbands, wives and kids for reaping great rewards from being associated with and/or to those rogues.

The only point I would make is turn that hatred into positive redress and legal action and don't let it just fester or simply evaporate away. Make your formal complaints if that's what you need to do for in doing so you will kick start a myriad of much needed karmic events.

Network with fellow mindsets and empower yourself in firm assurance that you're no longer that lone foot soldier that you'd lead yourself to believe you are, because at the point you empower your psyche to engage in seeking redress, you've morphed into a dynamic and cataclysmic particle of change.

That will prove to you once and for all, that you're a very real, dramatic, even majestic vanquisher of what is an insidious blight upon society i.e. our shockingly poor and unresponsive medical model, industry and the shits who work within it who are happy to destroy far too many peoples' lives.

I am the master of my own health, for I take my quality of health seriously

Personal Notes

I am the master of my own happiness, for its in my interests to live life to the full

Personal Notes

I am the master of my own health, for I take my quality of health seriously

Personal Notes

I am the master of my own happiness, for its in my interests to live life to the full

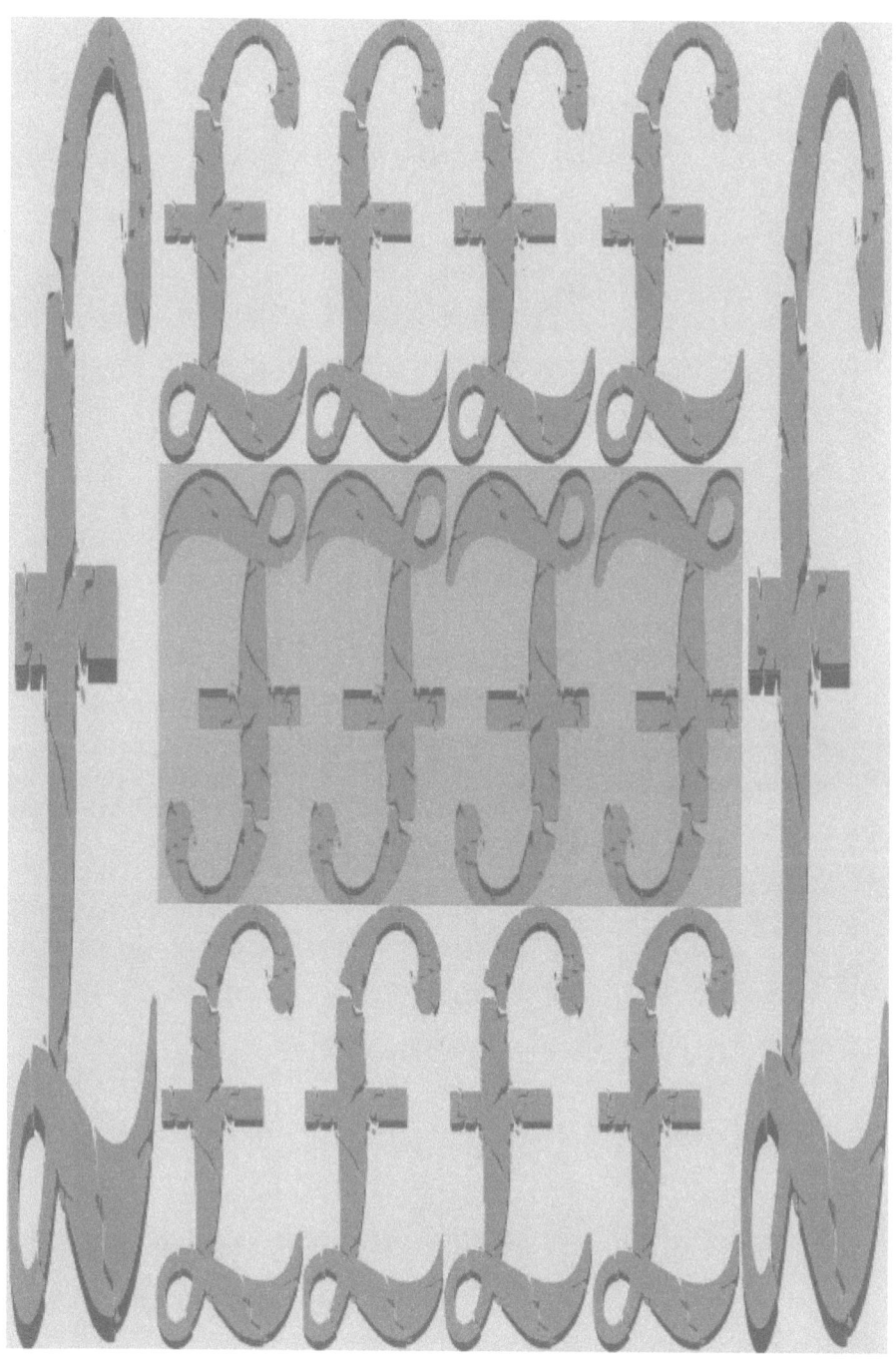

I am the master of my own health, for I take my quality of health seriously

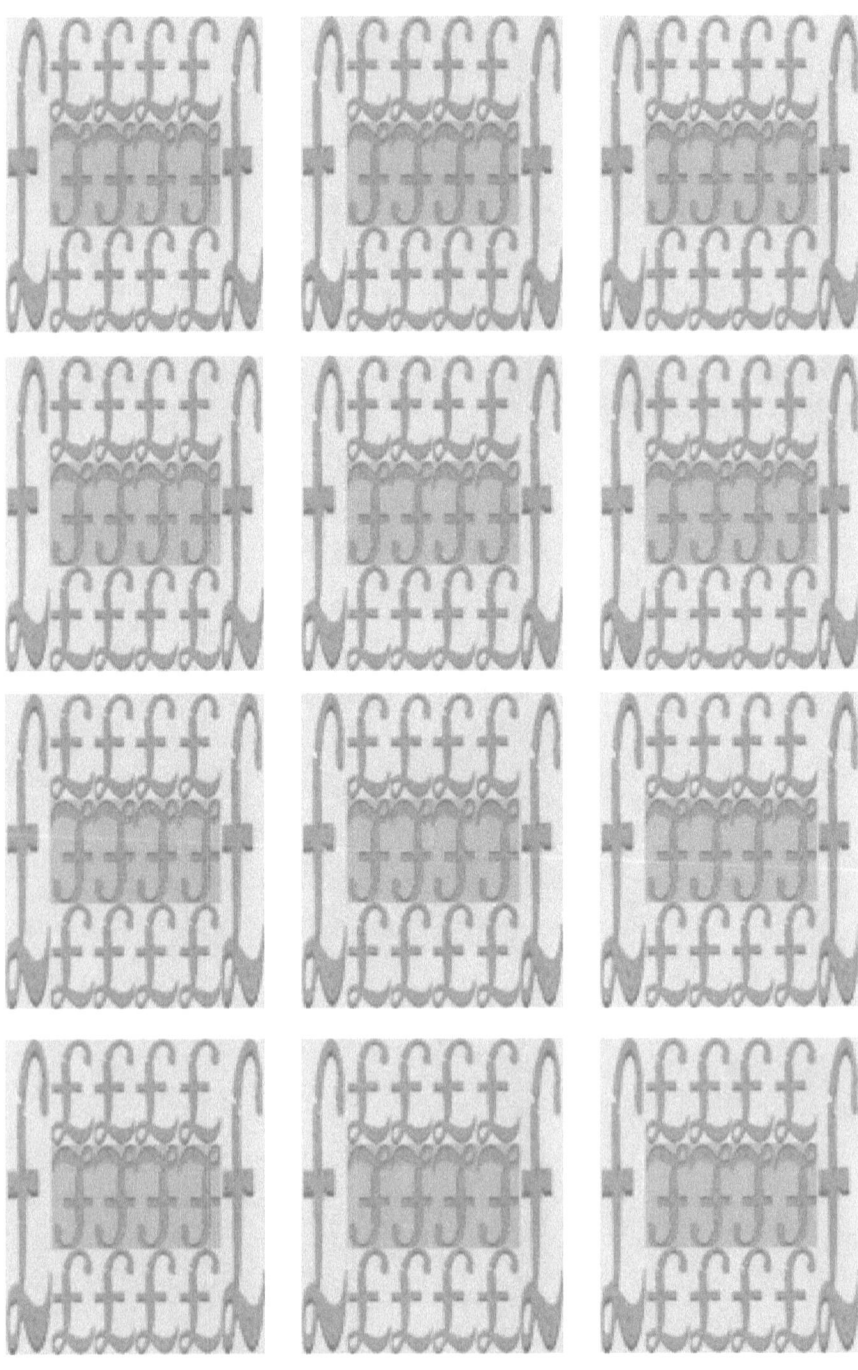

I am the master of my own happiness, for its in my interests to live life to the full

PUTTING A PRICE ON ILLNESS

What price good health eh? That is a question that some may find difficult to answer. You see, putting a price on good health, the price of freedom, of relaxation, of contentment, of security, of wellbeing is like putting a price on the sun, moon and stars. We see them almost every day and yet their value indeterminable or frequently underestimated simply because we've never had a time when they've not been by our side.

Yet every day we hear about films stars securing £20 million for one film, young 16 year old guys signing multi million pound football contracts whilst their older peers are transferred for anything between £10 and £60 million pounds. It's no longer unusual for a mediocre star to be paid between £40.000.00 to £80.00000 a week and that doesn't include the raft of sponsorship deals that they sign.

But who is it that determines these values, is it the result of a standard evaluation formula? Well no it's actually agents and media interests that drive this process and as for skills, well they come in third in the majority of instances at best. Its possible to be a complete flop these days and leave your sporting career behind without any fears, simply because you only need to sign one contract and you're sure to have been made a millionaire.

I am the master of my own health, for I take my quality of health seriously

That's why I don't have any difficulty in putting a price on poor health, or in particular my health that was destroyed by sheer incompetence. You see; I know I had the potential to do many things, to be an Olympian, an extremely wealthy businessman, a politician or a corporate leader of any one of a number of institutions.

But I didn't manage to realise my birth right because my health was removed from my life through ignorance at a very early age and compounded for most of my life thereafter. Today I find it quite bizarre watching our modern football stars, when they pull up with a strain on Saturday, because by Sunday morning they're in having a scan. And by the following week they're playing again if their treatment goes well and whilst that's great for them, it seems implicitly perverse to me.

How can a man kicking a ball get such brilliant treatment whilst another man must fight for his life and recognition of simply appalling symptoms? How can a man be ignored, rubbished and let down when he has an artery in his brain slamming into his neurological nerves, when a guy with a strain gets world class support?

Well the answers not as clear cut as we first might believe. Despite what we may think, it's not simply down to money, although money does have the ability to open doors. Nevertheless; the reality is that the science of sports medicine and clinical care is streets ahead of the shit that we the general public receive. You see; in sports medicine we have a situation where anything and everything is possible, where techniques and procedures are developed at exponential rates. Yet in mainstream medical care all we have delivering our clinical services are charlatans, luddites and rogues rolling out techniques which are decades out of date.

I am the master of my own happiness, for its in my interests to live life to the full

Well I've had a lot of time to think about my health and:

(a) How I was let down.

(b) How I fought for my life.

(c) How much damage my body has incurred.

(d) How much suffering I've endured.

And

- What lies before me now and in the future?

And

- What I've lost and am likely to keep on losing as I continue to age.

I am the master of my own health, for I take my quality of health seriously

Compare that to the pampered highly paid blokes I love to watch every week who get paid obscene amounts of money for simply doing something that they love i.e. playing football. The cost of my damaged health is very low when spread over fifty years. My costs are broken down into five stages with each one being a critical part of my life for a whole host of reasons.

- **16 to 26:-** This was the child moving into manhood and the impacts that my health had upon my well being and career. All of which were compromised by the impacts that my health had upon my whole well being.

- **27 to 37:-** This was the period of my first personal expansion, where home, family, children and career are all or should have be developing rapidly along the same time line. All of which were compromised by the impacts that my health had upon my whole well being.

- **38 to 48:-** This should have been the period that I moved into greater professional presence, where rewards should have been greater including the preparation for future requirements. All of which were compromised by the impacts that my health had upon my whole well being, career and the sheer amount of suffering endured.

- **49 to 59:-** This should have been the period that I moved into several boardrooms with exceptional professional presence, where rewards should have been great including the preparation for future requirements. All of which will be compromised by the impacts that my health had upon my whole well being, career, status and the collateral damage that had been done to my entire body.

- **60 to 70:-** This should have been the period that I moved into gentle retirement, where rewards of my professional career should have provided a high level of comfort. All of which will be compromised by the impacts that my health has had and will continue to do so as I age, plus the lack or earnings derived from a stalled career and significantly lower professional status.

Now whilst I've no agent or any media interests in my personal case I've nevertheless applied a few subjective formulas in my spread sheet on the next page, because you know what? I was worth a whole lot more than I ever received and that's a very bitter pill to have to swallow.

So then I argue that the total cost of my suffering assuming I live to 70 is £89 million which works out at £1.6 million a year, which is a significantly lower cost than my working class peers, who fortunately for them make it big in the glorious game e.g. a footballer earning £5 million a year with ease.

I don't think that £89 million is obscene for all the suffering and the destruction of my body that I've endured, including the associated loss of earnings, loss of home, loss of pensions, and shortened life span when an ignorant GP can earn during his or her career; over £20 million for a few years training and a simple 40/50 hour week.

You see the very same highly paid shits who are daily responsible for so much suffering for people like me and you are very good at making out how badly they're done to. However the very real and unsavory fact of the matter is that they're paid obscene amounts of money for very low skills, whilst systematically crucifying people like you, me and us every single day of their shoddy and disgraceful careers. And do you know what? That really give me the hump!

I am the master of my own happiness, for its in my interests to live life to the full

	Cost	Hours	Days	Weeks	Years	Totals	Accumulative Total
Age 16 to 26							
Emotional & Physical Suffering	20.00	14.00	7.00	52.00	10.00		1,019,200.00
Loss of earnings	15.00	1.00	7.00	52.00	10.00		54,600.00
Medical Treatment Expenses	40.00	1.00	1.00	52.00	10.00		20,800.00
Medication Travel Expenses	10.00	1.00	1.00	52.00	10.00		5,200.00
Impact Upon Sporting Activities	25.00	1.00	1.00	52.00	10.00		13,000.00
Impact Upon Career Activities	40.00	1.00	1.00	52.00	10.00	Sub-total	20,800.00
							1,133,600.00
Age 27 to 37							
Emotional & Physical Suffering	60.00	14.00	7.00	52.00	10.00		3,057,600.00
Loss of earnings	250.00	1.00	7.00	52.00	10.00		910,000.00
Medical Treatment Expenses	60.00	1.00	1.00	52.00	10.00		31,200.00
Medication Travel Expenses	30.00	1.00	1.00	52.00	10.00		15,600.00
Impact Upon Sporting Activities	70.00	1.00	1.00	52.00	10.00		36,400.00
Impact Upon Career Activities	800.00	1.00	1.00	52.00	10.00		416,000.00
Impact Upon Pension	80.00	1.00	1.00	52.00	10.00	Sub-total	41,600.00
							4,508,400.00
Age 38 to 48							
Emotional & Physical Suffering	350.00	24.00	7.00	52.00	10.00		30,576,000.00
Loss of earnings	320.00	1.00	7.00	52.00	10.00		1,164,800.00
Medical Treatment Expenses	250.00	1.00	1.00	52.00	10.00		130,000.00
Medication Travel Expenses	70.00	1.00	1.00	52.00	10.00		36,400.00
Impact Upon Sporting Activities	300.00	1.00	1.00	52.00	10.00		156,000.00
Impact Upon Career Activities	800.00	1.00	1.00	52.00	10.00		416,000.00
Impact Upon Pension	200.00	1.00	1.00	52.00	10.00		104,000.00
Property Equity Lost	580.00	1.00	1.00	52.00	10.00	Sub-total	301,600.00
							32,884,800.00
Age 49 to 59							
Emotional & Physical Suffering	320.00	18.00	7.00	52.00	10.00		20,966,400.00
Loss of earnings	450.00	1.00	7.00	52.00	10.00		1,638,000.00
Medical Treatment Expenses	80.00	1.00	1.00	52.00	10.00		41,600.00
Medication Travel Expenses	20.00	1.00	1.00	52.00	10.00		10,400.00
Impact Upon Sporting Activities	300.00	1.00	1.00	52.00	10.00		156,000.00
Impact Upon Career Activities	1,500.00	1.00	1.00	52.00	10.00		780,000.00
Impact Upon Pension	400.00	1.00	1.00	52.00	10.00		208,000.00
Property Equity Lost	580.00	1.00	1.00	52.00	10.00	Sub-total	301,600.00
							24,102,000.00
Age 60 to 70							
Emotional & Physical Suffering	500.00	14.00	7.00	52.00	10.00		25,480,000.00
Loss of earnings	120.00	1.00	7.00	52.00	10.00		436,800.00
Medical Treatment Expenses	100.00	1.00	1.00	52.00	10.00		52,000.00
Medication Travel Expenses	20.00	1.00	1.00	52.00	10.00		10,400.00
Impact Upon Sporting Activities	100.00	1.00	1.00	52.00	10.00		52,000.00
Impact Upon Career Activities	200.00	1.00	1.00	52.00	10.00		104,000.00
Impact Upon Pension	200.00	1.00	1.00	52.00	10.00		104,000.00
Property Equity Lost	580.00	1.00	1.00	52.00	10.00	Sub-total	301,600.00
							26,540,800.00
						Total	£89,169,600.00

Personal Notes

I am the master of my own health, for I take my quality of health seriously

I am the master of my own happiness, for its in my interests to live life to the full

Personal Notes

I am the master of my own health, for I take my quality of health seriously

Personal Notes

I am the master of my own happiness, for its in my interests to live life to the full

I am the master of my own health, for I take my quality of health seriously

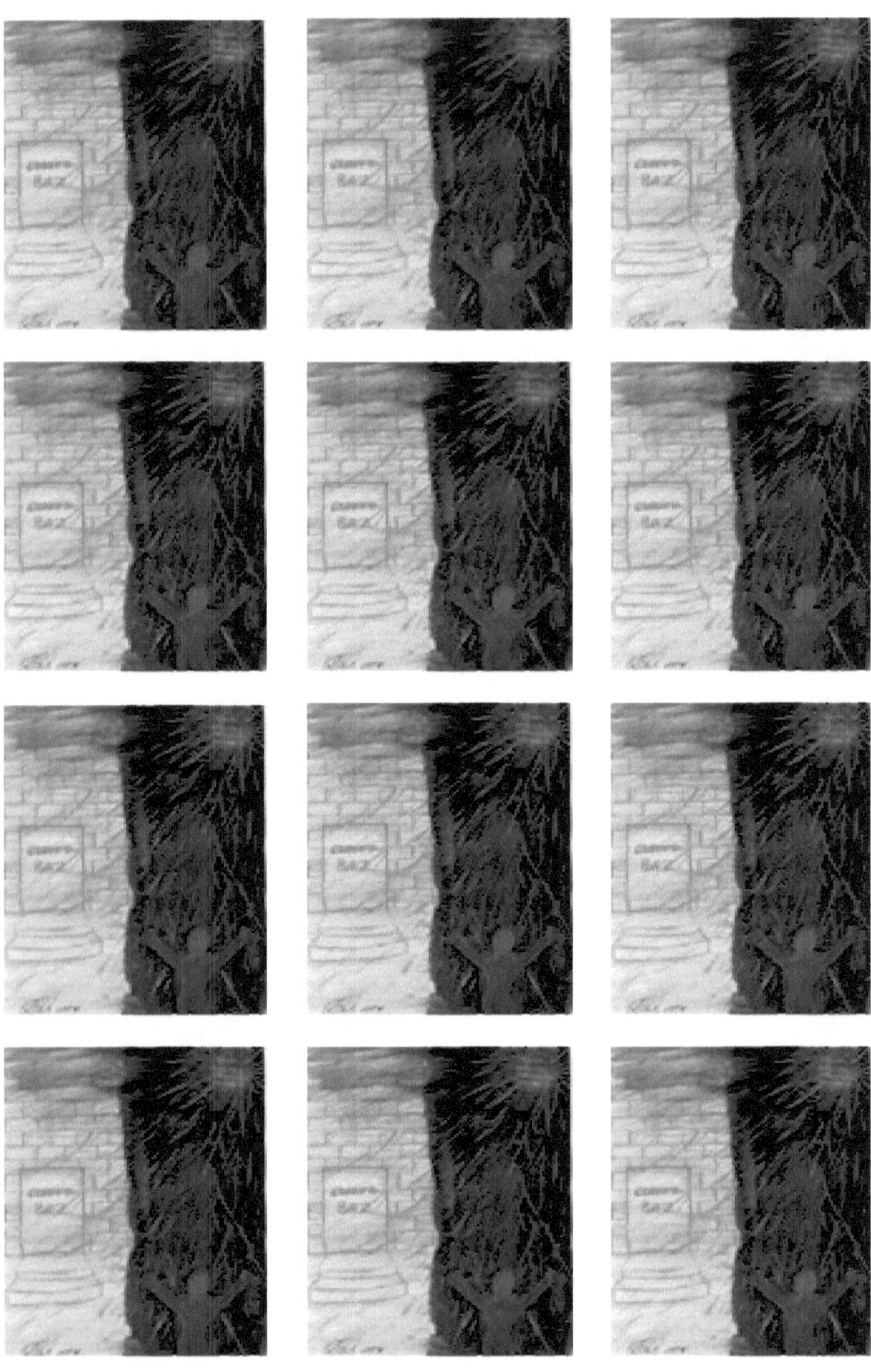

I am the master of my own happiness, for its in my interests to live life to the full

FRIENDS FOREVER OR UNTIL YOU GET TOO ILL BAZ

I've never felt the need to be part of a pack, to conform to someone else's agenda, nevertheless I

- Like people.
- Love life.

And

- Continuously seek to always broaden my horizons.

I'm neither a loner nor a socialite, wherever I am in the world, I'm able to integrate easily into that community. I embrace new experiences and reject social or historical ignorance's, yet I'm my own man:

- I have a keen sense of honour and fun.
- I do not discriminate in the moment in terms of race or creed.

And

- I will help any man or woman who needs my help.

I am the master of my own health, for I take my quality of health seriously

I am blessed to have the friends that I have and grateful that my illness enabled me to see my blessings for what they truly were. You see, during my life I've helped hundreds of people in thought, word and deed and because of that I've been humbled, astonished and even rewarded in so many different ways. Interestingly though, I've also been frequently hurt by the thoughtlessness, selfishness and despicable conduct of some of those who have sought my help. No more so than as my health declined. You see, prior to my decline, I'd spent my entire life:

- Supporting, sponsoring many good causes.

- Mentoring deadbeats back into work.

- Helping people move home and even helping to refurbish their homes at times.

- Given people lots of money during their difficult times and most never even thought or sought to repay me back.

- Writing CV's and references for hundreds of people, sometimes being woken by them in the early hours of the morning desperate for a CV rework so that they had something to hand over the very next morning for the job that they so desperately needed.

- Employed the virtually unemployable on some of my larger jobs and always given jobs to the local lads where and when I could.

- Given freely of my time normally at my own personal expense as and when people needed help or in put from me.

In my despair however, I received not a call, not a text, not a card or a letter for any of those souls that I'd helped in the past. Instead my payback was to find out that the majority either turned their back or simply turned their attention to ridiculing me e.g.

- As my health declined I helped one guy in particular a TV repair technician who pleaded with me to help him because he desperately wanted to work in the nuclear industry. So I re-wrote his CV, mentored him through several interview processes, gave him references and in essence I reinvented him in terms of his professional credentials. I placed him in his first real job and at the point he secured his dream job in the Nuclear Industry, he simply walked by me in the street as if I didn't exist. All I can say is shame on you dude and I hope you can handle your karmic payback.

- The several charities that I'd supported simply dropped me like a hot potatoe because I was of no further use.

- My extended family and wider circle of so called friends just whispered behind my back, cackling their ignorant thoughts but offering zero support.

- The builder whom I sponsored to the tune of 2.5k to kick start his failing business simply dived into doorways rather than attempt to engage with me.

- The fell club that I'd supported for the best part of ten years, not one of my so called fell running buddies reached out and attempted to contact me, albeit that one of my team mates Gary Byers was very considerate every time I met him in the street.

I am the master of my own health, for I take my quality of health seriously

- The numerous women that I'd helped through their difficult tricky times simply passed me in the street by dipping their eyes.

Because of those experiences

- It remains simply shocking to me to this day, just how sickeningly shallow most mortals or so called friends can be, as our life or our health or a combination of both fall apart with high visibility.

But I can't change any of that, the generosity I gave freely or the hurt that was my payment in return, simply because I don't feel that I can ever change who I am save to say, that I'm much better these days at defusing and not allowing people to drop their problems onto me. I will offer advice if asked for it, but if people need help to change then the first thing they need to understand is that change must come from within i.e. THEM and not from me, because I'm not prepared to shoulder anyone else responsibilities or concerns any longer. Because I have far too many deep hut and let down t-shirts hanging up in my emotional wardrobe and to be honest I don't want any further additions.

I am the master of my own happiness, for its in my interests to live life to the full

Nevertheless a big part of the process in my recovery was to try to understand why I'd encountered what I had i.e. the best and worst of all things, truly brilliant friends and lizards simply masquerading as friends.

Such that when we look at the 'Oxford Dictionary' we read that a friend is: *a person known well to another and regarded with liking, affection and loyalty, an ally in a fight or a cause.* Well there is no doubt in my mind therefore that the few who stayed with me were indeed very good friends. Because they laughed, cried and died with me many times but they never gave up on me, but my friends were few in number i.e.

- John Brenan, lifelong friend, we connected on every possible level, work, politics and morality etc.

- Janice Curwen, John's partner and mother to the engaging Ben and the feisty Kim.

- Fred Anderson, my boyhood sporting hero who went on to become my fell running mentor and loyal loyal friend.

- Paul Berry, my first sports massage specialist and good mate, fantastic sense of humour and just loves a hug.

- Dave Beattie, my Glasgow Rangers brother in arms, uncompromising, passionate, sincere and a fantastic slant on life and indeed a king of sporting satires.

What of the people who abandoned me 'my fair weather friends' well actually I realise now they we never anything more than, floaters, and Machiavellians, cunning amoral and simply opportunistic aliens. As for their part in my life, well the blame resides firmly with me. I simply wasn't strong enough to act upon my gut feelings and keep my distance from them. I made a very real mortal mistake, I gave of myself far to easily, far too many times, to individuals and organisations who were not deserving of me or my decency. Such is the way of things I guess and only my illnesses let me see that. In making connections we can all make some very big mistakes that remain invisible until our vision not our eyes enable us to see.

Mortality can be a real leveller, you see when our health fails, for the first time in our lives we're able to validate fully who's by our side and who's been simply with us for the ride. Chronic or terminal illness tests us all, it tests our own physical and emotional strength, it tests friendships and relationships, it in invades every aspect of our living, breathing, functioning psyche. There is nothing that the imposition of chronic illness does not breathe its damp, stagnant breath upon, bringing about: misery, alienation, challenges and change.

Staying with a friend during a period of chronic illness must be one of the most difficult things that we as mortals ever have to do, because we've forged connections on one level and then we are plunged into uncertainty, complexities and concerns. For some it's far too much for them, for others they can handle it for a while, whilst for others the thought of abandoning their friend in need simply never crosses their decency of mind. My friends did things for me that are upon reflection simply staggering to this day, they:

I am the master of my own happiness, for its in my interests to live life to the full

- Welcomed me into their homes.

- Listened to me, my ideas, my beliefs and my despairs.

- Raised concerns with the medical industry on my behalf.

- Gave me money, food, shelter and asked for nothing in return.

But more importantly they;

- Were my only points of contact in my isolated and very desperate world!

And yet the saddest thing that has ever happened to me in my entire life was the day I lost forever, my best friend John Brenan. You see, as my condition severely declined, I was rushed off to London by my then girlfriend Karina. Feeling that I would never see Cumbria again, I did all that I could do as the spiritual guy and simply thanked all my friends and said my last goodbyes.

But I didn't die, because I'd connected with Dr Sarah Myhill and she took my clinical care onboard and with her help I sort of recovered from the 6.5 stone wreck that had left Cumbria, into a 9 stone yet still desperately ill young man.

To my complete shock upon returning back to Cumbria for a brief visit prior to relocating down to Shaftesbury to undergo extensive herbal treatment. I found that my best friends door was closed to me, calls and texts were not returned and whilst at first I was simply perplexed by this, within a few days I realised that he too had now abandoned me.

I am the master of my own health, for I take my quality of health seriously

I've never felt hurt like that before, it was a sense of complete bewilderment and complete devastation at a time when just being in my body drew upon all of my strength just to cope. To this day, whilst I understand his reasoning for the decision he took, his handling of the situation was tasteless and not something I can ever forgive. Because it was so shocking and not what I expected or deserved from him.

The background was that John's partner Janice was going through a bad time herself and so she simply couldn't handle me being around any longer which is understandable I suppose. But what hurt me the most was that instead of John simply calling me, texting me or pulling me to one side, he said nothing, yet the rules of our engagement had changed, except I was the only one who didn't know they'd changed.

At that hollow point where I realised things had changed I did all I could do at that time. I sent him an email notifying him by text, and made it quite clear that I understood that he didn't want me anywhere near his home and that was now fine by me.

Fifteen minutes after that email was sent he arrived outside my mother's home and asked if he could have a chat with me outside, he was nervous and not like my old friend at all, his words were brisk as he said only this: 'Baz I have no idea what you're suffering marra or where that is taking you too, but I need to protect my family and I can't go any further with you, so I'm wishing you the best of luck marra I really am'.

I am the master of my own happiness, for its in my interests to live life to the full

At that point he just extended his hand and for some reason in my confusion I let him shake mine. No other words were spoken and I simply turned my back on him and at that point our lifelong friendship came crashing to an end. It was a very sad time for me and I'm sure for him too the fall-out of which I'm sure he would agree is that we both know now, just how illness can destroy so many things.

Chronic illness pushes us and the people close to us to the very limits of our personal capabilities. Yet it also allows all parties to see each other in different lights, to see our differences, our strengths and weaknesses, in essence it provides us with hitherto unreachable personal insight. I once had nothing but the highest regard and respect for my best friend John, for the way he approached and conducted his life. But on the day we parted company for ever, all that respect I had for him simply evaporated away like morning dew when baked in the morning's bright sunshine. On that morning it was as if our friendship had never been there, simply a delusion, an illusion or a dream that I'd had.

So whilst he will always be a very real part of my former life, a kindred soul that I encountered and connected with on so many levels, a man of great decency, generosity and humility. He will never be my friend again and that's for sure; for when we destroy the foundations of a building, we all must understand that no building ever sits securely again.

We could never be the friends that we once were, for my trust of him has been destroyed completely and whilst we could attempt to do a little bit of patch work here and there. The reality is we're both far too real to know that the past is past and for all concerned it's often best left there to simply dissolve away.

I am the master of my own health, for I take my quality of health seriously

We're on completely different paths now because John chose it that way, he not me, decided that our connection must end and I'm sure that wasn't easy for him.

But hey it's not all doom and gloom I'm sure he and his family are doing very well for themselves because he's a highly successful guy in his own right. And whilst we will never ever have a laugh together or talk about matters of state, it really is okay now as I'm sure he would agree, because the death of friendships, like the death of a soul, are only parts of the bigger scheme of things.

When we're dealt a bum hand, we only have two choices, we either stick or play it's as simple as that, because we frequently can never choose our playing partners or dealers anyway. I don't ever expect to see, meet or greet John or any of his family again and I'm confident that he is of the same opinion; we have nothing in common now in any way shape or form, and that's just how powerful a karmic clearing can be.

Whilst it's sad that my chronic illness and his personal circumstances lead to the destruction of a very special connection, a connection which guided us both through some difficult and enjoyable life experiences together. I'm frequently reminded of John's very own words: 'shit just happens sometimes marra' and of course he's right so when the shit does hit the proverbial fan, then it's time to evaluate and reformulate all our perception and if we can move forward with the minimum of resistance.

I am the master of my own happiness, for its in my interests to live life to the full

In closing this chapter I think the final point I need to make is that we all need friends, no matter who we think we are, because we need friends to:

- Laugh with.

- Grow with.

- Cry with.

And

- Enjoy all of the great things of life with.

The truth of the matter however is that none of us will ever truly know how good our friends or our friendships are until all either ours or their chips are down. Nevertheless, as a great romantic I accept that nothing stays the same forever and that all things change, and I suspect that is one of the most rewarding facets and blessings of life.

You see, it doesn't matter if we've moved on and leave former friends, friendships and fond situations behind, the fact that we once had them indicates to me just how blessed we were at that particular moment in time.

During the darkest days in our lives, if we can count one single friend by our side, then I would suggest that our life and the way we've chosen to live our life has been of far greater importance than we could ever imagine at that time. Because the fact that we've a friend by our side says to me, that we've connected with a kindred soul in much lighter and brighter times.

I am the master of my own health, for I take my quality of health seriously

People come in and out of our lives for all sorts of reasons, but the ones that hold us when we fall, feed us when we're hungry, love us for who we are without any shadow of a doubt stand head and shoulders above the best of any other mortals we encounter.

The rest I would suggest are nothing more than froth merchants and really not worth a moment of our precious time, you see, it's not what a man or women says he or she will do for you that's important when the shit hits the fan. It's the things that they do, the reasons they do things for you and the fact that they hold no hidden agendas that truly sets them apart from their peers.

I'm a strange guy in many ways and I will always hold both hands up to that. But wherever I go, whatever I do, I know that I'm a very sincere, very genuine and implicitly reliable friend and I've never forgotten the poignancy of a film that I saw way back as a child with my earth god and granddad stating: **'No man is a failure who has friends'** *It's a Wonderful Life (1947) Staring: James Stewart, Donna Reed and Director: Frank Capra.*

I am the master of my own happiness, for its in my interests to live life to the full

Well on that emotive statement no man is a failure who has friends all I can say is; look to your left, look to your right and consider this from time to time, who amongst the people I associate with now is a truly good friend of mine.

Above all things be very mindful of who those friends are and their role in your life for one day you might just discover what they really are. At which point you will truly know which ones are your friend and which ones are the froth merchants who've simply wasted far too much of your valuable time.

May we all be blessed and bring blessings upon the lives of others through the mutuality of; unconditional friendship and on that final aspiration I'll close this simple chapter in the unequivocal realisation that in terms of mutual friendships, I've been one truly unlucky yet truly lucky guy.

I am the master of my own health, for I take my quality of health seriously

Personal Notes

I am the master of my own happiness, for its in my interests to live life to the full

Personal Notes

I am the master of my own health, for I take my quality of health seriously

Personal Notes

I am the master of my own happiness, for its in my interests to live life to the full

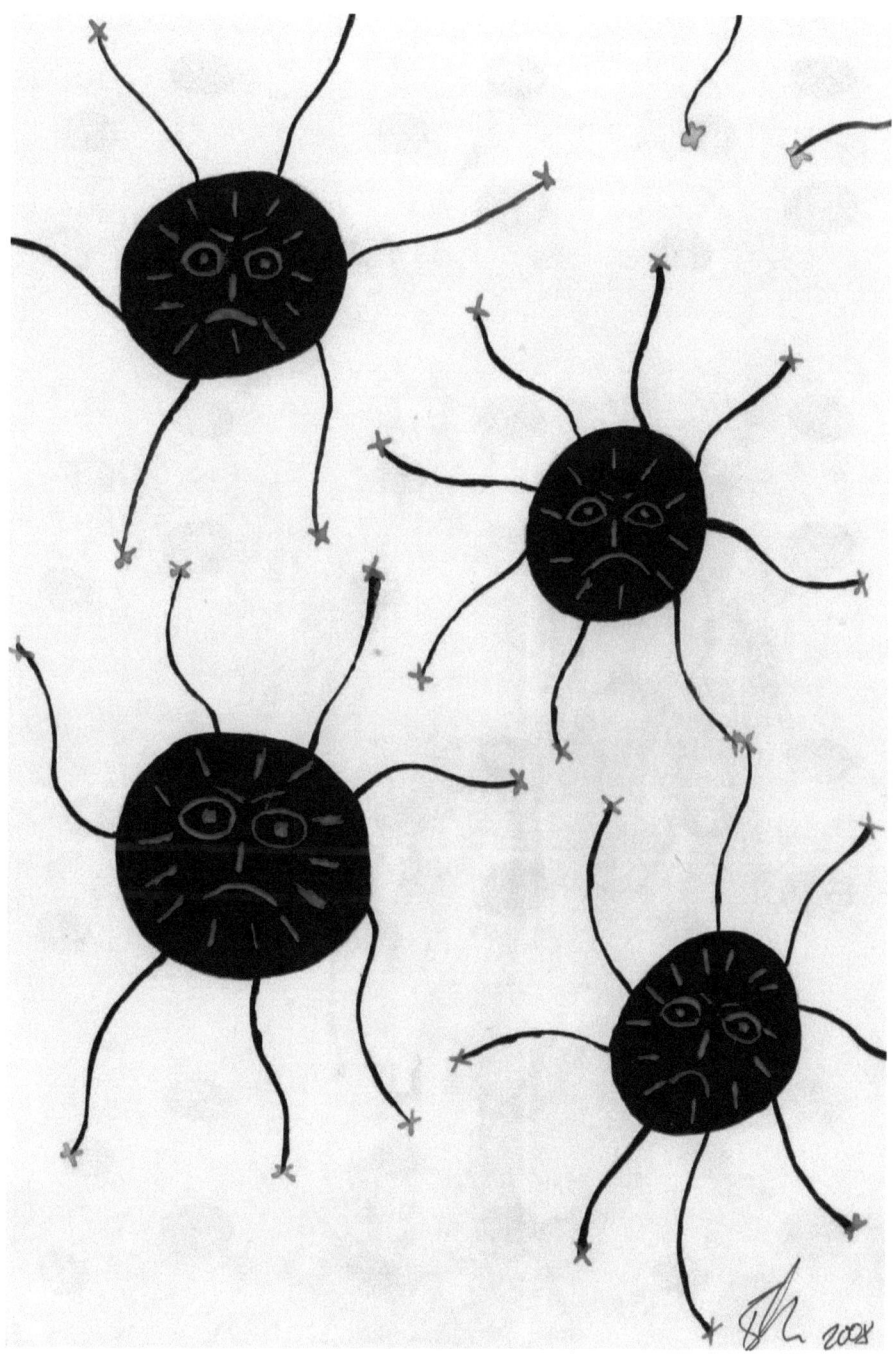

I am the master of my own health, for I take my quality of health seriously

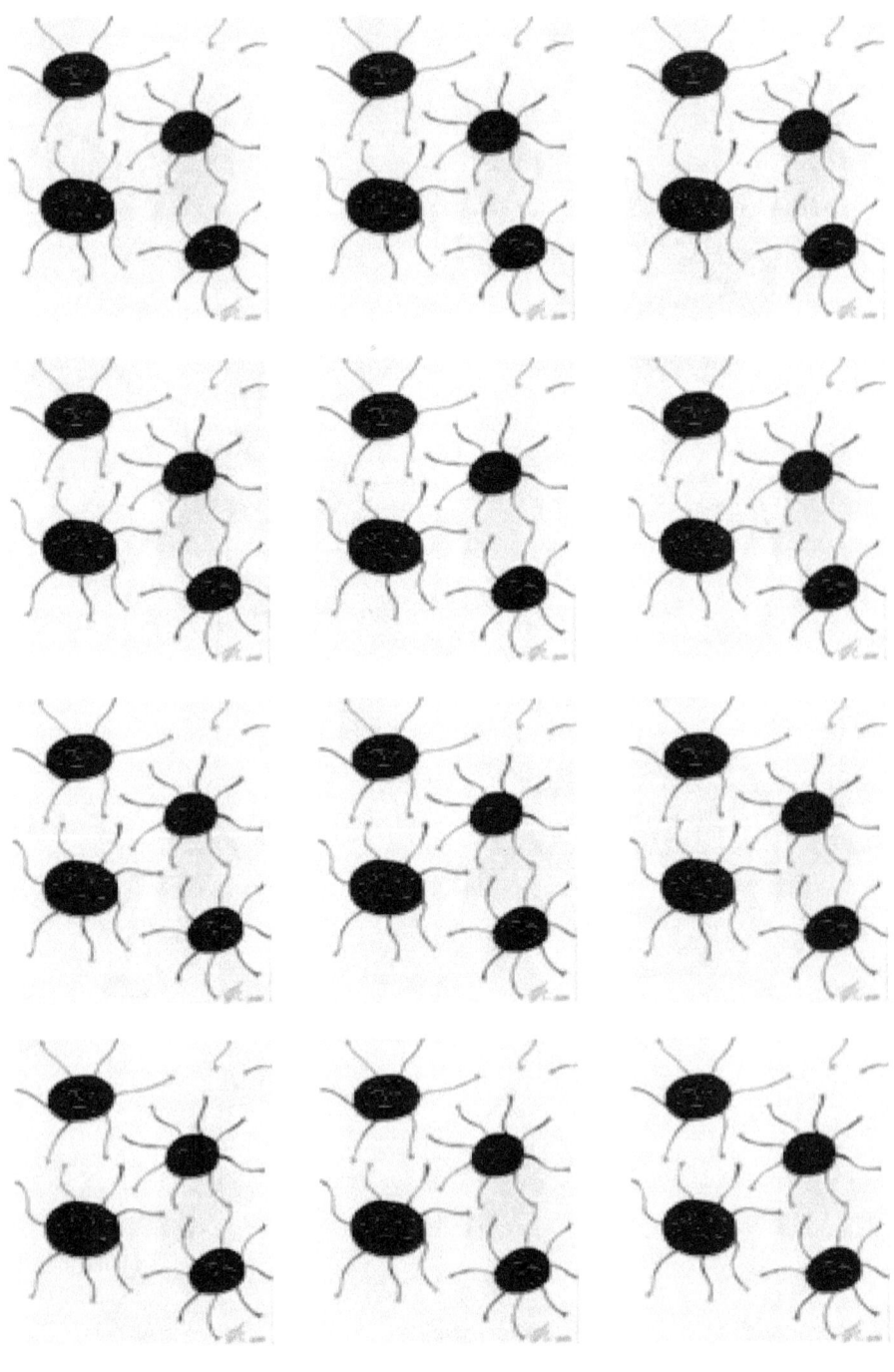

I am the master of my own happiness, for its in my interests to live life to the full

WHEN HARPIES ARE YOUR ONLY COMPANIONS

Harpies were the spirits of sudden, sharp gusts of wind. They were known as the hounds of Zeus and were dispatched by the Gods to snatch away people and things from the earth. Sudden, mysterious disappearances were often attributed to the Harpyiai. The Harpies were once sent by Zeus to plague King Phineus of Thrake as punishment for revealing the secrets of the Gods. Whenever a plate of food was set before him, the Harpies would swoop down and snatch it away, befouling any scraps left behind. Jason and his Argonauts sort of put paid to a couple of them for a while, but hey that was a Greek trilogy not my reality, there was no Jason or his Argonauts there for me. No matter how much I prayed during the darkest years of my illness, my reward was nothing more than to be greeted with greater ignorance, greater intolerance and symptoms that:

- Refused to respond to any form of intervention.

- Continued to worsen and change for no apparent reason.

My illness simply pushed me into places that no man should have to go to, it pushed me in to deep dark pits, each one with a deeper darker pit of its own inside. And I was forced to descend helpless into all those pits, petrified, completely distort yet always alone.

My faith in all I believed in was shattered to its core, it was like the higher force that I'd always believed in had simply abandoned me to the harpies of the night. As I screamed in mortal agony for help, the light and all its so called majesty simply sat back whilst the darkness feasted upon me with delight.

To truly understand the depth of my feelings now, it's important that I explain the position that I came from prior to my illness. As a child, I saw spirit, e.g. I communicated with my oldest brother William from the age of four or five. I quickly learned however that it was neither cool nor safe to let people know who or what I could see.

It was okay when I was able to let channelled thoughts resonate with people who needed to hear what they needed to hear. Having such a gift is an extraordinary burden however, because you're stuck between two worlds, each with a message to give, but each with limitations on accessing, delivering or welcoming those messages.

At the age of four we moved into a new property on woodhouse, in fact it was 16 Fell View Avenue and on the very first night I was immediately targeted and assaulted by a dark spirit. Can you imagine that? I was scared witless and had no one to talk to, yet knowing that I was going to have to live with something so vile and obscene, for what I felt in my little child's brain for the rest of my life. Anyway, by night three my little big brother came back to me but now he was surrounded by a very very bright light.

I am the master of my own happiness, for its in my interests to live life to the full

I had no idea what the light was it had no shape or form, but it transpired later that the light's only role appeared to protect me from the dark spirit that was for some reason after me. The dark spirit made its presence very clear in the house and soon everyone knew it was there, it would slam things around, move things and generally be a pain in the arse day and night.

Incredulous as it may sound, even though my mum knew we had a problem upstairs, every night she would send me up there for her nightdress which she'd left in her bed. Every night that bloody horrible thing would just jump out on me, snarl at me and scare the life out of me. I would jump from as high a step as possible on the stairs just to get back down and into the light. No matter how much I pleaded with my mum not to make me go upstairs for the nightie my mum would simply say don't be so stupid and then simply make me go.

My brother and sister would always be so relieved and happy that it was me who'd been sent upstairs and not them. One night though my mum asked my sister for some extraordinary reason to go upstairs for the nightie and she just broke down in hysterics and threw herself to the ground.

It was from that point only that it became accepted that we indeed had a problem that couldn't be ignored. So my mum pulled the church into the problem and lots of things were done, prayers where offered and bibles were placed by our beds but the dark spirit simply snarled in the corner of the bedroom that I shared with my surviving brother.

It was made very clear to us by my mum that no one should be told about the problem upstairs, because if we did we would never get out of the council house and onto Kells where my dad was from and always wanted to return to. So that is precisely what we did, we never uttered a word about our problem to anyone for many many years.

I am the master of my own health, for I take my quality of health seriously

At the age of eight I was by my bed saying my prayers as I did every night when suddenly the room went cold and when I looked to my right the snarling dark sprit just thrust itself at me. At that point, there was a thunderous white flash and the dark spirit disappeared. Behind me stood my little big brother William who simply pointed to my bed, and so I quickly jumped into it at which point he sat on the edge of my bed.

He was not a little baby anymore, yet he was neither a boy nor a man, he was just, well, I don't know, just my little big brother William beaming a fantastic big smile at me. I never saw the dark spirit again although whenever it was around, my bed would sink as if someone was sitting on it and as soon as I looked out our William would smile back at me.

Now none of that story was ever told whilst I lived at home, for it was far too dangerous to even consider informing my mum of such happenings of our William in my life. So for the rest of my time in that house, whenever anyone mentioned that someone had sat on their bed the night before I would simply play the family game of; shit how scary is that? Knowing full well the actual score!

I am the master of my own happiness, for its in my interests to live life to the full

From my infancy until 2005 I saw spirit, I saw the lost souls, I saw the angels, and I saw far too many harpies. You see from 1996, the presence of harpies in my life simply increased in frequency and intensity year upon year.

I would feel ill for several days and then I would be confronted by one or perhaps two and therein would have to do battle with them in whatever form that needed to take. I saw them everywhere, and as my health declined and that pushed me further and further into the abyss I saw no more light workers or angles just harpies to the left, right, back and front of me.

I was alone; I couldn't tell anyone close to me, even worse very few in the realms of spirituality could understand precisely what was happening to me or how to help me protect myself. One so called expert even asked me never to come to his premises again, because he'd never experienced such a level of dark energy that I'd apparently brought in with me. I said to him, 'I can see that you know that I'm fighting for my soul here so why won't you help me?' whereupon he lowered his head and said, 'sorry, I'm so sorry but it's all far too much for me'.

Some however tried their best to help me yet found they were unable to do so and I was frequently asked if I'd ever studied the occult because the darkness had sort of enveloped me. I screamed and begged the higher light forces to come in and help me, until September of 2004 when I finally gave up and at that point for the first time in my life the darkness simply swamped all over me.

I am the master of my own health, for I take my quality of health seriously

I've never felt such fear, such terror, I just wanted so badly out of my body and two days later I committed suicide. Yes I committed suicide, there was no attempt, it was real, I'd simply had enough of life, enough of pain, enough of the light force and more importantly I'd had enough of me.

But for me there was to be no end to my suffering, because by some perverse/sick fluke I was rescued and forced to endure even deeper and more isolatory misery, suffering and insurmountable despair. My faith in divinity and my faith in mortality have been shattered beyond any of my former comprehensions as a result of my life passage.

I've never intentionally set out to harm anyone, I've never hindered the progress of anyone, I've always given from a pure heart and yet the support that I've had from the forces of light and the universe in general has been spectacularly sparse. My view now is screw spirituality and spiritual growth through emotional and physical pain; I'll take success in mortality until the light force of spirituality decides to participate fully in ALL the rigors of mortality and the pain of living a mortal life.

I'm simply not interested in people who've experienced cursory life challenging problems, quoting extracts from e.g. 'The Power of Now: A Guide to Spiritual Enlightenment by Eckhart Tolle'. I live my life by the same values I brought with me, I acknowledge my mortality, express my spirituality, but I'm no clone of any new age spiritual splinter group. I am a man of my own time, a man with lots of issues, a man with lots of pasts, but I've lost my faith in mortality, divinity and the ultimate spiritual progression of man.

I am the master of my own happiness, for its in my interests to live life to the full

So if you wish to engage with me now on be that: spiritual matters or not, it's important to note that you'd better be personally well experienced, in all matters of life and death and above all, 100% your own man or woman. Because unless I believe in you or who you think you are; I'm not interested in exploring anything you have to say on matters spirituality or mortality in point of fact.

I say that because I was born and lived for many years in a polarized, insular and ignorant backwater where absolute 'cretins' felt they had the right to say anything they wanted to say to you. Be that, articulating their flawed perception of you, to you, or even daring to impose their own bigoted views upon you.

Many was the time that some ignorant West Cumbrian cretin would jump out on me in the street, in the pub and in the work place spewing their bile, 'Who does thou think thou bloody is marra etc, etc,' and I always did my level best to try to explain who I was to them. I did so because I foolishly thought that I had an obligation to lighten their load, to enable them to be more than they thought they could be. That I have to say was just part of my overall spiritual beliefs.

But I'm no longer able to buy into the spiritual progression clap trap that I bought into way back in my youth. It's a fact that we cannot project ourselves out of famine, it's a fact that we cannot change anything we've already completed and it's a fact that for some of us, mortality is just a complete pain. The only thing we can ever do is realise that we're trapped in mortality for a short time only and in that pain we will find love, fear, further pain and personal growth if we're lucky.

I am the master of my own health, for I take my quality of health seriously

The sad thing for me these days is that whilst illness hasn't really changed my generosity and intent. What really pisses me off these days now and it never did before, is that I can no longer accept talent-less, greedy, disgusting 'cretins' living off the fat of the land. Whilst people I consider kindred souls can make absolutely no progress at all. There is no grace in suffering, no renewal through a life filled with pain and there is absolutely no growth at all for me now in a life filled only with misery when what we all need is security for our mind, body and soul.

Mortality really sucks and all the froth in between is as forgettable as: a desolate lonely tear or a prayer that's never heard. It's as forgettable as the call we never made, the love we never had, the things we should have said and the lives we should have saved.

The only things that gives mortality any notability at all, is the way that we: touch people's hearts, bring smiles to a face and how hard we're prepared to work for and towards all that we passionately believe in.

Personal Notes

I am the master of my own health, for I take my quality of health seriously

Personal Notes

I am the master of my own happiness, for its in my interests to live life to the full

I am the master of my own health, for I take my quality of health seriously

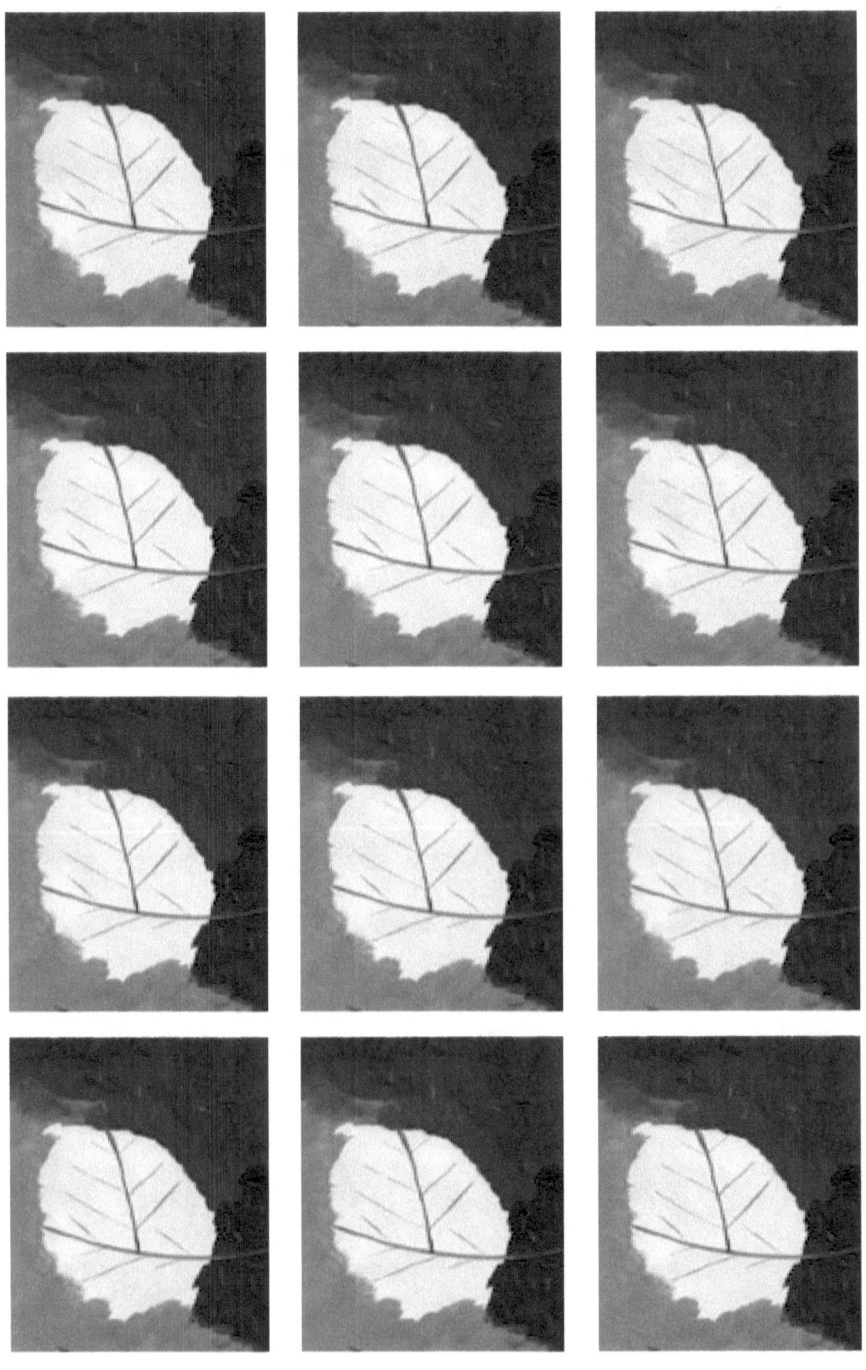

I am the master of my own happiness, for its in my interests to live life to the full

Exploring My Own Mortality

What do you say about yourself when you've already bared your soul? Well I guess all anyone can ever do is tell it as it is. I'm a working class guy with nothing more than a desire to do well in all I undertake. I trained as a plumber and worked for the best part of ten years as a pipefitter in a heavy chemical process industry. I've self funded all my own professional training and qualifications culminating thus far, with my highest qualification being the award of a Master of Science degree from the University of Manchester in 1999. I've worked at every conceivable level in industry and management from shop floor to reporting solely to numerous board rooms.

Despite my appalling health conditions I have an impressive track record of successes, and in general my colleagues have always applauded my technical competence, candour, work ethics and general lighthearted disposition. I have absolutely no medical qualifications and no desire to acquire the same, I've had a belly full of the medical industry after enough suffering to last me several hundred years.

I've been a fell runner, a doer, a carer and a lover, I've been a giver, a supporter, a motivator and creator in fact I've been many things to both myself and my fellow man. But one thing I've always been despite my tests, my disappointments and my despair, is a man above all things who's been true to himself.

I am the master of my own health, for I take my quality of health seriously

I've been blessed with great tenacity and an ability to learn and despite all that the universe has conspired to throw at me I've always given one hundred per cent of me, not one hundred and one or ninety nine per cent but everything that it's possible to give. So that at the ripe old age of 47 I now truly understand that to ask one hundred percent of one hundred per cent is more than enough to ask of any living man. For if any man says he's with you one hundred and ten percent then you know he's a liar, because most of us operate at sixty percent or less almost one hundred percent of the time.

I've battled back from appalling illness; I've battled with the medical industry and society's perceptions of me. I've done what no man that I've ever met could possibly do unaided. I've taken my conditions, the establishment and the universe head on and whilst my quality of life is still dreadful I know that I've done all that I can do.

Every organ and every cell in my body has been damaged I have a Posterior Inferior Cerebella Artery slamming into my vestibular bundle and brain stem with every beat of my heart. Most days my life is simply dreadful, and I would be happy not to be in my body at all and yet some days I just think when all said and done, by simply writing my books I've sort of really won this battle.

But the reality is that none of us ever win, and whilst some of us have a trouble free passage blessed with rewards and great glory, some of on the other hand have simply the shit that we call mortality to deal with day after day. I for one have had more than enough of mortality for within its magnificence and beauty resides the reality of its sheer insanity and highly predictable and incongruent stupidity.

I am the master of my own happiness, for its in my interests to live life to the full

Only those truly touched by personal mortality understand that it's nothing more than physical insanity. A moment in time, so dreadful, so appalling, so unforgiving and so very stupid, to the point that one wonders if there really is any point. Such has been my experience of mortality that I hope and pray that at some point in the collective cosmic process, that, mortality in its current projection is finally eclipsed for all time by something far more worthwhile and rewarding for everyone who is forced to experience it.

You see; I don't know anyone who's worked as hard as me and yet failed so badly to create a platform of financial security for myself. I don't know anyone who's endured the depth of abuse and suffering from the medical industry that I have and yet I've never received any recognition or reward for all my own endeavours in pursuit of securing a recovery. I don't know anyone who has failed as badly as I have to achieve the sort of professional recognition and standing that someone with my credentials should have achieved with ease.

In fact when I look at my life, even through sanguine eyes, I wonder why I've only ever been entitled to 3rd, 4th or 5th best all of the time, when crueler, less talented and even those of incongruent and fatuous dispositions appear to secure with ease that which is always out of my reach.

Am I bitter? Am I deluded? Or do I think that things will ever change? Well in answer, I'm certainly hurt about my lot in this life, however having studied my own psychology for the best part of 30 years in truth, no I'm not deluded at all. However I accepted a long time ago that things will never change for me, you see; we're born; blessed, lucky or doomed to have a blighted and unfulfilling life and there's absolutely nothing that we as mere mortals can do about that.

I am the master of my own health, for I take my quality of health seriously

To those who wonder what sort of man wrote this book albeit good or bad? I say only this, we all have stories to tell, experiences to live, loves to share, and battles to win, so stop looking for answers in me or your kith and kin and start finding the answers that you hold deep within you. Barry Hardy at worst is here to antagonise you or serve merely as a pointer on your path to your own personal greatness or place of serenity and for me it really is nothing more complicated than that.

Nevertheless on a more personal level I'm really unsure these days whether I've been poisoned forever by the sheer hell that can be mortality or I've simply become extremely macabre. But I've never been so aware of the fragility, complexity, stupidity and ultimate finality of this transient state of being called mortality. A seemingly impenetrable and sordid stench which invades every aspect of my psyche imploring me to conclude that:

- My innocence as a child was too short.
- My confusion as an adolescent was too complicated.
- My stress as a young man implicitly unnecessary.
- My suffering in my middles ages completely insane.
- My security in what's left of my life nonexistent.
- In totality I wonder just what the 'fuck' my mortality is all about.

I am the master of my own happiness, for its in my interests to live life to the full

Personal Notes

I am the master of my own health, for I take my quality of health seriously

Personal Notes

I am the master of my own happiness, for its in my interests to live life to the full

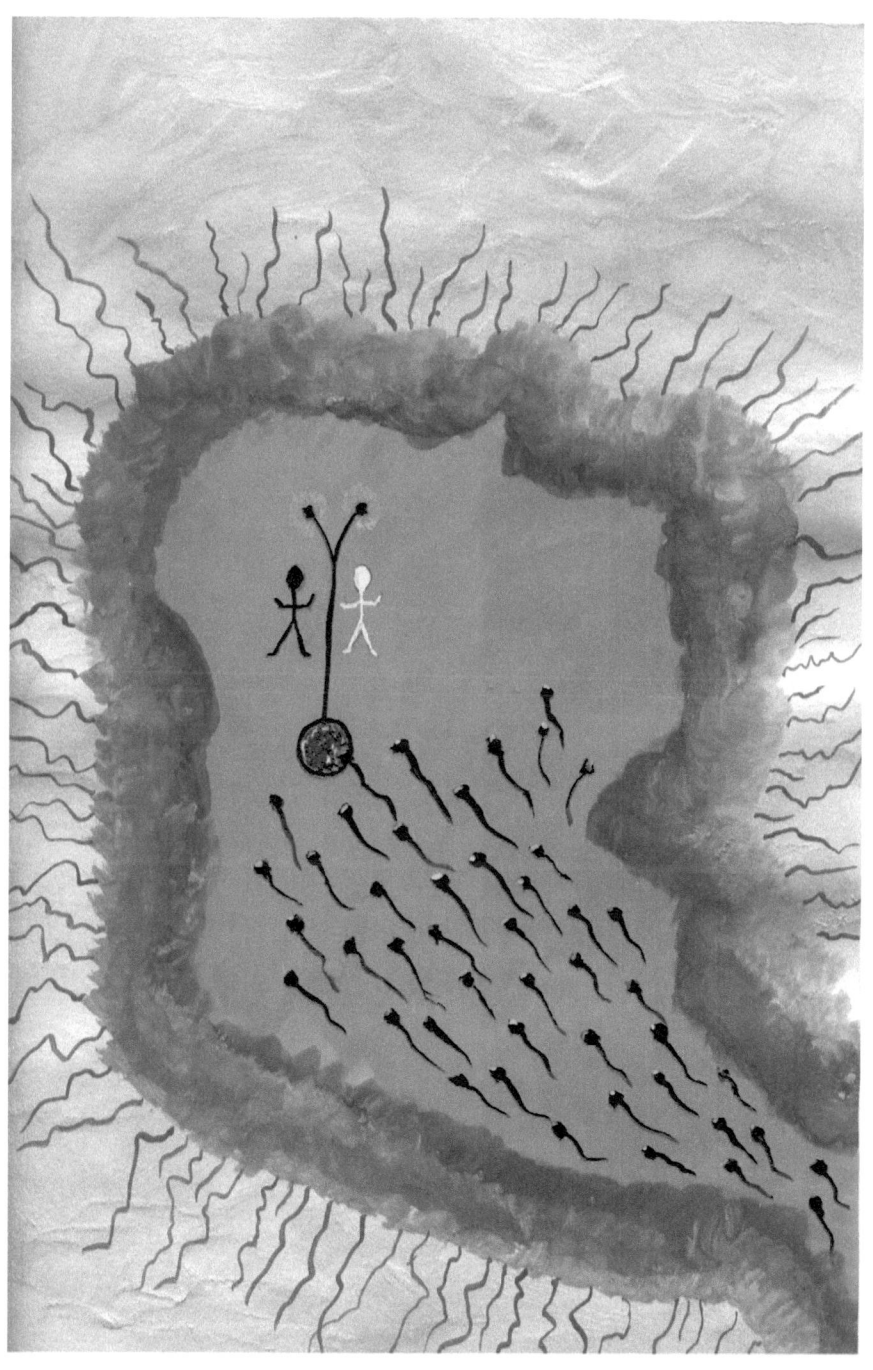

I am the master of my own health, for I take my quality of health seriously

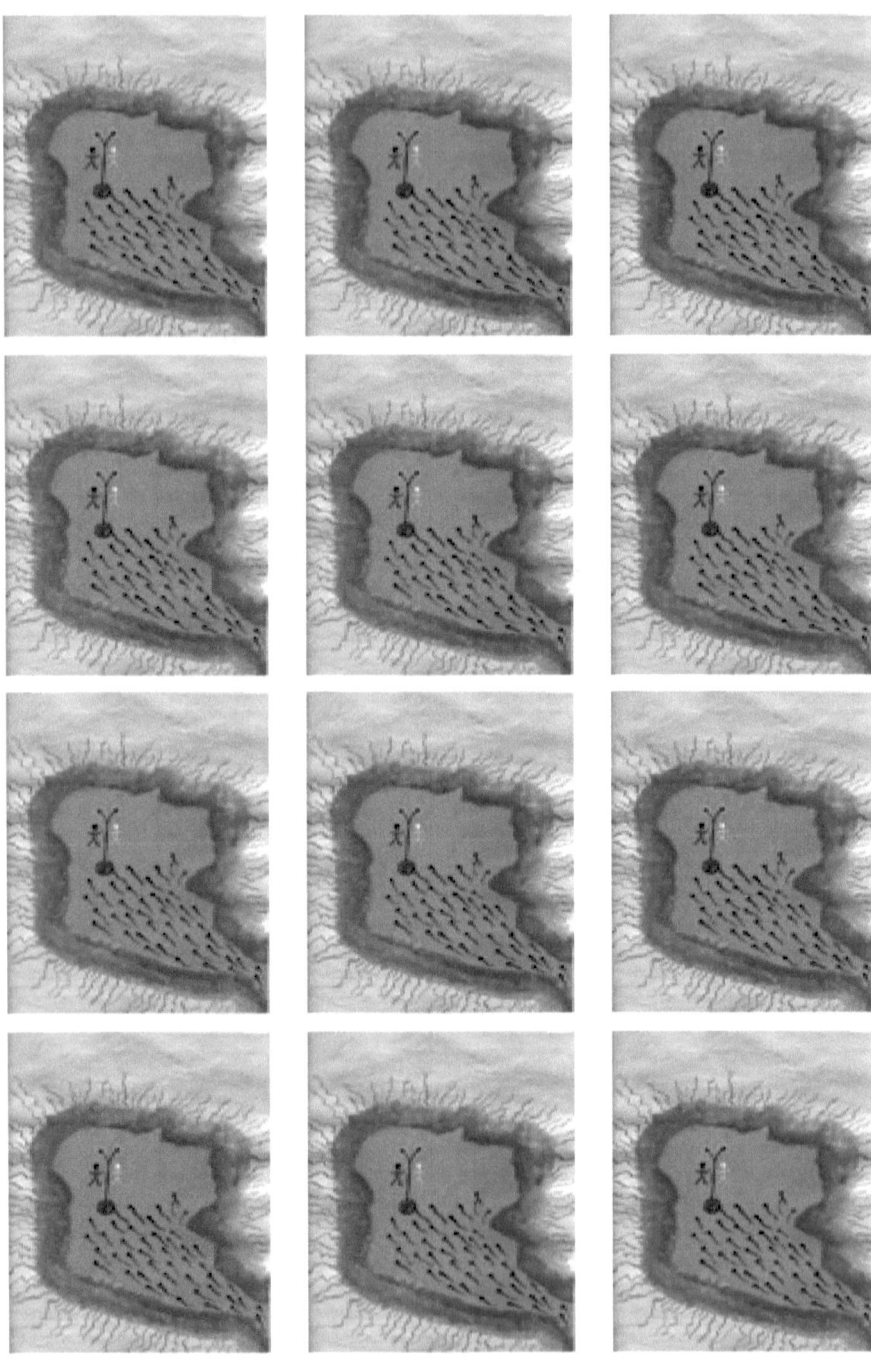

I am the master of my own happiness, for its in my interests to live life to the full

A FEW CLOSING THOUGHTS

It doesn't matter which way we look at life in terms of the bigger scheme of things because the reality is that we're all trapped in mortality despite how immortal we may believe that we are. It is the innate fragility of mortality which is the great leveller of men, because no man ever really knows what's about to jump out on him. One moment everything is fine the next we're faced with:

- Chronic ill Health.
- Chronic Disability.
- Surgery.
- Death.

That is just the way it is and no man or woman walking this green planet is above the process or processes of mortality. Because of that we must accept at some point or at the very least come to terms with all our mortal frailties and eventualities including the fact that we will ALL die. All that we can ever hope during our own personal conclusion is that, its peaceful and that we leave our body in the knowledge that we've lived a good productive life and that we've treated and been treated with a degree of dignity and respect from our fellow man.

I am the master of my own health, for I take my quality of health seriously

The real difficulty for me is that in our conclusion there is always the potential for the medical world to become involved and ultimately end up playing a leading role. So where do I sit in terms of the medical industry given the theme of this book? Well exactly where my opening text in this chapter states. I am a mortal and as a mortal I must accept all things mortal. Be that the frailty of my own body or the frailty of the men and woman charged with the responsibility for helping me with my mortality.

As mortals we're never able to take just one path through mortality because events, eventualities and karmic situations completely outside of our control always impose contradictions upon us. We might strive for a given path only to find some way down the road that it's not as rewarding as we had lead ourselves to believe. Equally the universe often conspires to place us back once more amongst energies that we'd sort to leave behind.

Being trapped within mortality at times can be a very challenging existence and only those who've grown through adversity will ever truly understand that place. It's a place that has no reason, it's a place where beliefs are shattered, and it's a place where we as mortals truly understand the reality behind mortality. I believe as a mortal that there is always the potential for me to place my life in the hands of an industry that I completely despise i.e. the medical industry.

But why you may ask? Well it's as simple as this; there are times in all our mortalities when we have very little choice at all and when we reach that journeys end, all we can do is give way to our mortality and the insanity and cruelty of men.

I am the master of my own happiness, for its in my interests to live life to the full

In vibrancy however I neither trust nor respect the medical industry and it's as simple as that. The industry is full of contradictions, full of illusions, full of cruelty, full of incompetence and full of mortals. I will have no faith in any man or woman working within or supporting the medical industry until that industry is able to prove to me that there is an appetite within the same for change. For that industry to move away from protectionist cultures and move closer to a service delivery based upon, quality, expertise and ownership of all front end and back end service provision.

My personal life passage has been too difficult, my suffering was to prolonged and the abuse I endured from those charged with the responsibility to help me was moralistically wrong. During the production of this book I watched the Kevin Smith, 1999 film Dogma and was somewhat reminded again of the complexity and even sheer stupidity of the concept of universal divinity.

In that film there are angels of all denominations happy to inflict suffering upon mortals and where God is portrayed as a complete simpleton to say the very least. It was during that film that I was vividly reminded again as if there was a need for me to reconnect the abstract clarity between light, right, darkness and wrong.

You see, given the hellish experiences that were thrust upon me; universal divinity is a far more complex dynamic than simply light, right, darkness and wrong. I've lived in a mortal abyss for far too many years and because of that I can never return to the innocent that I once was, or accept that I needed to experience so much evil or mortal despair.

I am the master of my own health, for I take my quality of health seriously

Equally I cannot change the man I've always been and that's reflected in my daily needs, aspirations, dreams and prayers. But why I need to say my prayer every day now is completely beyond me. However if I was to be very gentle with myself I suspect at its root is the little boy deep within me, simply crying out to be listened to, helped and loved by someone or anything outside of his control.

Who really knows what the act of giving up prayers is all about, whether it has validity or not, all that I can say is that if it helps us at times to lower our heavy mortal loads, then perhaps at times offering up our heartfelt prayers is some little way is indeed worthwhile.

As for me, well I believe that in every man there resides a god prince and dark lord, each with tremendous and equal potential, where the only thing that ever differentiates between those expressions at any stage in our lives is the choices that we as mortals make and it doesn't get any more complicated than that. I am by nature a man of peace, a man of love and a man who chooses always to walk in the light, yet my path has been a very hard and at times a very unrewarding and lonely path and now as I enter my 47th year of age I really struggle to make any sense of that.

I am the master of my own happiness, for its in my interests to live life to the full

However after thirty years of despair I'm of the opinion now that there is no great secret to a happy life, whether we commit to prayer or not it is a FACT that some are blessed with lots of luck whilst others are simply not. Because of that I've sort of colluded that: eagles fly with eagles, crows fly only with crows, whereas rogues on the other hand feel much happier when they can imprison the light of heart in the cesspits' they call home.

That's just the way life goes I'm afraid and we just have to make the best of whatever we've been dealt, the key as ever is to retain that essential bright spark which is our personal integrity. You see, life is hard, life is cruel, life is unfair, life is love and life is always the beginning of the end. And on that final point all I'll say is, have a great day, a great life and never forget that there's nothing to fear in this life at all except the fear that we generate through our own silly and highly fatuous or incongruent thoughts. So please try to remember that, because life is far too short to simply lose the plot or give up and lose our way through unnecessary mind manufactured strife. But maybe my comfort blanket is my own little prayer!

I am the master of my own health, for I take my quality of health seriously

My morning and evening prayer go something like this:

Still my mind yet let me grow; fill me with hope when I can't take any more.

Hold my heart in a place of peace yet allow me to find myself, through, personal release.

Guide my path when I am blind and always allow the light to shine.

Forgive me when my anger flows and show me how to heal my woes.

Be even handed when you assess my life and protect me from any further strife.

Let me rest when my work is done and forgive me if I'm guilty of committing wrongs.

Heal their pain when I have gone and let them know it's not for too long.

Hear this prayer for I do not hide, please send forth release my spiritual guides.

I am the master of my own happiness, for its in my interests to live life to the full

Personal Notes

I am the master of my own health, for I take my quality of health seriously

Personal Notes

I am the master of my own happiness, for its in my interests to live life to the full

Authors notes

I am the master of my own health, for I take my quality of health seriously

I am the master of my own happiness, for its in my interests to live life to the full

Personal Insight and Ownership

I'm aware that I've scared and troubled many people in the past with my ability to: analyse, condemn, congratulate and even poke fun at myself in the pursuit of reality and my own personal progression. I'm a very big believer that personal insight and personal ownership of all our mortal endeavours is the key to a truly considered life. Therefore if the tone, substance and/or in-depth of personal expression or certain aspects of my personal life are too much for any of my readers. I would respectfully suggest that perhaps its time for them to stop reading and start writing, for the expression of repression certainly offers release as far as I understand, from the tension we all as mortals appear to manufacture with ease.

Medics and the Medical/Clinical World

The medical world is full of humans each with their own unique gifts, skills and personal flaws and it's because the medical world is full of mortals and not earth God's that they fail us so badly day after day. But don't just sit back any longer when you're abused, let down or failed by anyone in the medical/clinical world. Sue them and bring them and their industry to account if you desire, for in doing so you will not only help yourself via the pursuit of redress, but indirectly you'll play a very big part in helping the entire human race.

I am the master of my own health, for I take my quality of health seriously

The Great Psychological Bluff and Scandal

If we allow others to cloud our realities in terms of who we are and what we're actually experiencing with inappropriate postulations about the state of our psychology, be under no illusion we fail ourselves completely at every conceivable level. On matters of psychology when pursuing well-being, listen to your antagonists but choose not to hear when you're being written as another psychological basket case. Because I'm confident you'll discover if you test your body thoroughly, that it's your body that's at fault not your emotions or mind. At that point all psychological assertions can be met head on as you pursue a meaningful life.

Eminently Solvable Conditions

When you're health conditions are being fudged and written off as illnesses that have only names with no treatment or resolution options open or offered to you to help you get by or simply cope. You really have only two options open to you and that is to stick with what you've got if that's all you can do or you can test and test until your condition or conditions are identified. We are all the sole guardians of our own mortality; therefore we can either relinquish our responsibility to the uncaring and obscene or we can fight for what is our mortal right, the right to decency and an acceptable quality of life.

I am the master of my own happiness, for its in my interests to live life to the full

Depression Expression

There is no insanity at all in depression expression save only for the sheer depth of suffering its victims incur. Because the reality is that depression expression can be eradicated in days, not weeks, months or years when the physical generators, precursors and accelerators of depression expression are treated and removed. All that is needed is a shift in perceptions, a position significantly enhanced by holistic treatment results.

Stressful Resolution

Whilst the majority of us have experienced some degree of stress at some point in our life, very few of us realise that it's so predictable, so treatable and so recoverable from, hence nothing whatsoever for us all to get stressed about. Once you understand the dynamics, your stress levels will fall and at that point you will wonder why you allowed yourself to get so stressed in the first place or indeed at all.

Wellness

There is no great secret to wellness over and above understanding the root cause of any decline from wellness into un-wellness. But that root-cause analysis is not determined by non intrusive subjective analysis, because it can only be determined by holistic, scientific testing and analysis. Anything less than that is mere supposition, supposition however has never cured anyone or created a state of considered wellbeing, but it has forced many poor mortals like you, me and us, to give up completely on the idea of a satisfying mortality. But no longer yeah?

I am the master of my own health, for I take my quality of health seriously

Divine or Higher Force

We all at some point need someone or something to pray to, no matter what race or creed we originate from. But the reality is when all said and done, we all as mortals are the only living beings able to solve complex mortal mysteries, so whilst it's okay I suspect to offer up prayers. I think it best that we all put our faith in ourselves and the endeavours of our fellow men.

I am the master of my own happiness, for its in my interests to live life to the full

Book Images & Contributors

All flow diagrams	Barry Hardy September 2008
All schematics	Barry Hardy September 2008
All book graphics	Barry Hardy September 2008
Raphael	Jesse Garrick November 1994
Empowerment	Barry Hardy September 2008
Earth God	Barry Hardy September 2008
Luddites	Barry Hardy September 2008
Journey	Barry Hardy September 2008
Psychology	Barry Hardy September 2008
Hypocrites	Barry Hardy September 2008
Lymes	Barry Hardy September 2008
Depression Expression	Barry Hardy September 2008
Stop Stressing	Barry Hardy September 2008
Thyroidman	Barry Hardy September 2008
Fibroman	Barry Hardy September 2008
Sillynames	Barry Hardy September 2008
TSB Soup	Barry Hardy September 2008

I am the master of my own health, for I take my quality of health seriously

Time Bombs	Barry Hardy September 2008
Genetics	Barry Hardy September 2008
Toxic Body	Barry Hardy September 2008
Expensive illness	Barry Hardy September 2008
Insane Testing	Barry Hardy September 2008
Analytics	Barry Hardy September 2008
Internet	Barry Hardy September 2008
Friends	Barry Hardy September 2008
Harpies	Barry Hardy September 2008
Explorer	Barry Hardy September 2008
Irony	Barry Hardy September 2008
Mind Anger	Barry Hardy September 2008
Honourable Past	Barry Hardy September 2008
Treatment	Barry Hardy September 2008
Health Wealth	Barry Hardy September 2008
My Mortality	Barry Hardy September 2008
Numpties	Barry Hardy September 2008
Prayer	Barry Hardy September 2008
Conclusion	Barry Hardy September 2008

I am the master of my own happiness, for its in my interests to live life to the full

Web sites you may wish to explore

The information provided here is for research only; no responsibility will be accepted for the scope or content of any of these web sites.

1. www.doctormyhill.co.uk
2. www.biolab.co.uk/
3. www.thyroiduk.org/
4. www.rife.org
5. www.marshallprotocol.com
6. www.nutramedix.com
7. www.mickeltherapy.com
8. www.homeopathy-soh.org/
9. www.moodcure.com/
10. www.reikifed.co.uk/
11. www.thyroidtears.co.uk/
12. www.meassociation.org.uk/
13. www.paulocoelho.com/ *(My favourite Author)*
14. www.rangers.co.uk *(My favourite football team)*

I am the master of my own health, for I take my quality of health seriously

DECENCY WARNING

This warning is repeated and placed at the back of this book because if you're like my daughter you're sure to start at the back of this book and I certainly don't wish to offend any back book readers either. Therefore please don't read this book if you are easily offended by:

- Strong views.
- Strong language.
- Grammatical inconsistencies.

Or

- Personal suffering freely expressed.

I am the master of my own happiness, for its in my interests to live life to the full

Personal Notes

I am the master of my own health, for I take my quality of health seriously

Personal Notes

I am the master of my own happiness, for its in my interests to live life to the full

Personal Notes

I am the master of my own health, for I take my quality of health seriously

Personal Notes

I am the master of my own happiness, for its in my interests to live life to the full

Personal Notes

I am the master of my own health, for I take my quality of health seriously

Personal Notes

I am the master of my own happiness, for its in my interests to live life to the full

Personal Notes

I am the master of my own health, for I take my quality of health seriously

Personal Notes

I am the master of my own happiness, for its in my interests to live life to the full

www.ingramcontent.com/pod-product-compliance
Lightning Source LLC
Chambersburg PA
CBHW020631300426
44112CB00007B/82